*more...*

*Organized to be the Best!* is an invaluable training tool that I use with participants in Personal Productivity Management training programs at the Jet Propulsion Laboratory. Each participant receives a copy of the book, which serves as both training material during the program and a take-away resource they use after the program. What's great about this book is that it shows such a wide variety of useful ideas and has something for everyone. It has both depth and breadth and does not have to be read sequentially.

> **–Nancy Ferguson**, Training Specialist, Jet Propulsion Laboratory
> Pasadena, California

I'm enjoying your book and I'm now applying what I have learned...The book is very well written and organized. I'm making it required reading for my staff, too.

> **–Nancy Stockinger**, Vice President, Human Resource Services
> Security Pacific Corp., Los Angeles, California

Takes a hands-on approach...includes a "Quick Scan" summary of each chapter, annotated resource guides and complete index–a model of the organization it teaches. Use it for sessions on time management, productivity and office management.

> **–The Training Store catalog**, Harrisburg, Pennsylvania

The impact of the time I spent with you continues to multiply. As you recommended, I set up a daily/monthly tickler file system to improve follow-up on the growing number of projects that I manage. I've trained myself to check it each day. It has really helped me stay on top of deadlines. Then working with my staff we created a tickler slip system we could all use. I am now delegating more confidently because I have an organized way of following up with people. I am saving time because I have the tools to move through my paperwork more quickly. Thanks for your ideas, coaching and advice!

> **–Terry Preuit**, Training Director, Los Angeles, California

This book has truly made it possible for me to increase my productivity by one and a half fold. My filing system is manageable and understandable for the first time in my life.

> **–Robert Simon, M.D.**, Chairman of the Board, International Medical Corps, and Chairman, Department of Emergency Medicine, Cook County Hospital, Chicago, Illinois

Every present and future leader who aspires to excellence should read *Organized to be the Best!* It is truly a hands-on masterpiece.

> **–Joe Batten**, Author of *Tough-Minded Leadership*, Des Moines, Iowa

In just one hour, Susan Silver can transform your office.
  −**Karen Otazo**, Manager, Human Resources Development, ARCO
  Los Angeles, California

I've already gone through half of your book and have found the material really helpful, especially the time management and IBM PC organization. This ought to be standard issue for administrative people.
  −**Alan C. Macdonald**, Vice President, Citibank, New York City

Susan Silver offers a wealth of practical advice and ideas from which even the most diligently organized of us can benefit.
  −**Sanford C. Sigoloff**, President and CEO, Sigoloff & Associates, Inc.
  Los Angeles, California

Thank you for bringing the "Organized to be the Best!" program to Teledyne Systems Company. The two-part custom training program provided the participants with useful ideas and information that they were able to readily apply.
  −**Janet Cordera**, Past Vice President, Northridge Management Club
  Teledyne Systems Company, Northridge, California

*Organized to be the Best!* is one of the few books I keep referring back to for organizing ideas and product resources. It's an excellent resource book with numerous illustrations of office products and accessories and good suggestions on how to use them. It's also the only book of its kind to cover organizing of computer files. I've recommended it to over a thousand clients and students.
  −**Harriet Schechter**, Professional Organizer and Owner, The Miracle
  Worker Organizing Service, San Diego, California

Your book is great, fills a gap and is readily useful to organizer colleagues.
  −**Paulette Ensign**, President, Organizing Solutions
  Bedford Hills, New York

You have written a very useful and easily accessed guide for helping the public get organized, but also, for organizers or the organized public to continue to use as a reference for deciding which organizing tool to use.
  −**Maxine Ordesky**, President, Organized Designs
  Beverly Hills, California

*Organized to be the Best!* will help anyone achieve his or her goals. I heartily recommend it.
  −**Robert Kotler, M.D.**, FACS, Author, *The Consumer's Guide to Cosmetic Facial Surgery*, Los Angeles, California

As an attorney in a solo practice, I'm trying to make the office more efficient. The book was helpful for my legal assistant and me to organize our work and our office. It gets right down to the brass tacks.

−**Shirley A. Bass**, Attorney at Law, Portland, Oregon

Your book is definitely unique in its approach. I learned a lot from your abundance of pictorial examples and the specific naming of products and where to locate them. I don't recall ever seeing that done before. You did a great job on the book.

−**Nancy Reiser**, Development Director, Florentine Opera of Milwaukee
Milwaukee, Wisconsin

I was literally drowning in paperwork six months ago. Then I bought your book. It was the perfect solution. So far, I have put to use at least one suggestion from each of your chapters. Order is finally being created from chaos. And, I really love your practical approach to keeping your readers up to date on new office products via illustrations and diagrams. I can now just photocopy the appropriate picture and hand it to my assistant to order. Thank you for a terrific book.

−**Kori Lee Garner**, Reference Librarian, University Library
California State University, Fullerton

From advice on managing time, to assistance on creating efficient work space, *Organized to be the Best!* has it all. It showed me how to tame my chaotic schedule, clear the clutter from my home office and generally bring order to my life...the most helpful book on the subject that I've come across.

−**Elane Osborn**, Novelist, *Skylark*, Reno, Nevada

I've read and implemented many of the wonderful ideas presented in your book. Your ideas have reduced the stress in my life and made me much more successful in my professional career. I'm a believer.

−**M. Susan Stegall**, Senior Consultant, Chi Laboratory Systems
Ann Arbor, Michigan

Your book was a delight to read and a tremendous help to me in setting up my home office. Your suggestions were most valuable in helping me decide upon an arrangement of furniture and resources. I was able to create an efficient filing system. I enjoy working in my office and feel I can accomplish much more because I have planned well for my needs.

−**Ilana Hoffman**, Mother and Community Volunteer, Portland, Oregon

I attended a most helpful three-hour workshop called "The Positively Organized! Office" taught by Susan Silver. The program was very focused and easy to understand. I was taught in three hours what I've struggled with for seven years.

−**Carrie Ann Ruiz**, Owner, All That Video, Bakersfield, California

I skimmed several chapters of Susan Silver's book and suddenly "got religion"—decided to bite the bullet and get my papers in order. I spent one successful hour following Susan's routines and plan to keep that orderly motion going.

–**Betty B. Gross**, Founder, Westchester Lyme Disease Support Group
Irvington-on-Hudson, New York

I have a long-standing prejudice that I understand my daily routines fairly well, and that help from consultants will not be too helpful. In relation to your book, this turns out not to be true. I read it a chapter at a time, over the last month, and I found it very helpful. What did I like? First, in time management, I liked the notion of A, B and C priorities. Second, keeping track of paperwork is a big problem for me because I have a multi-dimensional job and many interests. Two little things helped: 1) my desktop file rack is for *active working files* only and 2) taking five or ten minutes at the end of a day to put papers away makes it easier to be creative tomorrow.

–**Peter Lev, Ph.D.**, Associate Professor
Towson State University, Towson, Maryland

What a pleasure to tell you how much I enjoyed reading *Organized to be the Best!* I'm very excited about the useful information it contains; it has given me the inspiration to actually put your ideas into use, *right now!*

–**Eadye Martinson**, Executive Secretary, INTERMEC Corporation
Everett, Washington

Thanks so much for your help in getting my office to function again...Your book has done wonders for me.

–**Nora M. Wasserman**, Division Secretary, Long Island University
Brooklyn, New York

Two hours with Susan changed my life. I turned a wasted room into a wonderful working environment. I had thought I should be able to do it myself. Wrong! Her guidance was what I needed.

–**Sharon Bloom, Ph.D.**, Psychotherapist, Los Angeles, California

I really enjoyed your book. It was inspiring. I was able to read the required chapters, do the exercises and focus on several other interesting topics–in less than two hours!

–**Becky Shelton**, Vice President and Sales Manager, Union Bank
Los Angeles, California

It's obvious there's much work and love put into *Organized to be the Best!* It's a motivating book and the resources are excellent!

–**Elaine Wilkes**, Vice President of Sales, Slides in a Day
Los Angeles, California

We all felt the opportunities presented by you for organizing our daily life in the office were without equal. Thank you for increasing our office's efficiency, positively! Your sessions were a catalyst in which our entire staff responded so enthusiastically that we are still buzzing over your presentation, discussions and the projects you inspired. And I have a new "bible"—your book!

    **—Robert Aronoff**, Controller, Weight Watchers of Southern Calif.

Thank you for your book. Even the title is an inspiration to get started. In addition to providing a wealth of information, it is also well written and enjoyable to read. And when I go to an office supply store I can now point to the organizer I want to buy; I just bring your book along and point to the illustrations.

    **—Patricia L. Stewart**, Marketing Program Manager, AT&T
    Parsippany, New Jersey

The book looks great! Such detail! If a person can't get organized with this advice, he/she must be hopeless.

    **—Trish Lester**, President, Lester Creative Group, Newhall, California

Thanks for a terrific job on your mini seminar at our annual management conference.

    **—Barbara Klemm**, Director of Conferences, Credit Union Executives
    Society, Madison, Wisconsin

Susan has a remarkable talent for identifying habits and work conditions which are unnecessary complications and prevent you from becoming more productive. She has a first-rate ability for selecting the tools or ideas that are best suited to your style and needs. Add to this the fact that she is a delight to work with and you have an invaluable consultant who can make a real difference in your productivity.

    **—Waltona Manion**, President, The Manion Firm, Public Relations
    San Diego, California

# Organized
## To Be The
# *Best!*

New Timesaving Ways
To Simplify And Improve
How You Work

## SUSAN SILVER

ADAMS-HALL PUBLISHING
Los Angeles

Requests for such permissions should be addressed to:

Adams-Hall Publishing
PO Box 491002
Los Angeles, CA 90049

Library of Congress Cataloging-in-Publication Data

Silver, Susan
    Organized to be the best! : new timesaving ways to simplify and improve how you work.
        p.    cm.
    Includes index.
    ISBN 0-944708-22-6
    1. Business records-Management-Data processing.  2. Information resources management.  3. Time management.  I. Title.
HF5736.S54    1991
650.1--dc20                                         90-26452
                                                        CIP
Cover Design by Robert Steven Pawlak

Printed in the United States of America
10  9  8  7

Second Edition

# CONTENTS

# ACKNOWLEDGMENTS

Perhaps acknowledgments for a second edition of a book may seem unnecessary or even a bit redundant. That's assuming such an edition has only gone through minor revisions.

In the case of *this* second edition, however, the opposite is true. Because this new edition is completely revised, expanded and updated with 40 to 50 percent new material, the editorial and production process has once again been a tremendous undertaking and has involved the talents and skills of many individuals.

Let me begin by thanking those who reviewed the advance proof. My deepest appreciation goes to Edward Bales, Fred DeLuca, Scott McNealy, Robert Osterhoff, Joel Slutzky and Lillian Vernon for making time in their busy schedules to read the manuscript and offer praiseworthy comments.

Many thanks go to my copy editor, Ralph F. Marks, whose clear eye, attention to detail and diplomatic comments and suggestions greatly enhanced this edition.

It has been my special pleasure to work closely with two talented individuals during book production. Robert Steven Pawlak, San Francisco book designer, did a wonderful job on the cover and the interior design elements. It's always a pleasure to work with Los Angeles production artist June Winson.

Once again, I appreciate all of the firms who supplied line art, halftones or photographs for the book. I especially appreciate the following individuals who "went back to the drawing board" to provide custom art for the book: Sunny Banfield and Felice Willat, Day Runner, Inc.; Natalie Rzonca and Keith Snyder, Day-Timers, Inc.; and Jenny Burton and Winter Horton, Franklin International Institute.

I remain grateful for the ongoing professionalism and perseverance displayed by Adams-Hall Publishing and their distributor, Publishers Group West. In particular, I'd like to thank Charlie Winton and Susan Reich at PGW for their special work.

Over the last several years the quality of my work (and this second edition) has developed in relation to several professional associations and relationships with colleagues and clients. I would like to acknowledge the National Association of Professional Organizers, the National Speakers Association, the Quality & Productivity Management Association and the Community Alliance for Total Quality.

And on a more personal note, I gratefully acknowledge my parents, the rest of my family and my wonderful friends, whose support gives me balance, perspective and joy. A special thank you to Emily for her loving support, as well as the many hours she spent assisting with fact checking on this edition. This book is dedicated to Charlie, whose memory lives on.

And the best for last: thank you to my dear husband, Don, who is my partner in love and life.

Susan Silver
Santa Monica, California

# INTRODUCTION

# HOW TO BENEFIT
# FROM THIS BOOK

This book is the answer for you if *any* of the following questions are true. Are you

- usually swamped with paperwork?
- struggling with too many priorities and/or feeling out of control or overwhelmed with your workload?
- working in a chaotic or cluttered environment?
- projecting a less than successful, competent, professional image to your clientele, your colleagues or yourself?
- not using your personal computer as efficiently as possible?
- working with others without a common sense of purpose, pride and teamwork?
- just looking for more ideas to help you grow professionally and personally in order to further fine tune your work style?

Nearly everyone says, "Boy, could I use *you!*" when they hear of my business called Positively Organized!

Most people will go on to joke about the sorry state of their desk and office and how they've simply got to get more organized. You're not alone if you're always putting organization on the back burner. ("Someday, when I have some time, I'll clean out these drawers.") The problem is "someday" never comes and paper builds and builds until you've created a mountain out of a molehill.

But like many people, you, too, may have kidded yourself into thinking all you need to get organized are some good intentions, a little willpower and a free Saturday. All common sense, right? But if all it took were common sense, it would be common practice.

The secret to organizing your desk, your work space, yourself and your co-workers is much more than common sense. It's *learning and applying specific skills, systems and shortcuts.*

## THE POSITIVELY ORGANIZED! PROGRAM FOR ACTION

This book is different from all others because it is *interactive.* This book is as close as possible to having a personal consultation with me right now. Together we will use the Positively Organized! Program for Action. Tried and tested over the years, this is a proven program designed for professionals who already possess strong determination and clear goals. I always use it in my consulting/coaching work as well as my training programs. The Positively Organized! Program recognizes the level of success you have already achieved and keeps on building and refining. It also gives you immediate access to *solutions*–specific tips, techniques and tools you can use.

### WE'RE A TEAM

In the Positively Organized! Program, you are the player and I am the coach. As a coach I require your full attention and commitment and I, in turn, will help you see what could be working better for you. I will point out the best strategies around so that you won't have to waste your precious time and energy reinventing the organization wheel.

Take what you *read* and translate it into *action.* You'll be able to create a simple plan of action for tackling your desk, work surfaces, drawers (never again will you have to use them to clear your desk when you're expecting visitors!), paperwork, projects, filing cabinets or storage areas.

Or maybe you and a colleague will read this book and together you'll create a joint action plan to improve a communication system, implement a fail-safe method for follow-up or create an office paperwork procedure that simplifies how you work.

## WHAT'S IN IT FOR YOU

This book will help you do what you've always wanted to do. You'll reduce your stress, find extra hours in the day for the most important activities in your life and achieve more of your goals. You'll accelerate your performance, productivity and your own personal sense of achievement.

If your share this information with others, you have a chance to improve quality, service and teamwork where you work.

You'll also discover handy desk accessories and helpful office products, including many for your personal computer.

And you'll learn that more important than having the right equipment and tools is having the right *habits* to use the tools. You'll create your *own* personal organization system–because there's *no one right way to get organized.* We're all different and this book recognizes and appreciates those differences.

Even if you have the previous edition of this book, you'll discover all kinds of new products and ideas in this edition because there's no one right way to write a book either. Just as I encourage all of my clients to continue striving to be the best they can be, so, too, I work at making each succeeding edition the best it can be. And it appears to be working; you're reading a nationally award-winning book that has been selected as a main selection by several book clubs and continues to receive praise from readers just like you.

Just follow the advice of leadership expert Danny Cox when approaching a learning opportunity such as this book: "If you get one good idea that improves your effectiveness you've paid for your investment many times over." It's my goal that you'll get *many* good ideas but the real trick is to *apply* those ideas.

## HOW TO SAVE TIME
## WHEN READING THIS BOOK

This book is easy to use and will save you time because it has been specially designed for you, the busy professional. Special features make this book instantly accessible and usable. There is a complete table of contents and a useful index for easy reference. Also, there are brief "Quick Scan" summaries at the beginning of each chapter, distinct subheads in the chapters to help you read more quickly and plentiful resource guides at the end of Chapters 2 through 13.

And what's more, **you don't have to read the whole book!** Outside of Chapters 1, 2 and 14 (which are "required reading"), read only those chapters that apply to you.

The "Quick Survey" in Chapter 1 will let you see immediately where to fine tune and where to do a complete overhaul. After the survey, go to the table of contents and mark those chapters that relate most directly to the items you marked that need improvement. The "Quick Scan" summary at the beginning of a chapter will help confirm whether you should read the chapter. Whichever chapters you select, *be sure to read Chapter 14* to actually put the ideas from this book into action.

All you need right now is a pen, pencil or highlighter for marking key points and the eagerness to get started. Getting started, as you probably know, is the hardest part. On your mark, get set, get organized!

# 1

# HOW TO BE
# POSITIVELY
# ORGANIZED!

*Quick Scan: This chapter is "required reading" because it helps pinpoint where you are now and where you'd like to be with your organizational skills. Through the Quick Survey, you'll assess your organizational strengths and weaknesses. Next, you'll identify your goals and values. Finally, you'll reassess your survey results in light of your goals.*

Take a deep breath and relax. *Positively Organized!* does *not* mean being *compulsively* or *perfectly organized*. It's being **only as organized as you need to be.**

Your own style and degree of organization will depend on a number of factors—your level of activity, whether you have any support staff, the image you want to project, if you deal face to face with the public and how you like to work. It's up to you just how much organization you need.

It's *not* just having your papers in order; much more important is whether your priorities are in order. It's a question of *balance* between the details and the big picture, the micro and the macro.

5

## HOW ORGANIZED ARE YOU AT WORK?

As a consultant I usually begin working with clients by giving them a quick survey, which helps them determine their own organizational strengths and weaknesses. Here's one for you that ties in with the subject areas covered in this book.

Read and react quickly to each of the following items and check off the appropriate letter that describes how effectively you handle each item below—O for Outstanding, S for Satisfactory or N for Needs Improvement. If an item is not applicable to you, write N/A.

**Figure 1-1. A QUICK SELF SURVEY**

| ORGANIZATION AREA | Your Rating | | |
|---|---|---|---|
| | O | S | N |
| 1. Your system for planning, prioritizing and accomplishing work and achieving your goals. [Chapters 2, 3]................ | | | |
| 2. Your paperwork. [Chapters 4, 5, 9, 10, 11].................... | | | |
| 3. Dealing with interruptions. [Chapter 3]........................ | | | |
| 4. Your ability to easily access needed information. [Chapters 2-11]................ | | | |
| 5. Your telephone time. [Chapters 3, 11]......................... | | | |
| 6. Letting go of papers and possessions. [Chapters 4, 5, 10]........ | | | |
| 7. Your follow-ups. [Chapters 2, 3, 9]............................ | | | |
| 8. Your reading load. [Chapter 4]................................ | | | |
| 9. Your filing system. [Chapters 4, 5]........................... | | | |
| 10. Your desk or table top(s). [Chapters 4, 10, 11].............. | | | |
| 11. Your personal computer organization. [Chapters 6-9]............ | | | |
| 12. Making habit changes in how you do things. [Chapter 14]...... | | | |
| 13. Your attention to quality and/or service. [Chapters 2, 9, 13]... | | | |
| 14. The layout and location of your work space. [Chapter 11]...... | | | |
| 15. Your drawers, shelves, bookcases. [Chapters 10, 11]................ | | | |
| 16. Your furniture and equipment. [Chapter 11]............................ | | | |
| 17. Your accessibility to supplies. [Chapter 11]......................... | | | |
| 18. Your portable, on-the-go, traveling office. [Chapters 2, 12]..... | | | |
| 19. Office communications and teamwork [Chapters 12, 13].......... | | | |

## HOW TO SELECT THE AREAS
## MOST IMPORTANT TO YOU

Look at the "N's" you've checked. Decide which three N's are most important to you right now. Star these three items. Keep them in mind as you decide which chapters to read.

Take a moment now to reflect on what it would mean to you, your business, your career and your life to improve your top three starred items. Think about the *benefits* that you would experience. Take 60 seconds to jot down as many benefits that come to mind:

Put a star by the most important one.

## BENEFITS ARE THE KEY

Just why is visualizing and listing benefits so crucial? A benefit is the reason why you do something. It's the motivation behind an action or activity and it should be connected to at least one of your major goals. You'll need a *compelling* benefit to justify spending the time and effort required to organize anything. *If there's no real payoff to getting more organized, you won't.*

Organization gets put on the back burner because it doesn't *appear* to be a top priority. Your benefit has to be strong enough to make organization a top priority and to counteract all the reasons and excuses that justify this "back burner syndrome."

**Make organization a top priority.** Take it off the back burner and make time for it *every day.* Get into the organization habit. It will give you the professional edge, not to mention more control and less stress.

Once you've identified at least one top benefit, keep it uppermost in your mind. Second, keep reminding yourself about the benefit while you're reading this book and when you're applying what you read. You're very much like athletes in training who need to remind themselves constantly about what they want to achieve and why. You need to do the same.

## TARGETING CHALLENGING, ACHIEVABLE GOALS

Your benefits will come into focus more clearly once you've identified your current goals.

As Yogi Berra once said, "If you don't know where you're going, you'll end up some place else." This is the first secret to being organized–Positively Organized! All the organizational tools and techniques in the world and this book are useless if you don't know where you're headed, that is, what you want to accomplish at work and in your life.

Start with an up-to-date list of goals. Not having this list is like taking a trip without a map. Goals give you focus, purpose and direction. Goals help you *attain* something you don't have or *maintain* something you do. Effective goals are simple, clear-cut and direct. They should reflect both professional and personal values.

**Write down your goals on paper** periodically during the year (this means more than once!). Make appointments with yourself to plan your goals on paper. Twice a year may be sufficient–in January and then again in July. Others (Lee Iacocca included) prefer quarterly goals.

## HOW TO WRITE DOWN YOUR GOALS

Use the Goals Work Sheet in Figure 1-2 to identify the "what," "why" and "how" of each goal.

Begin by listing "what" you want to attain or maintain and the extent or degree of accomplishment. In describing your goal, ask yourself what you want to **do, be** or **have**. Be as specific as you can. Write your goal in the present tense, whether or not it is something in the future or is a part of your life right now. Write each goal as if it has already been achieved or fulfilled. Here are three "do, be, have" examples of personal and professional goals:

> **Do:** I exercise three times a week; I play volleyball on Sunday, tennis on Tuesday and racquetball on Thursday.
>
> **Be:** I am a peaceful person who greets problems as challenges and opportunities.

**Have:** I have a job in my chosen field that is financially and personally satisfying.

Answer "why" by listing any benefits and results you expect from accomplishing your goal. The "why" should also state the *value* this goal has for you in your life as a whole. If you choose goals that conflict with your life values, you'll be setting yourself up for sabotage and failure. Let's suppose, for example, one of your goals is to get a promotion within the next few years and to do so will require that you put in many more hours at work. But one of your values is to lead a balanced life that includes plenty of time spent with your family. You could have a conflicting situation on your hands.

Your goals need to be in harmony with your most important life values. Taking the "do" goal listed above, here are some benefits or results to be derived:

feeling fit
increased energy and vitality
getting those endorphins flowing
decreased stress
feeling more relaxed (exercise is one of the four natural
    tranquilizers—laughter, music and sex being the other three)
having more fun
better social life
balancing a hectic lifestyle

Answer "how" by listing specific ways you plan to achieve your goal—any strategies, action steps or tasks, in addition to the amount of time required (per day, week, month or year). Assigning deadlines—or "lifelines" as one person I know prefers to call them—will make your "hows" much more specific and helpful. Some specific "hows" for the "do" goal could include:

calling to make reservations
confirming tennis and racquetball times with partner
writing down activities and times in a calendar
putting out sports clothes the night before by the door

Now take five to ten minutes to complete the Goals Work Sheet in Figure 1-2 to quickly jot down three or more of your goals, including the "what," the "why" and the "how" for each one.

**Figure 1-2.** GOALS WORK SHEET
Date:_____

| WHAT is your goal? | WHY do you want this goal? | HOW will you proceed? |
|---|---|---|
| | | |

## THE POWER OF THE PEN

Putting your goals in writing helps affirm your *commitment*. Your chances of achieving your goals are much greater when you write them down. It makes your goals more real. It also helps plant them into your subconscious. One professional woman I know writes down her goals each year in January, seals them in an envelope, opens the envelope at the end of the year and discovers she has accomplished almost all of them.

## AIM HIGH

Second, who says you have to accomplish them all? There's a saying that goes like this, "If you accomplish everything you planned, then you haven't planned well enough." You *should* plan a little more than you may actually do; practice aiming high because you'll probably accomplish more than if you lower your expectations and make them "realistic." There's an Indian parable that explains why. The parable asks, "Is it not better to aim for the moon and hit an eagle than to aim for an eagle and hit a rock?"

## TECHNIQUES TO ENSURE SUCCESS

So aim high and use these eight ways to increase your chances of reaching your goals:

1. Put your goals in writing.
2. Take some action on your goals every day or at least every week.
3. Share them with one other person (and listen to theirs). But only share them with other people who also set goals of their own and reach them. Those are the kind of people who will be most supportive.
4. Read them daily before you do your planning and before you go to sleep.
5. Every week write down and accomplish smaller goals that relate to your long-term goals. List these weekly goals where you will see them every day.
6. Review and revise your goals at least twice a year, always making sure they reflect your deepest values.
7. Let them *inspire,* not haunt you.
8. Include both professional and *personal* goals to increase the balance of your life. Make sure, too, that your goals harmonize with those of your career, position or company; if they don't, you could experience some conflict in your life.

Now review your survey on page 6. Find your starred items and notice the chapter references. See which chapter numbers come up most often. Now go to the table of contents and select the most important chapters for you to read. Keep in mind, too, that you should make Chapter 2 and Chapter 14 part of your "required reading" no matter which "elective" chapters you choose to read.

Now look at your goals on page 10 and note which chapters will best help you reach your goals. And, remember, the idea isn't just to be organized. It's to become organized to be the best! That means the best *you* can be.

# Follistim™
## (follitropin beta for injection)

# TIME MANAGEMENT: WHAT YOU REALLY NEED TO KNOW

*Quick Scan: The second of three "required reading" chapters, this one gives you the secrets to getting the most important things done in your life. Learn the art of planning and prioritizing. See a wide variety of quality time management tools and why it's important to be using the right ones.*

**E**very problem with organization is in some way a problem with time. If your time isn't well organized, your papers, projects and priorities won't be either.

**Time management** is the foundation of good organization. Its purpose is to help you do the most important things in your life.

Many people think the purpose of time management is to get as much done as possible. Not so. Let me repeat: **it's getting the most important things done.**

Do you *often* have days when it feels as if you have accomplished nothing? If so, you aren't taking advantage of time management. You're not doing the most important tasks and activities.

Have you considered what "most important" means? Is it something that has an urgent deadline? Is it something your boss wants? Is it something *you* want that relates to one of your goals?

It can mean all of these. But watch out if you're only making *other people's demands* the most important things you do. To be your best, make time every day to accomplish something that *you* consider important.

Activities you deem important come out of the values and goals you identified in Chapter 1. (If you haven't read that "required" chapter please do so now.) Without clear-cut goals, your time management decisions will be made in a vacuum or else they will be all externally determined by outside circumstances and people. You won't be in charge. So take charge and start choosing activities that contribute to your long-term goals.

Time management is the great simplifier, putting things in focus and perspective. Time management is an awareness of time coupled with the ability to choose and control purposeful activities related to your goals.

Time management is making choices about activities that have meaning to you. These choices should balance short-term and long-term, urgent and less urgent, internal and external activities. Time management helps you control what you can, when you can.

Time management is also using the right tools and habits to improve *how* you do something. Effective time management tools and habits can improve the quality and quantity of your work, help you make better decisions and increase your performance.

## HOW TO PLAN AND PRIORITIZE

Planning and prioritizing are two essential habits that are the bread and butter of time management. Use them to balance long-term and short-term goals and activities.

Why take the *time* to plan and prioritize? Research indicates that for every hour of planning, you save three or four hours. Effective planning and prioritizing ("P and P" for short) will help you get the most important things done each day, week, month and year.

You've already started with long-term P and P in Chapter 1. Long-term goal setting is a real time-saver because it's a handy yardstick against which you can measure all your day-to-day P and P decisions.

## LEARNING YOUR ABCs AND NUMBERS

To master P and P, begin by learning to identify your "ABC" priorities. Author Edwin Bliss, in his wonderful book *Getting Things Done*, differentiates between these three priorities. He says A priorities are "important and urgent," as in crisis management. B priorities are "important but not urgent," as in long-term goals. You should try to spend most of your time on A's and B's. C priorities are "urgent but not important." Try to spend as little time on C's as possible.

You're probably pretty good at handling A's, which fall in the "fighting fires" category, but how many B's do you work on each day? **Make time every day to work on your important-but-not-urgent B priorities and goals.** A good source for these priorities are the goals you listed on your Goals Work Sheet in Chapter 1.

Another way to describe A, B and C priorities is to substitute these three words: "must," "should" and "could." In other words, an A priority is something you *must* do, a B priority is something you *should* do and a C priority is something you *could* do.

And here's a trick using numbers that I learned from colleague Marjorie Hansen Shaevitz when she and I appeared on the same college program. Using a scale from 1 to 10, she suggests asking yourself these two questions if you're indecisive about whether to do an activity:

1. How much do I really want to do this activity (against the backdrop of everything else that is going on)?
2. How important is this activity?

### ADD D, D AND D TO YOUR P AND P

To get the most important things done each day, add three other ingredients to your planning and prioritizing: **discipline, dedication,** and **desire.**

There is no substitute for a daily dose of **discipline.** Build planning into *every* work day and give it as much importance as if you were going away on a two-week vacation. (Did you ever notice how good you get at planning and prioritizing the day before you go away?)

Build a specific time slot into your daily schedule to work on top projects or priorities–and stick to it. For example, authors set aside certain hours of the day to write.

No matter what else happens, keeping that commitment to yourself will make you feel good about the day and your accomplishments. Nothing beats out single-mindedness of purpose when it comes to getting the most important things done.

What we're talking about is real **dedication** to your most important priorities. Start out the morning by asking yourself, "What are the most important items for me to handle today that would allow me to call this a successful day?"

And take time to acknowledge your accomplishments each day. Pat yourself on the back. This is a good way to spark your **desire**, which in turn will fuel your dedication and discipline. Keep relating your activities to your goals, which should also feed your desire.

## SIX WAYS TO MAXIMIZE YOUR P AND P
## WHEN YOU MAKE YOUR TO-DO LIST

Now that you've learned the ABCs of planning and prioritizing, you're ready to use them plus these six ways to improve your **to-do list**–a daily or weekly list of activities that reflects your goals and priorities and helps you see the most important things you need to accomplish:

1. **Plan tomorrow, today, and put your plan in writing.** Take five or ten minutes today to write tomorrow's to-do list so you can start tomorrow fresh. (If you're an early riser, set aside some quiet time at home or at work to plan before the day really gets going.) Planning and prioritizing on paper (or computer) lets you *see* what you need to accomplish and when.

2. **Revise your plan–stay flexible and use common sense!** Check today's list several times throughout the day and if necessary, rearrange, postpone and yes, even *procrastinate on purpose.* "Planned procrastination"–consciously choosing to put off–is what prioritizing is all about. Remember your to-do list is a guide and *no one gets everything done.* Use common sense as

you plan out your priorities. If something comes up during the day that bumps another item in importance, so be it. Write in pencil so you can easily erase and move items on your list. Weigh the value of doing an item at a particular point in time. For example, it may be better to call Joe Blow at 1:00 p.m. today, even though Joe is only a "B" priority, because you're sure to reach him at 1:00; otherwise you'll be playing telephone tag with him for the next two weeks—which would be a major time waster.

3. **Make at least one, screened-time appointment with yourself each day.** Give yourself at least one hour of "screened, prime time" every day to work on top priority work. "Screened time" is quiet, uninterrupted time allowing you to concentrate and "prime time" is the time of the day when you're most effective. You can screen your time by doing any of the following: coming in an hour early, staying an hour later, having your calls screened by a secretary or colleague (and offering to do the same for them), working in another location (at home or a quiet, inaccessible office), closing your door, activating your voice mail system or your answering machine and writing in a one-hour appointment with yourself on your calendar.

4. **Consolidate activities and avoid "laundry listing."** If you're tired of making long, laundry lists of unrelated to-do's, then shorten your lists and group like items together. Have one section of your to-do list for scheduled appointments. Try grouping activities by category (such as "calls" and "correspondence"). Use priority groupings where you first list your top A priorities of the day—limit the number to three or four—and then list your B priorities.

5. **Make time every day to work on B priorities.** These are the priorities that most closely tie in with your goals. But most people tend to put B's on the back burner, selecting only the more pressing, fire-fighting A priorities.

6. **Write down several key goals, activities or projects for the week.** Select no more than four and write them some place where you'll see them every day as you do your daily planning.

# HOW TO CHOOSE
# THE BEST TIME MANAGEMENT TOOLS

There is no one best time management tool. There are, however, the best tools for *you* at this point in your life and career to help you plan, prioritize and get the most important things done.

One thing is certain. The more complex and demanding your life and career become, the more you need time management tools that can help you keep track of the complex demands on your time.

Select the least number of tools. The simpler, the better. But don't force yourself to use a tool that you've outgrown or that no longer meets your needs.

You'll see a wide variety of tools, many of which can be used alone or with other tools. Some tools, such as a notebook organizer or computerized time management program, contain many tools already built in.

What's so great about today's time management tools and systems is that you have great flexibility to put together the components *you* need. Remember, too, not to feel guilty if you don't want to use all of the components. Use only what you need.

In this section we'll look at six main types of time management tools: calendars, to-do lists, master lists, tickler systems, computerized time management programs and planners/organizers. Be thinking about the following criteria as you evaluate time management tools:

**Size**–what's the right one for you?
**Portability**–how portable does it have to be?
**Features and adaptability**–how important are they to you, as well as others with whom you work?
**Looks, image and appeal**–what is appropriate for your position and lifestyle?

## CALENDARS

The most basic planning and scheduling tool is the calendar, which can track future dates, events, meetings and appointments over a long range of time–at least a year out at a time.

Everyone needs a calendar but not everyone is using the right calendar or using it correctly. Calendars come in all shapes, sizes and configurations and often by many a name: date books, diaries, appointment books, desk calendars, desk pad calendars and wall calendars. Calendars are often part of other planning tools such as notebook organizers or computer time management programs, which will be discussed shortly.

Don't underestimate the importance of your calendar selection. Since this is an item you use daily, you should give your selection some thought. Don't be afraid to change to a different one, even in mid-year. Ask yourself these five questions:

1. Do you have more than one calendar?
2. Is your calendar either too small or too big?
3. Is it easy to miss seeing important dates (because they're hard to spot, there isn't enough room or your calendar is too cluttered)?
4. Are you afraid of losing your calendar?
5. Is it troublesome to carry it with you when you're away from the office?

If you have one or more "yes" responses, consider reevaluating your choice of calendar according to these criteria:

• You should not have more than one calendar unless you have a staff person and/or a foolproof routine to maintain the additional one. (Keep personal and professional items on the same calendar.)
• Select a calendar whose size and style are adequate for your work and appointment load. Don't force yourself to use a calendar you've outgrown even if it is the middle of the year; switch to another one.
• Maintain a reliable backup system. What would happen if you lost your calendar? Do you have photocopies of the most important pages?
• Your calendar should be accessible to you, both in and out of the office.
• Your calendar should have the right "look" for your profession and it should appeal to you in terms of appearance and ease of use.

If you're trying to cram too much information into your calendar or appointment book, consider a larger format or a different time management tool, such as a planner or an organizer. A calendar is for mapping out long-range plans; it's not generally the ideal tool for detailed, daily planning. If you're continually using many slips of paper to make notes to yourself because your calendar simply isn't big enough, you're ready for a change.

Allow me to comment on the desk pad calendar. I'm not fond of this calendar because it's so big, it's not portable, it adds to desktop clutter, it often becomes a big doodling pad, there's no place to conveniently store past month sheets and it's not the most professional looking tool you can get. (Other than that, I love it!)

## TO-DO LISTS

Most people should use some kind of to-do list for daily or weekly planning at work and/or in their personal life.

If your work is very routine or very physical, it's possible you wouldn't need this tool. If you're a teller, a baker or a mechanic you probably wouldn't need this on the job. But if you have a lot of other things to remember to do in connection with your job, it might be helpful to write them down on a to-do list. And if you have a busy personal life, a to-do list is essential.

A good to-do list should have two basic sections—a place for scheduled activities and a place for your nonscheduled activities. Scheduled activities include appointments as well as blocks of time you set aside to do specific types of work, e.g., projects, paperwork and planning. Nonscheduled activities are items on your to-do list that aren't scheduled to be done at any particular time of day. Choose forms in stationery stores and catalogs that provide these two important sections. You can buy these commercial to-do list forms separately or as part of a time management system or organizer. Figure 2-1 shows an example of Day Runner's daily planning form and Figure 2-2 shows the Personal Resource System two-page-per-day planning forms.

It's important to see both your scheduled and nonscheduled activities at the same time and have them next to one another. Whenever possible or feasible, make your nonscheduled tasks into scheduled ones because they're more likely to get done when you've attached a time frame or deadline. When you set time aside to accomplish a task, you're more likely to do it than if it's just an

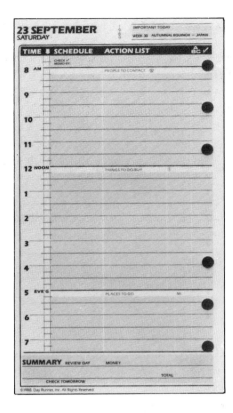

**Figure 2-1.** Day Runner's daily planning form comes dated as shown here or undated and includes space for both your "schedule" and "action list."

unscheduled item on a to-do list. If you've set aside time to do tasks and you have trouble gauging time, use an electronic countdown timer from Radio Shack to help you stick to your schedule.

If you get tired of transferring today's uncompleted to-do's to the next day's list, consider using a two-page-per-week format (Figure 2-3). You'll have a little less space to write, but you won't have to keep rewriting to-do's. You can also see your entire week, including any items that are incomplete.

```
_____ SCHEDULE YOUR DAY _____

  Today's Actions Determine Tomorrow's Results
  ☐ Review Goals          ☐ Select Items To Do        ☐ Visualize Day's Results
  ☐ Transfer Appointments ☐ Review Other
  ☐ Select Project Items  ☐ Prioritize Daily Activities ☐ Review Finances

  THIS WEEK'S GOAL _____


  _____


  SCHEDULE
  _____    3:00 _____
                           3: _____
  8:00 _____    4:00 _____
  8: _____    4: _____
  9:00 _____    5:00 _____
  9: _____    5: _____
  10:00 _____    6:00 _____
  10: _____    6: _____
  11:00 _____    7:00 _____
  11: _____    7: _____
  12:00 _____    8:00 _____
  12: _____    8: _____
  1:00 _____
  1: _____    _____
  2:00 _____    COMPLETE THE DAY
  2: _____    ☐ Identify Any Incomplete Items And Transfer
                           ☐ Acknowledge Results Produced Today
                           ☐ Schedule Tomorrow
  TODAY'S NOTES _____

  _____

  _____

  _____

  _____

  _____

  _____

  _____
```

No. 160                                              ©1980 PRS, Inc.

**Figure 2-2.** The Personal Resource System daily planning forms (on this page and the next) include sections that relate directly to goals, projects and results. You can also group activities together by type, e.g., "schedule," "do" and "call."

DAILY ACTIVITIES

Day/Date

THOUGHT FOR THE DAY

TODAY'S PRIORITY

DO

CALL

No. 160                                              ©1980 PRS, Inc.

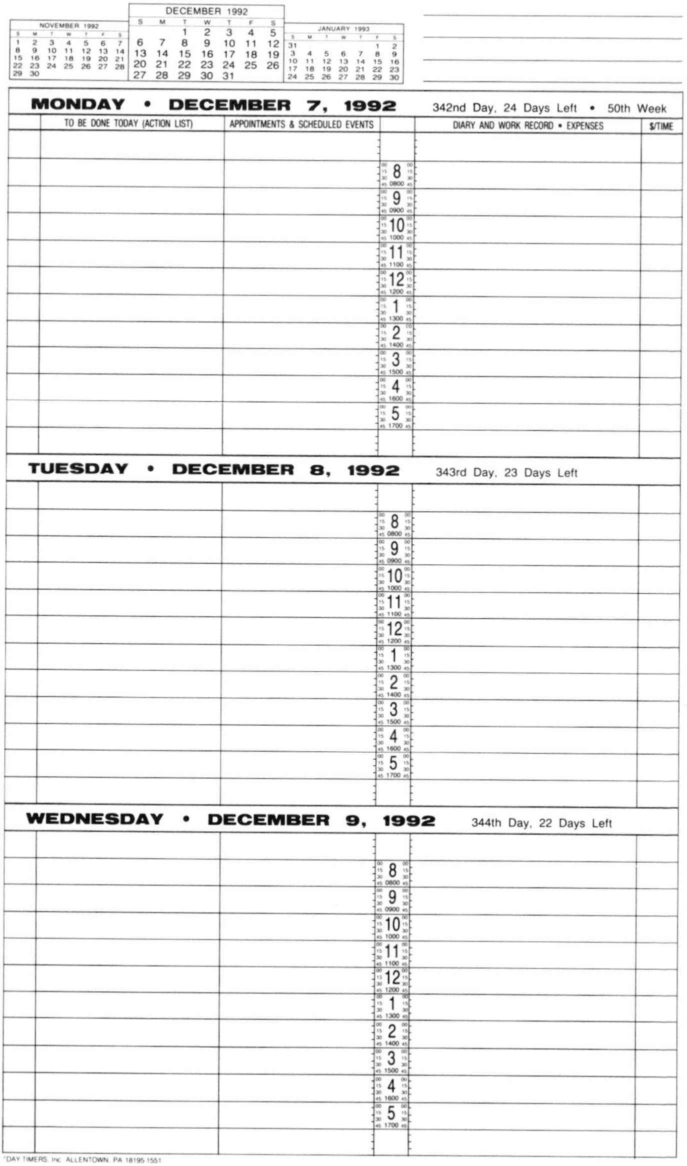

**Figure 2-3.** The Day-Timer Two-Page-Per-Week format (on this page and the next) shows you the entire week. Notice there are three divided sections per day. Use the first one for to do's, the second for appointments and the third for such items as services performed, expenses incurred or telephone calls made. (Illustrations courtesy of Day-Timers, Inc., Allentown, PA 18195-1551)

**THURSDAY • DECEMBER 10, 1992**   345th Day, 21 Days Left

| TO BE DONE TODAY (ACTION LIST) | APPOINTMENTS & SCHEDULED EVENTS | | DIARY AND WORK RECORD • EXPENSES | $/TIME |
|---|---|---|---|---|
| | | 8 0800 | | |
| | | 9 0900 | | |
| | | 10 1000 | | |
| | | 11 1100 | | |
| | | 12 1200 | | |
| | | 1 1300 | | |
| | | 2 1400 | | |
| | | 3 1500 | | |
| | | 4 1600 | | |
| | | 5 1700 | | |

**FRIDAY • DECEMBER 11, 1992**   346th Day, 20 Days Left

| | | 8 0800 | | |
|---|---|---|---|---|
| | | 9 0900 | | |
| | | 10 1000 | | |
| | | 11 1100 | | |
| | | 12 1200 | | |
| | | 1 1300 | | |
| | | 2 1400 | | |
| | | 3 1500 | | |
| | | 4 1600 | | |
| | | 5 1700 | | |

**SATURDAY • DECEMBER 12, 1992**   347th Day, 19 Days Left

| | | 8 0800 | | |
|---|---|---|---|---|
| | | 9 0900 | | |
| | | 10 1000 | | |
| | | 11 1100 | | |
| | | 12 1200 | | |

**SUNDAY • DECEMBER 13, 1992**   348th Day, 18 Days Left

| | | 8 0800 | | |
|---|---|---|---|---|
| | | 9 0900 | | |
| | | 10 1000 | | |
| | | 11 1100 | | |
| | | 12 1200 | | |

## MASTER LISTS AND OTHER BIG PICTURE PLANNING TOOLS

If you have a large number of projects, activities and tasks (as compared to meetings and appointments, which go on a calendar), it may be helpful to group these items in special places other than calendars or daily to-do lists.

A **master list** is useful for listing activities that will occur over a period of time, from one week to several months. A master list serves three functions. First, it consolidates ideas you've been storing in your head and on your desk into one source. Second, it gives you an overview and some perspective of the "big picture." Third, you can use it to select items to put on your daily list.

To make your master list more effective, categorize and prioritize it. Some people simply flag the most important items with a red star. You may want to combine a red star with a start date or a due date.

Others prefer to have separate lists. Some of my clients create two lists, one for personal and another for professional. Some create a separate list for each project, case or type of work. Usually the fewer lists the better, but the trick is to remember to *use* them. The more lists you have, the easier it is to forget to use one of them.

Whenever possible, put your master list on *one* sheet of paper. See Figure 2-4 for an example of a simple master list in chart form that groups activities by type and priority. List your activities on the chart in pencil (to write really small and get more items on a page, use a mechanical lead pencil with 0.5mm lead). Writing in pencil lets you erase and rewrite items when your priorities change. Remember to include some kind of deadline or time frame because almost nothing gets done without one. If you carry an organizer, hole punch your list and file it under "M" for "Master List"; that way you'll always have it with you.

Many commercial time management systems, planners and organizers provide their own master list sections or special planning forms. Success desk calendars and Day-Timer systems come with **monthly master lists** (see Figures 2-5 and 2-6). This kind of master list is helpful if you like to group activities by the month.

If most of your items extend beyond a month, however, you may find yourself having to spend time transferring items to the next

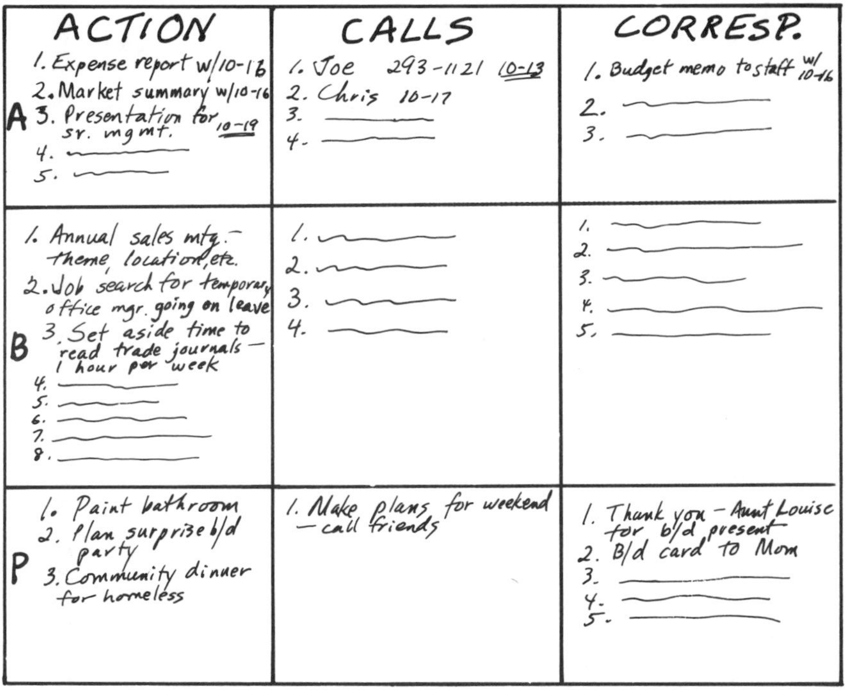

| ACTION | CALLS | CORRESP. |
|---|---|---|
| A 1. Expense report w/10-18<br>2. Market summary w/10-16<br>3. Presentation for sr. mgmt. 10-19<br>4.<br>5. | 1. Joe 293-1121 10-13<br>2. Chris 10-17<br>3.<br>4. | 1. Budget memo to staff w/10-16<br>2.<br>3. |
| B 1. Annual sales mtg. - theme, location, etc.<br>2. Job search for temporary office mgr. going on leave<br>3. Set aside time to read trade journals - 1 hour per week<br>4.<br>5.<br>6.<br>7.<br>8. | 1.<br>2.<br>3.<br>4. | 1.<br>2.<br>3.<br>4.<br>5. |
| P 1. Paint bathroom<br>2. Plan surprise b/d party<br>3. Community dinner for homeless | 1. Make plans for weekend - call friends | 1. Thank you - Aunt Louise for b/d present<br>2. B/d card to Mom<br>3.<br>4.<br>5. |

**Figure 2-4.** This master list chart groups three main types of activities in the vertical columns—"Action" or project items, "Calls" and "Correspondence." The horizontal columns group activities into "A," "B" and "P" (for Personal) priorities.

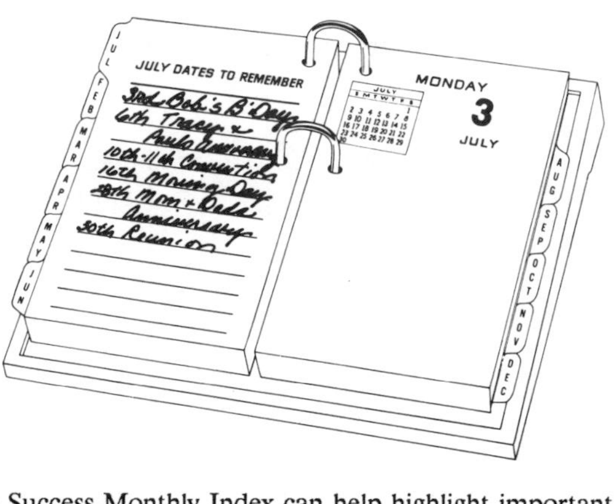

**Figure 2-5.** The Success Monthly Index can help highlight important dates as well as things to do. It functions as a monthly master list for their two-page-per-day desk calendar and has a reusable, write-on, wipe-off surface.

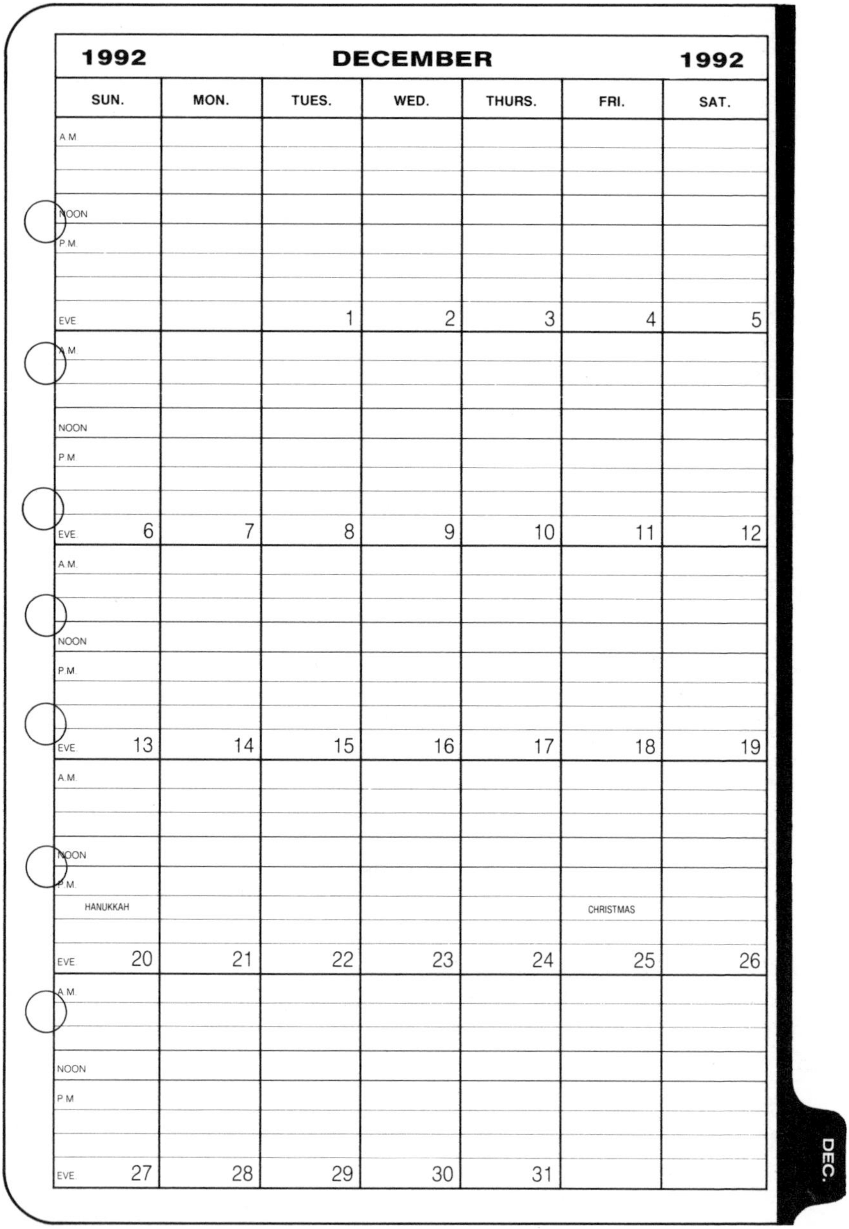

| 1992 | | | DECEMBER | | | 1992 |
|------|------|------|------|------|------|------|
| SUN. | MON. | TUES. | WED. | THURS. | FRI. | SAT. |
| A M<br><br>NOON<br>P.M.<br><br>EVE | | 1 | 2 | 3 | 4 | 5 |
| A M<br><br>NOON<br>P.M.<br><br>EVE  6 | 7 | 8 | 9 | 10 | 11 | 12 |
| A M<br><br>NOON<br>P.M.<br><br>EVE  13 | 14 | 15 | 16 | 17 | 18 | 19 |
| A M<br><br>NOON<br>P.M.<br>HANUKKAH<br><br>EVE  20 | 21 | 22 | 23 | 24 | CHRISTMAS<br>25 | 26 |
| A M<br><br>NOON<br>P M<br><br>EVE  27 | 28 | 29 | 30 | 31 | | |

DEC.

**Figure 2-6.** This combination monthly tabbed calendar page on the front (above) and master list on the back (see next page) monthly calendar page comes with the loose-leaf style Day-Timer diary.

# TO BE DONE IN DECEMBER

| ITEM NO. | NUMBER EACH ITEM | ITEM NO. | NUMBER EACH ITEM |
|---|---|---|---|
| | | | |
| | | | |
| | | | |
| | | | |
| | | | |
| | | | |
| | | | |
| | | | |
| | | | |
| | | | |
| | | | |
| | | | |
| | | | |
| | | | |
| | | | |
| | | | |
| | | | |
| | | | |
| | | | |
| | | | |
| | | | |
| | | | |
| | | | |
| | | | |
| | | | |
| | | | |
| | | | |
| | | | |
| | | | |
| | | | |
| | | | |
| | | | |
| | | | |
| | | | |
| | | | |
| | | | |
| | | | |
| | | | |
| | | | |
| | | | |
| | | | |
| | | | |
| | | | |
| | | | |
| | | | |
| | | | |
| | | | |

DEC

month's list. You may prefer Personal Resource Systems' open-ended time frame "Items to Do" form (Figure 2-7) where you list and prioritize future to-do's on the front and any notes about particular items on the back. Here you have a form for a concise list that isn't cluttered with any extraneous written notes or reminders.

If you work on projects with many detailed steps, use a **project sheet** or **project planner** in addition to or instead of a master list. Make a simple list for each project or buy project planning forms that are commercially prepared (see Caddylak Systems, Day Runner, Day-Timers and Personal Resource Systems listed in the chapter resource guide). Figure 2-8 shows two by Day-Timers. See also Chapter 9 for some other examples of project forms.

Memogenda is a thin, spiral bound book that is a great combination master list and project planner. You can keep an up-to-date listing of all the things you have to do in one convenient, compact, lightweight source. Particularly useful if you travel, the Memogenda (shown in Figure 2-9) is an indispensable planning tool for professional speaker Jeanne Robertson who is on the road much of the time.

The Executive ScanCard System is a compact, portable approach to project management. Available in many different sizes, the system features portfolio or notebook style cases with pockets for project cards, which you scan regularly to determine future planning or action steps you need to take. (See Figure 2-10.)

If you work with others on joint projects, you may prefer large **wall charts** or **visual control boards** that display activities or specific project tasks for many people to see at one time. Different varieties include "write-on-wipe-off" boards and magnetic boards with movable strips and cards. If portability is not a factor, these boards can be just the thing. See also Chapter 9 for more information on charts.

## TICKLER SYSTEMS

Almost all of us need to have our memories reminded or "tickled." A **tickler system** is a reminder system that tickles your memory.

A calendar and a to-do list are the simplest tickler systems just about everyone uses. But you need more than these tools if you have many, many reminders or follow-ups that are too numerous or tedious to write down in the ways we've discussed up to now.

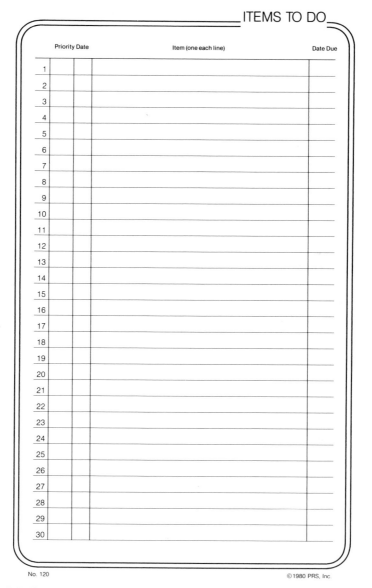

Figure 2-7. The Personal Resource System Items To Do form lets you list one item per line and has you put any notes about a particular item number on the back (see next page), thereby keeping the notes convenient but not cluttered.

## NOTES FOR TO DO'S

| Item # | Additional Information |
| --- | --- |
| | |

No. 120

**PROJECT DESCRIPTION**

Project # _____ Project Title _____
Description _____
_____
_____
_____
_____
_____

Project # _____ Project Title _____
Description _____
_____
_____
_____
_____
_____

Project # _____ Project Title _____
Description _____
_____
_____
_____
_____
_____

Project # _____ Project Title _____
Description _____
_____
_____
_____
_____
_____

Project # _____ Project Title _____
Description _____
_____
_____
_____
_____
_____

Project # _____ Project Title _____
Description _____
_____
_____
_____
_____

1987, 1990. DAY-TIMERS, Inc. ALLENTOWN, PA  •  STYLE L543  •  PRODUCT NO. 90689          PRINTED IN USA

**Figure 2-8.** Here are two project forms by Day-Timers. The form on this page gives you an overview summary of all ongoing projects. The form on the next page lets you take a project and plan out the necessary tasks and steps.

1. PROJECT NAME _____

2. ASSIGNED TO _____ 3. RESPONSIBILITY _____

4. COMPLETION _____ 5. REVIEW DATES _____

No. _____

2.     3.

BACKGROUND

PURPOSE—RESULTS TO BE ACCOMPLISHED

DETAILS

©1985, 1989, DAY-TIMERS, Inc. ALLENTOWN, PA • STYLE L544 • PRODUCT NO. 90671     PRINTED IN USA

MEMOGENDA.  Typical Entries

| | REF | ITEM—ONE LINE TO EACH | DUE | X T O | DATE |
|---|---|---|---|---|---|
| 1 | P42 | attorney      appt 2 pm | 2-16 | | |
| 2 | | Bank Statement | | X | 2-12 |
| 3 | | Third Quater adv. Plans | | | |
| 4 | | Production meeting 2 pm | 2-18 | | |
| 5 | | Check Sales Policies    Put off a few days | | T | P-28 |
| 6 | LG | Dividend Meeting 10 AM | 2:20 | | |
| 7 | | Trip Expenses | | X | 2-10 |
| 8 | CgB | Costs on Item A-62    Referred to department head. | | | |
| 9 | | Birthday Jim Smith    Taken care of. | 2-16 | X | 2-12 |
| 10 | FK | How many replacements | | | |
| 11 | | aniversary wife | 3-6 | | |
| 12 | LC | J. P. Mordant 416-6241    More information on left page. | | X | 2-10 |
| 13 | P46 | Long term plan    Check page-46 every few days. | | T | P-26 |
| 14 | P42 | Development Notes    Special sheet. | | T | P 32 |
| 15 | | See Mordant plant | 2-20 | | |
| 16 | RTL | Inventory Equipment | 6-30 | | |

Note above table: X - Completed  T - Transferred  O - Abandoned

**Figure 2-9.** Here is a half page from the Memogenda system listing typical tasks and activities to remember.

A **tickler card system** is useful if you regularly follow up with certain people over a period of time or have particular tasks to do on a project on certain days. A tickler card system typically consists of plain or colored index cards, monthly and 1-31 index guides and an index file box.

A tickler card system is particularly useful for sales follow-up. You could use it for a prospect who isn't ready to buy your product or service today but could be ready over the next several months. You'd first prepare a prospect card with the person's name, address and phone number. Then you'd place the card behind a numbered tab (if you're calling within the next 31 days) or behind the tab for the month you plan to make the call. Each time you call or write you make a notation on the card and indicate your next follow-up

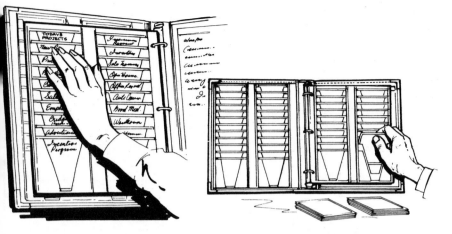

**Figure 2-10.** The Executive ScanCard System helps you handle large numbers of projects simultaneously by having you scan project cards for the next action steps.

action. The card keeps moving through the system until you decide to remove it.

The **tickler slip system** works in much the same way as the card system except you use preprinted, NCR (no carbon required) forms. Because you can make several copies of the original form, this system is particularly useful for activities such as delegations that involve other people. For example, if a co-worker has agreed to complete a report for you, you would jot down the co-worker's name and number, the report name and the due date on the slip. You could keep the original and give the copy to the co-worker. You'd file your slip behind the due date (or a few days before) in your tickler slip system file box and your co-worker would do the same. Ideally, the party most responsible for the activity (in this case your co-worker) would complete the report and give you a copy with the tickler slip attached. If the co-worker does not follow through, your system is a backup that makes sure nothing slips through the cracks. But when both parties are using the system, greater accountability and responsibility is usually the result.

The tickler system that we use in our office is called a **desk file** or **sorter.** The desk file opens like a book and has an expandable binding on the spine. Our model has both 1-31 *and* January to December tabs. I use it every day for follow-ups and action items that are connected to some paperwork, such as a letter or notes. (I also use it for birthday cards to be mailed.) I keep the desk file conveniently located on a corner of my desk.

The **accordion file** is similar to the desk file except it is enclosed on three sides and usually has a flap that folds over. I find it less convenient than the desk file/sorter. And if it's less convenient, you'll be less likely to use it. If, however, your tickler needs to be portable, the accordion file could be a wise choice. (Both the desk and accordion file come in other nontickler styles and have other uses that are discussed in Chapters 5 and 9.)

A **file folder tickler system** is very similar to the desk file/sorter and accordion file in that it usually has file folders labeled January to December and 1-31 and it, too, is designed to handle paper triggered actions. You can have more flexibility for the names of your tabs, e.g., you could use weekly tabs. This system can sit inside a desk drawer or in an upright rack or caddy on a nearby credenza, return or table. Again, it's not quite as convenient as the desk file/sorter and some people are afraid that if it's out of sight in a file drawer that they'll forget all about it. Once it's a habit, however, and part of your daily routine, that shouldn't be problem.

See Chapter 9 for more ideas on how to use tickler systems and to see illustrations and specific product sources.

## COMPUTERIZED TIME MANAGEMENT PROGRAMS

If you have a computer that you use all the time in your office, it may make sense to buy a computer-based time management program. Such a program usually comes with many different time management features, including calendar/scheduling, to-do list and tickler functions.

You can print out "hard copies" of your schedule on paper. It's also easy to make backup copies for added protection.

An especially nice feature of a computerized program is that you can quickly search for information in a variety of ways. Let's suppose you want to find every contact you've had with a particular customer. You can search that customer by name and within seconds find the information you need.

In general, the time management programs designed for your office or laptop computer are far superior to the new, hand-held computers. Since many of these hand-held computers aren't equipped with the standard QWERTY keyboard (which allows you to use the touch typing method), keyboard entry is laborious at best. And even with those that have the QWERTY, the scaled-down size still makes typing difficult. (See Chapter 12 for more information on "palmtops.")

If you're near a computer most of the day and you like computing, try one of these popular programs listed in the chapter resource guide: Metro, OnTime and PrimeTime.

## PLANNERS AND ORGANIZERS

Like computer time management programs, planners and organizers are becoming more and more versatile and packed with many different features. The difference is that planners and organizers are manual tools and are generally more portable.

### WHAT TO LOOK FOR IN A PLANNER

When you need more than a calendar or appointment book but less than a full blown organizer, a planner may be the perfect solution. And in fact, every organizer should include a good planner as its main feature.

A good planner combines both long- and short-range planning. For long-range planning, you should be able to see the major events of the year and/or each month of the year. For short-range planning, you should have planning pages that present either the entire week (which is my preference) or separate pages for each day.

Your planner should have enough writing space. If you're adding notes all over the place, you could either be short on space or the format isn't working for you.

Decide whether you want a dated or undated planner. With the latter you have to spend more time writing in the dates, but you also won't waste any sections of your planner if you should purchase it after the year has begun. With loose-leaf planners that isn't a problem, unless dated sheets are prepackaged by year or quarter.

If your planner comes with a telephone directory, try to find one with sections for *each* letter of the alphabet rather than two letters combined.

The size of your planner may pose some problems. You may want it to be small and compact enough to carry with you yet large enough to carry standard size papers. A tradeoff may be necessary. Choose the most important size considerations. Lean toward the *size you will use* and select a planner that has the most important features to you.

## DO YOU REALLY NEED AN ORGANIZER?

Usually housed in plush ring binders, organizers help professionals manage both time and information. Organizers incorporate a variety of planning and scheduling tools, including calendars; daily to-do sheets; weekly, monthly and yearly projections; master lists; and schedules for special projects and activities.

Other features usually include a phone directory, sections for "fingertip information" referred to frequently, record keeping tools, special compartments for credit cards and cash, pen and pencil holders and combination calculator/rulers. (See Figures 2-11, 2-12 and 2-13 for some examples of organizer accessories.) Organizers are "Swiss army desks" equipped with all the essentials professionals need close at hand. You need never be at a loss for important resource or scheduling information—particularly vital if you're out of your office frequently.

Figure 2-11. The Day Runner Classic organizer

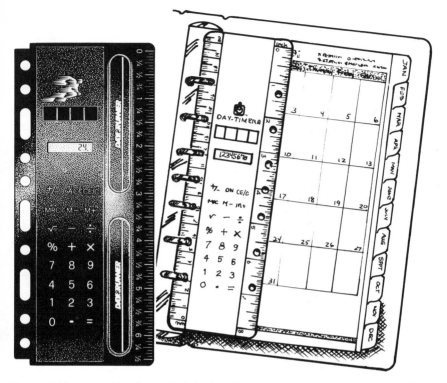

**Figure 2-12.** A combination ruler/calculator is a new accessory for your organizer. Shown here are the Day Runner version on the left, which also comes with two snap-out red and blue pens, and the Day-Timer version on the right. Both are hole-punched, include inches and centimeters and are solar-powered.

A variety of styles and sizes adapt to many different professional needs. Some are small enough to fit in a coat or shirt pocket; others fit in a briefcase or purse; still others are self-contained mini-briefcases that can be carried on the shoulder with a strap. Many come in leather and make for professional accessories that are functional as well as attractive.

The organizer is my personal time management favorite but it's not for everyone (nor is any tool for that matter). If you're at your desk most of the day and don't move around from office to office or meeting to meeting, you may not need the portability and compactness of the organizer. Some people don't need to have that much information at their fingertips and find notebook organizers

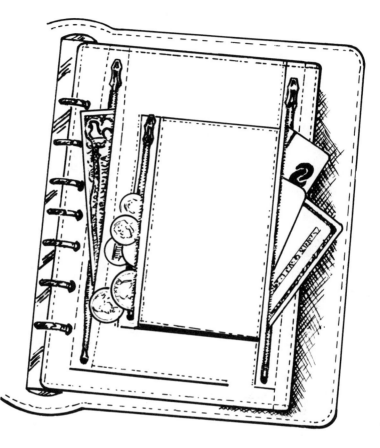

**Figure 2-13.** The "Carry-All" Multi-Zippered Holder is a Day-Timer organizer accessory I've used for years. (Illustration courtesy of Day-Timers, Inc., Allentown, PA 18195-1551)

bulky and cumbersome. Some see organizers as too "trendy" for their taste.

Others ask, "What would you do if you lost it?" Here are three measures to prevent the dire consequences of such a disaster. First, always photocopy any critical material and store it in a safe location. Second, use a computerized time management program (such as On Time or Primetime, listed in the resource guide) and a computerized personal database program (such as Address Book Plus and DynoDex, discussed in Chapter 9). With this option, you would print out your hard copies (which you can use in your organizer) and make regular floppy disk backups. Third, write the following statement on a business card that you laminate and attach to the inside front cover of your organizer: "REWARD: $150 for returning this lost book."

## RESOURCE GUIDE

Time management is an ongoing challenge and adventure. There are no magic wands but hopefully this listing will open your eyes to the many exciting solutions that are available.

## TIME MANAGEMENT TOOLS AND SYSTEMS

Practically every time I turn around, I see a new time management tool or system. The following are among the best I've seen. See also Chapter 9 for additional ideas.

**AT-A-GLANCE** is a well-known brand name for calendars, appointment books and wall charts. Two organizers, the M.B.O. ("Management By Organization") and the TimeTactics systems, are also available. 607/563-9411
Keith Clark
101 O'Neil Road
Sidney, NY 13838

**Caddylak Systems** is a catalog featuring wall planning systems and charts; time management forms. 800/523-8060
131 Heartland Blvd.
Brentwood, NY 11717

**Day Runner** notebook organizer/planners are available nationally in department and stationery stores in an affordable, versatile range of styles, sizes and features. (See Figure 2-14.) 800/232-9786 or 213/837-6900
Day Runner, Inc.
3562 Eastham Dr., Culver City, CA 90232

**Day-Timers, Inc.** planners and work organizers come in many different sizes and formats. Free catalog. 215/395-5884
Day-Timers, Inc.

**Figure 2-14.** Day Runner makes many different styles and sizes of organizer. Shown here is the Entrepreneur briefcase style (open and closed), which holds 8½-by-11-inch paper.

PO Box 2368
Allentown, PA 18001

**Executive ScanCard System** is a card/notebook organizer in several styles and sizes to track major activities related to projects with color-coded cards. Options include appointments calendar, Month-at-a-Glance Planner, telephone index, business card holder, letter size pad, inside storage pockets, pen loops and calculator. You can keep up to 200 project cards in view, depending on the model you select. 800/848-2618 or in Canada, 800/447-5552; 614/469-3100
The Executive Gallery, Inc.
380 Dublin Avenue
Columbus, OH 43215

**Filofax** small planners incorporate date book, project, expense and phone/address information in compact, attractive, leather binders. Available in department and stationery stores. 800/345-6798 or 203/353-9777 (to get names of stores in your area that carry Filofax) Filofax Inc.

**Figure 2-15.** The Shoulder Binder by Franklin is a convenient way for a woman to carry both her organizer and a few personal items in the outside purse pocket. I use this binder every day and I never need to carry an additional handbag or briefcase.

500 West Ave.
Stamford, CT 06902-6325

The **Franklin Day Planner** is a full-featured organizer system. The Franklin catalog offers a nice selection of high quality binders (including one with a shoulder strap and outside purse pocket as shown in Figure 2-15) as well as special forms and training materials.
800/654-1776 or 801/975-1776
Franklin International Institute, Inc.
PO Box 25127
Salt Lake City, UT 84125-0127

**Memindex Desk Planning Guide** is a dated, color-coded, one-page-per-day planner with special yearly, monthly and weekly planning sections. The binder is 7 by 7½ by 1½ inches. The 500-name-

address-phone insert is extra ($7.95). Ranges from $19.95 for vinyl to $37.95 for leather. 800/828-5885; in New York: 716/342-7890
149 Carter Street
Rochester, NY 14601

**Memindex Pocket Planning Guide** is a wallet style planner that lets you carry one month at a time, a yearly planner and phone/address booklet. Each day of the month is tabbed and has two pages that include space for appointments, notes, expenses. Ranges from $27.95 in vinyl to $42.95 in leather. (See Memindex above.)

**Memogenda** is a system for keeping track of your to-do's and for getting them done. **Zipagenda** is a zippered case that contains the Memogenda system and allows you to store additional papers.
615/833-4101
Norwood Products Co.
1012-N Thompson Lane
Nashville, TN 37211-2627

**Metro**, a time/desktop management computer program for IBM compatible computers, has a complete and flexible calendar function with many features. The program handles several calendars and schedules on a daily, weekly or monthly basis. A mini time-and-billing program with a built-in timer will track time for 100 clients, projects or activities. $85. 800/345-1043
Lotus Development Corp.
55 Cambridge Parkway
Cambridge, MA 02142

**The #1 Personal Management System**, a compact time management system, emphasizes positive development of habits. 817/754-3209
American Leadership Institute
PO Box 8690
Waco, TX 76714-8690

**OnTime** is an easy-to-learn and easy-to-use computer time management program that features a lifetime calendar (through the year 2079), calendar/to-do list printouts (in a variety of formats), tickler alarm system, automatic entry of recurring events (such as weekly staff meetings), automatic rollover of uncompleted to-do list tasks and keyword searching. $69.95. 800/521-9314 or 313/559-5955
Campbell Services, Inc.

Software Division
21700 Northwestern Hwy., Suite 1070
Southfield, MI 48075

The **Personal Resource System** is a cleanly designed, leather, zippered notebook organizer system that comes with an instruction booklet and tape. It now comes in two sizes, 5½ by 8½ or 8½ by 11 inches. There's also the new "Personal Pocket Companion," perfect for travel or for places you don't want to carry your entire organizer. New forms include the "Personal Reference Series," featuring handy medical, family and household information sheets. 800/542-8488 or in California, 800/255-9018; 619/259-6001
Personal Resource Systems, Inc.
PO Box 2529
Del Mar, CA 92014

**Planner Pad** (Figure 2-16) is a weekly planner in different sizes that has sections for things-to-do, appointments, expenses and space for your own categories. It helps you think in terms of categories and priorities. 402/592-0666
Planner Pads, Inc.
PO Box 27187
Omaha, NE 68127-0187

**Primetime 1.2** is a well-designed time management program that helps you set goals, organize and prioritize tasks on your to-do lists, keep a chronological record of your accomplishments and remember delegations and deadlines. $99.95. 800/777-8860 or 714/556-6523
Primetime, Inc.
PO Box 27967
Santa Ana, CA 92799-79671

**QUO VADIS** planners are readily available in stationery stores and allow you to plan by the week. I particularly like their **Prenote**, **Trinote** (see Figure 2-17) and **RAF Businessnote** planners. 800/535-5656 or 716/648-2602
QUO VADIS
120 Elmview Avenue
Hamburg, NY 14075-3770

**Remarkable Products** is a mail-order catalog featuring organizing boards, charts, forms and supplies. 201/784-0900

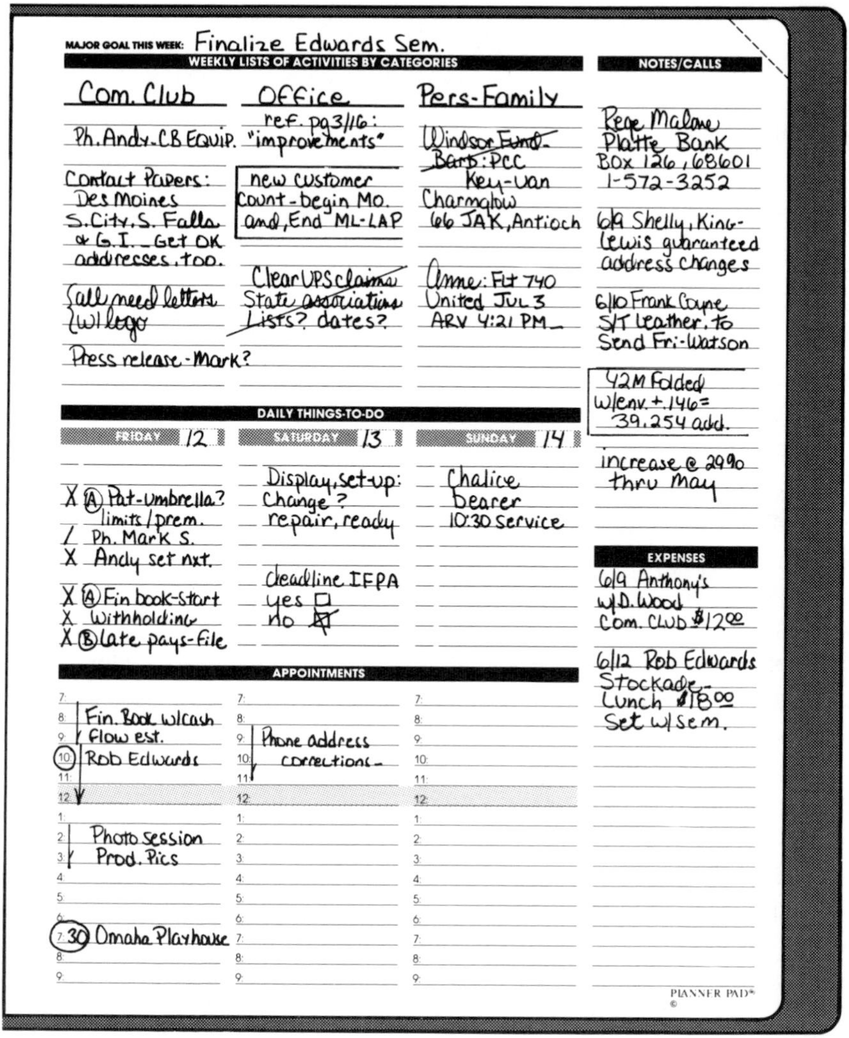

**Figure 2-16.** Here is Planner Pad's right-hand page (the left-hand page has Monday through Thursday). Planner pad is a combination appointment book, daily to-do list and weekly master list. Note the columns across the top that allow you to create your own categories of to-do's for the week.

245 Pegasus Avenue
Northvale, NJ 07647

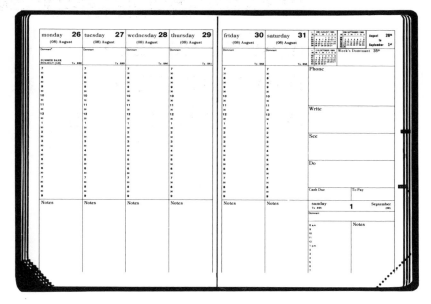

**Figure 2-17.** The Quo Vadis Trinote Agenda Planning Diary lets you do daily and weekly planning and keep track of appointments as well as to-do's by category.

**Success** is known for its appointment books and desk calendars. I like the **Monthly Index** accessory that goes with the desk calendars. 800/558-0466 or 404/988-9955
Success Calendars
1827 Powers Ferry Road, Bldg. 23
Marietta, GA 30067

The **Time/Design Management System** is an integrated organizer that has planning, project and reference sections. The Activities Checklist is a clever master list form that helps with daily planning and eliminates unnecessary rewriting. 800/637-9942 or 213/312-0288
11835 W. Olympic Blvd., Ste. 450
Los Angeles, CA 90064-5005

**WHO-WHAT-WHEN** is easy-to-use people, project and time management software. $295. 800/777-7907 or 415/626-4244
Chronos Software Inc.
555 De Haro St., Ste. 240
San Francisco, CA 94107

# HOW TO HANDLE
# TOO MUCH TO DO
# IN TOO LITTLE TIME

*Quick Scan: If you have an increasingly busy schedule in your professional and/or personal life, you'll discover time-tested tips on managing interruptions, telephone time, delegation, multiple priorities and the "rushing game." See how to better balance the "great juggling act," make room for your personal life and start using ten terrific time-savers.*

**R**arely, if ever, do people I meet have the luxury of working at a leisurely pace. There are always countless deadlines and shifting priorities, which all add up to mounting pressure.

The issue is not how much you have to do but rather how much you have to do that is really *important.* You learned how to sort the important from the less important in Chapter 1 and Chapter 2. You also learned how to organize work into categories and priorities so that you could *see* what you had to do.

The next step is to take a good hard look at *how* you work. See if there are better ways for you to get things done.

49

each call. Your area should have enough writing surface and be close to files and other telephone information you may need. Telephone equipment should ideally include: a clock (or if necessary, several clocks for different time zones); a timer (if you have trouble keeping track of time and length of calls); a voice mail system or a telephone answering machine; a speaker phone with on-hook dialing, automatic on-hook re-dialing and automatic memory dialing; and a telephone headset if you're on the phone at least two hours every day and/or you need your hands free for writing or typing while on the phone.

I've used a headset for years. I use the Plantronics SP headset (Figure 3-1). The small $89 price tag is certainly worth it for convenience as well as for your health, too. A telephone headset can help prevent neck and back aches and trips to the chiropractor. Plantronics makes headsets that are compatible with every phone system. Their toll-free number is 800/544-4660.

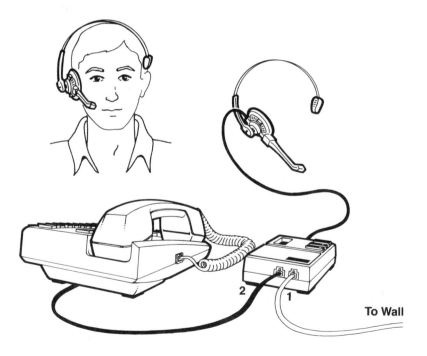

**Figure 3-1.** The Plantronics SP telephone headset

Use the speaker phone when you're on hold so you can do other work while waiting. You can also use it for a conference call in your office, provided that confidentiality isn't a problem and the speaker phone echo doesn't bother the person(s) on the other end.

## TWO: TAKE CONTROL THROUGH PREPARATION AND PLANNING

The key to mastering the telephone is doing much of your telephone work in advance, making more outgoing calls and taking fewer incoming calls. Whenever possible, set up telephone appointments. Prioritize and consolidate all callbacks. Prepare for each outgoing call or telephone appointment by having all the necessary material in front of you and *writing down* in advance any key questions or areas to cover as well as a projected time limit for each call.

Planning the time you call can be critical in preventing telephone tag. The busiest time for business calls is usually Monday morning, between 9 and 11 a.m. Sometimes calling before 9:00 or after 5:00 is a good time to catch those hard-to-reach people.

## THREE: WHAT YOU SAY GOES A LONG WAY WITH A PTA

Do you have a "Positive Telephone Attitude"? A PTA is essential for building rapport and good working relationships.

In particular, there is nothing like the power of praise when you're trying to accomplish your goals through the telephone. Acknowledge good telephone behavior by those who assist you, be they colleagues, contacts, prospects, receptionists or your own staff members.

I make a big point of thanking assistants or secretaries who have gone out of their way to take down a long message or connect me with someone who's been difficult to reach. I often will tell their boss. Fund raiser Suzanne Marx sends thank-you notes to secretaries and hotel operators as well.

A PTA also includes helpfulness and follow-through. A well-intentioned PTA becomes hollow indeed if what was promised isn't delivered.

## FOUR: USE CONCISE COMMUNICATION

Be specific when you communicate. Corporate communications consultant Dr. Allen Weiner of CDA in Sherman Oaks, California, teaches professionals "bottom line communicating," which is similar to Dragnet Sergeant Friday's, "Just the facts, ma'am." Nothing will speed up a call like getting to the point sooner.

Try these two proven techniques: first, set time limits up front (e.g., "I've got five minutes to talk") and second, outline your calls (e.g., "I'd like to discuss these two questions...").

Even your voice mail or telephone answering machine message should be as concise as possible. We get a lot of compliments on ours: "Thank you for calling Positively Organized! Please leave your name, number *and the best time to call you back.*"

## FIVE: TAKE NOTES AND TAKE ACTION

Take notes during the call if you think you may need to refer back to the call in the future. Don't rely on a good memory and don't be tempted by the thought, "I'll remember this call."

I use an 8½-by-11-inch sheet of paper (as compared to slips of paper that can get lost). Always date the entry, list the party, who initiated the call, any main points to be covered and list comments *as you go.* I like to number comments as well.

Right after the call, underline key points and take any necessary follow-up steps, such as transferring information to your calendar or listing the next action step on a tickler card. (For more information on tickler cards, see Chapter 9.)

## SIX: TRAIN YOUR TELEPHONE TEAM

If you're fortunate enough to have someone else in your office handling your telephone, you have an opportunity to boost your effectiveness, provided you *train* that person how to screen and prioritize calls, take messages and use all of the effective telephone habits listed here. Give the person a copy of George Walther's wonderful book, *Phone Power.* (You should read it first yourself.)

# HOW TO DELEGATE YOUR WAY TO SUCCESS (EVEN IF YOU'RE NOT IN A POSITION TO DELEGATE)

Whether or not you're in a position to delegate, delegation is a tool to help you increase your work output and performance in the least amount of time—provided you know how to use it and you understand what delegation really means. For the delegator, it's giving people things you don't want to do, or often, things you *do*.

In fact, according to Ben Tyler, past Burlington Industries Transportation Division president, "It's giving up things you enjoy to someone else and recognizing that not only can they do it, but sadly, they can do it better." For the delegate, delegation is an opportunity to grow and develop and to shine.

Effective delegation requires these four steps:

1. Organize.
2. Train.
3. Entrust.
4. Follow up and evaluate.

First, organize yourself. You need to see the whole picture in order to make delegation decisions. Think through the process. You'll also need a good personal organization system in order to follow up later. Top designer and entrepreneur Calvin Klein says he organizes himself first so he can delegate effectively to others.

Second, train your delegate. The amount of training and direction will vary according to the delegate's abilities and the nature of the assignment. Take time to clearly teach the delegate how to do something. Helping people be the best they can be is the highest and most productive level of delegation.

Third, entrust your delegate with the assignment. Resist the temptation of peeking over shoulders. By the way, the dictionary definition of the verb "delegate" is "to entrust to another."

Fourth, follow up, evaluate and *praise a job well done*. Of course, you can't do this step if you haven't mastered step number one. So we've come full circle, back to organization.

If you find it tough getting people to follow through and give you things on time, do what Revlon's Kathy Meyer-Poppe does. She tells them, "This is what I need and this is the date I need it by." Then she writes it on her calendar and her staff knows she's done so. They also know she will ask for it if it isn't done. But usually she doesn't have to ask. She says, "They know it's truly important when I say, for example, I need this by next Friday–that I'm not just blowing in the wind." She stays flexible, too; if her request is unrealistic, her staff will tell her and together they'll pick a new goal and agree on it. At times she may suggest they reprioritize their work.

## REVERSE DELEGATION

When Meyer-Poppe's staff comes back to her to negotiate work assignments or deadlines, they are practicing a type of **reverse delegation**. This tool works best when you're organized and can clearly see the important things you have to do, how long they will take and how they relate to the goals of your delegator, your department and yourself.

This type of reverse delegation occurs when a person gives a delegated task back to the delegator. It requires great tact and diplomacy and communication skills. It also requires a thorough understanding of goals and objectives for the company or office and for the delegator. There has to be a real *benefit* for the delegator whenever you reverse delegate.

When I was the communications manager for an aerospace company, my boss wanted me to get involved in coordinating one of his new pet projects–the creation of a historical aviation museum. Since I had no interest in his project and saw no relation in it to either my job or career, I suggested that he involve someone else who was far more qualified than I. Coming up with the name of someone else was an easy task; the company historian worked right within our department and was a natural for this project. I didn't know it at the time, but I was practicing reverse delegation.

There's one other type of reverse delegation that you should always practice whenever you're given an assignment or project. Take each of the four steps of effective delegation–organize, train, entrust and evaluate–and make sure *you* are doing them. Organize yourself, get any necessary training or information, get the trust or authority to do a job and finally, make sure *you* follow through on evaluating the job with your boss. This type of reverse delegation is a marvelous communication and self-marketing tool; it can show your boss just how well you work, not to mention how dependable and organized you are!

## HOW TO JUGGLE MULTIPLE PRIORITIES

When you handle many different projects, priorities and deadlines, you're very much like the juggler from Vaudeville who would run around keeping a dozen plates spinning on sticks. Do you often feel like the juggler pictured in Figure 3-2?

**Figure 3-2.** Illustration is courtesy of Executive ScanCard Systems

Sure, you can try to keep up this act all day, but you'll certainly burn out before too long. Unfortunately, this method is used by far too many people. To prevent burn out, here are four tips that can help. (The first three recap key ideas you learned in Chapter 2.)

First, **plan and prioritize on a daily basis** and if necessary, several times a day. Do your main planning for the day, *the day before*. Then stay flexible in order to reprioritize, if necessary, throughout the day.

Second, **use the right planning tools** that give you enough of an overview. I'm not talking about a flood of reminder notes scattered all over your desk. Such tools could include a wall chart that shows upcoming deadlines, a project or time management software program that lets you see priorities in a variety of ways or a master list.

Third, to prevent having to remember too many things in your head, **use an appropriate follow-up system.** A tickler system that you use every day, for example, can save a lot of wear and tear on your gray matter.

Fourth, **use effective communication tools, techniques and systems** with those people making demands on you. Get clarity from others in terms of the real, not imagined, urgency of each request. Have others use a special written form that indicates both the nature of the request and the time frame for its completion. (Figure 13-3 in Chapter 13 is a sample of such a form.) A written request doesn't interrupt you and lets you plan and prioritize similar requests and time frames more easily.

If several people from the same department or office are making conflicting demands on your time, bring it up at a staff meeting for a brainstorming session. Often, people may not be aware of the severity of the problem. Involve them in a cooperative way, not through finger-pointing, but through an exchange of ideas that can solve a problem. (For more on problem solving, communication and teamwork, also see Chapter 13.)

## HOW TO AVOID RUSHING

If rushing makes you crazy, make a commitment to stop doing it whenever possible. As a famous Simon and Garfunkle song says, "Slow down, you move too fast."

I keep reading articles in the paper about life in the fast lane. The more we do in our lives, the faster we need to do it. One recent newspaper story reported that even some microwavable foods aren't fast enough; if a meal has a two-step cooking process, consumer dissatisfaction sets in, even if the total cooking time amounts to no more than five minutes.

Some rushing may be unavoidable. Beware though if it's a regular habit of yours. In most cases, advance planning can prevent most cases of rushing.

Be realistic about time by becoming more *aware* of time. Be honest with yourself about how long an activity will *really* take. Estimate the minimum amount of time and a maximum and then allow an amount in the middle.

Things usually take longer than we think (the unexpected almost always comes up). And yet, Parkinson's Law says that work expands to fill the time available, which is to say that if you allow too much time to do something, you'll do it in that period of time. Sometimes the opposite is also true: work contracts to fill the time available; it's amazing how much you can get done quickly when you have to.

Follow your own time clock but speed it up and slow it down when necessary. If you practice setting your own realistic deadlines and time frames, and sticking to them, you will soon accomplish so much more and with less rushing.

My own mother used to rush all the time (and be late for almost everything) until she decided that the associated stress was just too much. She now allows more time to get ready for appointments and commitments and also does more advance planning. The combination results in less stress and greater respect from clients, friends and her daughter, the organizer.

## TEN TERRIFIC TIME AND ENERGY SAVERS FOR TERRIBLY BUSY PEOPLE

Here are ten things you may like to try to help you save time and energy and create more balance (they work for me):

1. Carry a planner all the time and write things down right away.
2. Consolidate similar activities, such as errands, telephone calls, correspondence or errands and do them together. You'll save time starting and stopping different kinds of activities.
3. Buy in bulk. Whether you're getting office supplies, gifts or cards, it's more efficient to buy for long-range needs than to frequently run out to buy individual items.
4. Call to confirm appointments. Always call doctors to see if they're running on schedule before you go there.
5. Use voice mail/telephone answering machines for screening calls and preventing unnecessary interruptions. Ask callers to leave you the best time(s) to call them back.
6. Sometimes do two things at once, such as listening to a self-improvement tape while commuting, or reading while waiting in line.
7. Never leave a room empty handed. Before leaving a room at home, ask yourself if there is something you can take with you that belongs where you're going.
8. Be creative, open-minded and look for better ways of doing things. Did you know you can buy stamps through the mail as

well as by phone? (The latter operates 24 hours a day, takes credit cards and works by calling 1/800/STAMP-24.) Share ideas with your friends and colleagues. How do *they* organize their day and life?

9. Don't rush. There's a saying that the faster you go, the slower you are going to get there. It's the old tortoise and the hare story.

10. Make time for yourself every day ideally but certainly every week at the very least. Plan things you look forward to, that nourish you. They will revitalize you with energy to spare.

## HOW TO FINISH YOUR WORK AND STILL HAVE TIME FOR A PERSONAL LIFE

If your work hangs over you like a dark cloud and follows you wherever you go, it's time to stand back and gain some perspective.

I'm not concerned about an occasional heavy schedule or major deadline. But if you think about work all the time, take work home every night or suffer from insomnia over work-related problems, you need a break!

In fact, you need more than a break; you need **balance.** Granted, your need for balance will be different at various times in your life. But the first step is developing some awareness when you're losing your balance and then to take some realistic steps.

For some people, it's helpful to add more structure to your schedule. Establish a quitting time each day and stick to it! That's more difficult than it seems for the workaholics among us.

If you must take work home, make an appointment with yourself. Decide to spend thirty minutes and thirty minutes only, for example, reviewing that report for tomorrow's staff meeting. (If necessary, use a timer.)

Make sure, too, you're not just playing a martyr role by taking on too much work or that you're giving in too much to your perfectionism ("no one else can do this as well as I"). Time management expert Mark Sanborn counters the myth that everything worth doing is worth doing well. He says, "Some things are worth doing well, some things are worth doing *very* well and some things are just worth doing."

Make an effort to talk openly with your boss or co-workers about your heavy work load. Don't just assume that there's no solution.

## WHEN TOO MUCH IS JUST TOO MUCH

It does help to have a cooperative boss or co-worker. If you're working, however, with someone who's out to sabotage you or the company, or you truly do have too much to do and too little time, it may be best to look for a different working situation altogether. This is a last resort but consider it if you've tried the time management tools and techniques in this chapter, all to no avail.

In every seminar I give there's at least one person in one of these "impossible situations," with an autocratic boss or a highly bureaucratic structure where no amount of organization could help. If you're in such a situation, it may be better to cut your losses and bail out.

## RESOURCE GUIDE

## TIME/SELF-MANAGEMENT BOOKS AND TAPES

Time management is the process of making the most of your life in the time available. When fully understood, the concept of time management embraces self- and life-management. How you manage time outside of work has a direct relationship to time management at work and vice versa. The following books and tapes will help you make the most of *all* the time in your life, especially if you lead a busy life.

**CareerTracking: 26 Success Shortcuts to the Top** by Jimmy Calano and Jeff Salzman (New York: Simon and Schuster, 1988). The authors have summarized the best of what they've read, heard, seen and experienced on the subject of career success. The book is easy to read, easy to use and will save you time on your way to the top and *at* the top as well. Hardback, $15.95. Available from CareerTrack, 3085 Center Green Dr., Boulder, CO 80301, 800/334-1018 or 303/447-2300

**Creative Time-Plus** offers three excellent tape cassette albums for busy people by home-organizing expert Ann Gambrell: "Quick Meals," "Paperwork, Paperwork" and "Clutter Control." $29.95 for each three-cassette album. Available from Creative Time-Plus, 2667 Monterey St., Torrance, CA 90503, 213/212-0917

**Feeling Good: The New Mood Therapy** by David D. Burns, M.D. (New York: New American Library, 1981). If negativity, criticism, procrastination, perfectionism, mood swings or depression are frequent or even occasional companions, effective time management will be next to impossible. This is a breakthrough book that offers clinically tested, practical solutions presented in an inspiring, compassionate style. It's easy to read and use. Paperback, $5.95

**Getting Organized: The Easy Way to Put Your Life in Order** by Stephanie Winston (New York: Warner Books, 1989). Here's a great book to help you better manage personal areas of your life from financial planning to meal planning. Learn also to maximize storage space, organize your kitchen, run a household and even teach your child to organize. Paperback, $9.95

**Getting Things Done** by Edwin Bliss (New York: Scribner/Macmillan 1983). Literally the ABCs of time management, Bliss takes time management and organization topics such as "Deadlines," "Goals" and "Priorities," puts them in alphabetical order and succinctly provides practical and entertaining gems of wisdom. Paperback, $6.95

**How to Create Balance at Work, at Home, in Your Life** by Bee Epstein, Ph.D. is a dynamic, six-cassette program for working women. Epstein herself is a model of balance and success. This is a great program to enhance your life. Available from Adams-Hall Publishing, PO Box 491002, Los Angeles, CA 90049. $49

**How to Get Control of Your Time and Your Life** by Alan Lakein (New York: NAL, 1989). This classic time management book is particularly useful in helping you sort out your life goals. Paperback, $4.50

**How to Get Organized When You Don't Have the Time** by Stephanie Culp (Cincinnati: Writer's Digest Books, 1986). Culp makes time management and getting organized *fun.* In her down-to-earth, humorous style, Culp cuts through with plenty of practical ideas to organize the time and space in your personal life. Paperback. $10.95

**Managing Your Time, Your Energy and Your Relationships** by Mark Sanborn is a fast-paced six-cassette audio album that shows you how to get more done by managing not only your time and energy but that of your employees. Available from ManagersEdge Corp., Box 1347, Englewood, CO 80150, 800/776-5771 or 303/778-1692. $69 plus $3 shipping and handling

**ManagersEdge Monthly Cassette Program,** ManagersEdge Corp. (see previous listing). Each month, subscribers receive a 60-minute cassette featuring professional business consultants and trainers discussing time management, managing people and communication. $119.40 per year

**Newstrack Executive Tape Service,** ManagersEdge Corp. (see previous listing). Bi-weekly tape cassette series that summarizes major newspaper and magazine articles related to business. $249 per year

**Nightingale-Conant** business and motivational audiocassettes. An excellent selection of tape programs to get and keep you inspired to and from work. 800/323-5552

**Organize Yourself!** by Ronni Eisenberg (New York: Collier Books/Macmillan, 1986). Eisenberg's book is an easy-to-read, easy-to-use guide for organizing your personal life. Paperback, $7.95

**The Organized Executive: New Ways to Manage Time, Paper and People** by Stephanie Winston (New York: Warner Books, 1985). Not just for the executive, this classic provides nuts 'n bolts techniques to streamline your work flow and office. Paperback, $7.95

**Phone Power** by George Walther (New York: Berkley Books, 1987). A great book to teach you just about everything when it comes to the telephone. Paperback, $3.50

**The Psychology of Achievement** by Brian Tracy is a six-cassette program that distills the key ingredients of high achievement. Brian Tracy presents proven, practical methods and techniques that high achievers regularly use in their lives and careers. Available from Brian Tracy Learning Systems, 462 Stevens Avenue, Suite 202, Solana Beach, CA 92075-2065, 800/542-4252 (outside California), 619/481-2977 (inside California). $55

**Rogers Records** is a series of handy personal, household and financial record keeping booklets. Available through J.P. Roberts Company, 1205 Schaller Rd., Verona, WI 53593

**Soundview Executive Book Summaries** sends two or three eight-page summaries of business books and three one-page book reviews every month to subscribers. You can also buy back copies of summaries. $69.50 per year. 800/521-1227 or 802/453-4062
5 Main St.
Bristol, VT 05443

**The Superwoman Syndrome** by Marjorie Hansen Shaevitz (New York: Warner Books, 1985). This wonderful book is for women who want more balance and control in their life. Paperback. $3.95.

**Taming the Paper Tiger: Organizing the Paper in Your Life** by Barbara Hemphill (Washington, D.C.: Hemphill & Associates, Inc.). This is a delightful, easy-to-read guide with charming illustrations and many useful tips and techniques. Available through Hemphill & Associates, 2000 Pennsylvania Ave., N.W., Ste. 171, Washington, D.C. 20006, 202/387-8007. Paperback, $11.95

**What It Takes: Good News From 100 of America's Top Professional and Business Women** by Lee Gardenswartz and Anita Rowe (New York: Doubleday, 1987). An inspiring work, this book shows how women at the top arrange their lives to achieve their goals and how you can assess your own aptitude for success. Hardback, $16.95. Available by calling 213/823-2466 or writing 13470 Washington Blvd., Ste. 204, Marina Del Rey, California 90292.

**Working From Home, Third Edition: Everything You Need to Know About Living and Working Under the Same Roof** by Paul and Sarah Edwards (Los Angeles: Jeremy P. Tarcher, 1990). The Edwards have revised and expanded their power-packed sourcebook that provides many time- and energy-saving shortcuts for the small entrepreneur or anyone who works at home. Paperback, $14.95

**Working Smart: How to Accomplish More in Half the Time** by Michael LeBoeuf (New York: Warner Books, 1988). This classic continues to sell strong and with good reason: this is a must-read book that hits the core of essential work habits you need to develop on the job. Paperback. $4.95.

# MASTERING
# YOUR DESK
# AND THE
# PAPER JUNGLE

*Quick Scan: If you're inundated with the "pile system" on your desk, if your work area is steadily shrinking into non-existence, if desktop clutter has got you down and under, this chapter's for you. Learn why your desk represents the single most important part of your office, how to make it work for you and what to do about paperwork.*

Do you know where your desk is? This question is usually good for some chuckles at my seminars. The problem is most people can't even *find* their desk. It's under here somewhere...

You're not alone. You and 60 million other people in the U.S. have a desk of some kind. When I refer to a desk, I mean *any* piece of furniture that is used as your primary working surface. It may be a large executive model with many drawers in a traditional office or a simple work table at a computer work station.

Chances are good you spend many hours every day at your desk. Why not have it be the best looking, best functioning desk around?

## THE MYTH OF THE MESSY DESK

No matter what you've seen on coffee cups, **a clean desk is the not the sign of an empty mind!** I know those coffee cup cliches will try to tell you otherwise. But don't be fooled. Most people think and act more clearly at a clean, well organized desk.

Don't fall prey to false notion that a messy desk means you're busy because you *look* busy. The reasoning is that if you *look* busy, you're productive. Take the advice of B. W. Luscher, Jr., from the U.S. Postal Service, who warns: "Don't confuse activity with productivity."

Far from indicating productivity, a messy desk signals a lack of dependability, control and focus, not to mention incomplete work, missed deadlines and lost information. One manager told me about an employee who had a ton of stuff on her desk. As the manager put it, "All those piles of paper told me she was in trouble."

While the woman was on vacation, the manager went in and saw a six-month-old check lying there with a bunch of invoices. He also discovered an important letter to 20 people that had never gone out. The letter was to announce a meeting the *manager* had planned. The manager found the 20 letters stuck in a drawer together with papers to be filed. All the letters had been typed and the envelopes addressed. All the employee had had to do was mail the letters! When the employee returned from vacation, she was devastated to learn of her mistake–she could have sworn she had mailed the letters months ago.

What was her problem? The manager says it was a combination of many things. She was very social, always wanting to know what was going on with other people and didn't take care of her own business. The manager observed, "You've got to worry first about what's on your own desk." He also said, "You've got to be a team player and let someone know if you're falling behind." In a nutshell, what she didn't have were the right organizational systems–the right tools and habits that signify a pro who is organized to be the best.

The fact is you are *not* more productive when you're working out of a cluttered desk. Besides feeling stress, you're continually distracted by all the different papers, piles and objects that keep pulling at you. It's easy to go into sensory overload as your eyes keep flitting from thing to thing and your mind keeps worrying whether you're working on the *right* task. No wonder you're exhausted at the end of each day!

Think of a clean desk as a little gift you give yourself.

## NOT A STORAGE LOCKER

**Do not use your desktop for storage.** It's a *work* surface, not a storage locker. Keep it clear, ready for action. Your desktop is *prime* work space and should contain only those items you use every day, such as your phone, calendar or planner and clock. Keep your desk as clean as possible.

But how clean is clean? That depends on a number of factors. First, consider who sees your desk. Colleagues? Clients? Customers? Patients? What kind of image do you want to create before these people? It's quite possible your desk should be spotless before the public but can be more of a workhorse before other staff members.

Incidentally, if you're concerned with image, consider this: research reveals that the cleanest desks belong to those individuals higher up in the organization. If you're on an upwardly mobile career path, have your desk look the part.

Second, consider what your level of aesthetics and function dictates. Start to become conscious of what *your* ideal level of order is and work toward it.

Some people really are more comfortable with clutter and claim they would dry up in an orderly, "sterile" environment. Neatness counts but neat isn't always organized or necessary. If you're one of those people who prefers "organized clutter," more power to you.

Most people, though, have simply never tried working in a clutter-free setting for more than a day or so. The expression "try it, you'll like it" certainly applies here.

## HOW TO TURN YOUR DESK
## INTO A SELF-CLEANING OVEN

Clients chuckle knowingly whenever I tell them, "Your desk is not a self-cleaning oven." They realize that they need to *do* something. Even with a self-cleaning oven, there are steps you need to take for it to work effectively: wipe up major spills, remove cookware and set the controls. So, too, there are steps to take with your desk to make it more automatic.

## CLEAR A PATH

The first step is "clearing a path," as one of my clients described the process of thinning out the paper jungle and cleaning out the dead wood from her desktop and work area.

Think of yourself as an air traffic controller and your desktop as the runway. You're in charge. *You* determine which papers, piles, and projects can land on your desk–and stay there.

### USE THE ACCESSIBILITY PRINCIPLE

I once had a client who sent me a snapshot of his terribly cluttered desk and office before we began working together. The caption read, "My office...where everything in the whole damn world is at my fingertips!"

Don't use your desk as one giant tickler system. You needn't be afraid that if papers and projects are out of sight, they'll be out of mind provided you do two things:

1. Set up an appropriate **time management system** as described in Chapter 2.
2. Set up a **daily paperwork system**, which will be described shortly in this chapter.

Beware the feeling that everything has to be accessible. How many of those things on your desktop do you actually use every day? Every week? Every month? Every year? Make a list of the things you use every day. Of those things, which need to be sitting on your desktop? See if there isn't a better place, one that's accessible, but not on top of you.

Accessibility is the key word. Frequency of use should determine accessibility. How often are you using all of your items? Maybe you started out using an item every day in the past and at some point you stopped. But there the item remains. As a general rule, **the more often you use an item, the more accessible it should be.** Take the Accessibility Survey in Figure 4-1.

**Figure 4-1.** ACCESSIBILITY SURVEY
List in the space below the things on your desk that you use...

**Daily:**



**Several Times a Week:**



**Once a Week:**



**Once a Month:**



**A Few Times a Year:**



**Rarely or Never:**




   Remember, frequency of use determines the proximity and accessibility an item should have. Keep close at hand only those things you're using every day or several times a week.

## BEGIN TO SORT

The Accessibility Principle lets you see the big picture on your desk. Now you're ready to start sorting and grouping papers and other items on your desk, such as supplies and mementos, using another principle: **things that you use together or that require similar action, go together.**

As you sort through papers and other items, start grouping them in broad categories by asking yourself questions such as the following:

1. Do you see active paperwork or files you're using daily or several times a week? Put them on one area of your desk for now. Attach a self-adhesive, removable sticker to label this and the other temporary piles you will sort.
2. Do you see "reminder" papers with information that should be recorded elsewhere, such as your calendar, planner, phone book or computer? If you can do it quickly, transfer this information; if not, stack these papers together.
3. Are there any items of indecision that are sitting on your desk because you haven't decided when to handle them or what to do with them? These items make up what attorney Robert Span calls the "problem pile." Pull them together.
4. Do you see reference or resource items that somehow landed on your desk and remained? File them now if you can do it quickly or put them in an area or box for filing later.
5. Is there material to read—maybe magazines, books or reports? Separate personal from professional reading. When possible, tear out articles you wish to read and toss the rest of the publication.
6. Are there personal items related to a hobby or an interest that belong elsewhere?
7. Are there any supplies and equipment on your desk? Separate them by function and by frequency of use.

The trick is to start categorizing and prioritizing everything on your desk, focusing most of your attention on the active, action paperwork and projects and clearing away the clutter. Using your Accessibility Survey and this initial sorting process, see how many things you can remove from your desktop and store in other places. Even for items you use every day, don't clutter your primary work surface by putting them all on your desktop. They could still be very accessible in a drawer, on a credenza or on a table to the side. Remove any items you don't use.

## SET UP A DAILY PAPERWORK SYSTEM

Now that you've cleared away some items and have begun to sort your desktop paperwork, you may be wondering, "Now where I am going to put this stuff?" When you don't know where to put papers, they inevitably end up staying on your desk or in the in-box on your desk. You may also be making extensive use of the "pile system," which has a way of spreading to every available horizontal surface in your work area.

Let's face it: most of us were never "paper trained." Setting up appropriate categories and containers in a **daily paperwork system** can help. The daily paperwork system doesn't take the place of your filing system, which is discussed in detail in Chapter 5. The daily paperwork system is for *active* paperwork that you process on a *daily* basis. It is a set of tools and habits to help you manage your mail, paperwork, projects and desk.

Begin by categorizing types of papers that come your way most often. Typical categories might include: "Action" (this week), "Financial," "Correspondence," "Calls," "Staff," "Reading," "Filing" and "Pending." You might also include specific category names for *active* projects you're using on a *daily* basis. Using the initial groupings you've already created as a guide, list basic category names you could use for your everyday paperwork in the space below:

If you're having trouble thinking of ones that fit your needs, try this simple exercise. Next time you process your mail and other paperwork, have some 3-by-5-inch index cards handy. Go through your paperwork, making decisions about what to keep and what to toss. (For many people this is the most difficult part. Be willing to get in the habit of freely tossing—more on this in Chapter 10). On an index card, jot down the major category for each type of paper you're keeping (e.g., "Reports," "Must do today"). A broad category name will often describe the general type of activity or level of urgency. Do this for a few days or for one day if you have a lot of mail and paperwork.

Go through the cards and **select the broadest, most general categories you'll use every day.** See if some of them can be combined. A category is a good one if you'll use it just about every day. Remember the purpose of these categories is for general sorting, not filing of paperwork.

Once you've decided on your basic categories, set up the tools of your daily paperwork system using existing file folders, boxes, caddies or organizers. Label these containers with your categories. Ideally, get as much off your desk as possible. Containers should be accessible but they shouldn't crowd your space.

Set up a trial paperwork system. Buy a package of assorted colored, "third-cut," manila folders at your local stationery store. See what you already have on hand in terms of boxes, trays and caddies. Don't invest in a lot of equipment; remember this is just a trial system. Some people, after getting all inspired about organization, rush out and buy too many accessories without first thinking through the system. I've walked into offices of some new clients only to find five name and address files, ten letter trays and dozens of file folders—all of which had had "good intentions" but have since been abandoned. The supplies are not the system. They are *part* of the system. They are only the tools.

**Start with a simple system.** Select the smallest number of tools and label them with your category names. Arrange them in an easy-to-use, accessible location. A couple of pointers may be helpful. First, use *vertical* systems whenever possible, as horizontal ones tend to promote the "pile system" of stacking papers. (See Figure 4-2 for examples of vertical, desktop active file organizers.) Second, try the system out for two to three weeks, make refinements and *then* purchase any additional supplies you need.

Your daily paperwork system doesn't have to be visible; some of the best ones are "invisible." Use prime filing space in your desk or in an arm's-reach filing cabinet or credenza. If out of sight means out of mind, then perhaps a more visible system is indeed a good idea for you. But if you're the type of person who gets anxious just looking at paperwork, then design a more hidden, yet accessible, system and start using your time management tools to jot down things to do and remember.

A couple of tools may be particularly useful in your daily paperwork system. I use the **desk file/sorter tickler system** that is described in Chapters 2 and 9 to sort what would otherwise be miscellaneous follow-ups into an organized, chronological system. The **Pendaflex Sort-Pal** (Figure 4-3) is an expanding sorter file that organizes papers requiring specific routine actions, such as faxing, photocopying or signature. The **Pendaflex Hanging Expandable File** (Figure 4-4) fits inside your file drawer and has nine expandable filing sections that grow as your daily paperwork system grows.

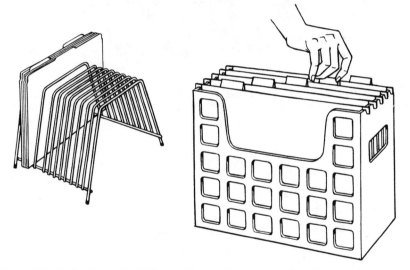

**Figure 4-2.** Colored manila folders for your daily paperwork system work great in a vertical wire rack (on the left). If you prefer a desktop file organizer that accommodates hanging file folders, consider the Oxford DecoFlex by Esselte Pendaflex, which comes with five different-colored hanging folders.

## SURVEY YOUR WORK SURFACE

Now that you've cleared a path and set up a daily paperwork system, look at your desktop. **Do you have enough work surface?** Many people put up with a desk that is too small to begin with and becomes smaller and smaller as the paper jungle takes over. Now that you've cleared a path, try out your desktop for several days. See if you now have enough space to work.

**Figure 4-3.** The Pendaflex Sort-Pal is a great paper sorter to handle routine action items. It comes with six preprinted tabbed sections and includes blank labels to customize your own headings.

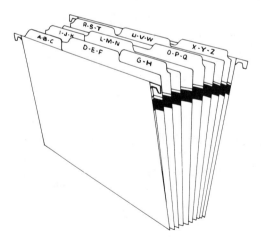

**Figure 4-4.** The Pendaflex Hanging Expandable File is a handy tool for your daily paperwork system and comes with blank, self-adhesive labels so you can make custom headings for your paperwork categories.

Most people need at least two work surfaces in their office (not counting a return or table for typewriter or computer). The second surface should be accessible, placed within an easy swivel of your chair–behind you or at your side.

Don't use the extra work surface as a storage depot or junk table. This surface should only hold things that you use daily or several times a week. This surface is great for holding active, working file folders that sit vertically in upright caddies. You might use this surface for your stapler, tape and other supplies as well as reference materials, in-out boxes, mementos and index card files. Part or all of this second surface could be designated a telephone station. A nearby table top, a credenza or even a two-drawer filing cabinet can work great as secondary work surfaces. If you prefer that spotless, executive, clean desk look, put items *inside* your furniture.

## MAKE APPOINTMENTS WITH YOURSELF

Setting up the *tools* of a daily paperwork system is only half the story; setting up *regular routines and habits* is the other half. Any organizational system, by the way, consists of two components–tools and habits. I often use this simple equation in my seminars:

a system = tools + habits

The trick to making your daily paperwork system work is simply, to work the system! Here are some habits and routines that can help you work the system–circle any that you could use:

• Schedule appointments with yourself to process paperwork. One training manager I coached schedules "personal administrative time" every week to work in her office. This time has become a "safety net" that allows her to stay in control of paperwork and priorities. She meets with her secretary every Monday to block out her self appointments on their respective calendars. They both try to protect these appointments.
• Open and sort your mail every day you're in the office.
• If possible, have someone else open and sort your mail.
• Make a decision about each paper that crosses your desk the first time it crosses your desk. For the papers you're keeping, decide if they can be handled *now* or *later*. If a paper will take only a minute or two, do it now. If you're deferring papers for

a later time, resist sticking them back in the pile or the in-box. Decide *when* you'll be handling each one and *where* each should go in terms of its function and meaning to you–i.e., where's the first place you're likely to look for the item and retrieve it for action?

• Make separate reading appointments with yourself to keep up with professional reading. If your day is just too hectic, make a reading appointment with yourself on your personal time. One professional working parent I coached has made Wednesday night "Reading Night" where she, her husband and their eight-year-old son curl up and read instead of watch television.

• When you read, try these tips: separate professional from personal interest reading; make clear decisions whether what you're reading is *worth your time;* read more quickly by reading selectively–check out headlines, subheads, first and last paragraphs; try using a timer or give yourself reading goals, e.g, two journals in twenty minutes; to increase your motivation, tell yourself positive messages about reading, e.g, how reading helps you control your paperwork, saves you time, helps you learn more about your field and makes you feel more professional.

• Keep it clean! At the very least, clean your desk and work area before you go. Or try the CAYGO habit–Clean As You GO–to prevent paper buildup during the day. And if filing is a real chore use FAYGO–File As You GO or do as Bill Butler from BCG International does–clean a file a day.

• Use time management tools such as your calendar, master list or organizer to record key information from papers that you can then toss.

• Consolidate information. Use notebooks, charts, forms, tickler systems and a good deskside filing system. (And read chapters 5 and 9.)

## FIVE EASY WAYS
## TO ORGANIZE YOUR TAX PAPERWORK

Here's a good way to apply the principles, tools and techniques we've discussed thus far, especially if you sweat it out at tax time spending precious weekends trying to catch up on a year's worth of tax-related paperwork and record keeping. Follow these five simple steps:

1. **Create a pleasant, well-equipped work area.** Whether it's a nook, cranny or corner or an office with a door, your work area should be conducive to doing tax paperwork. It should contain all necessary supplies and equipment—such as calculator, pencil, paper and files—within arm's reach. Make sure you have enough work space to spread out your paperwork. (For more on "work space basics," see Chapter 11.)

2. **Set up a simple daily paperwork system to store current bills, checks, receipts and records.** Notice the emphasis on *current.* Generally, you'll want to keep the current year's paperwork together, especially any tax deductible expense records. File current paperwork so that it's accessible. Select the right filing tools. If you're tight on space or you need portable containers, consider lightweight, plastic file boxes with handles. For faster filing, use different colored folders for different categories. (See also Chapter 5 on filing.)

3. **Separate and store past years' taxes and records.** Most records should be grouped by the tax year and stored separately from current records. Records that you'd refer to by category, such as those for car repair, home improvement and investments, should probably not be filed by the tax year. The main point is keep current records, or those you use most often, most accessible and file inactive information in your filing cabinet or in file storage boxes.

4. **Do record keeping as you go.** Once you've organized your physical records and papers, you're ready for a written record keeping system. Keeping your checkbook register up to date is an important step. But if you have a lot of deductions, you'll want to organize and track this information by category as it occurs. Record keeping books can help. If you deduct car or travel expenses, for example, use handy auto expense booklets, which are small enough to fit inside your glove compartment, briefcase or pocket.

5. **To make your system work, be sure to work the system!** Make weekly or monthly appointments with yourself and write them

down on your calendar. Create a routine and then reward yourself each time you stick to your routine.

## OTHER WAYS TO PUT PAPER IN ITS PLACE!

Are you suffering from a paper mill logjam? If so, you may have a tremendous amount of paperwork to process in your job and/or you probably have some *difficulty making decisions.*

## START MAKING DECISIONS

If you're always drowning in paperwork, chances are you tend to avoid decisions. See if one or more of the following seven symptoms apply to you:

1. You're insatiably curious and love to learn new things to the point of distraction.
2. Perfectionism tends to rule in your life.
3. Everything always takes longer than you thought it would.
4. You're creative.
5. You distrust structure and/or authority.
6. You're afraid of making a mistake and taking risks.
7. **You don't have a current, written list of goals that you refer to every day.**

All of these can contribute to decision-making difficulties concerning paper. But remember, number seven is the most important. Making decisions about paper shouldn't be arbitrary. They need to relate specifically to your values and goals in life.

Without goals as a guideline, as a yardstick, it is very difficult to make decisions, including decisions about those papers on your desk.

Difficult decisions about paper often signal ambivalence or conflict about what you want to do now and in the future. "I might need this someday" is such a haunting thought, especially when goals are fuzzy at best. Remind yourself frequently about your goals–every time, in fact, you pick up a paper, a piece of mail, a file folder, whatever. Remind yourself whenever you *put down a paper without making a decision.* And remember, almost always the worst decision you can make is *not* to make a decision because this equation is almost always true: **No Paperwork Decision = Greater Paperwork Buildup.** (See also Chapter 1 on goals and Chapter 10 on collecting.)

## PREVENTING AND CONQUERING LONG-TERM PAPER BUILDUP

Certainly, decision making will be a contributing factor to preventing paper buildup.

Controlling your mail will also be a factor. According to the best-seller *50 Simple Things You Can Do to Save the Earth*, "Americans receive enough junk mail in one day to produce enough energy to heat 250,000 homes." Here are some tips to gain more control over your mail monster:

- Cut subscriptions to magazines and/or share your subscriptions with others.
- Write to the Mail Preference Service of the Direct Marketing Association to remove your name from many national mailing lists: 11 West 42nd St., PO Box 3861, New York, NY 10163-3861.
- Reduce memberships in associations that no longer meet your needs.
- If you're not superstitious, try writing "deceased, remove from mailing list" on mailings that can be returned to the sender.

Some people will go to great lengths to avoid getting mail. I had an interesting encounter with a computer marketing director who had just returned from a trade show to stacks of mail in her office. I called to tell her I would be sending some copy for her approval through the mail. She suggested I fax it or "Fed X" it, anything, as long as it wasn't through the mail. When I explained that it was more convenient for me to mail it, she insisted I address it to someone else in her company (presumably so she wouldn't lose it!).

For existing long-term paper, you have these four options available:

1. Trash it.
2. Quickly box and store it now and plan to sort it later as a long-term project after reading chapters 10 and 14.
3. Read chapters 10 and 14 to do something about it now.

4. Create a workable filing system that accommodates resource and reference information you want to keep. Go directly to Chapter 5.

Choose an option based on how *important* these papers are to you. **Are they worth your time?**

## RESOURCE GUIDE

### PAPER MANAGEMENT SUPPLIES AND ACCESSORIES

The selected office products here are handy, dandy items you may wish to add to your work area. Most of these supplies are available in a good office products catalog or store (unless otherwise noted). Good office supply catalogs with hundreds of pages usually have two indexes–one listing manufacturers and the other listing general types of products. I've used general headings you're most likely to see in these catalogs.

### BINDERS AND ACCESSORIES

Besides file folders (which are discussed in detail in Chapter 5), there are many other options to store and organize paperwork.

The **notebook** or **binder** in all its different sizes is still one of the best organizational and storage devices around for paper resources and records *referred to frequently*. Sure, it's easier to throw something in a file, but when you go to find it, the notebook wins hands down.

Use binders to store articles and clippings, updates, product literature, samples, ideas, active client summary sheets, the latest professional or trade information–the list is endless.

As a professional speaker and writer, I keep an **anecdote notebook** with alphabetical tabbed dividers. Under each letter of the alphabet, I have key subject words that begin with that letter. For example, under the letter "I" are the subjects, "Information Management," "Inspiration" and "Insurance." Blank sheets of white paper are labeled with the key words. Short clippings are cut and pasted onto the appropriate page. Longer articles I want to keep are labeled with key words and placed in plastic sleeves.

You say you hate hole punching? Then buy the three-hole pre-punched plastic sleeves with a margin that allow you to store 8½-

by-11-inch papers without additional punching. They're called either **plastic sleeves** or **top loading sheet protectors** and are enclosed on three sides and "load" through the open end on top. See Figure 4-5 for an illustration of 20th Century plastic sleeves.

C-LINE makes them in several styles: clear, colored or clear with a colored edge. C-LINE also makes a combination sheet protector with tabs for indexing called "Tabbed Toppers." Or, if you prefer, you can use Avery's Extra Wide Index dividers specially designed for binders containing oversized sheet protectors. The point is if you're using sheet protectors and index divider tabs together, make sure the tabs are not hidden from view.

**Pocket dividers** are handy for material that is smaller than the standard page size and that you don't want to hole punch.

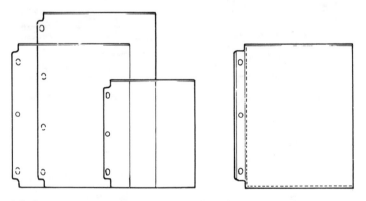

**Figure 4-5.** Sheet protectors such as these by 20th Century Plastics allow you to store 8½-by-11-inch papers in protective sleeves that are sealed on three sides and large enough so you don't have to hole-punch the papers.

If you need to organize duplicate sets of binders with tabs but you don't want to bother with typing and inserting labels repeatedly into plastic binder tabs, consider one of the multi-colored index systems on the market that let you simplify the job considerably. (See Figure 4-6.) The process is simple: you type a master contents page that aligns with the tabs and then you photocopy the page onto blank contents pages. Avery and Wilson Jones make these versatile indexes.

Avery Ready Index is available in either the standard 8½-by-11-inch or 9¼-by-11-inch sizes for binders with oversized items such as

**Figure 4-6.** Avery Ready Index lets you easily make multiple sets of binder contents pages using a typewriter and copier.

sheet protectors. There are a wide variety of styles, including numerical, monthly or alphabetical.

WilsonJones "MultiDex" features a slide out Quick Reference Table of Contents that allows you to see titles without having to flip back to the contents page in the front of the binder. It's available in five different numerical sets–5, 8, 10, 12 and 15.

"Eurofiles" is a time- and space-saving open shelf filing system whose main component is the Eurofiles binder, which features a two-ring mechanism designed to let you access, insert and remove documents easily. The system includes press-on index tabs customized for your business or professional needs. Also available are accessories for filing photos, bulky documents and important originals without without hole punching. See Figure 4-7 for an illustration of the binder and the open shelf system. For more information contact Bindertek (Sausalito, California, 800/456-3453).

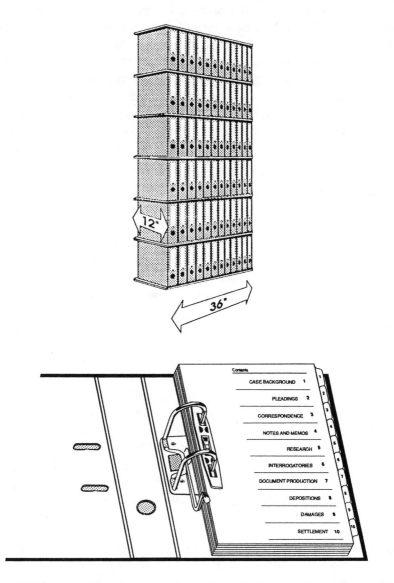

**Figure 4-7.** Eurofiles open shelf system and a Eurofiles binder shown with legal tabs

For a whole variety of preprinted tabs for nearly every area of law, consider those by Legal Tabs Co. (in Basalt, Colorado, 800/322-3022). The tabs are available on the bottom or on the side, plain or punched (3-hole side or 2-hole top). You can use them in binders or in file folders to organize your legal documents.

To easily make your own custom tabs for notebook dividers, look for Avery's IndexMaker, which comes with tabbed, reinforced dividers and clear labels, ready for photocopying or laser printing. You apply the self-adhesive labels directly onto the divider tabs.

## BUSINESS CARD ACCESSORIES

If you attend many meetings and you want a more organized way to keep business cards, start a **business card notebook** with plastic business card sleeves that are tabbed. Label the tabs with either letters of the alphabet or names of organizations and associations. Before you go to a meeting, scan the cards and any notes you made on them.

Izer International (Los Angeles, 1/800/422-4432 or 213/655-3868) makes Cardwear Hardware business card organizers, one of which fits right into a 5½-by-8½-inch, three-ring, daily planner or organizer. It comes with two, side-by-side filers with 50-card capacity, plus blank tabbed dividers and labels to create a customized portable filing system for key contacts and clients. See Figure 4-8.

Cardwear Hardware makes a special, self-adhesive strip that you can easily attach to a business card, which will then adapt to your rotary card file. DO-IT Corporation (South Haven, Michigan, 1/800/426-4822) also makes such strips called "AD-A-TAB card tabs" and they come in the standard card file size and also the larger 3-by-5-inch size, which is the one I use. See Figure 4-9.

Day Runner Inc. makes a loose-leaf business card accessory called Cardfiler Plus that fits right inside your organizer. As shown in Figure 4-10, Cardfiler Plus uses a business card as is, without having to recopy the information. Just put a special glue strip on the Cardfiler page and press the business card in place. There's preprinted space for notes and follow-up details. Whether you organize the card sheets alphabetically or by category, you have a very useful manual database that's portable, too. Cardfiler Plus comes in two sizes: 5½ by 8½ inches and 3¾ by 6¾ inches.

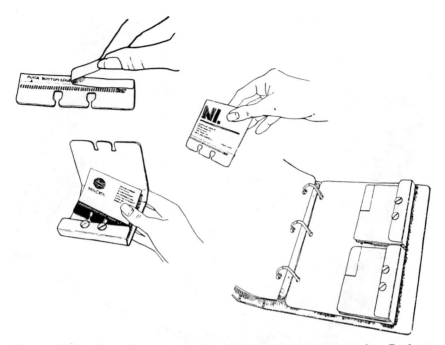

**Figure 4-8.** Cardwear Hardware business card management accessories: Cardwear Strip that affixes instantly to business cards; Cardwear Case, a pocket-sized card file; Cardwear Organizer for daily planners

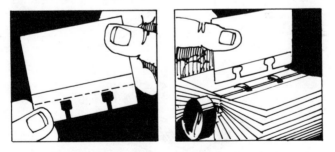

**Figure 4-9.** An AD-A-TAB card tab is a transparent strip that affixes to business cards to make them fit rotary card files.

For my business cards, I use three approaches: my computer database program, PC-File (discussed in Chapter 9), a phone book section in my organizer and a Rolodex card file. I use the 3-by-5-inch size Rolodex covered VIP file (Figure 4-11). The cards are

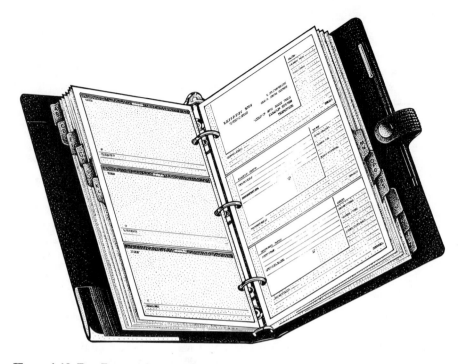

**Figure 4-10.** Day Runner Cardfiler Plus is a database for business cards that fits right in your organizer.

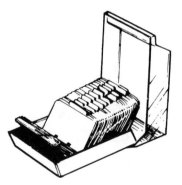

**Figure 4-11.** The Rolodex covered VIP file is the card file I use.

large enough to hold stapled or glued business cards (without having to recopy the information). There's also room for brief notes.

Rolodex makes a variety of different business card files as well as some useful accessories. To turn your file into more of a resource database, insert special Rolodex plastic divider tabs to divide up your Rolodex into different categories. Use an alphabetical system within those categories, not the entire Rolodex. With several different subject categories, it's often easier to look up listings, rather than trying to remember exact names. You can organize your file with Rolodex colored cards and/or colored plastic card protectors. If your system is used all the time, get the Rolodex plastic sleeve card protectors, which are available in clear as well as colors.

To further expand the usefulness of your card file as a database, consider adding one or more of the Rolodex Resource Files. These are compact directories preprinted on Rolodex cards. The City Directory, available for more than 30 cities, includes more than 1,500 listings from business services to nightlife. The Toll-Free Directory puts more than 800 toll-free numbers at your fingertips for categories such as airlines, business services and catalogs. The Executive Secretary combines reference information such as travel planning, office services and grammar tips along with monthly tickler and personal organizer sections. All three of these directories range in price from $9.95 to $15.00.

While the most common brand name, Rolodex is not the only brand of card file. There are many brands as well as styles from which to choose. Compare card files made by Bates, Eldon and Rubbermaid (available in office supply stores and catalogs). Cardwear Hardware, discussed previously, is a good alternative, too.

## CLIPS

To temporarily group and secure papers, nothing beats the paper clip. What you may not realize, however, is the variety of clips now available.

See Figure 4-12 for a sampling of multi-purpose clips. Labelon Owl Clips are rectangular clips that hold papers securely and will not catch on other adjacent papers. This type of clip comes in three sizes. Labelon Triumph Clamps hold bulky papers securely. **Binder clip** is the generic name for what is probably the most secure, slip-proof clip you can buy. Use binder clips for loose bulky papers that need to be held securely. For a touch of class, W.T. Rogers makes binder clips in gold as well as several colors. Baumgarten now makes a plastic binder clip. **Plastic paper clips**, such as Baumgarten Arrow

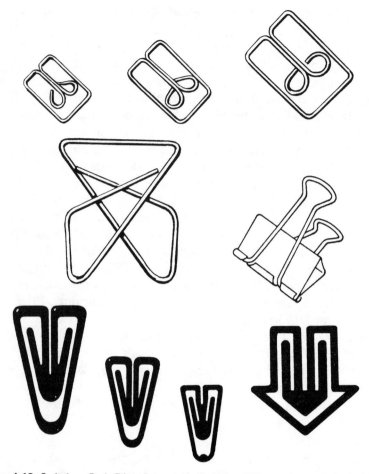

**Figure 4-12.** Labelon Owl Clips (top row), Labelon Triumph Clamp (middle left), metal binder clip (middle right) and Baumgarten Plastklips and Arrow Klip

and Plastiklips Klips should be used around computers because metal clips can become magnetized and can destroy computer data. They come in a variety of colors and so can be used for color coding different papers. Baumgarten Plastiklips and Arrow Klips come in a wide variety of colors and sizes. Use Arrow Klips for clipping as well as highlighting and color coding papers.

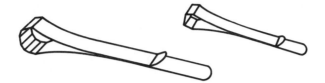

**Figure 4-13.** W.T. Rogers Banker's clasp

**Figure 4-14.** W.T. Rogers square magnetic clips

The **banker's clasp** (Figure 4-13) has a strong grip and is useful for holding bulky papers. The raised short end allows you to easily and quickly slip the clip onto papers.

**Magnetic clips** (shown in Figure 4-14) attach to the sides of metal file cabinets or cabinets and are handy for attaching notes or information.

**MasterClip** (Figure 4-15) is a multi-purpose clip useful for highlighting and color coding documents in files and binders. It's available from INNOLOG Inc., PO Box 93967, Los Angeles, CA 90093, 213/851-6215.

## COLOR CODING

For color coding and drawing attention, here are additional products that will help:

**Redi-Tags** (Figure 4-16) are removable, reusable color-coded tags that have a reusable adhesive on half the tag. They come in 16 different colors, three sizes and many preprinted phrases. There are alphabetical tags for each letter of the alphabet. There is a "general office" series with such tags as "FILE," "FYI," and "RUSH!" There's also a medical series that includes "DIAGNOSIS NEEDED," "SIGN ORDERS" and "COMPLETE HISTORY & PHYSICAL." If your

**Figure 4-15.** The MasterClip can be used to highlight and color code papers in a variety of applications.

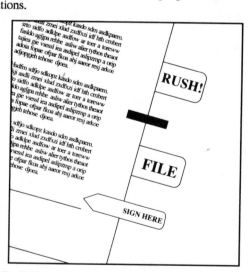

**Figure 4-16.** Use Redi-Tags to attract attention. Simply tag where action is needed and remove the tag when the task is finished or the reference is no longer necessary.

local office supply store or catalog doesn't have this item, call 714/894-4727 for a store location near you.

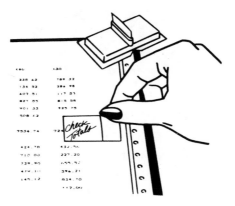

**Figure 4-17.** In seven colors, these convenient, easy-to-use Post-It Brand Tape Flags keep your paperwork organized. Use them for quick reference, easy retrieval and handy reminders. They are ideal for color coding, organizing and indexing.

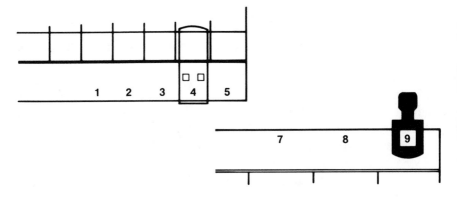

**Figure 4-18.** Labelon Cellugraf Plastic Signals (upper) are transparent (as shown) and are available in 16 colors. Labelon Graffco Nu-Vise Metal Signals stand above a card or folder edge, come in 12 colors and are available in numbered, alphabetical and calendar styles.

**Post-It Brand Tape Flags** by 3M (Figure 4-17) are now available with their own dispensers. Half of the tape flag is colored; the other half is a transparent surface upon which you can write with pencil or pen.

**Signals,** (see Figure 4-18) are made of plastic or metal and clip securely to record cards, folders or papers to "signal" next action date, type of activity or level of urgency.

**Figure 4-19.** Stabilo faxmarker

Avery's **See-Through Color Dots** are useful for highlighting directly on an item, such as maps, blueprints and graphs, where it's important the information not be obscured. Available in four colors, these 3/4-inch dots are removable. One manager uses them on her voice mail log where red dots are for "immediate call backs," blue for "action items" to do now, green for "correspondence" where she needs to send something and yellow indicates "for information only" with no response needed on her part. (If you need more colors and can use permanent, opaque dots, look for Avery color coding labels, which come in 13 colors.)

You know about highlighter markers, but now there are special highlighters for fax paper (see Figure 4-19). The Stabilo **faxmarker** comes in six colors and is handy next to the fax machine to color code faxes by level of urgency, by department or by function. This highlighter will not eradicate, smudge or discolor messages. You could also use the Stabilo BOSS **dry highlighter**, which comes in five colors, and works like a colored pencil. It's good on very thin paper as well as fax and carbonless paper.

The CLICK Hi-Liter marker by Dennison is a retractable highlighter that comes in four colors.

To help you keep tabs on your paperwork, try Dennison SwifTabs or TABBIES index tabs (Figure 4-20). Both of these products are self-adhesive, durable, plastic tabs that come in a variety of colors and styles. They're also available with preprinted months, numbers or letters. You can write or type on them. Use them on such items as computer printouts, reports or on spiral bound books.

And if you're looking for one of the largest selections of colored envelopes and presentation folders and you want to buy in quantity, contact Hudson Envelope Corporation, 33 W. 17th St., New York, NY 10011, 212/691-3333. Hudson also has three retail outlets in New York City called JAM.

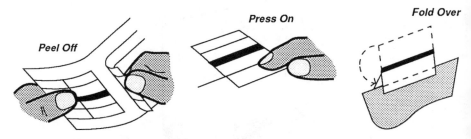

**Figure 4-20.** TABBIES self-adhesive index tabs (contact Xertrex International, 1530 W. Glenlake Ave., Itasca, IL 60143, 708/773-4160)

## DESK ACCESSORIES

In the office supply world, this category includes everything from basic desk or letter trays to designer desk sets with matching components. As a general guideline, I advise clients to use the *minimal* number of accessories and those with the *smallest* capacity. It's just too easy to start stockpiling stuff.

I also urge clients to lean toward *vertical* rather than *horizontal* containers and whenever possible, to put papers in files rather than piles. Of course, the type of paperwork will often determine which format you should use. A horizontal container often works best for frequently used forms, which often flop over in a vertical container.

But you'll generally want a vertical container for active files (look at the many examples in this section).

Your in-out box or basket system will most likely be horizontal because you're probably processing different sized papers. But remember these tips: keep the depth of containers to a minimum, maintain high access and visibility (the space between the trays on the sides should be open) and *clean out trays regularly.*

Balance good function with good design. Upon getting organized, some clients reward themselves with attractive desk accessories. Check out well-designed products by C-LINE, Eldon and Rubbermaid in office supply stores and catalogs. Also look at Hold Everything, the Williams-Sonoma store and mail-order catalog. Write them at Hold Everything, Mail Order Department, PO Box 7807, San Francisco, CA 94120-7807. The Reliable Home Office catalog

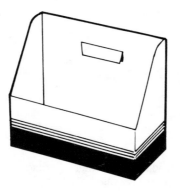

**Figure 4-21.** Fellowes Neat Ideas Folder Holder

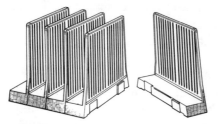

**Figure 4-22.** Eldon Add-A-File

is an excellent choice, too, at 1001 W. Van Buren, Chicago, IL 60607, 800/621-4344 or 312/666-1800.

### Desk Files

Take a look at some products to help you set up your daily paperwork system for your active working files and paperwork.

Fellowes Neat Ideas Folder Holder in Figure 4-21 is an economical way to keep active manila files close at hand. It's made of corrugated fiberboard and comes in letter or legal size.

If your work load fluctuates constantly, you may prefer a modular system that expands and contracts with your work. Such a system has components that snap together (see Figure 4-22).

**Step files** (Figures 4-23 and 4-24) give great visibility to your

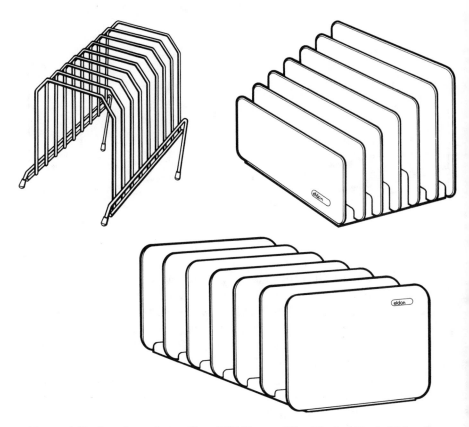

**Figure 4-23.** A variety of step files: W.T. Rogers Wire Vertical Rack, Eldon Step-Up Step Rack and Eldon Diagonal Files

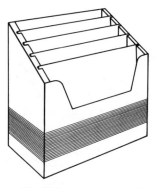

**Figure 4-24.** Fiberboard step file: Fellowes Premier Line Visible Folder Files

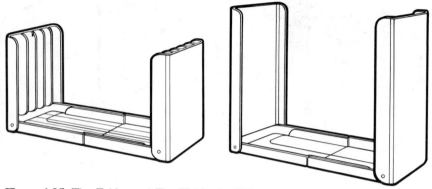

**Figure 4-25.** The Folder and The Holder by Eldon

working files. Most step files slant upwards but some slant sideways. Eldon Diagonal Files have pockets staggered sideways at 45-degree angles. The W.T. Rogers Vertical File is a wire step file that comes in chrome or three Epoxy coated colors. Fellowes' Premier Line Visible Folder Files is a low-cost step file made of corrugated fiberboard with five tiered compartments.

The Folder and The Holder by Eldon in Figure 4-25 make maximum use of limited space, accommodate letter or legal size folders and fold flat when not in use. The Folder holds manila folders and the Holder handles hanging file folders.

Earlier in the chapter you saw two examples of **desktop file organizers** for your daily paperwork system. Take a look at two more in Figure 4-26.

## OTHER ORGANIZERS

Here are some other items to organize your desk and paperwork, some of which may not be familiar to you.

A **collator** is designed to manually collate documents but I recommend it for large, bulky, *active* client or project files. It's great for CPA or legal files and comes in 12, 18 or 24 expanding sections. We use it in our office above our printer to store frequently used paper, letterhead and envelopes. See example in Figure 4-27.

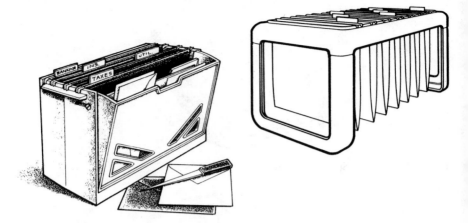

**Figure 4-26.** Rubbermaid Design-a-Space Daily File (left) is a portable filing organizer that's great for daily mail or paperwork. It's easy to carry with built-in handles on the sides. The expanding front provides easy access to the inside and serves as a short-term, mail/file pocket. If, however, you need a larger capacity for accessible, hanging folders consider the Eldon Hot Rack (right), which will hold up to 45 hanging folders.

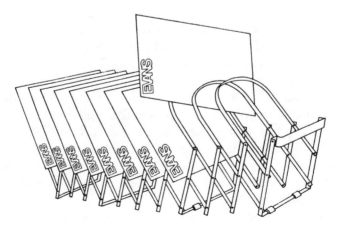

**Figure 4-27.** Evans Collator

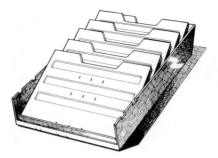

**Figure 4-28.** Eldon Stationery Tray

**Figure 4-29.** Eldon Versatilt

**Stationery holders** are great for letterhead, forms and envelopes and come in many different styles and formats. Some sit out in the open and others, like the Eldon Stationery Tray in Figure 4-28, fit inside standard desk drawers.

Many organizers, such as the Eldon Versatilt in Figure 4-29, are "versatile," allowing you to better organize and hold a variety of materials. This file and sorter system has dividers that can be positioned to accommodate different amounts of materials. Dividers can pivot, giving easier access to such items as diskettes, large index cards or forms. Locked vertically, dividers will separate file folders and other paperwork.

If you're short on work surface, try using **wall mount files.** Sometimes these files are referred to as **pockets** and they can be used on walls as well as on sides of desks and filing cabinets. They don't take up much space and they can hit the spot when you need a container for paperwork at the location where they will be used. For some examples, see the Eldon Hot Files and Pockets in Figure 4-30.

If you have lots of literature or inserts you're pulling together to put into kits or notebooks, consider **literature organizers and sorters.** Your selection will depend on a number of factors: the number of separate inserts you use, the quantity of each insert you need to have on hand, the space you have available, the frequency of use and your budget. (See Chapter 10 for illustrations of literature organizers and sorters.)

Don't forget your basic **letter trays,** which are useful for in-out boxes or to hold papers to be filed or read. Look for stacking letter trays that leave space betw·en trays and that use supports to connect trays. Some people prefer wire letter trays because you can easily see what's in them; others prefer plastic or wood trays that keep paperwork less visible. If aesthetics are important, select a line that has coordinated desk accessories. Consider getting shallow trays to prevent paper buildup unless you need deep ones for thick folders or reports. See the examples in Figures 4-31 and 4-32.

Eldon also makes a handy tray that sits on top of your computer terminal as shown in Figure 4-33.

To keep other materials, supplies and references neatly organized around your computer, on your desktop and in your desk drawer, consider the Oxford DecoRack, the Rubbermaid **magazine file** and the Eldon **drawer organizer** in Figure 4-34. To keep your drawer organizer from sliding around, use 3M brand Mounting Squares or Mounting Tape on the bottom.

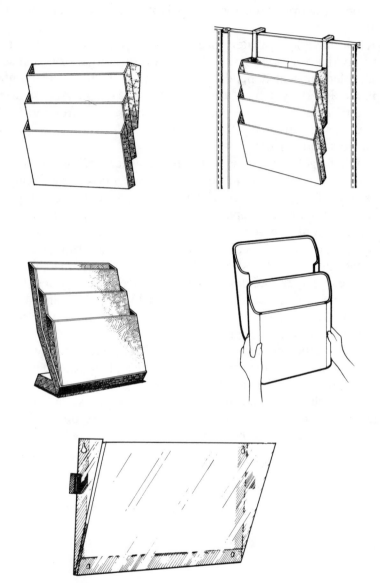

**Figure 4-30.** Eldon Hot Files and Pockets: Hot File Starter Set and Hot File Hanger Starter Set (top); Hot File Stand and Hot File II Add-On Pocket (middle); Magnetic Hot File (bottom)

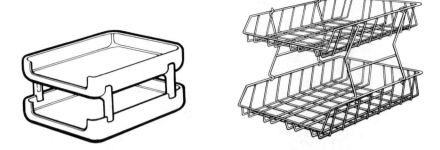

**Figure 4-31.** Eldon Image 1500 letter trays and W.T. Rogers wire desk trays

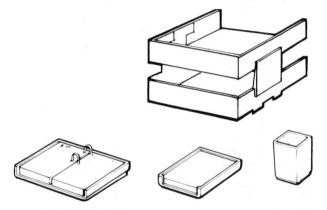

**Figure 4-32.** Rubbermaid Designer 2 letter trays shown with coordinated pencil cup, memo pad holder and calendar pad holder accessories.

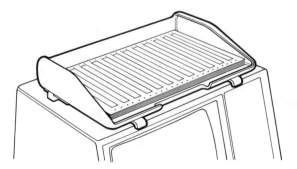

**Figure 4-33.** Eldon Stackable CRT letter tray

**Figure 4-34.** Oxford DecoRack by Esselte Pendaflex, the Rubbermaid Design-a-Space magazine file (bottom left) and the Eldon Catch'all drawer organizer (bottom right)

# 5

# A PRICELESS RESOURCE: CAPITALIZING ON UP-TO-DATE FILES

*Quick Scan: They're out of sight, out of mind. Or so you'd like to think until one fateful day when you can't find that all important document. Or until your files are so full that it's physically dangerous to pry open files to slip in just one more paper. Find out how to organize your files so that they become an ally, not an enemy. Discover which filing supplies can make a world of difference. While the main emphasis is on your own personal filing system, this chapter also includes information useful for larger or special office filing systems.*

For most people, paper files are like skeletons in the closet–bad secrets that no one likes to talk about. Who wants to admit that files are bulging with out-of-date papers, that they are difficult to handle and retrieve and that very often files are misplaced or even lost?

Then there are the *piles*–the papers that never make it into the files. They sit on desktops, in bookcases, on tables, on file cabinets, and yes, even on the floor. Let's see how your files stack up.

## HOW DO YOUR FILES STACK UP?

Here's a quick quiz to rate the state of your filing system. Check "yes" or "no" after each question.

|  | YES | NO |
|---|---|---|
| 1. Is filing a real chore?........................................................ |  |  |
| 2. Would it take a long while to catch up on your filing?.......... |  |  |
| 3. Do you often have trouble finding and retrieving papers —often enough to cause irritation?................................ |  |  |
| 4. Do you keep many papers and/or publications "just in case" someday you may need them?................................ |  |  |
| 5. Is your filing system characterized more by randomness......... than careful planning?........................................ |  |  |
| 6. Are your files inconveniently located?................................ |  |  |
| 7. Do you frequently have trouble deciding what to name files or where to file papers?................................ |  |  |
| 8. Is it difficult to tell what's in each file drawer without opening it up?................................................ |  |  |
| 9. Are you afraid to attempt retrieving a document from your files (or piles) while someone is waiting in your office or you're on the phone? (Would you prefer to look without the time pressure of "beat the clock"?)................ |  |  |
| 10. Are you copy machine happy—do you make unnecessary duplicates of papers?................................ |  |  |
| 11. Are all your filing cabinets/drawers stuffed to the gills?.......... |  |  |

If you have at least three "yes" responses, keep reading!

Below are some typical excuses I hear from people who explain why their files are usually not as functional as they should be. See if you relate to any of the following:

- I don't have a secretary.
- I don't have time/I'm too busy putting out fires.
- Setting up a system is menial, clerical work.
- It's not my job.
- I don't know what to call things.
- I'm creative and my work style is "organized chaos."

## THE THREE FILING PHOBIAS

Besides these excuses, there are three fears people have when it comes to files and piles. I call these fears the "3-D's" because they each start with the letter "D."

First, people are afraid of Decisions. If you don't know what to call papers, you'll end up calling them nothing. Papers then collect in unnamed stacks and piles, as well as in drawers and in-boxes.

Second, people are afraid of Discards. Heaven forbid you should throw anything out—you might need it someday.

Third, the fear of Disappearance haunts many. "Filing a paper in my system is like filing it in a black hole—never to be seen or heard from again," one new client told me.

Now that we've psychoanalyzed some filing phobias, here are some valid reasons for *making the time* to set up or revamp your deskside files. Check any that apply to you:

- You look and act more professional and competent when your information is organized.
- Organized information helps you plan your activities.
- It's easier to get work done.
- You feel better when you know where everything is. You have more control over your work.
- You save time looking for things.
- Accessible, fingertip information is a key resource for your productivity, professional image and peace of mind.
- Add some reasons of your own, making them relate specifically to your goals. What will a good filing system help you achieve or accomplish?
  - 
  - 

## FIVE EASY STEPS
## TO AN ORGANIZED FILING SYSTEM

Most people in the workplace are foggy when it comes to filing systems. They haven't been "office trained." They don't realize that the clerical work of filing is only a part of an organized filing system.

The *mental*, conceptual work is the most important aspect of a good system.

Most people also don't know where to start. What follows is a blueprint to guide you in designing or revamping your system. Here are the five main steps I use with clients:

1. Categorize any existing files as "active" or "inactive" and pull inactive files from your existing filing system.
2. Write out your filing system categories and subcategories *on paper*. Get input from any others who'll be using the system.
3. Physically set up the system. Have all supplies on hand as you prepare file labels and purge, consolidate and arrange file folders.
4. Put the finishing touches on your system. Label drawers and prepare a file index or chart for yourself and any others who have access to the system. If others are involved, introduce the system at a special training meeting.
5. Maintain your system by sticking to a routine.

We'll go into more detail about these five steps after becoming more familiar with the thought process behind every good filing system.

## A CLOSER LOOK AT THE FIVE-STEP PROCESS

There are three essential questions to answer about each paper or file:

1. **When** is it used? How many times a day, a week, a month, a year do you handle it?
2. **What** is it? Under what category(ies) does it belong?
3. **Where** should it go? Near your desk? In storage? In a filing cabinet? Which drawer? A notebook? The trash?

Steps One through Three will deal with these questions.

## STEP ONE: ACTIVE AND INACTIVE

Files should be categorized on the basis of *frequency*, that is *when* or how often they are used. There are two basic types: **active** and **inactive**, sometimes also called **open** and **closed**.

Active (or open files) belong in your office because you will refer to each of them at least several times a year. You will either add to these files or retrieve something from them. Examples include your financial records for this year and active client or customer files. **Working files** are active files that are used most often–daily or several times a week. They should be the most accessible to you at your desk or work station. They can go on a credenza, a side table next to your desk or inside the most accessible file drawer. The most active working files can be part of your daily paperwork system, described in Chapter 4.

Inactive, closed or storage files are used infrequently, if at all, and should usually be kept out of your office. If you opt to keep these files in your office, put them in the least accessible locations–in the rear of a file drawer, on a top shelf or in an area separate from your main work area. Whenever possible, remove files to someone else's office or to a designated storage area on or off site.

As you begin to sort through any existing files, be thinking of these two basic categories: active and inactive. Go through your existing files and weed out all the inactive ones and either discard or store them. By the way, this file sorting process should be done quickly by looking at file names only. *Do not sort through files individually at this time.*

Now that you've sorted through your files, you're ready to tackle any piles of paper you may have accumulated. Go through these piles *quickly*, pulling active and/or important papers. Don't spend hours and hours going through piles, however, or you'll never create your filing system. These five steps will help you streamline the process:

1. Get yourself a countdown timer. (An egg timer is fine or you may prefer an LCD countdown timer available at Radio Shack.)
2. Quickly sort through piles using the timer. This is not the time for a thorough analysis of each and every paper. As my friend and colleague Maxine Ordesky says, separate the treasures from the trash. For our purposes here, "treasures" are any papers that will go into active files or any important documents that you *must* save and file. Set aside for now "semi-precious" papers that may go into storage. As far as what "trash" to toss at this time, apply my two **Discard Dilemmas** rules:
   1) When in doubt, *save* legal, tax information.

2) When in doubt, *toss* resource information.

(For more information on purging, see Chapter 10.)

3. Clear the decks. Put your "semi-precious" papers temporarily in records storage boxes with lids (such as Fellowes Bankers Boxes). Label the outside of the box "Inactive Papers" and add any specific description of the contents, unless they're just miscellaneous. Try to keep the filing area as clear as possible–that way you'll be able to think and work more clearly.

4. For your "treasured" papers, think about category and file names and jot a name on each paper in pencil. If any of these papers could go in existing file folders, file them now. If they need folders of their own, quickly put these papers in folders and jot a name on the file folder tab in pencil. Or use removable Post-it brand File Folder Labels (Figure 5-1) for temporary labels. If you have no extra file folders on hand or there are too few papers for their own folder, then paper clip related papers together and jot a future file name down on the top paper or on a Post-it label in each grouping.

5. In summary: spend most of your time on *important* papers.

**Figure 5-1.** Post-it brand File Folder Labels are removable and can be used on both file folder and hanging file folder tabs that are third-cut. They're useful whenever you're setting up or revamping a filing system or for folder names that change frequently.

## STEP TWO: THE NAME GAME

Once you have the two most basic groupings of active and inactive, you are well on your way.

Now you're ready to identify *what* are the major areas or divisions of your work and/or your work-related information. Start thinking in terms of the largest, *broadest* categories for your active files.

One estate planning attorney who is a sole practitioner with a personal computer has designated four main areas of information: Clients, Business Operation, Estate Planning Information and Personal Computer Resources/References. A management consultant has these three categories: Business Administration (which includes client files), Resource Information (for seminars and articles) and Marketing/Business Development. A computer systems engineer has files for Communications, Software Applications and Hardware.

Here is a listing of general categories. Check any that might apply to your work. Add your own at the end. Remember to select the *broadest subject areas* (not necessarily specific file names) that apply to you.

Accounts, Customers, Clients or Patients
Background/History
Business Administration
Communications (in company or organization)
Contacts
Legislation
Management
Marketing
Products
Projects
Reference
Research
Resources
Samples
Staff
Support
Volunteers

To start breaking down these broad categories into subcategories and specific file names and to help you visualize their relationship to one another, you may want to try two exercises.

First, it may be helpful to make a picture or chart of your major category and subcategory names. You can draw an **organization chart**, also known as a "tree directory" in computer circles. Suppose you have three major categories called People, Products, Promotion. Your chart might look like the one in Figure 5-2.

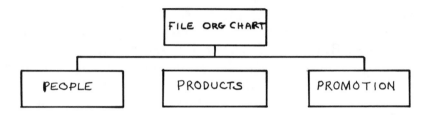

**Figure 5-2.** File Organization Chart

Writing in pencil, you would then draw lines and fill in the boxes with the next largest, broadest category names. Figure 5-3 shows how it might look now.

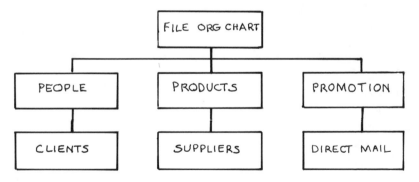

**Figure 5-3.** Expanded Organization Chart

A second exercise may be helpful if you're just setting up your system for the first time (or feel like it's the first time). Use **colored index cards** with one color for each of your major file categories. Put each file name on the appropriately colored card and put it with the other cards. Spread out the cards and arrange them alphabetically or by subject. You can use the cards later to make up your filing system labels and also right now as you design your system on paper.

## DESIGNING A SYSTEM ON PAPER

A filing system on paper serves as a blueprint that charts out all category, subcategory and file names and shows how they all fit together.

If you have a computer, a word processing program will be helpful at this step. Besides being able to easily move words around, many word processing programs such as WordPerfect let you sort (arrange) words alphabetically.

Start with one of your major category areas. Use the File Chart shown in Figure 5-4, which is a form to help you easily list your file categories and names and show how they are related. When completed, the chart will be an outline of your filing system.

**Figure 5-4.** FILE CHART

**MAJOR CATEGORY** (OR DRAWER NAME):

| HEADING | SUBHEAD | SUBHEAD |
|---|---|---|
|  |  |  |
|  |  |  |
|  |  |  |
|  |  |  |
|  |  |  |
|  |  |  |
|  |  |  |
|  |  |  |

Use the File Chart as a guide (photocopy it if you wish). Look at your existing file folders as well as the paper-clipped groupings and new folders you created in Step One. See if file names suggest themselves to you. Look for patterns, groupings, combinations that go together. Be creative but don't create file names that you won't remember later. Don't try to think of *every* file name right now; this is not your final system—it's only the beginning.

Using a pencil (or your computer), write down a major work category from your filing system. Now complete what you think will be the main headings. Leave plenty of space between headings as shown in the Figure 5-5 example. Select names for headings that make sense to *you* (and anyone else using the system). Stick with unadorned nouns for headings, if possible.

**Figure 5-5.** MAIN HEADINGS

**MAJOR CATEGORY** (OR DRAWER NAME): Resource Info.

| HEADING | SUBHEAD | SUBHEAD |
|---------|---------|---------|
| Contacts | | |
| Manuals | | |
| Products | | |

Look at Figure 5-6 to see two levels of subheads that have been added.

As you chart out headings and subheads you'll start to see which names belong together and which ones need additional subheads. You're creating your own file design. Don't get too carried away with elaborate headings and subheads. Often one heading and one level of subheads are plenty. Keep your design simple!

Now complete the file chart for one *major category only*. Then, when you're ready, do a chart for each of your other major categories in your filing system. Remember, nothing is etched in stone; your file chart is only a guide. If your file charts are on computer, you may now wish to alphabetize any headings or subheads that are actual names of clients, companies, vendors, etc., or you can wait to do it in Step Three.

**Figure 5-6.** ADDED SUBHEADS

**MAJOR CATEGORY** (OR DRAWER NAME): Resource Info.

| HEADING | SUBHEAD | SUBHEAD |
|---------|---------|---------|
| Contacts | Stores<br>Consultants<br>Service | Answers on Computers |
| Manuals | | |
| Products | Hardware<br>Software | |

# STEP THREE: PUTTING IT ALL TOGETHER

*Where* files will go in your system is a combination of *what* types of files they are, *who* uses them, *when* they are used and *how much room* you have. You should now know approximately how much room you have after having completed Steps One and Two because you've determined how often files will be used, purged your system of unnecessary inactive files and identified all your active file names.

One of the most important aspects of your filing system is location. Here are some guidelines to consider when deciding upon where to put your files:

- The more files are used, the closer they should be to your desk or main work area.
- Keep like files together. Group files by subject, type or frequency of use.
- Choose appropriate media to store your information–perhaps you want to use notebooks or boxes rather than file folders. Maybe you have large, bulky or odd-sized items that require special filing solutions.
- Security may be a factor; take any necessary precautions to secure confidential information.

Now you're ready to physically set up your system–a time-consuming task that's nice to share with someone else, if you have such luxury.

Decide if you want to use **color coding** in your system. A simple color-coding scheme by drawer or by major category can be helpful, especially when you go to refile a folder. We use blue hanging folder tabs and file folder labels for our business and administrative files, for example, and yellow ones for our resource information files. You're less likely to misfile a folder in the wrong drawer with color coding. You can also see at a glance the type(s) of folders in a particular drawer. (For more elaborate color coding, see "Special Office Filing and Information Management Systems" near the end of the chapter resource guide.)

Make sure you have the right supplies on hand (see also the chapter resource guide). Here's a typical "shopping list" I suggest to clients, followed by comments describing why these items are important:

- One box of hanging file folders, (generally 25 to a box), they come with or without tabs; get them without tabs if you're going to use color coding
- Hanging "box bottom" file folders, one-inch capacity, one box of 25, no tabs included
- Hanging box bottom file folders, two-inch capacity, one box of 25, no tabs
- Plastic tabs for any hanging folders that don't come with tabs. Tabs come in two-inch or 3½-inch lengths—I prefer the 3½-inch size; if you're going to color code your files, get colored plastic tabs or buy colored plastic windows (to use with any clear plastic tabs you may already have on hand).
- Third-cut *interior* folders, (100 per box); interior folders are cut lower than ordinary manilla folders so that the folders sit inside the hanging folders without sticking up; they come in a variety of colors; third-cut folders work with the standard file folder labels you'll be getting.
- Self-adhesive file folder labels; if you're color coding your files, buy the colored labels

To make full use of your headings and subheads, use **hanging file folders**, especially the one- and two-inch **box bottom folders**, which work great as your major headings. Inside each box bottom folder, place several **interior folders**, specially cut manila folders that can serve as subheads. If possible, avoid using only one interior folder per hanging folder; too many hanging folders will take up too much space and you also won't take advantage of the heading/subhead classification system, which adds to greater retrievability. (Check the resource guide for descriptions and pictures of these different folders.)

Pull out your File Chart (or your index cards, if you used them). Go through each heading and subhead and indicate which of the headings and subheads will take regular, one-inch or two-inch hanging folders. Put a "1" by any that you think will be up to one-inch thick and a "2" by any that will be up to two inches thick. Those with 1's will take one-inch box bottoms and those with 2's, two-inch box bottoms. Write "H" for any of the remaining headings or subheads that would take regular hanging folders; otherwise they would automatically get interior folders. (Most of your subheads will probably take interior folders.)

With your File Chart or index cards as a guide, type or print your hanging folder labels using all capital letters. (For more ideas about labeling, see Figure 5-7 as well as the resource guide section on "Labeling Systems.")

Insert the labels into the hanging folder plastic tabs (or if you're using Avery hanging file folder labels, attach them directly to the outside of the tab). Put in order the hanging folders you had marked on your File Chart. Insert the plastic tab on the inside front cover at the far left for headings. For hanging folders with subheads, you may wish to place the plastic tab a little over toward the right, as shown in Figure 5-8. Also note that you should stagger any tabs that would block other tabs. If your box bottom folders require that you insert cardboard reinforcement strips on the bottom, add them now. Set up your new hanging folders in a file drawer. Place existing file folders inside the new hanging folders.

Now type labels for new interior folders. Before you affix them on the interior folders, place the three types of folders in front of you: left-cut, center-cut and then right-cut (assuming you are using third-cut folders). Pull folders in order of left-cut, center-cut, and right-cut. Don't always start at the left every time you come to a

**Figure 5-7.** CREATIVE LABELS FOR HANGING FOLDERS

Colleague Beverly Clower of Office Overhaul uses a Kroy **lettering machine** to create large, legible labels. She uses 18- and 24-point size wheels in the Helvetica bold, all caps, font style. The 24-point size is for headings and the 18-point size is for major subheads. Kroy produces black lettering on clear (or white, if you prefer), self-adhesive strips cut to size. Each strip is then affixed to the white label insert.

If you have access to a **personal computer** with some desktop publishing capabilities, you could prepare your label names with the font and style of your choice. Print them directly on an 8½-by-11-inch sheet of "crack 'n peel" (self-adhesive paper used for labels). Avery's Labelpro software program is helpful if you have a laser printer.

Or if your printer won't accommodate crack 'n peel, print onto your normal paper, which will become the master. Then use the master to photocopy onto the crack 'n peel (make sure your copier will accept crack 'n peel—most high speed copiers should).

You might also try photocopying onto "65 lb. card stock," a heavier grade of paper that you could use instead of the furnished white label inserts. (Check compatibility of card stock with your copier.)

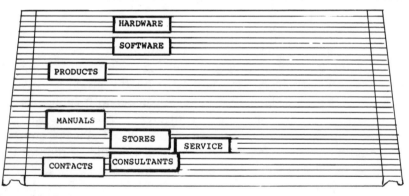

**Figure 5-8.** Position hanging folder tab headings on the left and subheads to the right. Notice that the tab subheads, "Consultants," "Service" and "Stores" are staggered for greater visibility.

new hanging folder; keep going where you left off. That way you won't end up with a lot of extra right- or center-cut folders when you're done. In addition, you will maintain good visibility in your system by staggering folders in this way. Now affix the labels.

For interior folders that you know will be handled frequently and will risk dog-earing, cover the label area with either self-adhesive plastic that you'll have to cut to size or, better yet, use pre-cut label protectors listed in the resource guide.

## ARRANGING FOLDERS

You can arrange your file folders in a number of ways: alphabetically, numerically or by frequency of use. You might even arrange your folders in a combination of ways. For example, you might use a basically alphabetical setup but group frequently used folders in a special, accessible location, for example, in the front of your file drawer.

Certain kinds of information work better alphabetically. For example, client or customer name files work best in an alphabetical system.

On the other hand, subject files do not always have to be in strict alphabetical order. It may be more convenient to place files you use more often in a more accessible location, irrespective of alphabetical sequence. Frequently used subhead files, too, may be placed out of alphabetical order within their hanging folders.

Numerical filing is a better method if you need to arrange files by date (e.g, purchase orders) or by number (legislative bills). Numerical filing is also useful when you want to keep files more confidential (it's more difficult to tell what's in a numerical file). A file index may be needed, however, in order to readily locate material. The index should be kept in a different location apart from the files to ensure their security.

Whichever method(s) you select, place all your interior folders into their respective hanging folders. Put any remaining, unfiled papers left over from Step One into appropriate folders.

## FINE TUNING

You may have noticed that your existing files haven't yet undergone a complete and thorough purge. There's a good reason for this. It's better to set up a *functional* system first and fine tune later. Do your fine tuning now.

Go carefully through each of your existing, *active* folders in your system. Do you really need this information? How accessible does it have to be? Could a folder be consolidated with another folder? Use a timer and allot a specified period of time, from 15 minutes to an hour and a half on a given day. Or try giving yourself a goal, say, five folders in fifteen minutes.

You may find you need to add new labels (or delete others). Add them to your File Chart in a different color. Don't take time out to type or print the labels right now. Jot down subheads in pencil on new folders.

When you have completed the purge for one complete subject area, type or print any remaining labels and attach them to the new folders.

## STEP FOUR: FINISHING TOUCHES

Now that you've physically set up your system, make sure you can tell the types of files you have in each drawer without having to open each one. You need a summary of your file drawer contents. Such a summary could be as simple as labeling each drawer with main headings.

Beverly Clower makes a "key to the files," which is a map or diagram of file cabinets and drawers. See Figure 5-9.

A simple listing on paper, such as your File Chart or a "file index," could suffice. Or keep a listing on your computer that can be easily updated. Be sure to print out at least one "hard copy" on paper.

Train anyone who will be using your filing system. Have a special meeting or training session to introduce the system. Distribute a file index, file chart, key to the files or other listing. If appropriate, show how to borrow files by leaving an **out guide** in the place of the missing file. See Figure 5-10.

## STEP FIVE: MAINTENANCE

The trick to a productive filing system is a regular maintenance program by you or someone you designate. Your program should be fairly routine and involve only a minimal amount of time—famous last words! But let's see how it can be done.

Start by making some decisions in advance about your file maintenance program. Answer the following questions:

1. Who's going to do your filing?
2. Will you file some or all papers "as you go"? Which ones?

KEY TO THE FILES

Cabinet 1:                          Cabinet 2:
Next to Shirley's Desk              Next to Ann's Desk

| | |
|---|---|
| OFFICE ADMINISTRATION GENERAL INFO/SOURCES | BOARD OF TRUSTEES MINUTE BOOKS COMMITTEES |
| INSURANCE PERSONNEL | CONTRIBUTIONS FINAN. ASSISTANCE |
| AGREEMENTS/CONTRACTS | ESTATE FILES |
| REPORTS/STUDIES | BUILDING PROJECTS |

Figure 5-9. A "key to the files," such as the one above, is distributed to everyone in an office using or accessing an office filing system.

3. If you plan to file papers in batches, how often and when specifically will filing occur?
4. How many times a year will you purge your files and transfer active files into storage? During which months or quarters?

Too many professionals and offices have *no* filing maintenance guidelines. Don't wait until an emergency, crammed file cabinets or a move forces you to take stock. It may be too late or you may be in the middle of a top priority project that prevents you from devoting what will now require a large chunk of time.

Set up your own maintenance system. Decide how many minutes a day or a week you (or someone you designate) will spend on it. Which day(s) will you choose and which time(s)? Be specific. Until your system becomes routine, write down your maintenance tasks on

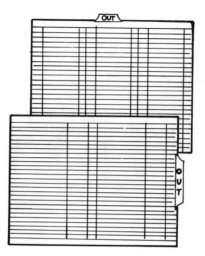

**Figure 5-10.** Two different styles of out guides, which function as library cards for your filing system

your daily to-do list or in your planner. Take a look at the Quick Chart (Figure 5-11) for other ideas.

The longer you wait to either set up or implement your maintenance system the easier it is for paper to accumulate once again. Get tough on paper!

The hardest part of maintaining your filing system is maintaining enough incentive. You have to believe this is a top priority or you'll keep putting it off. Filing systems often get put on the proverbial back burner until you've run out of filing space or a crisis occurs. Don't let that happen to you.

## THREE FILING TIPS
## EVERY MANAGER NEEDS TO KNOW

If you're a manager or you work for one, you need to help implement three key ideas related to your co-workers and your office filing system.

First, **take your office filing system seriously.** Filing is not just clerical busy work. It's a vital database without which your office or department could not function.

**Figure 5-11.** QUICK CHART: FILE MAINTENANCE TIPS

Here are some tips to make filing easier:
- Immediately after you read a paper or an article you want to save and file, jot down the subject or file name in the top right corner. This will save you time, especially if the paper is not filed right away so that you or an assistant don't have to re-read the paper before it's filed.
- If the information in the article will probably be obsolete after a period of time, indicate a discard date in the top left corner. This will help you easily toss old papers without having to reread them.
- As an experiment, keep track of papers or files that you actually go back and refer to. Jot down an "R date"—the date you referred back to a paper or file for information. At the top of the paper or file write "R" followed by the date. If you start to see several R dates, maybe you need to move this information so that it's more accessible. On the other hand, seeing no R dates, you may decide to discard more papers and files. If nothing else, R dates may show you how often or little you actually refer to files.

Evaluate your current systems, including the central filing system as well as individual filing systems. Begin by using the five steps we've just discussed. See if there's any duplication of effort, e.g., is everyone keeping a copy of internal memos that could be filed in one central location?

One manager, Kathryn Johnson, created the "vanguard system" in which each of her staff became a specialist in a particular subject area and maintained files in that subject. Because each staff member was "in the vanguard," filing became easier, reading loads were lighter and department morale was boosted.

Second, **reduce paper to be filed and stored through systematic records management/purging, paper reduction and recycling.**

Syntex, a pharmaceutical company based in Palo Alto, California, has records management guidelines with retention schedules that culminate in an annual event called "Pack Rat Day." This event encourages all departments to review their records for storage or disposal according to the company guidelines. Each department tracks all "pack rat material" on a log sheet, which, along with records for storage or shredding, are turned in to the Records Systems department, the sponsor of the event. There is a Pack Rat Day celebration with refreshments, live music and departmental "Reformed Pack Rat Awards."

For years, Northrop Corporation had "Operation Roundfile" every year in which employees cleaned out their files and offices, tossing as much paper as possible. More recently, the corporation has begun paper reduction programs throughout its divisions. One division has come up with a motto, "Paper doesn't grow on trees–it *is* trees." This division plans to reduce photocopies by 20 percent, lines of computer print by 50 percent and mailing lists by 25 percent and limit the distribution of internal memos to no more than 10 copies per memo.

Smart managers are recognizing that it's more productive and profitable for their organizations as well as for the environment to cut down on paperwork and paper-generated communications in the first place. Look for ways to communicate using less paper, e.g., through electronic mail, voice mail or routing one memo (instead of making copies of the memo).

Set up a policy to reduce paper in your office or organization. Adopt a **purge prevention policy** such as the one developed by Derrick Crandall, president of the American Recreation Coalition in Washington, D.C. Crandall implemented what he calls an "ongoing, self-policing, purge prevention policy" to limit office file cabinets to two lateral five-drawer units. He explains, "It's so easy to become a walking encyclopedia of nonessential stuff. It's more time effective to go elsewhere for information, even if it takes 24 hours to get it than having to purge files in two to three years. It's a terrible waste of time to prune that stuff–better to deal with it the first time around."

Many organizations have instituted major recycling programs, not only to recycle paper that would ordinarily be thrown away, but also to buy paper products, such as file folders, made from recycled fibers. As of this writing, Esselte Pendaflex Corporation has just introduced EarthWise, a complete line of filing supplies made from 100 percent recycled fiber, which should be available through your office supply dealer (or call Esselte at 516/741-3200). The Quill Corporation direct mail catalog now features recycled products, including file folders (708/634-4800).

To get a better idea of just how important recycling is with regard to conserving our natural resources and saving energy, money and landfill space, see Figure 5-12.

**Figure 5-12.** DO YOU KNOW THESE PAPER FACTS?

- Each American uses about 580 pounds of paper a year, the highest per capita consumption in the world.
- To produce one ton of virgin paper, it takes 3,699 pounds of wood, 216 pounds of lime, 360 pounds of salt cake, 76 pounds of soda ash, 24,000 gallons of water and 28 million BTUs of energy. This process also produces 84 pounds of air pollutants, 36 pounds of water pollutants and 176 pounds of solid waste.
- Each ton of paper made from recycled fibers saves approximately 17 trees, 4,100 kilowatts of energy, 7,000 gallons of water, 60 pounds of air pollutants and three cubic yards of landfill space.

Reprinted courtesy of Esselte Pendaflex.

The third filing tip is **value the importance of training**. Smooth functioning office filing systems don't happen by accident. They take careful planning and training.

Whenever more than one person is using an office filing system, you need to set up at least one training session and preferably two. The first session introduces the logistics of the system—how files are named and arranged and how and when they are filed and by whom. This is a good time to introduce the out guide and distribute a file index.

If you are at all concerned that there will be some resistance to the system, suggest that everyone "try it out" for the next couple of weeks and then meet again at a second meeting to discuss and evaluate the system. The more people are a part of any system, the more likely they are to accept it. You must, however, be open to their ideas.

If more managers would follow these simple tips, more offices would have better organized filing systems.

## RESOURCE GUIDE

## BOOKS AND BOOKLETS

**Alphabetic Filing Rules** published by the Association of Records Managers and Administrators (ARMA), 4200 Somerset Dr., Ste. 215, Prairie Village, KS 66208. This booklet provides guidelines for establishing a consistent, documented filing system, whether or not you have a manual or automated system. 800/422-2762 or 913/341-3808. $12 for members; $17 for non-members.

**How to File** published by Esselte Pendaflex Corp., Clinton Rd., Garden City, NY 11530. A great little full-color booklet with lots of photos, examples and information about filing tips, supplies and systems. 516/741-3200. Paper. Free.

**How to File and Find It** published by Quill Corp., 100 Schelter Rd., Lincolnshire, IL 60069-9585. This booklet provides step-by-step details on how to develop, organize and maintain an appropriate filing system for your office. It also includes some useful information on color coding and records management. 708/634-4800. Paper. Free.

**The Organized Executive: New Ways to Manage Time, Paper and People** by Stephanie Winston (New York: Warner Books, 1985). The chapter on filing is an excellent resource. Paperback $7.95.

**Records Management Handbook with Retention Schedules.** Fellowes Manufacturing Co., 1789 Norwood Ave., Itasca, IL 60143, 312/893-1600. While geared for large office filing systems, this booklet provides useful records retention/purging information applicable to smaller systems. Free.

**Technical Publications Catalog** lists the two dozen publications available from the Association of Records Managers and Administrators (ARMA), 4200 Somerset Dr., Ste. 215, Prairie Village, KS 66208, 800/422-2762 or 913/341-3808.

# FILING SUPPLIES
## FOLDERS

**Hanging folders** are the mainstay of frequently used filing systems. They provide easy access to paperwork, good visibility and an organized way to group files.

They are typically made of durable, two-tone green paper stock (many hanging folders also come in other colors and are made of other materials such as plastic or the more environmentally sound recycled fibers used in EarthWise folders).

Special scoring in the middle of the flaps and on the bottom makes these folders more useful (see Figure 5-13). Scoring in the middle allows you to bend back the flaps so that the folder can be propped open in the file drawer until contents are reinserted. Scoring and folding at the bottom let you square off the v-shape bottom to increase the folder's storage capacity.

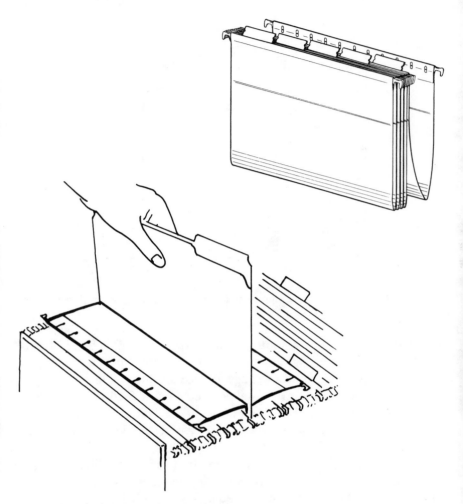

**Figure 5-13.** Hanging file folders (above) are shown with tabs and scoring in the middle and at the bottom. Below, scoring in the middle lets you bend back the flaps to "mark your place" in a filing drawer when you temporarily remove a file. (The Smead Flex-I-Vision hanging files are shown above, the Oxford Pendaflex hanging folder, below.)

To really increase the capacity so that you can more easily use the hanging folder as a container for several file folders (or for catalogs), use a **box bottom folder**, which, depending on the manufacturer, comes in one- to four-inch capacity, letter or legal

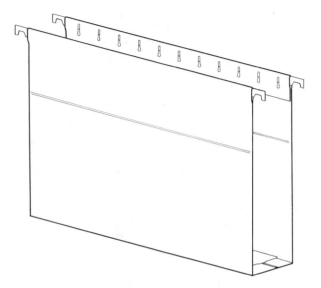

**Figure 5-14.** Box bottom folder with reinforcement strip at the bottom (Smead Flex-I-Vision box bottom)

size, and two-inch for computer printout size. Pendaflex box bottoms come in the standard green or in other colors. Special cardboard strips reinforce the "bottom" edge of box bottoms. On the Smead box bottom the strip is pre-installed. See Figure 5-14.

The Pendaflex Hanging Box File is a blue box bottom with sides that prevent papers and other materials from slipping out. See Figure 5-15.

Pendaflex hanging folders also come in a variety of different sizes to handle a variety of items, such as invoices, x-rays, computer printouts, checks and magnetic media.

The Pendaflex Hanging File Jacket in Figure 5-16 lets you file small items with standard-size papers so that they won't slip out. Notice the easy-access, cut-away front.

**Interior folders** are special file folders cut shorter to fit inside hanging folders without obscuring hanging folder tabs. Esselte Pendaflex Corp. makes them in two lines: the Pendaflex line, available in manila and nine two-tone colors, and the new EarthWise line, in five earth-tone colors.

**Figure 5-15.** Pendaflex Hanging Box File

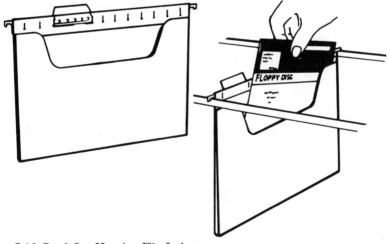

**Figure 5-16.** Pendaflex Hanging File Jacket

For manila folders that are handled frequently and are used more outside the filing cabinet than inside, consider getting those with **reinforced** tabs such as the one shown in Figure 5-17.

If you want papers you file to be more secure, less likely to fall out and easier to locate, consider two-hole punching papers in **fastener folders.** They're essential for important papers that have

**Figure 5-17.** This Smead manila folder with the reinforced "two-ply" tab has extra durability. Notice the scoring along the bottom which permits 3/4-inch expansion.

legal or tax implications where you just can't take a chance on losing any paper. Generally, you'll put papers in reverse chronological order–i.e., the most recent papers are on top. Hole-punched papers take up less space, which is particularly important in businesses where bulky files are the order of the day. See Figure 5-18 for examples of fastener folders. (You can buy folders with the fasteners already attached or buy the folders and fasteners separately, which is more economical.)

Wherever you'd use several fastener folders for one client or project, the **partition folder** is great. The partition folder, also called a **classification folder**, is made of heavy duty pressboard, and lets you group related papers together in different sections of the folder by either attaching two-hole-punched papers to fasteners on either side of each partition and/or by placing unpunched papers in between the partitions. Different styles are available from different manufacturers. You can get from one to three partitions, some of which are pocket dividers, (see Figure 5-19).

The Pendaflex Hanging Partition Folder (shown in Figure 5-20) is really two folders in one–a hanging folder and a partition folder. If you frequently pull files out of the filing cabinet and take them to different locations, you may want to use folders that have three sides to protect the contents. The **file jacket** comes in two styles–flat or expansion (see Figure 5-21). File jackets can be used within your filing system or as part of the daily paperwork system discussed in Chapter 4. Oxford file jackets come in manila and in ten colors.

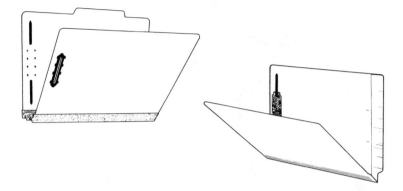

**Figure 5-18.** Smead folders with two different styles of pre-installed fastener: the "K" fastener (on left) is clinched into slots by eight tabs and the "B" fastener has a strong fiber base that bonds to inside surface of folder

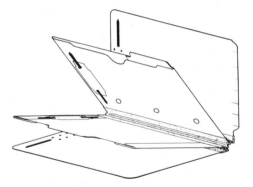

**Figure 5-19.** This Smead Classification Folder comes with pocket style dividers and is also available in four bright colors.

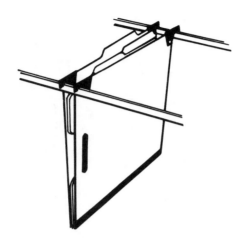

**Figure 5-20.** Pendaflex Hanging Partition Folder

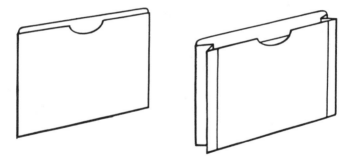

**Figure 5-21.** Oxford Manila File Jacket (left) and Expandable Manila File Jacket

Much sturdier than the file jacket, the **file pocket** in Figure 5-22 has accordion style sides called "gussets" that allow for more expansion and use. The file pocket can fit inside a file cabinet, on a shelf or in a metal collator (see Chapter 4). The file pocket will hold several related file folders together or other bulky materials, including catalogs and books.

The **expanding wallet** is similar to the file pocket except it usually has a flap with a clasp, tie or an elastic cord. It is useful for carrying, transporting or storing records. Wallets come with or without internal dividers or "pockets." I use wallets with pockets to

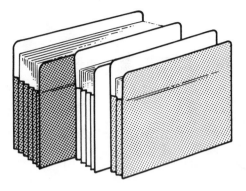

**Figure 5-22.** Wilson Jones ColorLife File Pockets come in three bright colors.

store my annual tax and business records. See Figure 5-23.

The **expanding file** is similar to the wallet in terms of construction, except it's larger and you can get it without a flap. The expanding file is a box-like, multi-pocket file with preprinted headings such as A-Z, 1-31 and Jan.-Dec. Figure 5-24 shows an example. If you're looking for an extremely durable material for an expanding file, check out CaseGuard in the All-state Legal Supply Co. catalog (800/222-0510; in New Jersey, 201/272-0800). Speaking of materials, take a look at Figure 5-25 to see the different types and grades of materials available for file folders.

## LABELING SYSTEMS

The labeling systems included in this section are useful for file folders as well as a variety of other office applications.

Dymo brand labeling tools (Figure 5-26) give you many low-cost options to print attractive labels for filing systems. Each tool comes with a dial you turn to select the correct letter or number you want to print. Clear as well as different-colored tapes are available in two styles: a medium-weight vinyl tape with printed, raised letters or a more expensive, thin plastic tape with flat, black lettering. Dymo label printers are made by the Boorum & Pease Division of the Esselte Pendaflex Corporation and should be available through most office supply dealers.

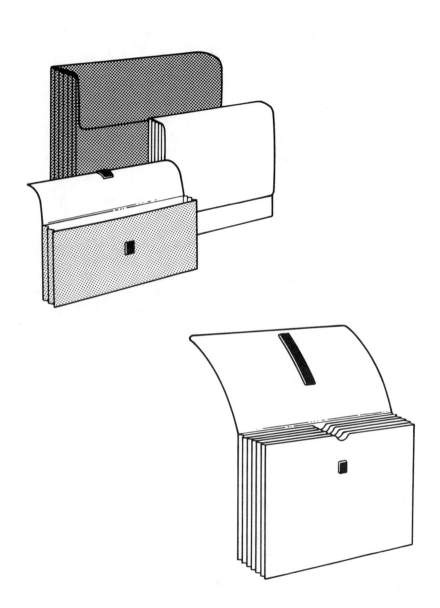

**Figure 5-23.** Wilson Jones ColorLife Expanding Wallets with single pocket and six-pocket styles include easy-to-use "Gripper" Velcro enclosures.

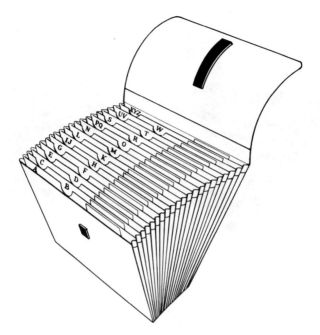

**Figure 5-24.** Wilson Jones ColorLife Expanding File

**Figure 5-25.** FILE FOLDER MATERIALS (Reprinted with permission of Esselte Pendaflex Corp.)

---

**3 COMMON TYPES OF PAPER FOR FOLDERS:**
**Manila** is semi-bleached stock that resists tearing, folding and bursting. It's available in 9½- and 11-point thicknesses (more about point sizes momentarily).
**Kraft** is durable, smooth, unbleached stock that offers greater strength and rigidity. The tan color resists soiling. It comes in 11 and 17 points.
**Pressboard** is hard, dense, long-lasting stock that offers superior strength and comes in 25 points.

MORE ABOUT POINTS AND FOLDER PAPER STOCK
Bearing in mind that a point represents a thickness of .001 inch....
9½ points   Medium weight.
11 points   Heavy weight. Available in manila and kraft.
17 points   Extra heavy weight. Available in kraft.
25 points   Superior weight and thickness. Available in pressboard.

---

Kroy's labeling and lettering systems range from portable models to more sophisticated keyboarded desktop systems (see Figure 5-27). You can make colored labels for not only filing systems but also for such items as maps, overhead transparencies and video disks.

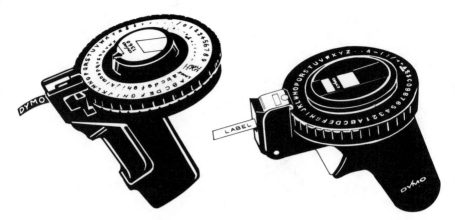

**Figure 5-26.** Dymo brand labeling tools can emboss or print labels, depending on the one that you select.

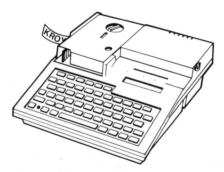

**Figure 5-27.** The Kroy DuraType 240 SE is about the size of a desktop calculator, has a typewriter-style keyboard and provides high-quality print on adhesive, laminated tape in a range of type styles and sizes. The retail price is $549. Contact Kroy at PO Box C-12279, Scottsdale, AZ 85267-2279 or call 800/729-5769 or 602/948-2222.

If you're going to be doing many file folder labels, look into either Avery LabelPro Software if you own an IBM or compatible personal computer and a laser or dot matrix printer and MacLabelPro if you own a Macintosh. The software has pre-set layouts for Avery laser labels, including file folder labels that come 30-up on an 8½-by-11 sheet, in five colors.

Sample labels for file folders as well as for a variety of other uses (such as disks and mailing addresses) are included with the software and the manual. LabelPro is a real time-saver and very reasonable at $99.95−assuming you don't have to go out and buy the computer and printer! For more information contact Avery Commercial Products Division, 818 Oak Park Rd., Covina, CA 91724, at 800/541-5507, the LabelPro Hot Line. By the way, there's also a free technical support help line should you need it.

## OTHER SUPPLIES

You'll need **hanging file frames** (see Figure 5-28) to support your hanging folders, unless your filing equipment already has them. Most come notched at half-inch intervals that you can break off to fit your drawer. But since most never break off easily, I recommend having your supplier cut them to size for you. Be sure to get the right size frame; Pendaflex drawer frames come in not only letter and legal but also check, invoice and jumbo x-ray sizes.

The Pendaflex Links and Stop Clamps shown in Figure 5-29 are useful accessories that will help you better manage and separate your hanging file folders. Made of stainless steel, links fasten hanging folders together to prevent between-folder misfiles. Stop clamps fasten to frame rails to separate groups of folders or to keep folders from sliding along the frame.

Smead makes **self-adhesive vinyl pockets** in two different sizes, which you can attach to the inside of file folders. These pockets can hold such items as business cards, microfiche, floppy disks and photos.

Hanging folder **tabs** generally come "fifth-cut" or "third-cut." The "cut" refers to the width of the tab in relation to the folder. A one-third cut tab, for example, is cut one-third the width of the folder, allowing the tabs of three folders filed back to back to be seen at one time. Since the tab is used for labeling, select the size that will best do the job. Use third-cut if you need a larger label surface.

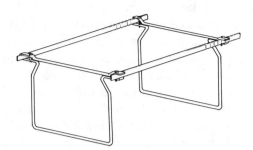

**Figure 5-28.** Smead Steel Frame for hanging file folders

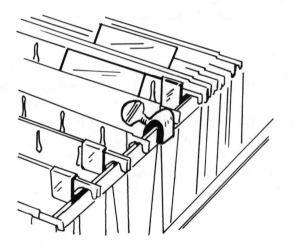

**Figure 5-29.** Pendaflex Links and Stop Clamp

Pendaflex Tabs come in clear (white) and seven colors—blue, green, orange, pink, red, violet and yellow. Or if you prefer, get the clear Pendaflex Snap-On Tabs. They're easier to attach but if you're using color coding, you'll need to also buy and insert Pendaflex Colored Plastic Windows. Use these windows, too, in any existing clear tabs that you'd like to color code. Pendaflex Printed Label Inserts let you save labeling time. Inserts are printed A-Z for name, subject and alphanumeric filing; states for geographic files; and months (Jan.-Dec.) and daily (numbered 1-31) for follow-up, sequential or chronological filing.

If you want a quicker way to label hanging folder tabs, use Avery Hanging File Folder Labels, which apply directly to one-fifth-cut plastic tabs. They come in 16 bright border colors and use a special adhesive for added durability.

**Label protectors** will help you keep file folder labels and tabs clean and resistent to wear and tear. Smead Seal & View Label Protectors, available in three sizes, are made of a transparent, Mylar laminate and should be available in your office supply catalog.

You can also get label protectors by mail order from the Finance Business Forms catalog (800/621-2184) and the SYCOM catalog (800/356-8141 or in Wisconsin, 800/356-9152). If you only need a few and don't mind cutting them yourself, look under "Sheet Protectors" in an office supply catalog and then look for clear, self-adhesive, plastic sheets that you can cut to size.

## SPECIAL OFFICE FILING
## AND INFORMATION MANAGEMENT SYSTEMS

If you're planning to design a filing system for a large office or an office with special information management needs, the products in this section could be helpful. Other places to look for local assistance with your filing or information needs is in the yellow pages under "Filing Equipment, Systems and Supplies," "Microfilming Service, Equipment and Supplies," "Optical Scanning Equipment," "Bar Code Scanning Equipment" and "Data Processing Equipment."

### MORE ON COLOR CODING

If your office is a medical office, for example, and has many, many files you'll probably select a more elaborate color-coded system that uses different combinations of colored, self-adhesive letters or numbers to quickly identify folders and prevent misfiles.

If you file patient files by their last name, for example, you would probably take the *first two letters* of their last name and put corresponding self-adhesive colored letters on the folders. Each letter of the alphabet in such a system has a color. For example all the "S's" are orange, the "I's" green and the "M's" purple.

Take my last name, "Silver." My folder would have an "SI" on it where the "S" is orange and the "I" is green. When you file or retrieve the "Silver" folder, it's much faster to go directly to "SI" than to check through all the last names that begin with "S."

If the next folder is "Smith," you'd see an orange "S" and a purple "M." Color coding file folders lets you find and file them more quickly.

There are other codes you can attach as well to folders, such as yearly codes or colors that signify a type of patient.

The following companies make a whole line of special color-coded tabs: ANCOM Business Systems (Brunswick, Ohio, 800/845-9010); Jeter Systems (Akron, Ohio, 800/321-8261); Smead (in Hastings, Minnesota, at 612/437-4111); TAB Products Co. (Palo Alto, California, 800/672-3109 ext. 3304 or in California, 800/742-0099 ext. 3304); and Wright Line (Worcester, Massachusetts, 800/225-7348). Many of these companies have local representatives to help you design your system.

## SPECIAL FILING EQUIPMENT

High-density mobile filing systems equipment, consisting of heavy lateral filing units that usually run on mechanical floor tracks and all but eliminate wasted aisle space, are useful for large, centralized filing systems. Three manufacturers of these systems are: Lundia (in Jacksonville, Illinois, 217/243-8585); The Spacesaver Group (in Fort Atkinson, Wisconsin, 800/492-3434, in Wisconsin, 414/563-5546); and White Office Systems (in Kenilworth, New Jersey, 201/272-8888). Jeter, TAB and Wright Line also offer special filing equipment that can handle both small and large systems.

Wright Line is best known for its computer media filing accessories and equipment that store and organize items such as printouts, computer tape reels and diskettes.

## AUTOMATED FILING SOLUTIONS

"File and Find" is a software program you can use on your IBM or compatible personal computer to help you index documents for future reference. You list the folders in your file cabinet and enter names of important documents you might want to retrieve in the future. For each document, you can list up to three search terms that will help you easily find it again. You can also print file folder labels of any size. The program is $49.95 and is available from the Power Up! catalog (San Mateo, California, 800/851-2917 or 800/223-1479).

If you already use a database management program, you could set up your own library catalog for your documents, files and other resource materials. Be sure to use key words and codes to indicate topic areas and types of materials. Also include the location where the item is filed. Consider other locations besides file folders–three-ring binders, spiral bound volumes or more permanently bound books with a "GBC" heat-sealed binding, for example. (GBC stands for General Binding Corporation, which is at One GBC Plaza, Northbrook, IL 60062, 708/272-3700–they make special binding machines.) Use an automatic page stamper to easily number pages incrementally.

For a more sophisticated document/file database, use a **CAR** or **Computer Assisted Retrieval** system that lets you locate documents through the use of computer-stored indexes. A CAR can be particularly helpful if you're using **micrographics** in your office–such as microfilm or microfiche. The Canon CAR System, for example, lets you index your documents as you transfer them to microfilm.

Micrographics offers options to copy paper documents onto more compact media where the information takes up less physical space and also is easily retrievable. A 4-by-6-inch piece of microfiche holds several hundred documents and a roll of microfilm holds 4,000 to 5,000 documents. **Optical disk technology** (discussed more fully in Chapter 8) can store 50,000 pages on one side of a disk.

**Optical Character Readers (OCRs)** or **scanners** are devices that work in conjunction with **page recognition software** to let you scan documents and transfer that information onto your hard disk.

The Canofile 250 made by Canon is a desktop electronic filing system that is comprised of a main unit with a mass storage built-in magneto optical disk drive and an optional keyboard and laser beam printer. A solution to large-volume filing, the system scans, stores, retrieves and prints out image information that would otherwise be stored in a filing cabinet.

# 6

# POWERFUL
# COMPUTING:
# ORGANIZING YOUR
# IBM PERSONAL
# COMPUTER FILES

*Quick Scan: Both you and your computer will never be the same when you learn the basics of organizing and managing your computer files. Gain full value from your automation tool by discovering different ways computer files can be organized on hard disks and floppies and which computer products can help. This chapter is for anyone who uses an IBM personal computer or compatible, has at least DOS version 2.1 (with or without Microsoft Windows) or OS/2 and has, or plans to have, a hard disk with or without Windows.*

One day, when the glow of using a computer wears off, you may discover you're having trouble getting around your computer. Files are hard to find. Naming and organizing your files is confusing. Somehow you thought the computer would make everything easier, certainly easier than dealing with all the paperwork on your desk and in your cabinets.

The bad news is that just like paper files, computer files need to be accessible, up-to-date, properly categorized and regularly maintained. Your computer can slow down dramatically whenever computer file organization and maintenance is poor (or nonexistent).

But the good news is both you and your computer will function better when your personal computer files are in good working order. And it's not hard to learn how to organize your files.

The hard part today is deciding among three organizational options based on your time, your money, your technical aptitude and your software needs.

If you're looking for the easiest, time-saving, most "user friendly" option *and* you have money for a 1 to 2MB (megabyte) 286 or 386 personal computer with DOS 3.1 or later, you'll probably want to get a software program called Microsoft Windows. This program doesn't replace DOS (Disk Operating System) but is a DOS "interface" that makes your computer screen look more like a Macintosh screen, lets you do "windows" (multiple screens or files open at once) and allows you to use a mouse. This interface is known as a "graphical user interface" or GUI.

Another GUI that is just as "friendly," but much more costly is OS/2. Actually, OS/2 is more than an interface; it's the second generation "*O*perating *S*ystem" that follows DOS. It requires that you buy very expensive hardware. To date, very few applications have been written to run under OS/2. Computer forecasters predict, however, that OS/2 will gobble up the operating system market by 1994 or 1995. Besides the GUI feature, both OS/2 and Microsoft Windows will let you do **multitasking**–running two or more programs at once and being able to switch easily between programs.

Both Windows and OS/2 require you to buy special versions of software programs that work under these environments if you want to do multitasking with those programs (but you can still use your existing programs, one at a time, with Windows or OS/2). Besides costing more money, many of these programs are not yet available. There are more programs, however, written for Windows than for OS/2 at the time of this writing.

If you don't have money to burn but still want ease of use, a third option is to continue using DOS and read this chapter. Here you'll discover software programs, as well as some basic background information on DOS, to help you better understand how to organize your computer.

If your computer has DOS 4.01 (in fact, if it has DOS 2.1 or higher), then you already have access to a built-in organization system called **tree-structured directories.** These directories make up a classification system that comes with your computer. They're called "tree-structured" because a diagram of them resembles a tree–an upside-down tree to be exact.

## STARTING AT THE ROOT OF THE MATTER

Just as you start with the root of a tree, so, too, tree-structured directories start with the **root directory.** This is the first and main directory; all other directories "branch off" from the root.

Technically, there is only one directory, the root directory. All the other directories are really **subdirectories.** All of your subdirectories grow and expand as you add files to them.

A directory or subdirectory (the terms are often used interchangeably) is a specific area on your disk that stores files, usually related files. Compare it to a drawer or a section of a drawer in your filing cabinet that holds a particular grouping of files. All subdirectories are related to one another, too, because in the tree-structured directory system, they all descend ultimately from the root directory. Some subdirectories are on the same level, some have their own subdirectories and those subdirectories can have their own subdirectories, ad infinitum.

If the terms "root directory" and "subdirectory" are still confusing, compare them to their counterparts in a paper filing system. Think of the root directory as your entire filing cabinet with no dividers for major sections or categories. All contents will be thrown together unless you include groupings such as dividers or drawers called subdirectories in the computer world.

The tree-structured directory system is similar to the one you set up for your paper files in Chapter 5. In a well-organized paper filing system you group related files together under headings and subheads. You do much the same thing with your computer files, whether they're on floppies or your hard disk, when you group them in subdirectories.

You can draw a picture of your tree-structured directories, just as you drew a chart for your paper files in Chapter 5. Think of this drawing as a "family tree" for your computer that shows how everything is related. The Directory Tree Chart in Figure 6-1, adapted from my computer's tree-structured directories, will help you see the relationships between five of my major subdirectories.

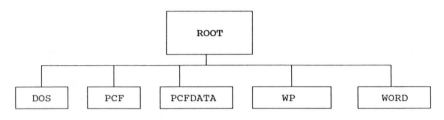

**Figure 6-1.** Directory Tree Chart adapted from my computer

## AN ORGANIZED ROOT DIRECTORY

The root directory is the place where files will automatically go until you set up your subdirectories. The purpose of the root directory, however, is *not* to store files. An organized root directory works like a table of contents for your entire hard disk.

Most importantly, **don't put all of your files in the root directory.** Just as you shouldn't put all your eggs in one basket, you're asking for trouble by putting all of your files in the root directory. For one thing, the root directory is limited as to the number of files it can hold. All your files simply wouldn't fit. And for another, even if your files didn't exceed the limit, you'd spend a lot of time trying to locate files. There is a better way to organize your system. Tree-structured directories let you group related files together so that your root directory doesn't become the local dumping ground. Your root directory should contain the names of your first-level subdirectories plus miscellaneous files that your programs require and three DOS files—command.com, config.sys and autoexec.bat. Put the rest of your DOS files in their own subdirectory branching off from the root directory called \DOS.

Most of all, remember that the root directory is not a place to put miscellaneous files. Check your root directory from time to time to make sure you haven't accidentally saved a file there that belongs in a subdirectory.

To see the files in your hard disk root directory from anywhere on your computer, go to any DOS prompt (e.g., **a>** or **c>**) and type **dir c:\** and tap **<ENTER>**. By the way, \ by itself means "root directory." The command **dir c:\** means display the listing for your root directory. If you want to see one screen at a time type **dir c:\ /p** ("p" stands for "pause"). To see the rest of the listing, tap any key to unfreeze the screen and continue scrolling. The listing will show files and/or subdirectories. **<DIR>** indicates a subdirectory.

Instead of scrolling down the screen, you can see the contents of the entire directory several columns *wide* by typing **dir c:\ /w** or if you want to include a pause: **dir c:\ /w/p**.

## ORGANIZING YOUR SUBDIRECTORIES

I suggest several guidelines when you name and organize your subdirectories. The most important one is this: **Keep your program files and data files separate.** Program files are the software programs you purchase and data files are what you create. There are a number of ways to separate and organize program and data files.

Ideally, put each program file in its own separate subdirectory (e.g., one for your word processing program and another for your spreadsheet program). You may also want to group these program subdirectories on their own "logical" drive as well because it simplifies backup routines (discussed in Chapter 8). A logical drive is an area of your hard disk that you've "partitioned off" or defined as "C," "D" or any other letter of the alphabet (except usually "A" or "B," which are generally reserved for your floppy drives). A "physical" drive means you actually have a separate physical drive. A floppy drive is a physical drive and two hard disks are two physical drives. But C and D drives that are both located on one physical hard disk are logical drives.

Group your data files on other separate subdirectories (e.g., one for each client or for the type of work) on another logical drive. If you are a professional writer, for example, keep your word processing program in its own subdirectory on one logical drive and keep your articles in at least one other subdirectory on another drive. As a professional writer as well as a consultant and speaker, I have subdirectories called "BOOK," "WRITE," "CONSULT" and

"SPEAK," all under my WordPerfect data subdirectory called "WP."
See Figure 6-2.

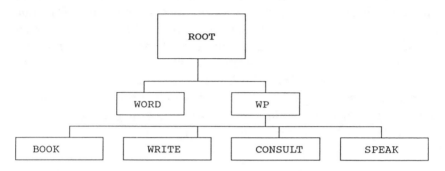

**Figure 6-2.** On my computer I keep my WordPerfect program in its own separate
subdirectory, "WORD." I keep data files in their own subdirectory called "WP," which
then in turn has grouped data files into their own task specific subdirectories. WORD
and WP are on the same level; the four subdirectories shown here are also all on the
same level, but one level down.

If you have too many subdirectories, however, you may want to
put your data subdirectories *under* their corresponding program
subdirectories. Taking the previous example, look at Figure 6-3 to
see how it would now look.

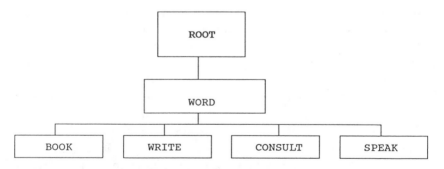

**Figure 6-3.** In this arrangement, the application program resides in the subdirectory,
"WORD." The data file subdirectories are under the WORD subdirectory.

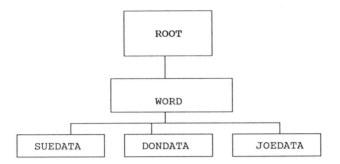

**Figure 6-4.** Subdirectory organization with shared computer word processing program

If you share your computer with other people who are using the same programs, it also makes sense to arrange program subdirectories followed by data subdirectories. For an example of what your subdirectory organization might look like, see Figure 6-4.

Another solution for multiple users would be to keep your programs in directories on your hard disk and have each individual put their own data files on separate floppies. Make sure your computer performance is fast enough and that each file will fit on just one floppy (unless you have a backup program that can split a file and copy it onto more than one floppy).

**If possible, don't go more than three levels down from your root directory.** Keep your subdirectory structure as simple as possible–simple enough to let you find and use files easily. As a general rule, **don't have any more than one screen full of data files per subdirectory.** When you have more than one screen full of names, it may be time to think of creating a new subdirectory–either a subordinate or a parallel one. Or, it may be time to delete files or move them into archival storage. If you really must have numerous files, just remember that this will slow you and your computer down considerably trying to locate them.

It may be helpful to design your subdirectory organization system on paper, or for an existing system, print it out from a file management program such as XTree that shows the subdirectory relationships graphically.

## IT'S ALL IN A NAME-A PATH NAME, THAT IS

One reason to keep your tree structure as simple as possible is to help simplify naming and locating individual files. Let's see why.

Just like a person, each individual file has both a name and an address. A computer file name is similar to a person's name in that both are made up of letters of the alphabet. A computer file name, however, can include numbers as well as letters but is limited in length. You can only use eight characters in a file name, plus a period followed by three additional characters for an "extension."

A name alone is not enough. Both a person and a file need more than a name to make them truly accessible. An *address* is necessary to locate a person as well as distinguish one person from another. John Jones on Maple Street isn't the same person as John Jones on Elm Street. An address is a *path* to someone's door, starting with the state, going to the city, then to the street and number and finally to the individual.

A computer file needs an "address," too. A **path name** is the address for a computer file. Your computer locates a file by following a path from the "drive" you're in (usually "A" or "B" for floppy drives and "C" or "D" for hard disk drives), on next to the root directory, then through any subdirectory name(s) and finally to the actual file name.

Just as the U.S. Postal Service likes to use certain abbreviations, so does your computer. When typing out a path name, start with the letter name of the drive you're in followed by a colon. Use a backslash symbol \ every time you want to indicate the different parts of your path name. The first backslash indicates the root directory. Each additional backslash tells the computer to go down to a new subdirectory level. The last name is the file name itself.

Here's an example. Go back to the chart in Figure 6-2. C:\WP\BOOK\CHAPT1.D1 is the full path name for my Chapter 1 file. C is the drive name for my hard disk, the first \ stands for the root directory, **WP** is the first-level subdirectory, **BOOK** is the second level subdirectory and **CHAPT1** is the actual file name with the **.D1** extension. The ".D1" extension, which means "Disk 1," lets me easily identify and back up all the D1 chapter files onto a backup floppy I call "Disk 1." I use a "D2" extension for all remaining book files that I back up onto "Disk 2."

And just as there can be a John Jones who lives on Maple as well as one who lives on Elm, so, too, you can have the same file name (or the same file) in two different subdirectories. If I wanted, I could have a copy of CHAPT1 in my WRITE subdirectory, too. The path name lets you locate the correct file. Your computer will not, however, let you create the same file name if it already exists in the same subdirectory you're in.

You also can't have two first-level subdirectories with the same name, for example, C:\BOOK and C:\BOOK. But with two different first level subdirectories, you could have two second level subdirectories, as well as files, with the same names. For example, the following would be acceptable:

C:\BOOK\LETTERS\MAY92 and C:\WRITE\LETTERS\MAY92

To keep your path names simple, however, keep down the number of subdirectory levels. Since many times you'll need to type out the complete path name to "call up" (retrieve) a file, you'll want to do as little typing as possible.

Fortunately, you don't always have to type out the full path name when you want to call it up. Just as sometimes when you're filling out a form, for example, a doctor's intake form, you might not need to list your state of residence. But you better know where you are at all times.

The same holds true for computers. **Know where you are**—especially which subdirectory you're in. Let's suppose you're in a particular subdirectory and you're using a file from that directory. If you want to switch to another file in the same directory, you need only specify the file name. But if you want to call up a file from a different directory, you have to follow the correct "path."

Let me show you what I mean. Once again, here's the full path name for the CHAPT1 file: C:\WP\BOOK\CHAPT1.D1. If you're in the CHAPT1 file but you want to call up CHAPT4, no problem. Simply save CHAPT1 and call up CHAPT4. (In some word processing programs, such as WordPerfect, you may not have to save a file first before calling up another; in WordPerfect, for example, you can either open a window or switch to a different screen to call up a different file.)

If, however, you want to call up a file called MEMOS91, which is located in the CONSULT subdirectory under the WP subdirectory on the C drive, you'll have to let the computer know you want to go to the CONSULT subdirectory.

To be sure, it's much easier calling up different files in different subdirectories when you're in the same program. Both CHAPT4 and MEMOS91 have at least one subdirectory in common—WP. It's kind of like living in the same city, but on different streets. Just as it's easy getting around city streets using local transportation, it's just as easy changing to a different subdirectory in the same program.

At other times, however, you may want to work on a file that's in another program. To do that, you may have to exit one program entirely, start another program and then make sure you're in the right subdirectory containing the file. A utility program, such as SoftwareCarousel, lets you temporarily exit a program you're working in, quickly switch to another program and be able to resume your place in the original program. Of course, if you're using multitasking through Windows or OS/2, switching is quite easy.

Build some consistency, rather than creativity, into your subdirectory and file names. Try to make directories parallel by using the same names and sequence of names. For example, if you have consulting clients, each client might get their own subdirectory with the following subdirectories: PROPOSAL (for proposals), CORR (for correspondence) and REPORTS. Use consistency in naming files, too. Use the same abbreviations, such as adding the ".ltr" extension to all files that are letters.

## MAY I SEE A MENU, PLEASE?

There's another easy way to switch into a different program subdirectory. After you boot up (start your computer) you could see a **menu** or listing of all your main computer application programs. If you don't have such a menu on your computer, consider buying a menu utility program or a DOS shell such as PC Tools Deluxe that can create menus. Such utilities are listed in the resource guide.

## MULTITASKING: BEYOND MENUS

A menu utility basically groups all of your applications together and lets you "point and shoot" to load a selected program. Multitasking goes beyond a menu in two important ways.

First and most important, in multitasking you can run a program in the "background" while you're working on another program in the "foreground." This means, for example, that you can continue to work on a report in your word processor at the same time your database management program is sorting names and addresses in alphabetical order.

Second, multitasking allows you to load more than one program so that you can switch rapidly among several programs. So when you choose a program, you don't have to wait for it to load–the computer can switch from one pre-loaded program to another. This is called "context switching" or "concurrency." The most common form of context switching is using pop-up programs such as calculators, notepads and calendars.

If you only work in one program or you rarely need to switch between programs, you don't need multitasking. But if you'd like to be able to switch frequently (and especially, do work in the background), multitasking is the way to go.

As of this writing, you have three options from which to choose:

1. Buy OS/2, the new IBM operating system.
2. Buy a multitasking software program, such as Windows 3.0 (make sure you have at least 2MB of memory on your computer); DESQview (which will run up to nine character-based applications, such as WordPerfect, Lotus 1-2-3 and Paradox); or an inexpensive utility such as Software Carousel
3. Buy a Macintosh that has Multi-Finder (and read Chapter 7).

## DOS IS NOT A DIRTY WORD

DOS is an essential program for your computer. DOS is a collection of commands that lets you operate your computer–specifically, your hard and floppy disks.

Think of DOS as a language with special words and codes that allows you to organize and coordinate all the operations related to your disks, your programs and your files. Compare DOS to a foreign language that helps you get around in a foreign country (in this case, your computer, which just may on occasion feel like a foreign country!). Knowing even a few key words and phrases can give you greater mobility, confidence and control. Control over what? In the computer environment you'll need control to effectively manage, store and retrieve information. DOS provides built-in file and information management tools. These tools help you control the information in your computer files. DOS lets you copy, erase, rename, back up, search, sort (in alphabetical or numerical order) and protect your files from accidental erasure.

What's more, DOS lets you list files in each directory, make a new directory, remove a directory and change to a different directory.

## FILE MANAGEMENT THAT KEEPS DOS TO A MINIMUM

Knowing how to take full advantage of DOS is a lot like auto mechanics; it might be nice to know your carburetor from your master cylinder and how to change your oil but you don't need to know the specifics of auto mechanics to drive your car.

It doesn't hurt to understand generally how DOS works but there are some wonderful file management utility programs that will do most DOS functions for you simply and easily–in plain English. And starting with version 4.0, DOS itself has become easier to use.

Whether you have a 4.0 version or a file management utility, knowing a few of the basic DOS commands can be very helpful and time efficient. There are a number of good DOS books and classes available. I recommend starting with *Running MS-DOS* by Van Wolverton. If you get really stuck, you can call Microsoft, the manufacturer of MS-DOS, on their new 900 support phone line staffed by eight technicians: 900/896-9000. At this writing, the first minute is free and then the charge is $2 a minute, which will appear on your phone bill. The service is available from 8 a.m. to 5 p.m., Pacific Time, Monday through Friday.

# FILE MANAGEMENT THAT USES
# DOS TO THE MAXIMUM

I must admit, there's a certain thrill learning to understand and use DOS. It's like cracking a secret code. In fact, DOS commands look an awful lot like code, rather than English.

But once you crack the code, you'll discover tempting shortcuts to incorporate into your computer routine. Take the **batch file**, for instance.

A batch file is like putting an automatic transmission into a stick-shift car; it does routine, repetitive tasks for you automatically. For example, it can automatically bring up a menu of your main programs on your screen shortly after you have started your computer. A batch file can help you simplify your work by reducing the number of keystrokes to perform a computer operation. A batch file contains a series of DOS commands or instructions to carry out an operational computer job such as starting your computer.

Every time you boot up (start) your computer, DOS follows a certain procedure. You can alter this procedure by creating a batch file called **AUTOEXEC.BAT** that has all the commands you want carried out. (In translating AUTOEXEC.BAT, you'll discover "AUTO" means "automatic"; "EXEC" means "execute" or carry out; and "BAT" means "batch" and has to appear as an extension on every batch file.).

Your AUTOEXEC.BAT file can include commands such as setting the date and time as well as taking you to your main menu of programs. If you are only using one program all the time, you could have AUTOEXEC.BAT take you right to that program. When you boot your computer, DOS automatically checks to see whether there is an AUTOEXEC.BAT file; if there isn't one, DOS carries out its own simple start-up procedure. The AUTOEXEC.BAT file lets you customize this procedure.

You may also want to include another useful command as part of your AUTOEXEC.BAT called **PROMPT $P$G**. No, this isn't a typo. This may well be one of the oddest *looking* commands but it certainly is one you should have. This funny-looking command tells you where you are in your tree-structured directory system when you're in DOS. It's like those directory maps in shopping malls showing all the stores and a little red dot that says, "You are here."

Normally, all you'd see on your computer screen is the letter of your default drive before a greater than sign. It would look like this: **C>** and is pronounced "C prompt." All you'd know is that you are in your C drive, as compared with say, your A or B drive.

With the PROMPT $P$G command added to your AUTOEXEC.BAT, however, instead of just seeing C> you'd be supplied with additional information about your current directory. Let's say you are in your root directory. Your location or "system prompt" would now read:

C:\>

As you may remember, the backslash symbol \ stands for the root directory. You now know that's where you are on the C drive. If you are in a subdirectory for your WordPerfect word processor (\wp) on the C drive, your system prompt in DOS might read:

C:\wp>

You can add PROMPT $P$G to your AUTOEXEC.BAT file through a word processing program such as WordPerfect or through Edlin, the built-in DOS text editor.

## A MORE USER-FRIENDLY DOS: IBM DOS 4.01

If you're really opposed to learning and typing odd-looking symbols and codes, IBM has made it easier for you through IBM DOS 4.01−a whole new generation of DOS.

Instead of having to remember DOS commands, you can easily select them from pull-down menus. You can even use a mouse to select the command or file management function you want.

While not as user-friendly as Windows 3.0 or OS/2, IBM DOS 4.01 includes pull-down menus and a graphic representation of your tree structured directories.

## RESOURCE GUIDE

## FILE MANAGEMENT UTILITY PROGRAMS

Also called "file managers" and "DOS shells," these programs let you move, delete, copy and rename files easily without having to master the DOS commands. You really want to have at least one of these invaluable programs when you're cleaning out your hard disk. (By the way, the terms "file manager" and "file management program" are also used for simple database programs, which are described in Chapter 9.)

**Direc-Tree Plus 5.4** is a *PC Magazine* Editor's Choice award winner and full-featured DOS shell that takes very little memory to run. $49.50 plus shipping; **Direc-Tree AutoPilot 6.0** has many added features and is $79.50 plus shipping. 800/755-3553 or 213/377-1640
Micro-Z Company
4 Santa Bella Rd.
Rolling Hills, CA 90274

**DOS2ools** has a full range of features and includes 43 programs. *PC Magazine* reviewer Vincent Puglia called DOS2ools "the most complete set of intelligent utilities I've ever encountered." 714/548-4886
E-X-E Software Systems
8855 Atlanta, #298
Huntington Beach, CA 92646

**KeepTrack Plus** has an excellent selective backup feature that lets you split files between disks. It also has a good range of file management features. $99 for Version 2.1 for DOS and $129 for Version 2.0 for OS/2. 800/748-6480 or 415/966-1900
The Finot Group
2680 Bayshore Parkway, Ste. 101
Mountain View, CA 94043

**PC Tools Deluxe** is a multi-award-winning utility program that is jam packed with DOS shell, disk backup, data recovery, application menu and desktop management features. It has received nearly every editorial award possible in its class. The latest version now has three user levels, beginning, intermediate and advanced. $149. 800/888-8199 or 503/690-8090
Central Point Software, Inc.
15220 N.W. Greenbrier Pkwy., #200
Beaverton, OR 97006-9937

**Q-DOS II** has speed plus versatile file management features and is easy to use, especially for novices. $79.95. 800/233-0383; 801/377-1288
Gazelle Systems

42 North University Ave., Ste. 10
Provo, UT 84601

**Tree86** is a power user's tool for advanced file management. Listed as one of five "most useful utilities" in an issue of *Personal Computing Magazine*, this program has pull-down menus, instant access to single or multiple drives, mouse support and text search. It is also network compatible. $89.95. 800/548-5019 or 713/953-1940
The Aldridge Co., Inc.
2500 CityWest Blvd., Suite 575
Houston, TX 77042

**XTree Gold 2.0** is the file manager I use (I have used XTree programs for more than five years). Considered to be the granddaddy of file managers, its visual representation of DOS' tree structure can't be beat. XTree Gold has added many new features since the original XTree was released in 1985: un-delete (retrieve files accidently deleted); pull-down menus; Open File (associate file and launch application without ever leaving XTreeGold); AutoView (view files in their native format, over 35 viewers included); and file compression with ZIP and ARC compatibility and an application menu that automatically searches your hard drive for over 700 applications and builds the menu for you. Plus, you can edit files, format floppies, log entire or partial drives and use split windows to view, compare and manipulate files—even those on different drives. Top personal computer magazines, such as *INFOWORLD* and *PC Magazine*, continue to praise XTree through the years. $149; upgrade is $35. 800/388-3949 or 805/541-0604
XTree Company
4330 Santa Fe Rd.
San Luis Obispo, CA 93401

## MENU UTILITY PROGRAMS

**Automenu** is considered a standard in this genre. $69.95. 800/662-4330 or 404/446-6611
Magee Enterprises, Inc.
PO Box 1587
Norcross, GA 30091

**Direct Access** is a menu system that organizes software programs on your hard disk into a user-defined menu. Features include automatic menu building, multiple menu options, mouse support, usage tracking and virus detection password protection. It was selected as *PC Magazine*'s Editor's Choice. The latest 5.0 version has been praised by *INFOWORLD* and *MIS Week*. Described as easy to use, the program comes with toll-free technical support, should you need it. $99. **Direct Net** is the network version, which is $245. 800/242-6368, 800/325-0471 in Canada or 715/832-7575
Delta Technology International
1621 Westgate Road
Eau Claire, WI 54703

**PowerMenu** is primarily menu software but also includes security password features and can track projects and usage costs. $89.95. 800/523-0764 or in California, 408/559-4545
Brown Bag Software, Inc.
2155 S. Bascom Ave., Ste. 105
Campbell, CA 95008

**Power Panel** is a *PC Magazine* Editor's Choice award winner that is ideal for novices. Mainly an applications menu system, the program also has file management features, a telecommunications module and desktop accessories (e.g., calculator, calendar and notepad). The program is designed to be used with a mouse. $69. 415/656-1117
Mouse Systems Corp.
47505 Seabridge Dr.
Fremont, CA 94538

**PreCursor**, Version 4.0 helps you design menus easily to organize your programs and batch files with unlimited menu selections. The program also has a password feature for security and computer usage tracking. It was selected as *PC Magazine*'s Editor's Choice. $96. 800/548-5019 or 713/953-1940 (See The Aldridge Co. under Tree86.)

## MULTITASKING SOFTWARE PROGRAMS

Multitasking programs offer you some exciting possibilities. Beware, though, that installing some of these programs can be complex. Here are ones that have received favorable reviews:

**Concurrent DOS 386** can support up to 10 users and is a cost-effective alternative to setting up a LAN (Local Area Network). $395. 800/443-4200 or 408/649-3896
Digital Research Inc.
Box DRI
70 Garden Court
Monterey, CA 93942

**DESQview: The Multiwindow Software Integrator** offers a mouse-and-windows environment that lets you operate up to nine programs simultaneously and switch quickly between programs. DESQview comes with **QEMM-386**, a memory manager, and **Manifest**, a system analyzer. $129.95. 213/392-9701
Quarterdeck Office Systems Inc.
150 Pico Blvd.
Santa Monica, CA 90405

**Headroom** is a memory manager that efficiently manages RAM-resident programs in extended memory, expanded memory and your hard disk so that you have enough memory to operate each one and switch between them. $129.95. 800/451-0551 or 718/262-8787
Helix Software Co., Inc.
83-65 Daniels St.
Briarwood, NY 11435

**PopDrop** is an easy-to-use PC memory utility that helps manage "pop-up" TSRs or RAM-resident programs and has received many favorable reviews from computer magazines. $49.95. 800/888-4437 or 305/445-0903
BLOC Publishing
800 SW 37th Ave., Ste. 765
Coral Gables, FL 33134

**PC-MOS** can support up to 25 users. $195, single-user version. 800/451-5465 or 404/448-5465
The Software Link Inc.
3577 Parkway Lane
Norcross, GA 30092

**SoftwareCarousel**, a program that provides concurrency for 10 different programs, in combination with **DoubleDOS**, a program that lets you do work in the background, provide an economical, multi-

tasking, concurrent environment. $89.95, SoftwareCarousel; $69.95, DoubleDos. 800/272-9900 or 603/627-9900
SoftLogic Solutions
One Perimeter Road
Manchester, NH 03103

**Switch-It** lets you switch between applications and pop-up programs without having to exit and save. $99.95. 800/848-0286 or 508/879-0744
Better Software Technology, Inc.
55 New York Ave.
Framingham, MA 01701

**Windows 3.0** has a graphic user interface that runs multiple MS-DOS applications and is getting rave reviews. $149. 206/882-8080
Microsoft Corp.
One Microsoft Way
Redmond, WA 98052-6399

## DATA ACCESS

**Extend-A-Name Plus** is a memory-resident program that lets you describe files with names up to 60 characters long and lets you group related file names into subdirectory "libraries." $89. 201/444-3228
World Software Corp.
124 Prospect St.
Ridgewood, NJ 07450

**Gofer** is a full-text retrieval software program that lets you find a word (or group of words) and copy it to another document. This program doesn't take up valuable space on your hard disk because it doesn't create an index. This memory-resident program works great for occasional searches or if you don't have hundreds of files to search. $59.95. 800/828-6293 or 716/248-9150
Microlytics
Two Tobey Village Office Park
Pittsford, NY 14534

**LIST** is a fast, inexpensive file search utility that scans forward, backward and sideways through files. This is a shareware program available directly from Vernon D. Buerg. $20. 707/778-1811

Vernon D. Buerg
139 White Oak Circle
Petaluma, CA 94952

**Magellan** was selected as the best text search utility by *PC Magazine*. It includes 40 different file viewers (which means it will show a file in WordPerfect format or Lotus 1-2-3 format, for example). You can also load the program related to the file you're viewing. Magellan also operates as a DOS shell with many file management features. It's particularly useful for examining and grouping files. $139. 800/343-5414 or 617/577-8500
Lotus Development Corp.
55 Cambridge Pkwy.
Cambridge, MA 02142

**ScreenExtender for WordPerfect 5.0/5.1** is a screen utility that lets you see the entire width of documents without scrolling and also displays italics, sub- and superscript, strikeout, double underline, small caps and bold underline. $79.95. 800/782-4792 or 804/977-7770
Stairway Software Inc.
700 Harris St., #204
Charlottesville, VA 22901

**Viewlink** provides access to related information across all of your existing software programs by linking information and files in unlimited ways, such as by content, date, name or any combination. The program lets you cross-file your work in different "views," without creating a separate copy that would take up valuable disk space. You can instantly view the contents of text files without starting the application that created them. The program continues to get great reviews. $149.95. 800/662-2652 or 206/483-8088
Traveling Software, Inc.
18702 North Creek Parkway
Bothell, WA 98011

**Zoo Keeper**, besides its clever name, is a clever way to locate files on your hard disk. Zoo Keeper lets you create 40-character descriptors for any of the files on your hard disk whose eight-character names may be a bit baffling. If you forget what you called a file, Zoo Keeper will look for your description of it. $75. 800/338-5943

Polaris Software
1820 S. Escondido, Ste. 102
Escondido, CA 92025

**ZyINDEX Professional** is a file-indexing program that creates an index of almost all the words or specified combinations of words in your files and their location. The program indexes up to 5000 files. $295. (ZyINDEX Plus indexes up to 15,000 files and multi-user systems and costs $695.) 800/544-6339

ZyLAB Corp.
100 Lexington Dr.
Buffalo Grove, IL 60089

## FURTHER READING

The following books, directories and magazines are excellent sources of computer information, providing news and views on the latest programs, updates and versions:

**Datapro Directory of Microcomputer Software** is a three-volume information service that is updated monthly. I found the loose-leaf format with tabbed dividers made this comprehensive resource particularly easy to use as I referred to it frequently to update software products for this book. More than 12,000 software packages are featured. Monthly updates and newsletters, along with access to the Datapro Telephone Inquiry Service, are included in the one-year subscription fee of $779. 800/328-2776 or 609/764-0100

Datapro, a unit of McGraw-Hill Information Services Co.
600 Delran Parkway
Delran, NJ 08075

**Hard Disk Management in the PC and MS-DOS Environment** by Thomas Sheldon (New York: McGraw-Hill, 1989). This book expands upon the organizational areas covered in this chapter. You'll learn more about DOS commands, tree-structured directories, menus, batch files, data protection strategies and organizing a hard disk to suit your needs. Paperback, $24.95

**IBM PC & Compatibles–Professional Set** is a three-volume information directory listing detailed descriptions of 18,000 products. $89.95. 800/843-MENU or 412/746-MENU

MENU Publishing

PO Box MENU
Pittsburgh, PA 15241

**Inside OS/2** by Gordon Letwin (Redmond: Microsoft Press, 1988). If you want to learn about the next generation of operating system software, take a look at this book. OS/2 picks up where DOS leaves off. Because the author helped design OS/2 software, he'll help you understand it–from the inside out. Paperback, $19.95

**MICROREF Quick Reference Guides and Keyboard Templates** will help you find and learn commands for DOS as well as popular software programs such as WordPerfect, Q&A, Lotus 1-2-3 and dBaseIV. The handy guides and templates are available at computer, software and book stores or can be ordered directly from the publisher. $19.95 or $24.95 for guides; $9.95 to $14.95 for templates. 800/333-0551
Educational Systems, Inc.
3175 Commercial Ave.
Northbrook, IL 60062

**PC Computing, America's Computing Magazine** is a monthly magazine on personal computing aimed more at active PC users than experts. It provides shortcuts and secrets designed to increase productivity. Annual subscription (12 issues) is $24.97. 800/365-2770
Ziff-Davis Publishing Co.
PO Box 50253
Boulder, CO 80321-0253

**PC Magazine, The Independent Guide to IBM-standard Personal Computing,** comes out every two weeks and features in-depth product reviews and industry trends. The "Editor's Choice" designation helps you quickly spot winning products and programs. A one-year subscription (22 issues) costs $39.97. 303/447-9330
PC Magazine
PO Box 54093
Boulder, CO 80322

**PC WORLD** is a monthly publication widely read by managers that offers consultation on selection and optimization of PC products. $29.90 for one year. 415/243-0500
PC WORLD
501 Second St.

San Francisco, CA 94107

**Running MS-DOS: 4th Edition** by Van Wolverton (Redmond: Microsoft Press, 1989). This book is considered the definitive source on MS-DOS. It's highly readable, with excellent illustrations. The well-organized chapters, table of contents and descriptive index make this book a handy reference source as well. Paperback, $39.95

**The Software Encyclopedia** comes out each year in two volumes. It lists more than 21,000 microcomputer software packages available for 14 different microcomputer hardware manufacturers (from Apple to Xerox). I used it to update this book and found it to be a very helpful, reliable resource. Paperback, $189.95. 800/521-8110; in New York, Alaska and Hawaii, call collect: 212/337-6934; in Canada: 800/537-8416; fax: 212/337-7157; outside U.S., fax: 0732-884079
Customer Service
R.R. Bowker Company
PO Box 762
New York, NY 10011

**Supercharging MS-DOS: 2nd Edition** by Van Wolverton (Redmond: Microsoft Press, 1989). The power user's guide to DOS, this book offers an array of programs, batch files and utilities to help you get the maximum in DOS efficiency, productivity and creativity. Paperback, $19.95

Note: Always check with vendors for the latest version of software products and the compatibility with your existing hardware and software.

# MAKING THE MOST
# OF YOUR
# MACINTOSH FILES

*Quick Scan: If you use a Macintosh Plus (Mac Plus), a Macintosh SE (MAC SE), or a Macintosh II (Mac II), this chapter will help you better manage all the documents and applications you're accumulating. Discover how to take full advantage of the file management features that are built right into the Mac. See how to make the best use of your hard disk and high-capacity, 3½-inch disks.*

Several years ago, Apple introduced a tool to help you better organize all of your application and document files. It's called the **Hierarchical File System** (HFS).

HFS is a filing system for your computer that lets you organize applications and documents inside file folders. Just as a good paper filing system groups related papers and files logically together, so, too, HFS encourages you to group related applications, documents and folders together. An "application" is a software program, a "document" is a file you create with an application and a "folder" is a holder for documents and applications. Folders are the building blocks of HFS. ("Files" refer to either documents or applications.)

Whether you're using high capacity floppy disks or a hard disk, HFS is a lifesaver. This filing system helps you better manage the large numbers of files and folders that come with the increased storage you now have available.

What's nice about HFS is that you have a system that lets you group files logically by categories (folders) and subcategories (folders "nested" inside folders) that make sense to you. This beats scrolling through a long list of several hundred files at a time, which is what Mac users had to do before HFS.

## HOW TO USE HFS

See if you have HFS on your Mac. How can you tell? If you're using at least System version 3.2 (which came out in 1986), you have it.

Next, make sure you are using the right System and the right **Finder**. As of this writing, you should be using at least System version 6.0.3, which is the recommended upgrade for all users (the latest is 6.0.5), and Finder version 6.1. If you're not, buy yourself the **Apple Macintosh System Software Update** (called the **System Update** for short), version 6.0. Or check with your dealer for the latest System Update that you need for your machine.

Both the System file and the Finder file are necessary to operate your Macintosh. These two files (together known as "System files") should reside in your System Folder. The System file contains HFS—and tells your Mac and all the applications you use how to organize and store files. The Finder uses information from the System file, including the HFS information, to help you work easily with disks, applications, folders and documents.

It's important to update your system files and make sure you aren't using multiple system files. One computer consultant told me the importance of this updating process. He said, "One of the first things I do with a client is check all version numbers of all the systems and utilities. I make sure there aren't duplicates. People often don't realize they're adding all these systems to their computer when they update their computer."

Dan Shoff, an Apple dealer senior systems consultant, explains why this is dangerous. He says, "The main problem we find is that customers load multiple System files onto their hard disk, which invariably causes their hard disks to crash–at which point customers get angry. It's very important to have only one set of System files–one system and one finder that are compatible with one another."

Shoff also points out that all machines don't necessarily need the latest versions. "It just depends on your machine and your applications."

If you've ever updated and upgraded your System and Finder before, you'll find upgrading with System Update 6.0 is much easier and simpler. The System Update also lets you keep intact any fonts, desk accessories and utilities that you've previously customized. System Update 6.0 costs $49 and is available from your Apple dealer. (If you don't want or need the documentation, you may be able to get the System Update by itself free of charge from dealers, user groups or on-line services.)

## HOW THE "HIERARCHY" IN HFS WORKS

HFS is a *hierarchical* system because it lets you group files and folders in a multi-level hierarchy. You see the first or top level of the hierarchy when you open a disk and you view all the applications, folders or documents in the **disk window**. Each of these folders, applications or documents you first see is at the first level (sometimes also known as the **root directory**). Refer to Figure 7-1 for an example of a disk window at the first level.

If you were to open up one of the folders, you would see the second level of the hierarchy. Open up a window for a second level folder and you'll see the third level. Figure 7-2 illustrates these "nested" folders at the three levels.

There is an easier way of moving through the different levels of your hierarchy within an application rather than double-clicking on folder names in a series of windows. First, pull down the File menu and select Open, which will open a **standard file dialog box** (as shown in Figure 7-3) and provide you a listing of the folder's contents. The dialog box only shows you what's in one level at a time–namely, files or folders. But by placing the mouse pointer on

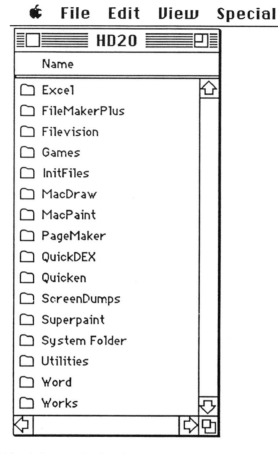

**Figure 7-1.** Disk window at the first level

the disk or folder icon at the top and holding down the mouse button, you can see the different levels of the hierarchy—that is, the different levels of the nested folders. (See Figure 7-4.)

What you get is a pull-down list (which looks similar to a pull-down menu). But instead of listing commands, the list shows you the path through the hierarchy, all the way back to the first level. (By the way, the first and highest level is always the last one on the pull-down list and is the name of the disk you're using.)

This little pull-down list shows you all the different levels in

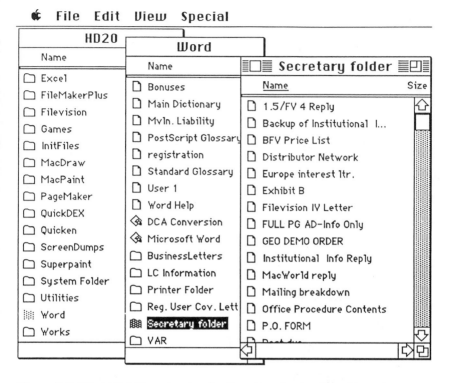

**Figure 7-2.** "Nested" folders showing the first three levels of the hierarchy

order. To get to a different level, you simply drag the mouse to the level you want (or from the keyboard, press the Command key and the Up or Down Arrow).

## NAMING NAMES

The name you give a document or folder may depend in part upon your use of dialog boxes and whether you're scrolling to see long lists of files and folders.

Bear in mind that file and folder names in dialog boxes are in alphabetical order but special characters (such as periods, commas and asterisks) and then numbers precede letters. The order goes like this: first, special characters; second, numbers; and third, letters.

This is good to know if you want to have the files you use most

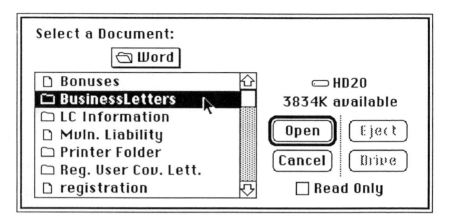

**Figure 7-3.** Standard file dialog box

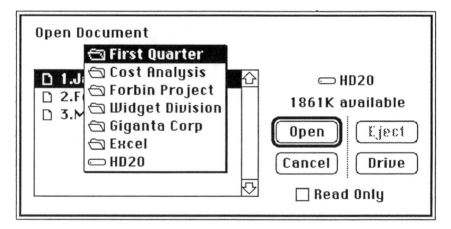

**Figure 7-4.** Different hierarchy levels using the mouse pointer on the folder icon

often at the top of the file dialog box. You simply tack on a special character or number to the name. For example, you could easily change the folder name "Report" to ".Report" or "1Report" to move up the folder in the dialog box. See Figure 7-5.

HFS lets you repeat file names, provided you put each of those files in different folders. Let's suppose you have three files called "Mileage Report." With HFS you could keep a Mileage Report in three different folders—for example, one for Mary, another for John

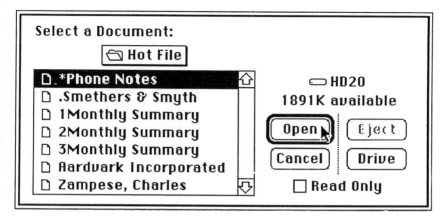

**Figure 7-5.** Use of special characters and numbers in names

and still a third for Chris.

HFS makes sure you don't replace any file you've previously created with the same name. You'll be asked whether you want to replace the existing file. If you click OK, you'll destroy the original file and replace it with the new one. Incidentally, it's not a good idea to give documents the same names as applications. Disks should also have their own individual names.

There are only a few restrictions to the names you choose. Remember not to use more than 27 characters (including spaces) for a disk name and no more than 31 characters for a document or folder name. Don't use colons in your names.

## PUTTING APPLICATIONS IN GOOD ORDER

There are three main locations in which you can place your applications: a disk window, the desktop and a folder.

## APPLICATIONS IN YOUR DISK WINDOW

Whether you're working on a hard disk or on a floppy disk, Figure 7-6 illustrates how you can place applications (depicted as application icons) in the window of the disk you're using. The disk window shows the top organizational level of HFS.

Applications stored outside a folder in your disk window should

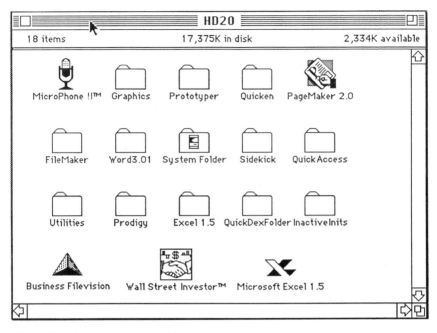

**Figure 7-6.** Applications in a disk window

generally be only for applications you use daily that don't have their own auxiliary files or utilities. Storing applications in this way makes saving files easier. You also won't have to navigate out of a folder when you open files inside an application.

I know one Mac user who keeps all his applications in the disk window. He places the ones he uses regularly in the visible part of the window and the ones he doesn't are kept out of sight, at the bottom of the window, available through scrolling. What he's doing is grouping them by frequency of use, using the standard, "By Icon" view.

If, however, you have an application that uses auxiliary files (such as a word processor that has extra dictionary files), you're not going to want to clutter up the disk window with all these files. You have a couple of options. You could place these auxiliary files in the System Folder, since the application will look there for them after not finding them at the application's location. Or you could put both the application and these files in their own folder—a method we'll be discussing shortly.

If you don't have a hard disk, you can put your applications on 3½-inch disks. If your computer has two 3½-inch disk drives, you could keep related applications on one disk, which would serve as your startup disk. Your applications would appear in the window of this disk. Documents could be kept separately on another disk.

If you only have one disk drive, you can create special disks organized by task that combine related applications and the documents created with them. Since each of these disks will also be serving as a startup disk, be sure to include the System Folder on each one. (The System Folder contains the System and Finder files.) Don't forget to leave at least 50K of available space on any startup disk.

## APPLICATIONS ON YOUR DESKTOP

If you use just a few applications on a regular basis, say four or less, consider moving those applications from your disk window onto the desktop itself. The desktop is the first thing you see after loading the Finder. You'll usually see a light gray surface that has a menu bar at the top, a disk icon in the top right corner and a trash can icon in the lower right corner. (I've changed the gray desktop to white for the illustrations.)

You'll save some keystrokes by not having to open your disk window each time you want to call up an application. It's also easier to find a few applications on your desktop rather than having to look through lots of application and folder icons in your disk window (see Figure 7-7). Be careful, however, you don't accidentally throw them in the trash can, which is nearby.

Your desktop can also be used to temporarily store a group of selected applications, as well as folders or documents, that you may be using on a particular day. What's nice is you can pull the icons you want from different disks and "drag" them all to the desktop. There's no need to keep windows open. It's easy to put the icons back; first select them, then select "Put Away" from the File menu and the Finder does the rest. It's like having all of your current paperwork and projects on your desk, right in front of you for easy access, and then having an assistant put everything away for you

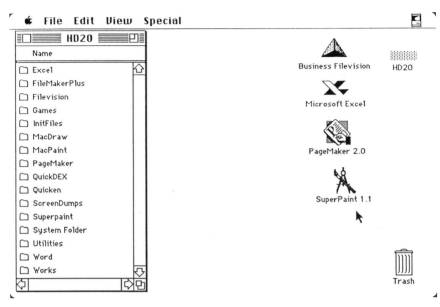

**Figure 7-7.** Applications on the desktop

when you're finished.

## APPLICATIONS IN FOLDERS

We've talked about storing frequently used applications (with their icons) outside folders on the desktop and in disk windows. Let's see some situations where you might want to store applications in folders (and then keep those folders in disk windows–the first level of HFS).

You should store most of your applications (including work applications and utilities) in folders. Documents, though, should generally not be kept in the same folder as applications. You could, however, have a folder for each application (and its supporting applications or utilities) and then nested folders for the application's documents. But you may be better off putting all applications in one folder and then setting up separate folders for each application's documents. These methods can work if your applications aren't sharing data.

Users whose work involves sharing of data often group related applications and documents in a project or task folder that describes a type of work that's being done. You might have a Presentations folder, for example.

If you have many project folders, however, that each need to use a particular application, you're probably not going to have space to keep more than one copy of that application on your disk. In that case, you could group similar applications together. A word processing application folder could contain a word processor, a spelling checker and an outlining program, for example.

Take a look at Figure 7-8 to see how applications can be stored in folders in the disk window, the top organizational level. Store utilities in their own folder, which you can keep inside the Application folder, or if you use utilities frequently, store the Utilities folder also in the disk window.

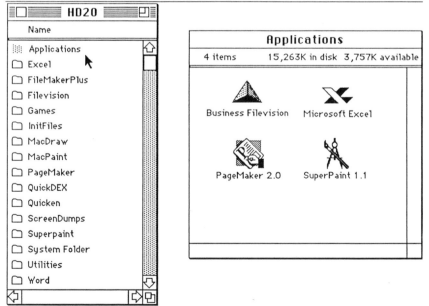

**Figure 7-8.** Applications in folders in the disk window

As you can see, you have quite a bit of flexibility with HFS. For additional flexibility, consider using **Multi-Finder,** which comes with the latest System Update. Multi-Finder can replace your Finder and give you the ability to load as many applications as memory will allow and to switch easily between them at the click of the mouse.

One word of warning: if you purchased any Mac software before January 1986, confirm compatibility of your software applications with HFS. Contact any manufacturers of software that could apply.

Here's an important tip: don't keep any applications you rarely use, especially space-hungry work applications, on your hard disk.

## DEALING WITH DOCUMENTS AND FOLDERS IN HFS

When it comes to organizing documents, just like applications, HFS gives you tremendous flexibility. With flexibility, however, comes the opportunity for too many choices and if you're not careful, chaos can quickly take over.

Organizing your documents with HFS is a lot like organizing your papers in a filing system. There's no one right way to set up a system. What's most important is thinking in terms of category names that have meaning to you. Where would *you* logically file and find documents and folders? Under what names?

You also want to make sure you don't accumulate too many documents in any one folder. When that happens, files become difficult to find. That's when you may need to subdivide large folders into smaller ones. But if you have too many small folders, your system can become too complex. It's all a matter of balance and good design whether you're using a paper filing system or the Macintosh Hierarchical Filing System.

To keep your HFS as simple and as accessible as possible, follow two guidelines. First, limit the number of documents you keep in each folder, especially any folder that you use frequently. Some experts suggest keeping no more than one dialog box full of files so that you don't have to scroll to another screen. Of course, you can always use the View menu to help you view the contents in a text view that compacts and groups more information in one window than you can see in a dialog box. Charles Rubin and Bencion Calica in their book *Macintosh Hard Disk Management* recommend that you create a new folder when you have more than 20 files on a disk or in a folder.

The fewer files you have in a folder, the faster it is to find files–especially the files you use most often. And that's the secret: keep files you use most often, most accessible. If a folder is crowded with files you rarely use, both you and your computer will slow down. Yes, you can use the Find File utility, but it won't be as fast for you as having a smaller, well-organized folder (and HFS) system. Get in the habit of moving old or rarely used files to archival or storage folders and disks.

Second, limit your number of nested folders. Although technically you can go more than 50 levels deep with HFS, beware of creating too complex a system that takes too much time to use. In general, you won't want to go more than three levels deep.

## CREATING FOLDERS

Start by setting up your first-level folders in your disk window. Use names that reflect the major kinds of work you do and how you like to group that work. General folders called "Correspondence," "Reports" and "Graphics" may be just fine. Perhaps, however, these may be too general and you'll need to go immediately to a second level of folder within each one to break it down further.

You might, instead, want to be more specific with your first-level folder names. For example, give them the names of specific projects, clients or customers. Then break each one down into second level folders that represent the different activities connected with each.

These second-level folder names can be identical, provided they're used in different first-level folders. Suppose I have two speaking engagements, one for ARCO and another for GE. My ARCO first-level folder could have three second-level folders called "Correspondence," "Notes" and "Seminar Materials" and so could my GE first-level folder.

## DESKTOP MANAGEMENT

As a Mac user you probably have two desktops: the traditional one where you do your paperwork and your Macintosh screen or working environment, which is also called a "desktop." We'll be looking at ways to manage your Macintosh desktop more effectively, so that you can do computer organizational tasks more easily and productively.

The Mac desktop is the main staging area for your computer work (just as your desktop may be the main area for your paperwork). The Finder is the system application used to create the desktop and manage what happens on the desktop, such as organizing documents, creating folders, viewing windows and starting applications.

## FIVE FINDER MENUS

You can do these and many other desktop management tasks using the commands or mini-applications located in five Finder pull down menus along the top edge of your desktop: **Apple, File, Edit, View** and **Special**.

### APPLE MENU

Mini-applications called **desk accessories** (DAs) are included in the Apple menu. Let's look at three that help with file management.

The **Control Panel** will let you design your own desktop, set the date and time and use a "RAM cache" to speed up your work. The Control Panel lets you choose these and other options to customize your computer to your specifications.

**Find File** helps you locate any application, folder, document or resource on a disk. It's particularly helpful in an HFS environment where you may have many files nested many levels deep in folders and when you just can't remember where you put a file. Find File not only locates a file for you but it furnishes a brief summary about it. You'll learn when you created the file, when you last modified it, the size of the file, the space the file takes up on your disk and where it's located. If you want, Find File will put the file right on your desktop. You can use Find File from the desktop or when you're in a file or an application.

**Scrapbook** is a desk accessory that lets you store bits and pieces of text and graphics that you use frequently or in many files. You might store such things as pictures, letterheads or boilerplate (standard portions of text that are plugged into different documents). Not only can you store text and graphics, you can cut, copy and paste them using the commands in the Edit menu (which we'll be discussing soon).

Incidentally, you can have up to 15 desk accessories in the Apple menu. You can install a DA (desk accessory) directly into an application using the Font/DA Mover program usually found in your System folder. An excellent utility called "Suitcase" allows you to go well beyond the 15-DA limit (see the chapter resource guide.)

## FILE MENU

This menu has ten useful file management commands, which are used with icons and windows (as opposed to documents, folders and applications).

**New Folder** creates a new folder to hold applications, documents or other folders.

**Open** is used with icons to open documents into windows and to start applications.

**Print** lets you print documents by first selecting their icons.

**Close** lets you close the active window, leaving a highlighted icon and the next active window, if there is one.

**Get Info** gives you a brief summary of a selected icon. You can add information of your own as well as edit certain items in the summary (lock/unlock, the application memory size and the text summary itself).

**Duplicate** makes copies of items you select.

**Put Away** returns items on the desktop back to their original folders or disks.

**Page Setup** is used with the Print Catalog command to print *directories*. A directory is a listing of the contents in a disk or folder. The listing could be alphabetical, pictorial (with icons) or chronological. Page Setup lets you select page specifications for directories only. It doesn't work with documents you want to print from the Finder. Each application has its own Page Setup command that governs its documents. When in other applications, the Page Setup command calls up an application-specific dialog box that contains other specifications besides those found in the Page Setup command used for directories.

**Print Catalog** prints the active directory window in any "view" you've selected for the window. (We'll discuss the View Menu shortly.)

**Eject** is used to eject the diskette that is currently selected, or if no disk drive is selected, the last one in the series of one or more drives.

## EDIT MENU

Besides helping you edit text in standard documents, the Edit Menu also is useful for editing three types of desktop management information: 1) the names of disks, applications, folders and documents; 2) the text in "Get Info" windows; and 3) the text and pictures in desk accessories such as Scrapbook and Note Pad.

Many of the Edit commands are used with the **Clipboard**, a special holding place for material you "cut and paste." The Clipboard (generally stored in the computer's memory) is used with the Scrapbook file (located on the current startup disk) by means of a desk accessory program such as Scrapbook (an Apple DA) or Smart Scrap. The Scrapbook file contains frequently used pictures and text.

**Undo** undoes one of the editing commands you just used from the Edit menu. It can undo something you just did in a desk application, such as typing something incorrectly.

**Cut** deletes material (text or graphics) and puts it in Clipboard. Any other previous material in Clipboard will be replaced.

**Copy** makes a copy of the selected material, which then goes to Clipboard. Once again, any previous material is replaced.

**Paste** inserts the material from Clipboard.

**Clear** deletes material without putting it in Clipboard.

**Select All** lets you select all the icons either in the active window or on the desktop.

**Show Clipboard** displays a window that shows you what's currently in Clipboard.

Incidentally, you may notice that most of the file and edit commands listed in the pull-down menu have a special symbol followed by a letter. That symbol stands for the Apple or command key. When you press the command key and at the same time type the appropriate letter, you can perform an edit function more quickly since you don't have to pull down the File or Edit menu each time. Since you probably use the file or edit commands very often, it makes sense to use these shortcuts.

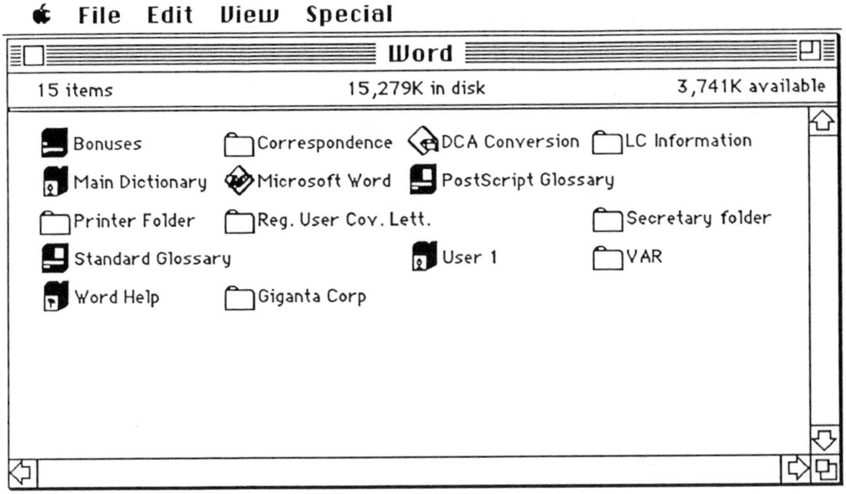

**&#xf8ff; File   Edit   Uiew   Special**

```
≣□≣═══════════════════ Word ═══════════════════□≣
║ ▢▢ ║                                              ⫿⫿≣
  15 items              15,279K in disk        3,741K available
┌─────────────────────────────────────────────────────────┐
│                                                        ⇧  │
│  ▪ Bonuses      ▢Correspondence ◁▪DCA Conversion ▢LC Information │
│  ▪ Main Dictionary ◈Microsoft Word ▪PostScript Glossary         │
│  ▢Printer Folder  ▢Reg. User Cov. Lett.        ▢Secretary folder │
│  ▪ Standard Glossary         ▪ User 1       ▢VAR               │
│  ▪ Word Help    ▢Giganta Corp                                   │
│                                                        ⇩  │
└─────────────────────────────────────────────────────────┘
 ◁▯                                                      ⇨▯
```

**Figure 7-9.** By Small Icon View

## VIEW MENU

This menu lets you see directories (listings) of disks and folders and even the trash in different "views." Through these different views, you can see more directory information at a glance and in more organized ways. The View menu makes it easier to find, copy, move and even rename files in your active directory window.

Each **By Small Icon** listing has a small icon on the left followed by its icon name. If you have many documents or applications, the By Small Icon view, shown in Figure 7-9, lets you see them quickly.

The **By Icon** view in Figure 7-10 resembles the desktop with its icon only display. This is a useful view if you only have a small number of applications, folders or documents.

**By Name** gives you an alphabetical listing as indicated in Figure 7-11. If you're good at remembering names–application, folder or file names, that is–then you should like this view.

**By Date** arranges your window contents chronologically by the date you most recently created or modified an application, folder or file. See example in Figure 7-12.

**By Size** lists applications and documents in order of their size so you can see which ones are taking up the most space. Folders are

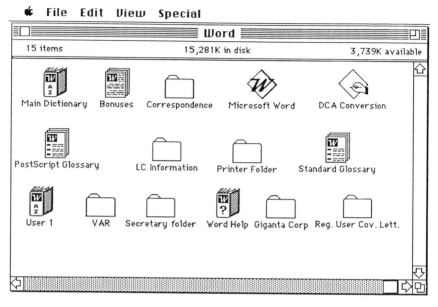

**Figure 7-10.** By Icon View

also listed but their size is not included. Folders are, however, listed alphabetically and they follow the listing of applications and documents. See Figure 7-13 for an example.

**By Kind** (Figure 7-14) groups applications, folders and documents separately. Each document also shows which application created it.

### SPECIAL MENU

Finally, the Special menu offers important desktop management tools.

**Clean Up** arranges icons neatly in an active directory window or on the desktop. Clean Up is used when the By Small Icon or By Icon view is in effect. Clean Up is called up by selecting the "Clean Up" command in the "Special" pull-down menu. If you hold down the Option key while selecting the Clean Up command, the icons in the selected window will be arranged more neatly and compactly within the window.

If you can't wait to "empty the trash" or you simply need more

**⌘  File   Edit   View   Special**

| Name | Size | Kind | Last Modified | |
|------|------|------|---------------|---|
| ☐ Bonuses | 4K | Microsoft Word d... | Thu, Sep 1, 1904 | 9:17 AM |
| ☐ Correspondence | -- | folder | Fri, Dec 2, 1988 | 5:42 PM |
| ☜ DCA Conversion | 72K | application | Sat, Jan 31, 1987 | 5:24 PM |
| ☐ Giganta Corp | -- | folder | Fri, Dec 2, 1988 | 6:52 PM |
| ☐ LC Information | -- | folder | Fri, Dec 2, 1988 | 5:33 PM |
| ☐ Main Dictionary | 161K | Microsoft Word d... | Sat, Jan 31, 1987 | 6:01 AM |
| ☜ Microsoft Word | 350K | application | Tue, Sep 6, 1904 | 9:42 AM |
| ☐ PostScript Glossary | 4K | Microsoft Word d... | Sat, Jan 31, 1987 | 10:19 AM |
| ☐ Printer Folder | -- | folder | Fri, Dec 2, 1988 | 4:26 PM |
| ☐ Reg. User Cov. Lett. | -- | folder | Fri, Dec 2, 1988 | 4:26 PM |
| ☐ Secretary folder | -- | folder | Fri, Dec 2, 1988 | 5:33 PM |
| ☐ Standard Glossary | 1K | Microsoft Word d... | Sat, Jan 31, 1987 | 7:41 AM |
| ☐ User 1 | 1K | Microsoft Word d... | Wed, Apr 27, 1988 | 2:43 PM |
| ☐ VAR | -- | folder | Fri, Dec 2, 1988 | 4:26 PM |
| ☐ Word Help | 113K | Microsoft Word d... | Sat, Jan 31, 1987 | 10:01 AM |

**Figure 7-11.** By Name View.

space on your disk immediately, then use **Empty Trash**. Of course, the trash is automatically emptied every time you shut down.

Use **Erase Disk** to delete the contents of a disk other than your startup disk. Erase Disk will also "initialize" a disk–prepare or format the disk so that it's ready to receive information.

**Set Startup** sets the conditions for the next restart of the computer. It allows you to specify being under the control of the Finder or under Multifinder. Under Finder, Set Startup takes you automatically to one pre-designated application after starting the computer (without stopping at the Finder first). Under Multifinder, Set Startup allows you to specify that several applications are to be loaded automatically upon startup.

**Use Minifinder...** lets you group together applications and documents you use most often or those you'd use together for a specific task.

Use **Restart** (on the Mac II) when you want to change to a different startup disk. Restart saves your latest information, ejects the disk you no longer want to use, empties the trash and restarts

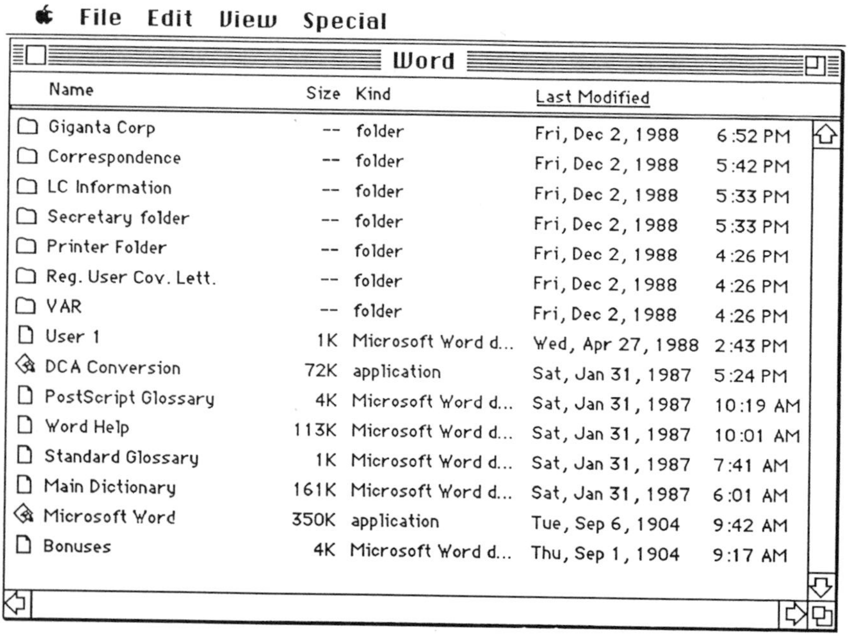

**&#xF8FF; File Edit View Special**

| Name | Size | Kind | Last Modified | |
|------|------|------|---------------|---|
| 🗀 Giganta Corp | -- | folder | Fri, Dec 2, 1988 | 6:52 PM |
| 🗀 Correspondence | -- | folder | Fri, Dec 2, 1988 | 5:42 PM |
| 🗀 LC Information | -- | folder | Fri, Dec 2, 1988 | 5:33 PM |
| 🗀 Secretary folder | -- | folder | Fri, Dec 2, 1988 | 5:33 PM |
| 🗀 Printer Folder | -- | folder | Fri, Dec 2, 1988 | 4:26 PM |
| 🗀 Reg. User Cov. Lett. | -- | folder | Fri, Dec 2, 1988 | 4:26 PM |
| 🗀 VAR | -- | folder | Fri, Dec 2, 1988 | 4:26 PM |
| 🗋 User 1 | 1K | Microsoft Word d... | Wed, Apr 27, 1988 | 2:43 PM |
| DCA Conversion | 72K | application | Sat, Jan 31, 1987 | 5:24 PM |
| 🗋 PostScript Glossary | 4K | Microsoft Word d... | Sat, Jan 31, 1987 | 10:19 AM |
| 🗋 Word Help | 113K | Microsoft Word d... | Sat, Jan 31, 1987 | 10:01 AM |
| 🗋 Standard Glossary | 1K | Microsoft Word d... | Sat, Jan 31, 1987 | 7:41 AM |
| 🗋 Main Dictionary | 161K | Microsoft Word d... | Sat, Jan 31, 1987 | 6:01 AM |
| Microsoft Word | 350K | application | Tue, Sep 6, 1904 | 9:42 AM |
| 🗋 Bonuses | 4K | Microsoft Word d... | Thu, Sep 1, 1904 | 9:17 AM |

**Figure 7-12.** By Date view

your computer.

You can also switch to a different startup disk by using either of the following:

- Hold down the Option key while you're opening an application that's on another startup disk. This is a useful way of switching if you're using a hard disk.
- Hold down the Option and Command keys while you're double-clicking the Finder icon on the disk you're switching to.

**Shut Down** prepares your computer for an orderly shut off. It turns off a Mac II, but not a Mac, a Mac Plus or a Mac SE.

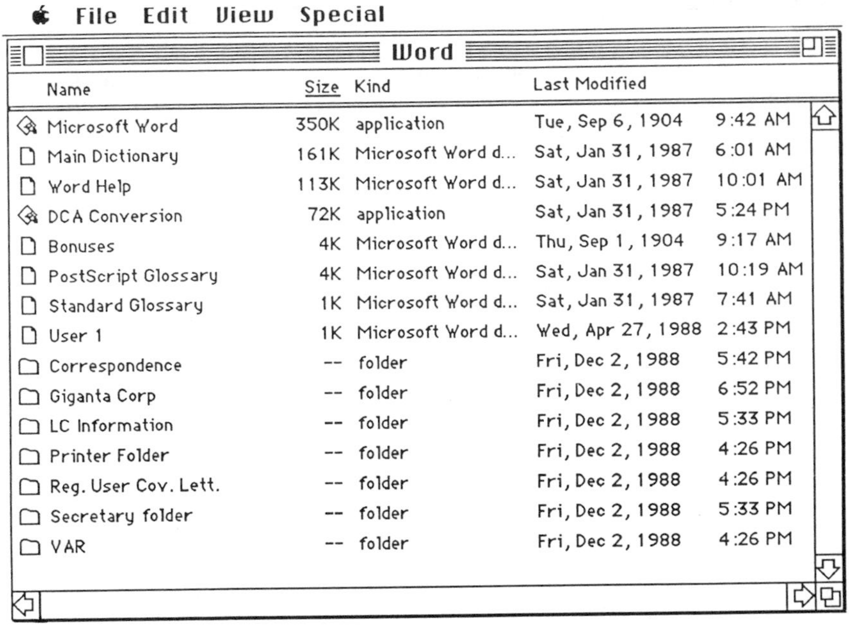

| 🍎  File   Edit   View   Special | | | |
|---|---|---|---|

**Word**

| Name | Size | Kind | Last Modified | |
|---|---|---|---|---|
| Microsoft Word | 350K | application | Tue, Sep 6, 1904 | 9:42 AM |
| Main Dictionary | 161K | Microsoft Word d... | Sat, Jan 31, 1987 | 6:01 AM |
| Word Help | 113K | Microsoft Word d... | Sat, Jan 31, 1987 | 10:01 AM |
| DCA Conversion | 72K | application | Sat, Jan 31, 1987 | 5:24 PM |
| Bonuses | 4K | Microsoft Word d... | Thu, Sep 1, 1904 | 9:17 AM |
| PostScript Glossary | 4K | Microsoft Word d... | Sat, Jan 31, 1987 | 10:19 AM |
| Standard Glossary | 1K | Microsoft Word d... | Sat, Jan 31, 1987 | 7:41 AM |
| User 1 | 1K | Microsoft Word d... | Wed, Apr 27, 1988 | 2:43 PM |
| Correspondence | -- | folder | Fri, Dec 2, 1988 | 5:42 PM |
| Giganta Corp | -- | folder | Fri, Dec 2, 1988 | 6:52 PM |
| LC Information | -- | folder | Fri, Dec 2, 1988 | 5:33 PM |
| Printer Folder | -- | folder | Fri, Dec 2, 1988 | 4:26 PM |
| Reg. User Cov. Lett. | -- | folder | Fri, Dec 2, 1988 | 4:26 PM |
| Secretary folder | -- | folder | Fri, Dec 2, 1988 | 5:33 PM |
| VAR | -- | folder | Fri, Dec 2, 1988 | 4:26 PM |

**Figure 7-13.** By Size view

## RESOURCE GUIDE

## DESKTOP AND FILE MANAGEMENT
## DESK ACCESSORIES AND UTILITIES

**DiskTools Plus**, is a powerful desk accessory that includes seven useful accessories. "DiskTools II," the major disk accessory in the program, greatly improves upon Finder; in fact, you may rarely need to use Finder again. DiskTools II uses simple, function icons to let you easily create folders; find, rename, copy, move or delete documents and applications; install files and applications without having to go through the folder structure; and find information about files. Other DAs include  "Calendar," "PhonePad," "Print Text" and "Windows."  $49.95. 415/571-7171 Ext. 263

Electronic Arts
1820 Campus Dr.
San Mateo, CA 94404

**DiskTop** is a useful DA that lets you do Finder functions without

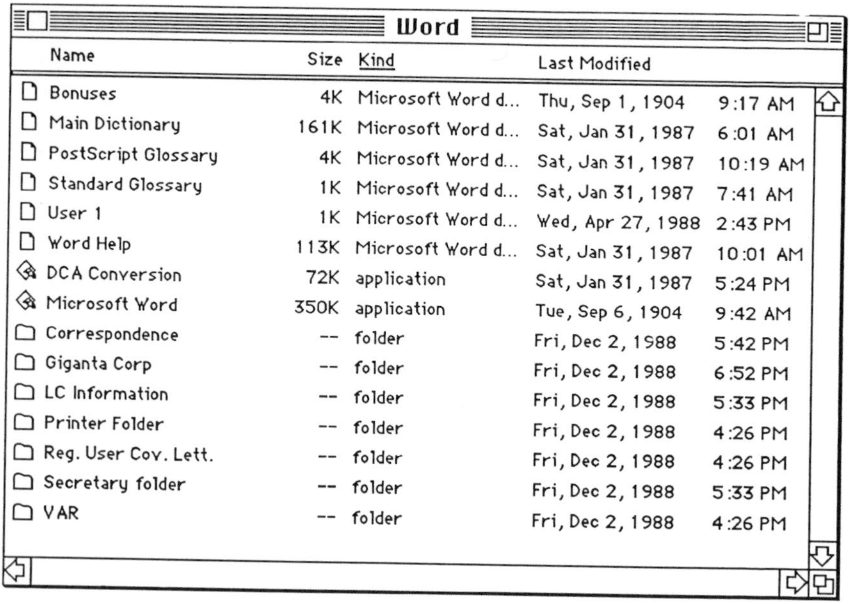

| Name | Size | Kind | Last Modified | |
|------|------|------|---------------|---|
| □ Bonuses | 4K | Microsoft Word d... | Thu, Sep 1, 1904 | 9:17 AM |
| □ Main Dictionary | 161K | Microsoft Word d... | Sat, Jan 31, 1987 | 6:01 AM |
| □ PostScript Glossary | 4K | Microsoft Word d... | Sat, Jan 31, 1987 | 10:19 AM |
| □ Standard Glossary | 1K | Microsoft Word d... | Sat, Jan 31, 1987 | 7:41 AM |
| □ User 1 | 1K | Microsoft Word d... | Wed, Apr 27, 1988 | 2:43 PM |
| □ Word Help | 113K | Microsoft Word d... | Sat, Jan 31, 1987 | 10:01 AM |
| ◈ DCA Conversion | 72K | application | Sat, Jan 31, 1987 | 5:24 PM |
| ◈ Microsoft Word | 350K | application | Tue, Sep 6, 1904 | 9:42 AM |
| □ Correspondence | -- | folder | Fri, Dec 2, 1988 | 5:42 PM |
| □ Giganta Corp | -- | folder | Fri, Dec 2, 1988 | 6:52 PM |
| □ LC Information | -- | folder | Fri, Dec 2, 1988 | 5:33 PM |
| □ Printer Folder | -- | folder | Fri, Dec 2, 1988 | 4:26 PM |
| □ Reg. User Cov. Lett. | -- | folder | Fri, Dec 2, 1988 | 4:26 PM |
| □ Secretary folder | -- | folder | Fri, Dec 2, 1988 | 5:33 PM |
| □ VAR | -- | folder | Fri, Dec 2, 1988 | 4:26 PM |

**Figure 7-14.** By Kind view

having to leave an application or document. $99.95. 515/224-1995
CE Software
PO Box 65663
W. Des Moines, IA 50265

**myDiskLabeler** is a disk labeling utility that easily lets you create meaningful and versatile disk labels. $80. 800/752-4400 or 509/458-6312
Williams & Macias, Inc.
3707 S. Godfrey
Spokane, WA 99204

**MasterJuggler** is a utility that lets you switch between applications and their windows, lets you access hundreds of Desk Accessories, fonts, FKeys and sounds and can open up to 12 files on multiple volumes. This program received a *MacUser* "Honorable Mention." $89.95. 713/353-4090
ALSoft, Inc.
PO Box 927
Spring, TX 77383

**QuicKeys** is a macro utility program that lets you bypass the mouse and more quickly perform commands and desktop management tasks. This program received a "95" out of 100 points from *MacGuide*. $99.95. CE Software (see Disktop above)

**SmartScrap & The Clipper II** are two excellent DAs that offer significant improvements to the standard Macintosh Scrapbook and Clipboard DAs. They provide multiple Scrapbooks and tools for cropping and scaling graphics. SmartScrap features a "Table of Contents" that displays many Scrapbook pages. SmartScrap lets you have many Scrapbook files on a disk and lets you select any portions of files. The Clipper lets you modify pictures in a variety of ways. $89.95. 802/865-9220
Solutions Inc.
PO Box 783
Williston, VT 05495

**Suitcase II** is a utility that overcomes the limitations of the Macintosh System file by allowing unlimited access to fonts, desk accessories, FKEYs and sounds, while freeing up System memory. $79. 800/873-4384 or 504/291-7221
Fifth Generation Systems, Inc.
10049 N. Reiger Rd.
Baton Rouge, LA 70809-4562

**Switcher Construction Kit** lets you switch between up to eight programs at the click of a mouse. If you use several programs every day, Switcher gives you the fastest method of calling them up. Through the special feature "Always Convert The Clipboard," you can easily cut and paste between applications. $19.95. 408/996-1010
Apple Computer, Inc.
20525 Mariani Avenue
Cupertino, CA 95014

**Virtual** is an operating system initializer that lets the Mac II run with 8MB of virtual memory on as little as 1MB of installed RAM if the Mac has a hard disk with 8MB of contiguous space available. This program received "five mice" from *MacUser*. $199. 415/324-0727
Connectix Corp.
125 Constitution Dr.
Menlo Park, CA 94025

# DATA ACCESS

**CanOpener** is a search-and-retrieval utility that can collect portions of searches in libraries that function like Scrapbook files. *MacUser* Magazine awarded this program "four mice." $125. 800/552-9157 or 914/747-3116
Abbott Systems, Inc.
62 Mountain Rd.
Pleasantville, NY 10570

**Eureka!** is a file-finding utility that's great for locating files whose names you may have forgotten or that may be buried deep within your HFS. It installs into a spare DA slot and can be selected from your Apple menu at any time. $24.95. 800/622-2888 or 813/884-3092
Personal Computer Peripherals Corp.
4710 Eisenhower Blvd., Ste. A4
Tampa, FL 33634

**Sonar** and **Sonar Professional** are fast, text retrieval programs that can search folders full of word-processed documents. They also do indexing. Sonar Professional is 25 times faster and contains many features not found on the regular version of Sonar. $295, Sonar; $795, Sonar Professional. 804/739-3200
Virginia Systems Software Services, Inc.
5509 W. Bay Court
Midlothian, VA 23113

# BOOKS, CATALOGS, REFERENCES

**Hard Disk Management for the Macintosh** by Nancy Andrews (New York: Bantam Books, 1987) is easy to read and understand. The book comes with three utilities, LOCKIT, WHEREIS and BACKUP. $34.95, paper

**MacGuide** is a terrific, semi-annual guide/magazine that features reviews and listings of more than 4,500 Macintosh products. The guide is very well organized with thorough reviews, helpful numerical ratings of products (by reviewers and often readers) and excellent feature articles. This is a user friendly publication that goes out of its way to help the reader. I especially like the cumulative listing of products by category, which contains condensed versions of all product reviews to date. I used this invaluable listing when selecting

products to include in this book. $9.95 for one issue, $19.90 for two issues, $19.50 for monthly updates or $39.40 for two issues and monthly updates. 800/873-1454 or 303/893-1454
MacGuide Magazine, Inc.
444 Seventeenth St., Ste. 200
PO Box 5937 T.A.
Denver, CO 80217

**The Macintosh Buyer's Guide** is an excellent resource for learning about software and hardware for the Mac. $20, newsstand price for one year; $14, subscription price for new subscribers. 800/262-3012
Redgate Communications Corp.
Attn: Circulation Dept.
660 Beachland Blvd.
Vero Beach, FL 32963-1794

**Macintosh Computers–Professional Set** is a two-volume information directory listing detailed descriptions of more than 4,500 programs. $89.95. 800/843-MENU or 412/746-MENU
MENU Publishing
PO Box MENU
Pittsburgh, PA 15241

**Macintosh Hard Disk Management** by Charles Rubin and Bencion Calica (Indianapolis: Hayden Books, 1988) is superb. Rubin and Bencion write clearly and the book has many helpful techniques, illustrations, examples and resources. $19.95, paper

**Macintosh Plus, Macintosh SE** and **Macintosh II manuals** are filled with excellent illustrations, examples and shortcuts. Sure the Mac is friendly enough so you don't *have* to read the manual, but you'll really benefit from doing so. At the very least, take a peek at the Contents pages and read selected chapters. Apple Computer, Inc. (see Switcher Construction Kit above)

**MacUser** is an excellent Macintosh monthly magazine that provides the latest in Macintosh software, peripherals and usage. This is a very practical, hands-on publication. $3.95 per newsstand copy; $19.97 for a one-year subscription (12 issues). 415/378-5600
MacUser
PO Box 52461
Boulder, CO 80321-2461

**Macworld** is a wonderful monthly magazine with top quality design and well-written columns and feature articles. $30 for a one-year subscription (12 issues). 800/525-0643: in Colorado, 303/447-9330
501 Second St.
San Francisco, CA 94107


Note: Always check with vendors for the latest version of software products and the compatibility with your existing hardware and software.

# 8

# THE BEST
# OF BOTH WORLDS:
# SPECIAL ORGANIZATION
# TIPS AND TOOLS FOR
# THE IBM AND THE MAC

*Quick Scan: Read this chapter if you want to protect yourself against computer disaster, because yes, it* can *happen to you. You'll learn the best protection for your personal computer comes from computer file maintenance, clean hard disks, organized floppies and a sound backup routine. Besides some simple techniques, you'll also discover some indispensable software programs that make it all much easier. Read this chapter whether you own a Macintosh, IBM or IBM compatible personal computer. Products are grouped by computer type in the chapter resource guide. (The term "IBM" is used throughout this chapter to denote both IBM and IBM compatible personal computers.)*

When it comes to good organization, computers are like file cabinets, only worse. If your file cabinets are jam packed, your hard and floppy disks are probably, too. But as long as you've got space on your disks, what's the problem? Let's see why you shouldn't wait until all your space is gone.

## THE REWARDS OF
## COMPUTER HOUSEKEEPING

Regular computer housekeeping, especially computer file maintenance, is essential to the health and performance of your computer. Not only will it be easier to find files, but you can improve the productivity and speed of your computer–particularly your hard disk.

What's more, if you never do maintenance and your hard disk fills up with files, you're just asking for a computer crash.

## BIGGER IS BETTER, RIGHT?

If you've ever been tempted to substitute a bigger hard disk for computer housekeeping chores, think again. You may have also been tempted at one time or another to buy another file cabinet for all your papers and files. Or perhaps you've bought a bigger house to accommodate all the "stuff" you've accumulated (you may remember the famous George Carlin routine).

If you're behind in your housekeeping, a bigger hard disk is just going to make matters worse. Just as with file cabinets, you can only tell how much space you need *after* you have purged your files. Once you've cleaned out your hard disk, see if you have 75 percent or more filled with current programs and files. If so, a larger or additional hard disk may be very appropriate.

By the way, when was the last time you cleaned out your hard disk? Have you *ever* cleaned it out? Since for most of us, out of sight means out of mind, it's particularly easy for computer files to accumulate.

There are three reasons to take the time and trouble to clean out your hard disk:

1. to speed up your computer
2. to speed *you* up (locating files becomes difficult when your IBM directories or Mac folders are full of files that you aren't using)
3. to make more room on your hard disk.

6.30.94

Cindy

# A SQUEAKY CLEAN HARD DISK

The best computer file maintenance is done as you go—deleting duplicates and out-of-date files, storing inactive files on backup media and having a backup routine that you use regularly. But if you're like most people, you probably will need to sit down once every six months to a year and do a thorough spring cleaning. Where do you begin and how do you proceed? Here are some useful steps:

- Before you do any "house cleaning," print a hard copy of your root directory so you can see at a glance all the names of your IBM subdirectories or your Mac first level folders.
- Go through each main IBM subdirectory or Mac folder and see if you recognize any files you can delete. (Now's the time to remove those extra backups that your word processor may automatically make.)
- Look more closely. Are there any files you're no longer using but you'd like to keep in archival storage? If so, back these up on floppies, tape or whatever backup medium you're using. Or perhaps you have a backup device or program that can "tag" these specific files and back them up collectively. For files that are very important, make *two* archival copies that are kept in different locations.
- Consolidate any files you can-i.e., group separate, related files together in one new file or a Mac folder. For example, instead of having every letter in a separate file, group all 1991 letters together or all letters to a client together. In the IBM environment, depending on your version of DOS, a file could take up to 8,000 bytes of memory even though it looks in your directory listing as if the file only has, say, 100 bytes. (Each file under DOS is allocated a certain minimum number of bytes, whether or not those bytes are actually used and whether or not those bytes appear to be included in the number of bytes next to the file name on your directory.)
- Examine your largest files and decide how often you use them. Perhaps they can be stored elsewhere.
- Look for any subdirectories or folders that only contain a few files. See if you can move these files elsewhere and delete these

subdirectories or folders, which even by themselves take up space.

• Print a hard copy of your latest **catalog** (a listing of all your directory or folder files) and keep them near your labeled backup media. If you back up your hard disk with a program that contains a catalog feature, print out the catalog when you complete your backup (I always do this after each full backup). If you're using 5¼-inch floppies, print out the directory listings and tape them to the jackets holding the floppies.

Just as with manual systems, try to keep most accessible only the files you're regularly using. Only these files should be kept in your current subdirectories or your Mac folders. It's so easy to start stockpiling files that you never use. When you do, you'll soon discover you have trouble finding files that are needed.

After eliminating, transferring and consolidating files, your computer may *appear* neat and tidy, but chances are that many files are probably **fragmented**, which means that the information in each file is scattered in different places over your disk. The more you use your hard disk, the slower it becomes. The reason for this is that every time you want to save information, your computer stores the information wherever it will fit.

Your computer stores pieces of information in **clusters,** wherever it can find room on your hard disk. The information in a file may start out as one cluster but through use, the file becomes many clusters that are scattered all over the hard disk. This results in slower access time, which you'll notice especially when you call up a file.

The more fragmented your files are, the more clusters you'll have on your hard disk, the more your computer slows down and the more you need to **optimize** your hard disk using a software program such as Disk Optimizer. Optimizing restores your hard disk's original speed by consolidating file clusters.

An optimizing program can reorganize the clusters on your hard disk, grouping them all together. Some experts suggest optimizing at least once a week. Optimizing not only keeps your access time from slowing down, but it also saves wear and tear on your computer. If your disk is optimized, your computer doesn't have to scramble around looking for all the clusters of a file and therefore, your computer doesn't have to work as hard.

Check the chapter resource guide under "Hard Disk Maintenance Utilities" for either a specific optimizing program or for a utility that contains an optimizing feature. If you're serious about keeping your hard disk humming, consider regularly using a more full-featured hard disk maintenance utility that can test and repair a host of maladies.

## FLOPPY ORGANIZATION

Most of our discussion about computer file organization has focused on your hard disk. But chances are good you'll still be using floppy diskettes (also called floppies, diskettes or simply disks) from time to time. Here are some tips to prevent you from floundering in floppies, as well as tips to save you time and aggravation.

As a general rule, separate program files from your data files. This can save you time during backup by letting you easily exclude program files (which don't usually change once you've installed them). Group data files together by subject, task or client or by a common IBM subdirectory or Mac folder name.

Keep floppies in plastic storage cases specially designed for floppy disks. Get the kind with plastic dividers and stick-on labels to group different types of files. For extra security, buy cases with locks and keys (see Figure 8-1).

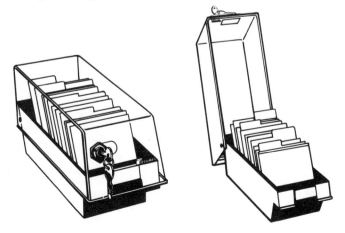

**Figure 8-1.** Fellowes Econo/Stor 40 Diskette Filing Tray

Keep a set of up-to-date, printed **directories** for all your floppies. As used here, a directory is a table of contents for your floppy. For the 5¼-inch floppy format, tape each floppy directory to its paper jacket. It's a good idea to keep a set of printed directories in a nearby notebook or folder, whether you're using 3½- or 5¼-inch floppies. Hard-copy directories can save you the time of inserting floppies and scanning the contents when you want to see what's on them.

If you have hundreds of files, you may want to consider color coding. You can use colored diskette labels or buy diskettes that come in colors. Sentinel and Verbatim make diskettes in 10 different colors.

For temporary labeling or color coding, use removable labels or dots or a strip of removable tape over a permanent label. Whenever you label a diskette, always date it. In fact, anytime you work on a disk, write the date of that work session on the label. Use a thin, permanent felt-tip marker, such as a Sharpie pen, instead of a pencil or ball-point pen, which could damage the diskette.

Speaking of damage, keep your floppies, especially your 5¼-inch ones, away from heat and magnetic fields. Avoid leaving floppy disks in your car or on top of your TV, monitor, modem or windowsill. Keep them away from telephones, stereos, headphones, magnetic paper clip holders, magnetic copy holders, metal paper clips, electric pencil sharpeners, electric cables and cords and all other devices that could have magnetic fields.

Worried about x-ray machines at airports? You don't have to be if you lay disks flat on the conveyor belt. Whatever you do, be careful about handing disks to a security guard, who may be standing at the back of the metal detector, where there are magnetic fields that could cause damage to data.

Be careful how you handle 5¼-inch floppies. Never bend or paper clip a disk jacket, which can prevent the disk from spinning freely in the drive. The best place to hold a 5¼-inch disk is at its corners. If you touch the disk itself, you may leave an oily residue from your fingers that can damage this disk as well as leave a residue on the drive's heads that could damage another disk.

If you use floppies often, consider using a floppy disk drive cleaning kit that cleans the drive heads. Don't use it too often, however; twice a year should be sufficient in most cases.

Remember, *all* disks wear out from normal use as well as from the passage of time. Never rely on only one disk to hold important information indefinitely–always have another copy and if you're really organized, make sure no disks are more than a year or two old.

And finally, when you buy diskettes, buy the best. You don't have to buy the most expensive, but whatever you do, avoid generic, dirt-cheap disks, that carry no manufacturer's name. These disks are said to have high failure rates–as high as 20 percent. High quality disks have no more than a one percent failure rate. Also, if you want to save some time, buy pre-formatted disks. 3M makes them in 3½- and 5¼-inch versions.

## BACK IT UP!

You can't talk about computer organization without talking about backups. For our discussion here, a backup is a duplicate copy of computer data (programs and files) that is stored on another medium besides the primary one you're using. There are two parts to making backups: establishing a **backup routine** and selecting a **backup device**. The backup device or medium you select isn't half as important as whether you actually use it.

## WHY BOTHER?

Why do you have to bother backing up your work when you have a hard disk–isn't it solid as a rock? Computer expert Paul Somerson responds by saying, "Hard disks used to be expensive and unreliable. That's all changed. Today they're inexpensive and unreliable."

You never backed up your filing cabinet; why should you back up your computer files? First, the chances of wiping out your computer data are much greater than losing your hard data. Second, it's so easy today to back up. (And why tempt fate anyway?)

Backups are *insurance* for valuable, current data that would either require more than an hour to re-enter or would be next to impossible to re-create exactly as inputted the first time. Whenever I'm producing original, creative material, I not only save it on my hard disk, I save it on a special backup floppy as well. That floppy goes home with me each night.

By the way, since I'm saving this material frequently and using two different media to do so–a procedure that requires many steps–I use a **macro** to automate the process. A macro is a quick, shorthand method of doing many computer steps with just a few keystrokes. With WordPerfect, my word processing program, I was able to create a "save" macro that lets me press just two keys (the Alt key and the letter "S") to quickly perform an operation that would normally require pressing at least 35 different keys!

Besides making additional copies of important information, backups can serve as **storage** for less important information that is not being used and is taking up too much space on your hard disk. Once you've backed up this archival information, then you can delete it from your hard disk or a working floppy. Make two archival backup copies if the information is very important and keep the copies in separate locations–for example, at home and at the office.

Good backups will let you conduct business as usual even if your hard disk crashes or your entire computer is in for repair. Don't wait until a crash to get serious about backing up. As writer Wes Nihei observed in *PC World*, "Backing up files is a lot like dental hygiene: by the time you get serious about flossing and brushing, it's usually too late."

## HOW OFTEN, HOW MUCH?

Your backup routine depends on how often files change, the number of files you modify a day, the kind of information or application and how easy your backup device is to use. It may also depend upon whether you keep any hard copy that would enable you to re-create computer files. Based on these criteria, check any of the following that you think would apply to your situation:

- Each day back up any data, IBM subdirectories or Mac folders or applications you have modified that day.
- Have two rotating sets of complete backups where the most current set is off site (at home, for example, if your office is not in your home). As soon as you make your most up-to-date backup, take it off site and bring back the older backup set.
- Do a full backup every day.
- Do a full backup every week.
- Do a full backup every month.

- Do a full backup every four to six months.
- Have three complete sets of programs and data: one you're working with and two current backups—one on site and an additional backup kept off site.
- Assuming your active program files are on one "logical drive" of your hard disk (as discussed in Chapter 6), do a full backup at least once a year and store it off site. It's faster to back up program files that are in one location and you're also backing up all that time-consuming customization you've done for each program.

Data processing departments generally keep daily files Monday through Thursday, make a weekly backup on Friday and do a monthly backup every fourth week. Copies of weekly and monthly backups are kept off site as well as on site. My recommendation is **always have at least one complete, current backup off site.**

## TYPES OF BACKUP

Your backup routine should include **selective** as well as **complete** or **full** backups. Complete or "full" backups are used to copy the entire contents of your hard disk and would be useful if you had a system failure and you had to restore the data on your hard disk.

Backup devices do complete backups in one of two ways: **image** or **file-by-file.** Image backups make a mirror-image copy of your hard disk, are very fast and can back up copy-protected programs. The disadvantage is that you might not be able to restore an image backup to a different hard disk other than the original. (If, for example, your hard disk crashes and can't be repaired, you may possibly be unable to transfer your image backup to a new hard disk.)

File-by-file backups, while slower, don't have that problem. Not only are they more reliable, they also make it easier to find backed-up files. You can also restore individual files without having to restore the entire hard disk. New technology is aiming for faster, file-by-file backups. File-by-file backups can be used for selective as well as complete backups.

Selective or partial backups are used to copy individual files, programs or data. An **incremental** backup is a type of selective backup that copies only files that have changed since your last backup. If your backup device can do incremental backups, you will save time—keep this feature in mind when you select a backup device. A **differential** backup is like an incremental backup except it will overwrite a previous version on your backup medium.

You would make incremental backups if you needed to save each version of a file because you might need to refer to one of these versions or you need an audit trail. If you don't need to see old versions, but only the current, most up-to-date version, use differential backups. I use differential backups because I generally work with the same files over and over and only need to see the latest versions. Differential backups save me time and space.

## ADDITIONAL TIPS FOR A BETTER BACKUP ROUTINE
Following these simple backup tips can save you many headaches down the long haul. Check off all the ones you already do; circle those you will incorporate into your routine after reading this section:

- Always back up new software.
- Always back up newly *installed* software, particularly if you made any special installation procedures. (Also keep a hard copy record of the answers you gave to installation questions in case you need to reinstall the program.)
- Make two backups of files that change every day. Make the backups as you go, saving each file twice, once on your hard disk and once again on a floppy. Or make your backups at the end of the day from a daily, written list of modified files.
- Carefully date and label all backup media; use color coding if necessary. If you make daily backups on floppies, use a different color label or diskette for each day of the week, for example, red for Monday's disk, orange for Tuesday's, etc.
- When you install a backup device, test it out with some junk files before betting your life on it.
- Use dated hard copy as important backup.
- Have at least two current sets of all important work—one should be off site.
- Try to select a backup program that can also be run from a floppy, such as Fastback Plus, and keep it with one set of

backup disks. That way you won't have to reinstall the program before restoring files.
- Whenever possible, exclude unnecessary files such as README, BAK or TMP files and do not back up system files.

## TYPES OF BACKUP AND STORAGE DEVICES

All backup devices are one of two types—disk or tape. Disk devices are generally faster in terms of backup speed than tape devices. It's also easier and faster to locate backed-up data on a disk. But disks usually cost more and hold less data than tapes. Tape backup devices use a magnetic tape similar to the kind used in audio recording. Most backup tapes are housed in cartridges.

Selection criteria as well as the two basic types of devices are described here. Specific brands and models receiving favorable computer magazine reviews are listed in the chapter resource guide.

### SELECTION CRITERIA

Before you select a backup device, consider the following criteria:

- ease of use (if it's not easy to learn and use, you won't bother with it)
- speed (how much of your time will it take?)
- capacity (how much do you need now and in the foreseeable future?)
- portability (are you going to be removing and transporting the device frequently and if so, how far?)
- operator monitored (or does it "run in the background" by itself?)
- compatibility (with other office computers)
- security
- performance
- reliability/verification (what kind of error checking does it have?)
- For IBM users: DOS or non-DOS format (often faster, more condensed and more reliable in a non-DOS format although you won't be able to use non-DOS files until they are "restored" back to a DOS format)
- additional hardware required (the cost factor aside, what kind of space do you have for more hardware?)

• file-by-file or image (you may need both, but at the very least have file-by-file)
• cost (what are your budget restrictions?)

Go back and check off all the criteria you *must* have and compare them to your budget and your information needs to determine the price you're willing to pay.

## DISK BACKUP DEVICES

Of the ten disk backup devices listed here, using **floppy disks** in combination with **DOS commands** is the least expensive disk backup device. Unfortunately, it's also the slowest.

Using **floppies** in conjunction with a **hard disk backup utility program** (also called **backup software**) is an inexpensive, reliable choice, though once again, not super fast. But if you have a fairly small hard disk, 10 or 20MB (MB means megabyte), or you use and back up only a small number of files, this could be a good choice. It has worked for me. When I had a 10MB hard disk, I backed it up in eight to 10 minutes using Fastback, a software program that continues to get good reviews. Now that I have a 40MB hard disk, I'm still using Fastback (although I've upgraded to Fastback Plus). I make differential backups daily in combination with full backups every quarter. (Backup utility programs such as Fastback can also be used with media other than floppies such as tape cartridges.)

**High-capacity 3½-inch barium-ferrite floppy disks and drives** offering from 2.8MB to 21.4MB of storage are coming on the market. The main advantage is greater capacity than regular floppies (the Stor/Mor can hold almost 10 times as much data). Sometimes this technology is faster than floppy disk technology, depending on the file size. It's more expensive than floppies, but much less expensive than many of the other backup devices in this section.

A **second hard disk** can function as a backup device as well as a duplicate computer system, provided you keep the second disk completely up to date. If your main hard disk should crash, you've got the second one ready to go. (Most likely you would have to send your hard disk, not the entire computer out for repair.) You can also get an **external hard disk** or another **internal hard disk** if you have room. Warning: Never rely solely on a second hard disk on site; you also better have a backup copy of data off site.

A **removable hard disk** gives you the speed and capacity of a conventional hard disk but adds portability. Such a hard disk is housed in a sealed unit and usually comes with its own internal or external drive. While faster than many other backup systems, removable hard disks, particularly older models, can be slower than the standard hard disk. That is changing, however, along with increasing storage capacity. Proteus Technology Corp. (800/782-8387) and Sysgen (800/821-2151) both make disks that can hold 150MB. Removable hard disks are faster and have longer media life than the next alternative, but they are considered to be much more fragile. ("Auto-parking" and "head-locking" features, however, have helped to minimize the fragility of removable hard disks.)

**Removable cartridge disk systems** use specially designed, more rugged "cartridge disks," which are like large capacity floppies housed in cartridges. These disks can hold from 10 to 44 megabytes each. The Bernoulli Box is an example. Cartridge disk systems provide removable, large capacity storage. These systems use their own controllers (compared to those that use floppy disk controllers) and can therefore, write more data on a disk.

There are two types of removable cartridge disk systems—flexible and hard. Removable flexible cartridges appear to be more durable.

While perhaps the most cost-effective solution for removable mass-storage, these systems are considered slow and somewhat susceptible to media wear.

**Hard disk cards**, also known simply as **hard cards**, are faster than cartridge disk systems, floppy disks or tape backup units. They are generally comparable in speed to hard disks, and like hard disks, have different speeds from which you can choose. Hard cards can hold as much as 80MB or even more. They are cost effective, too. Easy to install, a hard card slips into an empty computer slot.

A hard card is the equivalent of having a second hard disk. A hard card can be moved from computer to computer but switching it frequently is inconvenient. To use a hard card as your *only* backup storage device is foolhardy since you want media that you can and *will* store off site. Also be sure to check compatibility with your computer's controller as controller conflicts can be a problem. Plus

Development Corp. in Milpitas, California, is the leader in hard cards (800/624-5545).

If you need to backup or archive *hundreds of megabytes* or even *gigabytes*, **optical storage** may be the way to go. The newest type is the **erasable-optical (E-O) disk drive**, which is removable, has high storage capacity, from 500MB to 1GB (gigabyte), and unlike earlier optical disks, lets you write, erase and read data, much like a hard disk. E-O drives and disks don't come cheap—the drives range from $4,500 to $6,000 and the disks from $200 to $250. They also are subject to erasure if exposed to airport x-ray machines and magnetic forces. The "life expectancy" of these disks is at least 10 years. (Manufacturers of E-Os include Sony in Park Ridge, New Jersey, Canon in Lake Success, New York, and Advanced Graphics Applications Inc. in New York City.)

**WORM** (Write Once, Read Many) and **CD-ROM** (Compact Disk, Read Only Memory), two earlier optical technologies that are not erasable, still have their place. WORM is excellent as a secure, archival backup device that can't be altered. (By the way you can add data to a WORM on any unused portions but you can't overwrite existing data.) WORM capacity is up to 800MB for 5¼-inch disks and up to 3GB for 12-inch disks. WORM 5¼-inch drives cost $3,400 to $6,300 and disks are $200 to $250.

CD-ROM was the first optical disk on the market and is good for reference information that you need to access quickly and easily. CD-ROM can hold up to 700MB and is much less expensive than WORM. The drive costs $700 to $1,000 and disks range from $50 to $1,000. (You can also buy CD-ROM disks that already have reference information on them—from databases to dictionaries.)

### TAPE BACKUP DEVICES

If you're regularly backing up data that exceeds 40MB, it's probably time to use some kind of **tape backup system**, which includes a variety of special **tape drives** and **tape cartridges**. ("Open-reel" tape systems are the standard for mainframe computers.)

Tape backup is fairly fast and reliable but it has a number of disadvantages. For one thing, since tape drives, unlike hard disks and floppies, aren't "random access," you have to search sequentially through a tape to access the file you need. For another, many cartridges need formatting (i.e., preparing) before use, which takes time. Tape backup units also do not store or restore files as quickly as disk backup systems.

But you can't beat the *capacity* of tape systems. Today's low-cost tape drives use the standard quarter-inch tape cartridges and range from 40MB up to 120MB. The most common formats are "QIC-40" and "QIC-80" (QIC stands for Quarter-Inch Cartridge), although "QIC-150" is also becoming popular. The **DC 2000** (DC means "Data Cartridge") is the standard mini-cartridge tape backup system you'll probably want to get (it can hold up to 153MB). The DC 2000 is based on the **DC 6000**, which is a longer tape cartridge, has greater capacity (60MB to 525MB), has a faster data transfer rate, has been an industry standard and is more expensive.

You may want to avoid quarter-inch systems that use data compression because these tapes will be incompatible with other systems. Also, remember that tape cartridges don't last forever; *PC World* writer David Ferris estimates the average life span at 350 passes.

Be aware that even as you read this page, new and updated backup and storage technologies are emerging. There are even **backup services** that will back up *for* you–they're listed in the chapter resource guide.

## RESOURCE GUIDE

## IBM OR IBM COMPATIBLE PRODUCTS/SERVICES

### DISK BACKUP AND STORAGE DEVICES

**Bernoulli Box** is a removable cartridge disk system that continues to get good reviews. It consists of a special 10, 20 or 44MB cartridge disk inserted into its own disk drive. It comes with its own programs and clear documentation. Installation is easy. You can buy a one- or two-drive model (internal or external) ranging in price from $1,299 to $2,599. The "Universal Products" line easily adapts to both the IBM and the Mac and ranges in price from $1,399 to $2,599. 800/456-5522 or 801/778-1000
Iomega Corp.
1821 West 4000 South, Bldg. 4

Roy, UT 84067

**Hardcard II 40 and 80** are hard disk cards designed to work with fast, 16-bit machines and hold 40MB and 80MB respectively. 40MB, $849, 80MB, $999 (If you have a slower, 8-bit machine and/or need less storage capacity, Hardcard 20 and 40 are available at $749 and $849, respectively.) 408/434-6900
Plus Development Corp.
1778 McCarthy Blvd.
Milpitas, CA 95035-7421

**LaserStor Erasable** was selected as the "best all-around choice" by *PC World* among several erasable-optical disks. It's flexible and has good storage capacity (924MB). $7,995. 408/879-0300
Storage Dimensions
2145 Hamilton Ave.
San Jose, CA 95125

**Passport** is a removable hard disk selected as a *PC Magazine* "Editor's Choice." It is built for high performance and portability and includes auto-parking and head-locking to protect against head or disk damage. Internal unit, $659; external unit, $399; Micro Channel business PS/2 unit, $759; 20MB disk, $595; 40MB disk, $795. (See Plus Development Corp. under Hardcard above.)

**RHD-20** makes use of removable hard disk technology and uses a compact, 2½-inch, 20MB hard disk housed in a cartridge that works with its own drive. $640 to $695. 800/553-0337, 407/645-0001
DISCTEC
PO Box 1750
Winter Park, FL 32790

**Stor/Mor** makes use of a special high-capacity floppy disk (20MB) and drive. External unit with 8-bit controller, cable and one disk is $895; internal unit, $795. 404/923-6666
Q/COR
One Quad Way
Norcross, GA 30093-2919

## BACKUP UTILITY PROGRAMS

While most of these programs are designed to be used with floppy disks, some of them (such as Fastback Plus) can be used with other media, including tape cartridges.

**DMS/Intelligent Backup** rates high for beginners or busy professionals who don't have a lot of time. It is an automated program that reminds you when to do your next backup. It was a *PC Magazine* "Editor's Choice." $149. 916/635-5535
Sterling Software
11050 White Rock Road #100
Rancho Cordova, CA 95670-6095

**Fastback Plus** is a powerful, fast and flexible program that I'm using. I've been a Fastback user for years (I started with the standard version and was thrilled to upgrade to the "Plus" version). It does complete or selective backups and incremental backups. Fastback formats disks as it copies and will let you print a catalog of the backed up files. Besides the useful manual, there is a help line with "user friendly" assistance. The program has been selected as a *PC Magazine* "Editor's Choice" and as a *PC World* "Best Buy." $189. 800/873-4384 or 504/291-7221
Fifth Generation Systems
10049 N. Reiger Rd.
Baton Rouge, LA 70809

## TAPE BACKUP DEVICES

**ArchiveXL Model 5540** is a durable QIC-40 drive with good software, performance and solid construction. It was rated a "Best Buy" by *PC World*. $499. 800/237-4929 or 714/641-1230
Archive Corp.
1650 Sunflower Ave.
Costa Mesa, CA 92626

**Excel 40AT** was one of the fastest QIC-40 drives tested by *PC Magazine,* which selected this system as an "Editor's Choice." The software is easy to use for beginners as well as advanced users. $499. 800/821-0806 or 415/498-1111
Everex Systems Inc.
48431 Milmont Dr.

Fremont, CA 94538

**FileSafe 8000 Plus** was selected as a *PC Magazine* "Editor's Choice." It is fast in both backup and restore operations and has many features. It can store up to 152MB. $995. 800/458-0300 or 408/379-4300

Mountain Computer Inc.
240 Hacienda Ave.
Campbell, CA 95008-6687

**FSO 150e** is a QIC-150 tape drive using the DC 6000 quarter-inch cartridge and was selected a *PC Magazine* "Editor's Choice." It's fast, easy to use and includes support for QFA (Quick File Access), which lets you quickly restore a particular file on your tape. $1,795. 800/TAL-GRAS or 913/492-6002

Tallgrass Technologies Corp.
11100 West 82nd St.
Lenexa, KS 66214

**TG-1140** is a flexible QIC-40 system that adapts to a variety of different configurations that can give you storage capacity up to 120MB. It also includes a three-year warranty. $495. Tallgrass Technologies, see FSO 150e above.

## BACKUP SERVICES

If you just can't be bothered with backups or you need extra backup for vital information, consider one of these two services that will do it for you. They both archive files off site.

**Secure Data Network** charges start at $110 per month plus an initial $100 installation fee. 213/641-1300 in Los Angeles.

**Squibb DataSafe Systems** costs an initial $495 plus a monthly fee related to the amount of information you archive. For 10MB you'd spend about $53 per month. 800/648-5496 in Kingston, New York.

## HARD DISK AND DATA MAINTENANCE AND RECOVERY

A number of specialized programs and services will help you correct specific file and data problems you may encounter on your computer.

*Hard Disk Maintenance Utilities*

**Disk Optimizer** will speed up your hard disk by reorganizing scattered data into contiguous clusters. $69.95. 800/272-9900 or in New Hampshire, 603/627-9900
SoftLogic Solutions Inc.
One Perimeter Road
Manchester, NH 03103

**Disk Technician Advanced** makes hard disks factory-perfect every time you run it. It predicts, prevents and repairs problems which cause data loss, data corruption and crashes. SafePark, a RAM-resident head-parking program, is included to protect data against static electricity and other power-related problems. One reviewer wrote, "This could be the best investment you ever make." $149.95. 619/274-5000
Prime Solutions Inc.
1940 Garnet Ave.
San Diego, CA 92109

**OPTune** was selected a *PC World* "Best Buy" as a complete hard disk optimizer that's easy to use. $99.95. 800/233-0383 or 801/377-1288
Gazelle Systems
42 N. University Ave. #10
Provo, UT 84601

**PC-Kwik Power Disk** is a fast, hard disk defragmenting program. The Disk Explorer feature provides a disk map that lets you find the physical location of files and clusters. $79.95. 800/274-KWIK or 503/644-5644
Multisoft Corp.
15100 SW Koll Pkwy.
Beaverton, OR 97006

**PowerSave 500** is a UPS (uninterruptible power supply) on a card that monitors the output of your computer's power supply. It will provide up to 200 watts of power to your system should an unexpected power interruption occur. It will provide power long enough for the PowerSave software to save the data that is in your computer's memory at the time power is lost. $299.00. 800/999-6288 or 415/967-2302
Dakota Microsystems Inc.

301 E. Evelyn Ave., Bldg. A
Mountain View, CA 94041

**SpinRite II** is a utility program designed to tune up your hard disk and test it for flaws. It identifies, diagnoses and repairs every form of data and low-level format damage on standard DOS hard disks. It eliminates the cause of such common DOS errors as "Boot Failure," "Sector Not Found," "Bad Sector Error," "Probable Non-DOS Device" and all other "Abort, Retry, Ignore" style errors. It restores the drive's critical low-level format to better than new condition–dramatically increasing the drive's long-term reliability and extending its lifetime. It can find all evolving disk surface flaws, move endangered data to safety and prevent those flawed areas from being used again. $89. 800/736-0637 or 714/830-2200
Gibson Research Corp.
22991 LaCadena
Laguna Hills, CA 92653

### Data Recovery

**Mace Utilities** will recover deleted files and restore a formatted hard disk. It comes with all kinds of file management and hard disk maintenance utilities that will unfragment files and sort/squeeze directories. Mace Utilities has received the *PC Magazine* "Editor's Choice" designation. It's recommended more for power users than novices. $149. (See Fifth Generation Systems under Fastback Plus listed under IBM "Backup Utility Programs.")

### Data Recovery Services

If your hard disk has crashed and your data recovery program isn't able to retrieve valuable information, there's still hope–for a price. Here are some services that charge from $75 to $1,000 to recover data. Some of these services can also repair your disk. They may not be able to help, however, if your hard disk has suffered a major crash.

**Computer Peripheral Repair** charges $75 an hour, returns data within a week and repairs hard drives. 407/586-0011 in Hypoluxo, Florida

**Data Recovery Service** is in San Francisco. 415/585-7448

**Mace Data Recovery** charges $200 for the initial hard disk diagnosis and returns data in a few days. The average repair costs between $500 and $1,000 (including the $200 charge) and is determined by the complexity of the data, not the size of your hard disk. 503/488-5011 in Ashland, Oregon

**Mirror Technologies** charges by the size of the drive and returns data within five to 10 days. A 20MB drive would cost $117 but you can get a $30 discount if you also opted for hard disk repair, costing between $237 and $937. 612/633-4450 in Roseville, Minnesota

**Ontrack Data Recovery Inc.** charges $200 for an initial diagnosis and between $200 to $600 for data recovery. It takes three to five days. 800/752-1333 or 612/937-5161 in Eden Prairie, Minnesota

*Other*

**Cubit** expands the capacity of your hard disk (will also work for floppies) through data compression. It is based on the space-saving techniques used on mainframe computers. Cubit stores up to twice as much data on the same amount of disk space. You would use it for inactive or archived files. $69.95 (See Disk Optimizer under "Hard Disk Maintenance Utilities.")

**Diskette Manager 3** helps you print labels (both 5¼-inch and 3½-inch) and reports showing the contents of each diskette as well as your entire library. $39.95. 800/888-4437 or 305/445-0903
BLOC Publishing
800 Southwest 37th Ave., Ste. 765
Coral Gables, FL 33134

**FloppyDriver** is a speed-up utility that increases floppy drive performance by 500 percent and also lets you format floppies in the background. It's particularly useful for anyone with a laptop computer. It was recommended in a *PC World* article, "Software You Can Really Use." $89.95. 800/541-6579, 714/994-7400
Dariana Technology Group
7439 La Palma Ave. #278
Buena Park, CA 90620

**PC Librarian** is an archive management program that allows you to unclutter your hard disk by transferring inactive files to other storage media (such as floppies) and creating a catalog that stays on your

hard disk to manage these files. It's easy to use with pull-down menus and a graphical tree representation of your hard disk. $99. 800/892-0007 or 703/556-0007
United Software Security, Inc.
8133 Leesburg Pike, #380
Vienna, VA 22182

**PC Tools Deluxe** is a multi-award-winning utility program that defies classification. It combines disk-and-tape-backup with a DOS shell, disk compression, disk mechanic, data recovery and desktop management features. It has received nearly every editorial award possible. The latest version has three user levels: beginning, intermediate and advanced. It also has a version of Traveling Software's *LapLink* file-transfer program which lets you share files between laptop and desktop computers. $149. 800/888-8199 or 503/690-8090
Central Point Software Inc.
15220 N.W. Greenbrier Pkwy., #200
Beaverton, OR 97006-9937

**PKZIP PKUNZIP PKSFX** is a package of data compression and extraction utilities. It was featured as one of the best utilities in *PC Magazine*. $47 plus shipping and handling–$3.50, U.S., $5.00, overseas. 414/352-3670
PKWARE Inc.
7545 N. Port Washington Rd., Ste. 205
Glendale, WI 53217

## MACINTOSH PRODUCTS
### DISK BACKUP DEVICES
**The Bernoulli Box** disk cartridge/drive system offers models ranging from 10 to 44MB of backup storage. The Bernoulli Box disk cartridge system is a reliable, highly rated backup system. From $1,299 to $2,299. If you also own an IBM, consider the "Universal Products" line, which can back up both the Mac and IBM (price range is $1,399–$2,599 plus $49 for the MAC1B adapter kit). (See Bernoulli Box under IBM "Disk Backup and Storage Devices.")

## BACKUP UTILITY PROGRAMS

**Copy II for the Macintosh** is a program that makes archival backups and also copies software without making parameter changes. $39.95. (See Central Point Software under PC Tools Deluxe listed above under "Other.")

**DiskFit** is a hard disk backup utility that has received a 95 rating from *MacGuide Magazine* (on a scale of 1-100) and is touted in the book *Macintosh Hard Disk Management*. This program has many useful features. Files are backed up in Macintosh format so that you can more easily restore and use single files. The program lets you split a large file to more than one floppy. It does incremental backups and will print reports that list backed-up folders and files. But what's really exciting about the incremental backups is that they are done on your original complete backup set so that you use fewer disks than with other programs. The "Verify Writes" feature verifies that files are written correctly to disk. $74.95. 408/245-2202
SuperMac Technology
485 Portrero Ave.
Sunnyvale, CA 94086

**Fastback II** is fast backup software that combines maximum file selection flexibility with powerful backup and restore options that let you easily tailor the process to your needs. The typical backup rate is 1MB per minute and includes error detection and correction. You can fully customize your backup, which can include incremental backups as well as automatically scheduled, unattended backups. $189. (See Fifth Generation Systems under Fastback Plus listed under IBM "Backup Utility Programs.")

**HFS Backup** provides a long list of features plus ease of use and reliability. This program lets you define a "Backup Set," which specifies the folders and files you back up most often and can serve as a template for future backups. Two copies of the Backup Directory are included automatically whenever you back up. Useful features include backup customization; automatic disk formatting; and data verification. $49.95. 800/622-2888 or 813/884-3092
Personal Computer Peripherals Corp.
4710 Eisenhower Blvd., Ste. A4
Tampa, FL 33634

**SoftBackup Plus** works particularly well with floppies and tape media such as DC 2000 and Phillips cassettes. This program lets you use multiple tapes for backup. You can set up an automatic backup schedule. You can predesign different "scripts," or backup routines that back up different sets of files. $99.95. 408/745-0344
Diversified I/O, Inc.
766 San Aleso Ave.
Sunnyvale, CA 94086

## TAPE BACKUP DEVICE

**Tecmar QT-Mac Tape Drives** for backup and archival storage come in 40, 80 and 150MB capacities. $1,395 to $2,795. 800/624-8560 or 216/349-1009
Tecmar, Inc.
6225 Cochran Rd.
Solon, OH 44139

## HARD DISK AND DATA MAINTENANCE AND RECOVERY

A number of specialized programs and services will help you correct specific file and data problems you may encounter on your computer.

### Hard Disk Maintenance Utilities

**DiskExpress II** is a disk defragmentation utility that will optimize your hard disk (as well as floppies). The program can verify your disk directory, making sure that what your directory says is on the disk, is actually there. *MacGuide Magazine* gave this program a rating of 95, on a scale of 1 to 100. $39.95. 713/353-4090
ALSoft, Inc.
PO Box 927
Spring, TX 77383-0927

### Data Recovery Services

**Mirror Technologies**, charges by the size of the drive and returns data within five to 10 days. A 20MB drive would cost $117 but you can get a $30 discount if you also opted for hard disk repair, costing between $237 and $937. 612/633-4450 in Roseville, Minnesota.

See also **Computer Peripheral Repair** and **Ontrack Data Recovery Inc.**, which do both Macintosh and DOS machines and are listed earlier under IBM "Data Recovery Services."

### *Other*

**DiskQuick** is a lightning-fast catalog utility that has a database interface so you can quickly look up files in a catalog that has been downloaded to your database program. It comes with a clearly written manual. $49.95. 515/472-7256
Ideaform, Inc.
PO Box 1540
Fairfield, IA 52556

**Disk Ranger–Ranger Reader** is a fast catalog utility application that makes catalogs of the files on your hard and floppy disks. The application includes many features, including sorting capabilities, duplication elimination and disk label printing. $59.95. 303/422-0757
Graham Software Co.
8609 Ingalls Circle
Arvada, CO 80003

**myDiskLabeler III** is a disk labeling utility that easily lets you create meaningful and versatile disk labels and directory reports. $90. 800/752-4400 or 509/458-6312
Williams & Macias, Inc.
3707 S. Godfrey
Spokane, WA 99204

Note: Always check with vendors for the latest version of software products and the compatibility with your existing hardware and software.

# DETAILS, DETAILS: GETTING THEM UNDER CONTROL

*Quick Scan: Discover specific tools and systems to keep track of the detailed information related to projects, assignments, people, resources and records. If just too many of your office details are slipping through the proverbial cracks, you could profit from a simple system or two. Here are some ideas that can help.*

Let's face it. Life keeps getting more and more complicated each day. So many details to take care of and so much information to manage. How *do* you stay on top of it all?

Some people are lucky. They can delegate the details to someone else. But whether you can delegate or not, you still need a **detail orientation** to give you better **control over details.**

Why? If you're like most people, you probably do or supervise plenty of paperwork, record keeping and follow-up activities in your work, all of which generate many layers of information and details. When you manage details effectively, you're managing information and in doing so, you make a professional, lasting impression on people. It says you care about **quality** and **service.** It says you *care enough to follow up and follow through*–which is quite a feat in the midst of an ongoing information explosion that we all face each day.

Effective follow-up and follow-through require *systems* to organize details. Systems can be manual or computerized. Generally, it's best to start out using manual systems first (even if you have a computer). While complexity may necessitate a computerized system later on, start first with a manual one. The trick is to keep systems *simple*–as simple as possible.

Remember, too, a computer will not get you organized. Start planning logically and systematically on paper and then if necessary (and only if necessary) find a computer solution that conforms to you, not the other way around.

And should you happen to be fortunate enough to have an assistant, remember this: **when you have a good system in place, delegating is easy.**

## WORK AND PROJECT MANAGEMENT SHORTCUTS

Where most people get into trouble is trying to keep everything in their head. And then they get upset with themselves when they forget something using the infallible "mental note system."

The other ploy that has equally bad results is relying on countless written slips of paper on your desk, in your wallet and on your wall. The problem with paper slips is that they create clutter and stress in your life. They also tend to "slip" through the cracks and get lost–which is probably why they're called "slips" in the first place.

### TICKLER SYSTEMS

Assuming you read Chapter 2 (which was "required reading"), then you may recall a tickler system is a special reminder system that "tickles" your memory. There are many different types of ticklers as you know; now you'll see some of the specific ways you can apply them at work.

### CARD TICKLER SYSTEMS

Let's suppose you're in sales and you "prospect" or develop your market as part of your work. You may want to set up a **card tickler system**, using ruled, colored index cards along with cardboard file guides printed with the days of the month and the months of the year. Index cards come in different sizes—3 by 5, 4 by 6 and 5 by 8 inches. Decide what kind of data and how much you plan to write on each card.

You may prefer a commercial card tickler system such as TIC-LA-DEX (see Figures 9-1 and 9-2) that includes five, different colored, preprinted 3-by-5 cards and three sets of preprinted file guides—"1-31," "January to December" and "A-Z." Let me show you, step by step, how you can use this card tickler system.

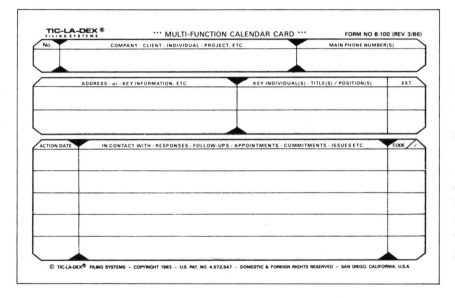

**Figure 9-1.** A TIC-LA-DEX card has preprinted sections on the front, which is shown here, as well as on the back.

If you were a professional speaker/writer/consultant, here's how you could use TIC-LA-DEX to systematically develop new speaking engagements, promote a writing career and stay in touch with clients. You could use four colors to code your market into the following categories:

1. red—speaking/training prospects
2. blue—consulting clients
3. green—writing contacts
4. yellow—networking contacts.

Let's see what you can write on each card. Begin with the name of the organization or the name of the individual, whichever name you're most likely to think of first. Then write the address and phone number and the key contacts and titles. Make a point of listing names of secretaries, receptionists or other staff members to whom you speak, too.

Write in an "action date" on the far left of the card for an action taken, e.g, actually talking to a key individual, as well as entering the date when leaving a message in their absence. The day you send out correspondence is an action date, too.

Keep a very brief summary of ongoing activity. For every attempted contact, write a date on the line at the far left under "Action Date." You may also want to use your own codes and abbreviations. I use "TT," which means "*T*elephone *T*o," and signifies I initiated the call. If I have to leave a message after I called, TT is followed by "LM," which indicates I "*L*eft *M*essage." LM will be followed by the name of individual in parentheses with whom I spoke. "Fol" plus a specific date and often a time indicates the next phone call *Fol*lowup or appointment.

When someone I've called isn't available, particularly someone I don't know well, I ask the receptionist or secretary to take down my name and company and indicate *I'll* call back, preferably at a specific time. I ask the receptionist or secretary what time would be best to call back. Then I jot down "IWCB," (*I* *W*ill *C*all *B*ack) on my card. This lets me put my name before a new contact or prospect without making any demands on the person. It's also good marketing to give my name repeated exposure and hence some familiarity. No call is ever wasted. It's a good way to make cold calls warmer.

You can file your TIC-LA-DEX cards in one of three places: behind a 1-31 card (for the 31 days of the current or following month), a month card (for the months further down the road) or an alphabetical card. If the next action on a card is to take place on a day of the current month, the card goes behind the correctly numbered day. If the next action should occur next month or later, the card goes behind the appropriate month. If the card has no known future followup but isn't ready to be removed from the system, the card is filed alphabetically by the name of the individual

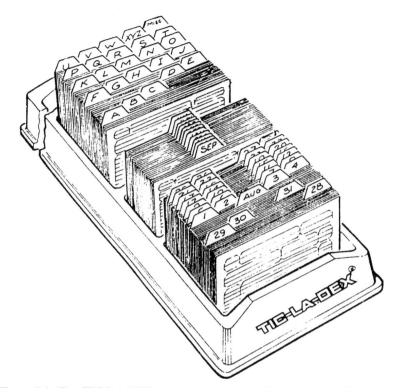

**Figure 9-2.** The TIC-LA-DEX system comes with 1-31, January to December and A-Z divider tabs.

or organization.

The cards are small (3 by 5 inches) but codes and abbreviations tell all of the action items at a glance. For more detailed information, you could keep a **prospect notebook** that contains correspondence and notes that are stapled together, hole punched and filed behind alphabetical tab dividers. There they remain until the prospect becomes a client, whereupon the material goes into a client file folder. The prospect notebook is the longhand version of your marketing activity; the index card tickler system is the shorthand. And if prospects should call *you* before the next follow-up date, you can quickly find the latest prospect information alphabetically in the prospect notebook.

## DESK FILES OR SORTERS AND ACCORDION FILES

If you don't like having to hole punch papers for your prospect notebook, use an alphabetical **desk file** (also called a **sorter**) or an **accordion file**. The desk file opens like a book and has an expandable binding on the spine. The accordion file is enclosed on three sides and usually has a flap that folds over. Both the desk file and the accordion file come in either alphabetical (A-Z) or numerical (1-31) styles. One desk file that we've been using in our office for several years has 1-31 as well as January to December tabs and works as a handy tickler system as well as a part of our daily paperwork system. I frequently recommend it to clients. See Figure 9-3.

## FILE FOLDER TICKLER SYSTEMS

Some people prefer a **file folder tickler system** that has file folders labeled both January to December and 1-31. A file folder tickler system can sit inside a desk drawer or in an upright rack or caddy on a nearby credenza, return or table.

There are many uses for such a system. One communications consultant I know uses a ruled sheet of paper in the front of each monthly folder to list follow-up calls for the month. He keeps corresponding notes for the calls inside an alphabetical notebook.

A file folder tickler system is also a great way to get reminder papers off your desk and into a chronological system. These are papers that require action on or by specific dates. They may include papers such as conference announcements, letters, memos, notes and even birthday or anniversary cards. If you like visual, tangible reminders, instead of a note jotted down in your calendar or planner, this system could be ideal for you.

Suppose you have some notes you'll need to use at a meeting on the ninth. Get those notes off your desk (or out of a generic, overflowing "pending file") and put them behind the "9" tab. A file folder tickler system is also handy for birthday cards filed on the day to be mailed or behind the appropriate month.

You can buy preprinted file guides or Pendaflex hanging folder label inserts in 1-31, A-Z and January-December styles. Pendaflex also makes Follow-up Tabs that run lengthwise across a hanging folder and have space for the file name plus two sliding signals that

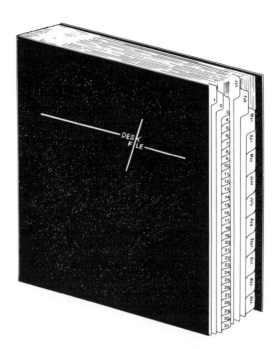

**Figure 9-3.** Combination 1-31 and January-December desk file by Smead

can be moved to indicate the month and the day of the month. Smead makes a Chan-L-Slide Follow-Up Folder (see Figure 9-4).

## TICKLER SLIP SYSTEM

If you have a very busy office in which you're responsible for many details and delegations, you may consider purchasing a **tickler slip system** such as LPI Tickler Record System. Although designed for attorneys, the Tickler Record System also works great for other busy professionals with many deadlines.

The three-part, NCR (*No Carbon Required*), color-coded tickler forms are versatile. Don't let the legal terms throw you; let them stand for the kinds of work *you* do. A "case" could just as easily be

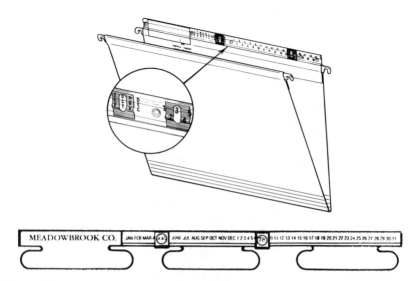

**Figure 9-4.** Smead Chan-L-Slide Follow-up Folder (top) and Pendaflex Follow-up Tab

™ **TICKLER RECORD**
© 1977 by Law Publications, A Division of All-state Legal Supply Co.
5910 Bowcroft St., Los Angeles, CA 90016
To reorder specify form E-120.

Client/
Case___*Smith vs. Jones*___ File No.__*7785*__
Event___*Motion to compel answers to*___
*interrogatories          Dept. 5*
Date of Event | *8/30/89          9 A.M.*
Reminder Dates(s)__*8/10/89*_____
Attorney Responsible__*Stephen Williams*__
Notes:__*See Rosen vs. Sparks for*__
*similar motion & points &*
*authorities*
☐ Done

**Figure 9-5.** LPI Tickler Record System slip is available through the All-state Legal Supply Co. catalog

a project or assignment and "attorney responsible" could be a staff member or colleague. See Figure 9-5 for a sample form.

The system is designed to be used with daily numerical and monthly card file guides along with alphabetical card file guides. The top white sheet is filed by the "Date of Event" or the final deadline or completion date. The middle yellow copy is filed by the first reminder date (there is room for three reminder dates). Having several different reminder dates helps prevent a form from getting lost in the system and a deadline from being missed. The pink copy is filed by the name of the client or project.

If you delegate to other people and want to keep track of their progress, consider using the system in another way. Give the original slip to your delegate, keep the yellow copy for yourself and file the pink copy alphabetically by client or project. You and your delegate should each file the slip by the date(s) action is necessary for you both. Perhaps for some people, you will only need to follow up on the due date; for others, such as trainees, you may need to follow up at each step.

If you work as part of an office team, you could adapt the Tickler Record System into a centralized tickler that is accessible to all team members. This adaptation works particularly well with sales teams. Each sales person, for example, writes a slip, keeps the original and files it inside their own deskside tickler system. The yellow copy goes into a central tickler system by date and the pink into a central alphabetical card file by client or project. One person monitors the central system and makes sure all follow-ups and deadlines are handled and reassigns activities if the responsible party is out of town or ill.

Two other tickler slip systems are also worthy of mention and are described and illustrated in the chapter resource guide under the "Tickler Systems" heading. They are SYCOM's That Reminds Me and Safeguard's General Reminder/Assignment System.

## CUSTOMIZING YOUR OWN TICKLER SYSTEM

Consider designing your own tickler system. One accounting firm created the simple tickler form shown in Figure 9-6 for use in its office file folder tickler system. Staff members complete the form, keep a copy and put the original in a centralized file folder tickler system arranged by the days of the month and the months of the

Today's date  _____

FOLLOW-UP REMINDER

Re:        _____          FOLLOW-UP DATES

Client:    _____

Client #   _____          _____

Subject:   _____          _____

Individual making request  _____

Remarks:   _____

           _____

           _____

           _____

           _____

           _____

           _____

**Figure 9-6.** Custom office tickler form used in an accounting office

year. One person in charge of the system makes sure that follow-through occurs.

When Terry Preuit was manager of Management Development at a restaurant chain, she worked with her staff to create their own customized tickler slip system. Their slip, which measures 8½ by 5½ inches, is a combination memo/assignment slip in four parts (see Figure 9-7). The sender keeps two copies, one to file by project (so all correspondence and due dates for the project are in one place) and one to file by date (as a standard tickler reminder). The receiver gets one copy. The department's program coordinator gets one copy that keeps her up to date on the status of all major assignments,

---

**MANAGEMENT DEVELOPMENT MEMO**

DATE: _____          DUE DATE:_____

TO: _____

FROM: _____

PROJECT: _____

INSTRUCTIONS/MESSAGE:

☐ See me to discuss details               ☐ Handle/then brief me afterwards
☐ Prepare response then we'll discuss     ☐ Handle/update at next meeting

_____

_____

_____

_____

_____

_____

_____

_____

☐ Done/Date:_____          ☐ See Back/Attached

ORIGINAL - RECEIVER    CANARY-SENDER/DATE FILE    PINK-SENDER/PROJECT FILE    GOLD-LAURA

---

**Figure 9-7.** Custom tickler slip designed by Terry Preuit and staff

helps her field questions when the rest of the staff are unavailable and in general, cuts down on "telephone tag."

If you handle reoccurring tasks, projects or reports each month, consider using the tickler card system developed by Judy Nowak, administrative assistant at Rockwell International. Judy uses two sets of 1-31 cards for two months in a row. When she completes a task on a card as it comes up chronologically, she immediately files the card behind the appropriate number for the next month when the task will come up again. In this way she "files as she goes" and doesn't have to file a whole group of cards at the beginning of the next month. She's all set to go.

Nowak also makes sure she never misses a deadline because she has a reminder card that she files a few days before the actual card comes up in her system. She moves both the reminder card and the task card to the next month's 1-31 set when the task is complete.

## COMPUTERIZED TICKLERS
## AND TIME MANAGEMENT PROGRAMS

If you're in your office most of the day and you use a computer, it may make sense to buy a time management program or a desktop management program that includes calendar tickler functions.

Some of these programs even have alarms that ring to remind you of appointments and deadlines. Some will remind your *computer* when to do things; for example, you can set the alarm clock so the computer dials a phone number at a certain time. Some programs have a "pre-reminder" capability that lets you place a pre-reminder two to five days before your final deadline. The pre-reminder stays on your calendar. Computer analyst and writer Lawrence Magid jokingly calls programs with alarms and reminders "nudgeware."

Besides an alarm feature, look at the flexibility of the program. Can you schedule appointments only by hour- or half-hour-increments? Can you schedule by 15-minute intervals? Can you schedule an appointment at a non-standard time, e.g., 3:20 p.m.? Does the program work on a 12- or 24-hour clock? Maybe you don't need this flexibility today, but perhaps you will down the road.

The program should let you make notes regarding your appointments or tasks. Some limit how long your notes can be—will it be enough for you?

If you manage or coordinate other people's activities, you may want to track their schedules. Select a program that lets you code the schedules of different people—a program such as Metro or Homebase.

Besides the extensive variety of desktop management programs with calendar/tickler utilities, there are programs on the market now that are specifically designed to help you better manage your time. Programs such as OnTime and PrimeTime are electronic calendars that have a key word search feature. If you plan to call client Joe Smith, you can search for any entries that contain "Joe Smith." Such programs let you print out a hard copy of your schedule to keep on your desk or take with you.

Los Angeles attorney Marty Weniz is enthusiastic about PrimeTime, which he reviewed for *The UCLA PC Users Group Newsletter*. He particularly likes the way the program handles "tasks"–i.e., your to-do list. PrimeTime automatically moves uncompleted tasks to the next day. PrimeTime also lets you prioritize your to-do list. According to Weniz, the most outstanding feature "is the ability to tell PrimeTime *when a task is due* and then to watch as each day automatically counts down until the due date is reached."

You can also specify your own time frames for task completion. Let's suppose you decide three projects should take one day, two weeks and three months, respectively. Just type in 1d, 2w and 3m and PrimeTime will automatically specify the exact date and day of the week. Says Weniz, "This feature alone is worth the price of the program."

There are appointment, assignment and address book features as well. The appointment feature lets you make ample notes, set alarms for reminders and easily change dates and times of appointments. The assignment feature lets you track delegations. An address book (referred to as "People/Phone"), lets you track 150 people by listing names, addresses, phone numbers and comments.

For a complete listing of computerized ticklers and time management programs, see the chapter resource guide.

## FORMS, CHECKLISTS AND CHARTS

It has been said that one person's form is another person's red tape. But a *well-designed* form is a clear, concise and useful summary of information at a glance. And contrary to popular belief, forms can actually help you *reduce* paperwork.

A good form *consolidates* information that is repetitive or otherwise would be scattered in many different places in your office (or someone else's). A good form saves you time flipping through many pieces of paper (or through many different computer screens). Use forms to track such things as work flow, projects, responsibilities, schedules and personnel. Use forms to simplify communication.

A clean, well-designed form is not only pleasing to the eye but is more likely to insure a quicker response. Form phobia really sets in only when clutter meets the eye. Figure 9-8 is a clean **invoice** created by industrial designer Rob Splane.

Checklists and charts are specific examples of forms. Checklists are old standbys that insure you won't forget something and often can be kept and referred to repeatedly. I have travel and seminar checklists that I use year after year.

Charts provide the added dimension of a diagram or graph that shows relationships between different components. It is more of a visual picture of information, almost like a map.

The chart is a two-dimensional form that shows relationships visually and graphically. The chart maps out details and the big picture at the same time. It summarizes information at a glance. The expense report chart in Figure 9-9 is a good example.

Let me share with you one of the greatest and *simplest* charts I use whenever I begin a project or a writing task. It's called a **mind map** and it was originally developed by Tony Buzan of the Learning Methods Group in England. I first heard about it at a professional communications meeting devoted to "writer's block."

The mind map is an effective way to free up your mind and let your ideas flow. Once you get the ideas out on paper, then you can add structure and sequence. It's a combination brainstorming and outlining tool where you can see your ideas and thought patterns more graphically. Figure 9-10 is a mind map for this chapter.

Charts are also good at showing numerical information, which, according to research, helps produce quicker, easier decisions. When information is expressed in numbers rather than words, complex decisions can be made 20 percent faster. It's also easier to evaluate many more factors and options with numbers than with words. There's an added strain when making decisions with words alone.

Use a standardized **checklist** to help you remember the repetitive tasks involved in similar projects. An aerospace company follows the checklist in Figure 9-11 for guests and visitors.

We use the **program tracking form** in Figure 9-12 to record important information and activities for each speaking engagement.

Create your own forms files in your file cabinet or on your computer. Collect samples of forms you like and those you often

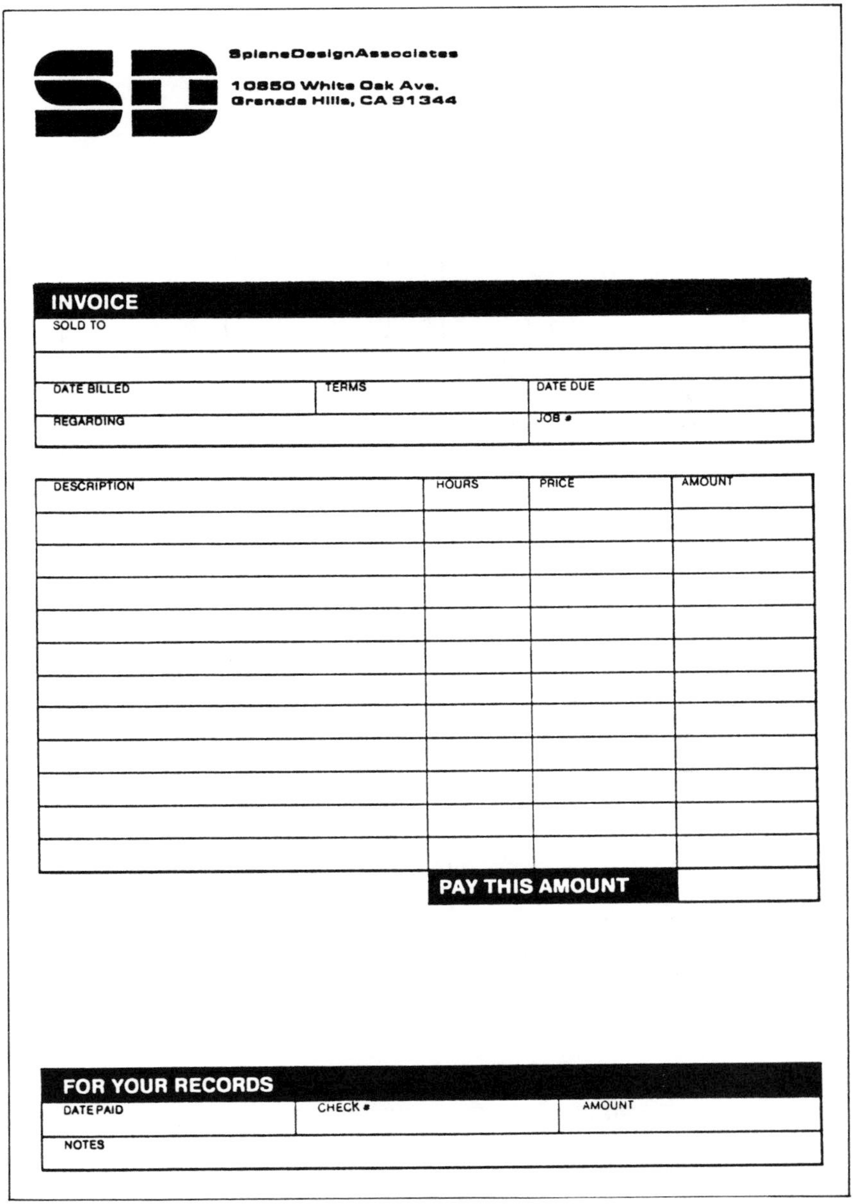

**SD** SplineDesignAssociates
10850 White Oak Ave.
Granada Hills, CA 91344

**INVOICE**

SOLD TO

| DATE BILLED | TERMS | DATE DUE |
|---|---|---|
| REGARDING | | JOB # |

| DESCRIPTION | HOURS | PRICE | AMOUNT |
|---|---|---|---|
| | | | |
| | | | |
| | | | |
| | | | |
| | | | |
| | | | |
| | | | |
| | | | |
| | | | |
| | | | |
| | | | |
| | PAY THIS AMOUNT | | |

**FOR YOUR RECORDS**

| DATE PAID | CHECK # | AMOUNT |
|---|---|---|
| NOTES | | |

Figure 9-8. Cleanly designed invoice form

**IWOSC EXPENSE REPORT** 85-01

date: _____

name: _____   position held: _____

address: _____   budget category(ies): _____

_____

phone: _____

month of expenditure:

PLEASE TOTAL YOUR EXPENSES IN EACH BUDGET CATEGORY AND LIST IN APPROPRIATE BOX BELOW

| item: | Jan | Feb | Mar | Apr | May | Jun | Jul | Aug | Sep | Oct | Nov | Dec |
|---|---|---|---|---|---|---|---|---|---|---|---|---|
| phone | | | | | | | | | | | | |
| prof. fees & services | | | | | | | | | | | | |
| room rental | | | | | | | | | | | | |
| printing & duplicating | | | | | | | | | | | | |
| postage & mail serv. | | | | | | | | | | | | |
| office supplies | | | | | | | | | | | | |
| entertain- ment | | | | | | | | | | | | |
| advertising & publicity | | | | | | | | | | | | |
| t-shirt manufac. | | | | | | | | | | | | |
| publications | | | | | | | | | | | | |
| bank charges | | | | | | | | | | | | |
| other | | | | | | | | | | | | |

total submitted: _____

COMMENTS: _____

_____

ATTACH ALL RECEIPTS!     signature _____

Figure 9-9. A simple expense report chart for members of IWOSC (Independent Writers of Southern California) who are reimbursed for expenses incurred throughout the year.

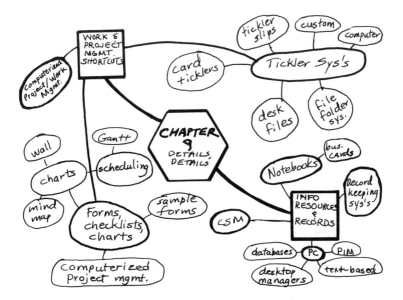

**Figure 9-10.** A mind map for this chapter

use. Make up a form to inventory all the forms you have in your office and when they're used. You may discover there are forms you should modify or eliminate altogether. My husband designed such a form when he worked as a summer intern for the federal government.

We keep some forms and form letters on computer. Our WordPerfect word processing program lets us easily create a special form letter called a **merge letter**. We keep related letters together in the same file. Using a special WordPerfect feature called a "document comment," we created a mini table of contents for standard follow-up letters we use in our office.

Speaking of computers, if you like and use forms, consider getting a **forms software** package. Forms software includes a variety of different programs. One type helps you design your own forms on screen and print them out on your printer. Another type helps you fill in preprinted forms that you use all the time, such as Federal Express forms, so that the information lines up correctly. More sophisticated forms software programs give you many options, including designing your own forms on screen, scanning an existing

PUBLIC AFFAIRS INTERNAL VISIT CHECKLIST

| ACTIVITY | RESPONSIBILITY | DATE | DONE |
|---|---|---|---|
| Invitation | | | |
| Receipt of Acceptance | | | |
| Reserve Room | | | |
| Develop Agenda | | | |
| VA to Marketing | | | |
| Contact Briefers | | | |
| Arrange Tour Leaders | | | |
| Hand-out Materials | | | |
| Gifts | | | |
| Badges | | | |
| Parking | | | |
| Transportation | | | |
| Bump Caps & Glasses | | | |
| Food | | | |
| Photographer | | | |
| Arrange for Films/Slides | | | |
| | | | |

Figure 9-11. Visitor checklist

form into your computer, filling out preprinted forms and linking your databases with your forms. (See the resource guide for examples of popular products.)

Don't let forms, checklists or charts scare you. They aren't straitjackets; rather they're guideposts to help you work through the maze of details in your office and your head.

In working with clients who have many ongoing projects where each project has most of the same tasks, I have developed the **checklist chart**. Figure 9-13 shows an example of the checklist chart

**Positively Organized!**®

PROGRAM TRACKING FORM                    Today's Date:

Date/#_____ Time_____ Title_____

Type of PO! Program_____ Type of Mtg_____#____

Fee/Contract Terms_____

Name of **Organization**_____

Key Contact/Title_____
                                                    Off #        Home #
Address_____

Other Contacts/Numbers_____

**Location** of Prog/Mtg_____Mgr/#_____

**Hotel** Reservations at_____By Org____GLA_____

Nearest Airport_____Distance to Mtg/Hotel_____

**Ground Transp.**_____

**Travel:** Drive/Fly  Booked on_____w/_____

| Departure Date | From City to City | At | ETA | Airline | # |
|---|---|---|---|---|---|
| Departure Date | From City to City | At | ETA | Airline | # |
| Departure Date | From City to City | At | ETA | Airline | # |

Deadline for Ticketing_____ Receive Tickets by_____ Fare $_____

Program Checklist

| Sent to Client | | Requested from Client | Date Rec'd |
|---|---|---|---|
| _____ Contract | _____ Intro | _____ Signed Contract | _____ |
| _____ Photo | _____ Invoice | _____ Deposit of $_____ | |
| _____ Bio | _____ TU Note | _____ Hotel Confirmation | _____ |
| _____ Blurb | | _____ Mtg brochure/map | _____ |
| _____ AV/Setup | | _____ Mtg agenda | _____ |
| _____ Handout for dup. | | _____ Trade pubs/bkg | _____ |
| _____ PR | | _____ Pre-program ques | _____ |
| _____ Pre-program Ques. | | _____ Fee/reim | _____ |
| | | _____ Letter of Rec. | _____ |
| | | _____ Referral | _____ |

**To Be Done**                          **By Date**    **Date Completed**
Write program_____
Prepare handout_____
Prepare/organize audio-visuals_____
Confirm a-v, setup, handouts one week before_____
Contact introducer/confirm has intro_____
Packout list/pack_____Wardrobe _____

3420 Ocean Park Blvd., Suite 3060  Santa Monica, California 90405-3305  213/452-6332

**Figure 9-12.** Program tracking form

PROGRAMS IN PROGRESS

| CLIENT NAME | PROGRAM DATE | AGREEMENT SENT | AGREEMENT RETURNED | DEPOSIT RECEIVED | INTRO. | ROOM SET-UP | PHOTO | HANDOUT | AIRLINE RESERVATIONS | FINAL PROG. C/L | MONTH-OUT CHECK | TAPES PACKED / SENT |
|---|---|---|---|---|---|---|---|---|---|---|---|---|
| | | | | | | | | | | | | |
| | | | | | | | | | | | | |
| | | | | | | | | | | | | |
| | | | | | | | | | | | | |
| | | | | | | | | | | | | |
| | | | | | | | | | | | | |
| | | | | | | | | | | | | |
| | | | | | | | | | | | | |
| | | | | | | | | | | | | |
| | | | | | | | | | | | | |
| | | | | | | | | | | | | |
| | | | | | | | | | | | | |
| | | | | | | | | | | | | |
| | | | | | | | | | | | | |
| | | | | | | | | | | | | |
| | | | | | | | | | | | | |

Figure 9-13. A checklist chart used by the office of speaker Danny Cox

I helped design for the office of professional speaker Danny Cox. The chart is a preprinted, 8½-by-11-inch form kept in a transparent plastic sleeve that sits conveniently on the desk of Tedi Patton, who uses it to coordinate all upcoming program details on a daily basis.

Since Cox travels so extensively, his office also uses a map of the United States that is dotted with his engagement locations. Self-adhesive dots indicate not only the location but the engagement dates. The map is a useful planning tool when the office gets calls from around the country asking when Cox will be "in their neighborhood."

**Calendar or scheduling charts** are a good way to show the relationship between periods of time and people, tasks or projects. Some scheduling charts list the months and weeks of the year. Such a chart can easily be turned into a **Gantt chart** or timeline that shows task start dates and deadlines and responsibilities. (Henry Gantt invented this useful chart while working for the government during World War I.) Day-Timers makes a variety of scheduling charts and forms that adapt elements from highly acclaimed project management tools such as Gantt charts, PERT charts (*P*erformance *E*valuation and *R*eview *T*echnique) and CPM (*C*ritical *P*ath *M*ethod). These tools show the steps and sequence that must occur for a project to be completed. Figure 9-14 shows the Day-Timers Yearly Schedule form that functions as a Gantt chart.

If you're comparing prices and features for products (such as computers) or services from suppliers (such as print shops) consider developing a simple chart so you can record the information as you go. It's a lot easier than whipping out all those notes later on. Your chart keeps you on track by reminding you to ask the same questions of everyone. Leave some blank spaces for additional questions that come up as you do your research.

Use **quadrille** or **graph paper** to make your own charts. The "non-repro blue" lines will not photocopy but they will guide you in drawing your own lines. They come in many different styles. See Figure 9-15 for some samples (check your office supply store or catalog for others).

If you need to track projects or personnel visually in such a way that you and/or other people can easily see the information, use **wall charts**. Also called **scheduling** or **visual control boards**, wall charts

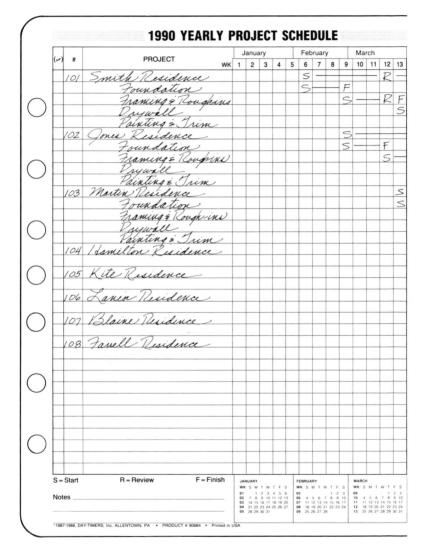

**Figure 9-14.** A portion of the Day-Timer Yearly Project Schedule

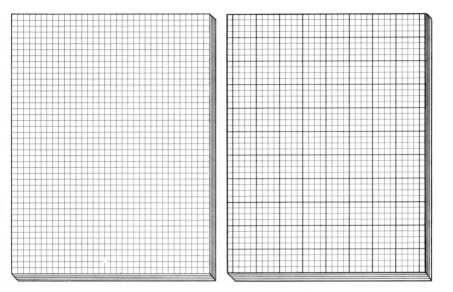

**Figure 9-15.** Ampad quadrille and cross-section graph pads

provide visibility to keep you on target. They're not the most attractive things in the world but if you have a work room or don't have to impress anyone with aesthetics, they are very functional.

Wall charts have an advantage over other systems because they crystallize your ideas, intentions and plans and make them visible. A wall chart gives you a visible game plan and very little escape. It's staring you straight in the face.

Color coding works great for wall charts. You can code people, types of activities, progress and deadlines.

Use wall charts to track one complex project, several simultaneous projects, a production schedule, your master calendar, personnel schedules and marketing or fund-raising campaigns. They come in many different sizes, styles, configurations and materials. **Magnetic** wall charts have different components that you can move around. See Figure 9-16.

Some people prefer the flexibility of a home-made chart such as the **action board** of nationally-known psychiatrist, author and talkshow host, Dr. David Viscott. You create the action board by putting up six or seven index cards on a wall or bulletin board. Each

**Figure 9-16.** Magna Visual Work/Plan Visual Organizer Kit

card stands for a different project and includes a key contact. Under each project card you put another index card that lists the next step to be taken on the project. Each project relates directly to your most important life goals.

If you don't want to permanently attach a chart to the wall, attach Wesystem's Track System instead (Figure 9-17). The four- or six-foot-long Track System holds maps, charts, posters, blueprints, schedules or drawings.

Turn to the "Forms, Checklists and Charts" section in the chapter resource guide for other ideas you can adapt.

## COMPUTERIZED PROJECT/WORK MANAGEMENT

If you need great control and flexibility over project planning and scheduling, consider **project management software programs** for the personal computer.

These programs combine charts and reports that let you see project information in a variety of ways. You can easily make changes such as automatically updating schedules. Reports are easy to generate and distribute. And it's easy to store completed projects

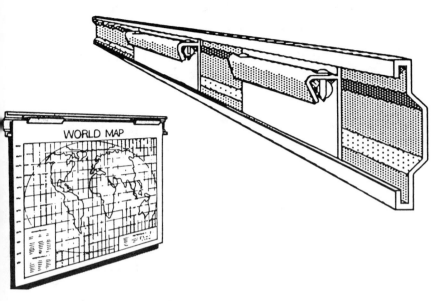

**Figure 9-17.** The Wesystem Track System

and schedules for reference later on—which means less reinventing of the wheel down the road.

Look for these features when you select a project management program: ease of learning (does it take a Ph.D. in computer sciences to grasp it?); ease of use; a good manual that's just the right size (if it's too hefty, forget it); good reviews by experts and/or people you know; and an easy-to-use tutorial. It's also a plus if the program can do both Gantt and PERT charts.

**Decision support software** is a relatively new genre software that can help improve the process of making complex decisions. Such software helps decision makers create uniform criteria and options. It's particularly helpful for making personnel decisions.

Popular project management and decision support programs are listed in the chapter resource guide under "Project Management Software" and "Other Work Management Tools."

# TOP TOOLS AND SYSTEMS TO MANAGE INFORMATION RESOURCES AND RECORDS

Each day as you're bombarded with more and more bits and pieces of information, it becomes a real challenge to organize all this information. Fortunately, you have many options.

## THE CRAWFORD SLIP METHOD

This is a special project management system that is particularly useful for putting together employee and procedures manuals. It was designed by Dr. C. C. Crawford, professor emeritus of Education and consultant to the Productivity Network of the USC School of Public Administration. The Crawford Slip Method (CSM) has a distinct methodology that is described in two booklets, both available from USC. CSM is an idea generator and organizer.

For anyone who loves slips of paper, this may be the system for you! (This is also one of the few paper slip systems of which I approve.) But not just any slip of paper will do: CSM specifies the precise *size* of paper you can use and just how and what you can write on each slip.

The slips, along with specially designed index cards, are used with custom cardboard trays with organizing slots. You can purchase the trays from USC for a minimal price ($7 each) and you can have the slips and cards cut to size by a print shop.

Briefly, here's how CSM works. One person acts as the facilitator for the members of a group, department or company who are guided in generating ideas for a manual. Each idea is written down on paper slips measuring 2 by 4¼ inches. The facilitator then sorts and organizes the collected slips into kindred piles of slips laid out on a table or using the cardboard tray slots. (See Figure 9-18.) Slips are further categorized behind colored, specially cut index cards that serve as guides. Once all the information has been collected and organized, it's a fairly simple task to transform the information into a written manual.

**Figure 9-18.** The Crawford Slip Method includes the "Think Tank," brainstorming specific, topic-centered ideas on paper slips and then sorting and organizing slips in a logical order.

## PERSONAL COMPUTER OPTIONS

### DATABASES

A computerized **database** is one of the best ways to gain control over and access to many records and resources. A database program lets you not only store but *sort* and call up information based on criteria that you select. It's the sorting capability of a computerized database that provides real information power.

There are different types and names for database management programs. The two simplest programs are called **file managers** or **file management programs**, not to be confused with utility programs bearing the same names described in Chapter 6. (I think it's awful that these terms are used interchangeably.)

Such programs have these names because they generally manage one file at a time. One file, however, can contain hundreds or even thousands of **records**. Each record is an entry consisting of different items or **fields** of information. Let's suppose you create a file of all your clients. Each client would be a different record in the file. The client's name, address, phone number are three different fields in the record. The blank form that appears on your computer screen showing the different fields before they're completed is a **data-entry form,** because you use it to *enter data* or information for each field.

The simplest file managers function as **mailing list programs,** which basically store names and addresses and print mailing labels. These programs either have or make use of **mail merge facilities** (which come with many of today's word processing programs), so that you can print labels and form letters.

**Contact management programs** or **contact managers** are easy-to-use database programs that are designed primarily for those in sales or for anyone who needs to stay in touch with at least 50 people on a regular basis. Such programs let you schedule and track calls, remind you with alarms when to do follow-up calls, encourage you to keep notes on calls and meetings with contacts and usually have an autodialer. (Telemagic and ACT! are examples of contact managers listed under the "Sales, Telemarketing and Contact Management" heading in the resource guide.)

The most sophisticated database management programs are the **relational databases.** Most of them are difficult to learn, some require a programmer and they tend to be expensive. What sets them apart besides these negatives, however, is their ability to work with more than one file at the same time. Relational databases can share related information between two or more files, keeping multiple files up to date with just one entry of data. Relational databases are great for inventory control and billing, for example.

Many file managers are starting to adopt some of the more sophisticated features of "high-end" relational database programs, while still maintaining ease in learning and use.

## DESKTOP MANAGERS OR ORGANIZERS

Sometimes also called "desktop utilities," these programs typically take items from your desk, such as a calendar, calculator, appointment book and business card file and computerize them. These programs often can do file management functions, too, such as naming, renaming, deleting or moving computer files. If you'll be storing less than 100 names, a desktop manager or organizer may indeed be more appropriate for you than a full-blown database program.

## TEXT-BASED PROGRAMS

When the resource information you want to store on computer isn't as structured as database records, you may prefer to use a **text-based management system**, also called a **text-based program** or a **textbase**. Such a program is much more *free-form* in nature, generally without pre-defined fields and records, and includes **free-form text databases** and **outliners**. A text-based program may be ideal if the information you're managing resides in long documents.

Text-based programs give you more flexibility, although frequently much less speed. You don't have to make your information conform to a database configuration. Search features are varied; some programs have you search on key words, others can search for "strings" of words or phrases.

As an organizer, I generally believe it's better to have some kind of structure, rather than a completely free-form database, particularly when there are common elements among the data you will enter. Free-form data may take longer to sort and retrieve. It may also be more difficult to clean out your floppies and hard disk later on as your free-form data accumulate. Restricted to special situations, however, such as speech writing, a text-based program could be just what you need. Just don't use it in place of a structured database because it's easier to use.

## PERSONAL INFORMATION MANAGERS

This is a new genre of software that combines elements of database programs, desktop managers and text-based programs. Personal information managers (called PIMs) let you store and arrange random bits of information such as notes, ideas, plans and activities in free-form style, linked loosely by categories that you create.

PIMs let you enter information as it occurs and then let you organize it later. They also provide speedy text retrieval capabilities. PIMs are not designed for people who need to do traditional, formal reports; rather they are for those who create and manage ideas.

The term "personal information manager" was first coined by Lotus Development Corp., who used it in conjunction with their

"Agenda" program. Lotus founder, Mitch Kapor, developed Agenda because he was looking for a better way to organize himself.

Often, however, you'll see the term PIM applied to other programs, such as desktop organizers, which manage "personal information" such as an address book or a daily schedule. Personally, I think it's all very confusing and yet, at the same time, very exciting as we explore ways to make information more and more accessible—no matter what we call information management programs. In general, however, PIMs are much more free-form in nature, rather than highly structured like a database.

## RECORD KEEPING SYSTEMS

Beyond the programs and products we've already discussed, a couple of other systems can help you track record keeping details. Let me tell you about a few of my favorites.

If you work with different clients or projects, the All-state Law Office Catalog has an easy manual system to keep track of billable time or expenses for clients or projects. No longer will you have to spend hours searching through your files, calendar, receipts and notes at billing time. (Although designed for attorneys, this system easily adapts to other professionals, such as consultants and writers.)

The system comes in two main styles: a time and service record system called the LPI (Law Publications Inc.) Time Record and a system that tracks costs and expenses called the LPI Expense Record. Both are "one-write" systems that are designed to be used "as you go" (which is the ideal way to use a system anyway).

Let's see how the Expense Record works. You chronologically record expenses as they occur on the two-part Expense Record form, shown in Figure 9-19. As you write on the top sheet, a piece of carbon paper transfers your records to the second sheet. The preprinted top sheet is die-cut into 15 self-adhesive labels. When the sheet is full, each of these labels can be peeled off and attached to their respective project, case or client sheets known as "Client/Case Costs Record" forms, which can be kept in a handy notebook arranged either alphabetically or chronologically. Bills or statements can be produced from these record forms. A carbon copy sheet un-

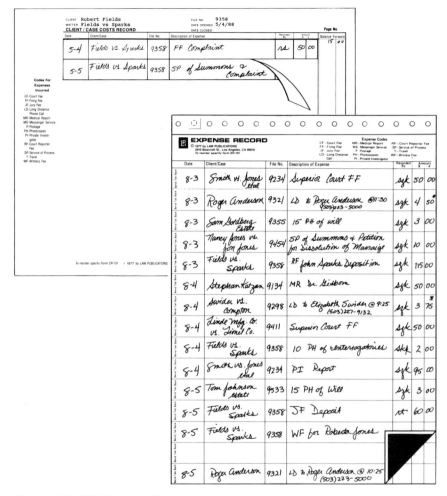

**Figure 9-19.** LPI Expense Record System

der the preprinted 15-label sheet remains as a permanent, chronological backup copy.

The Time Record works the same way as the Expense Record. Some of my clients have selected one or the other, depending upon the type of records they need to keep the most. Others like having the two different systems.

Builder/contractor Greg Bravard uses the Time Record to keep track of time and materials on building job sites. The Time Record form is attached to his clipboard, making for a convenient and portable system that's with him all the time.

Another "one-write" record keeping system that I recommend to clients is the Safeguard bookkeeping system (available in 200 formats). This is a simple-to-use manual system that is great for an entrepreneur or professional in private practice. We use it in our office. It actually makes bookkeeping *fun!*

The system comes with a "pegboard" or accounting board, imprinted checks in duplicate, journal sheets and sometimes special ledger sheets (depending on the style of system you select). First you set up your journal sheet (which is similar to an itemized check register). See Figure 9-20 for a sample journal sheet with some typical categories.

When you write a check, the information is automatically transferred in one-write fashion to the duplicate check as well as the journal underneath. Then you simply write the amount of the check under the appropriate column. At the end of a monthly cycle (or when the journal fills up) use a calculator with a tape to add up all the columns vertically and horizontally to make sure you're in balance. The duplicate copy of the check is attached to the paid bill.

If you select a different one-write system, make sure the checks don't have a black carbon strip on the back, which can interfere with endorsements. The new style of one-write checks has an invisible carbonless strip that provides high quality transfer of written information to journals, ledgers or duplicate copies beneath checks.

## RESOURCE GUIDE

(Note: software programs are considered IBM compatible unless specially listed under a "Macintosh" subheading or otherwise stated. If no addresses or phone numbers are listed, software and other products are widely available through dealers.)

## WORK AND PROJECT MANAGEMENT
### TICKLER SYSTEMS
*Manual*

**Desk Files/Sorters** are work organizers for sorting and storing paperwork that you refer to frequently. The 1-31 style and the

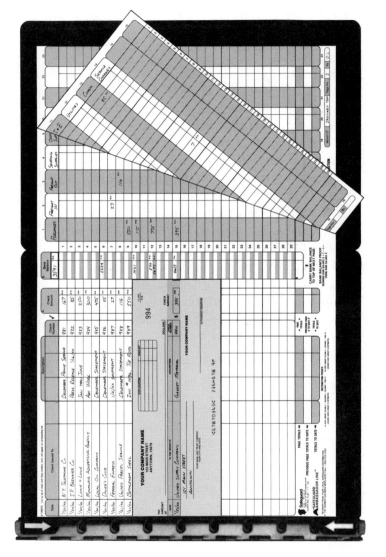

Figure 9-20. Safeguard Cash Disbursement System

1-31 plus January-December format work great as ticklers. The durable, plastic tabs are indexed front and back. The desk file opens like a book, and with the accordion gusset spine, there is a large storage capacity. About $11.00 for the 1-31 style and $15.00 for the 1-31 and January-December desk file. (See Figure 9-3 earlier in chapter.)

**General Reminder/Assignment System** by Safeguard is an easy-to-use method for organizing responsibilities, deadlines, delegations and appointments. This system is ideal for a wide variety of business and professional applications, including sales follow-ups, preventive maintenance schedules, job scheduling, tracking assignments and long range planning. Components include Assignment Slips (see Figure 9-21), Writing Board, Indexes (daily, monthly and alphabetical ones available), File Trays and Cross File Tray. 800/523-2422 (for the name of your local Safeguard consultant)
Safeguard Business Systems, Inc.
PO Box 7501
Fort Washington, PA 19034

**LPI Tickler Record System** is a three-part, NCR paper tickler slip system useful for a heavy load of deadlines and delegations involving other people. Designed for law offices, this system is applicable to many professions and offices. $45.95 for the "starter set." 800/222-0510 or 201/272-0800 or 609/921-0104
All-state Law Office Catalog
All-state Legal Supply Co.
One Commerce Dr.
Cranford, NJ 07016

**Memofile** is a combination 3-by-5-inch tickler card and planning system in one. The 365 daily cards are dated and tabbed. There are also 100 client/customer cards, 12 monthly tab cards, 52 weekly expense cards, an A-Z telephone index, A-Z guides, 100 blank record cards, a storage box and a card carrying case. You can carry up to two weeks of daily cards in the right side of the case and selected client/customer cards, telephone index and weekly expense cards on the left side. $34.95 to $42.95, depending on the material of the case. 800/828-5885 or in New York, 716/342-7890
Memindex
149 Carter Street

**Figure 9-21.** Safeguard General Reminder/Assignment System slip and writing board

Rochester, NY 14601

**Pendaflex Follow-up Tabs** and **Label Inserts** are useful supplies to help you create your own hanging file tickler system. The follow-up tabs run lengthwise across a hanging folder and have a space for the file name plus two sliding signals that can be moved to indicate the month and the day of the month. Preprinted file guides or Pendaflex hanging folder label inserts come in 1-31, A-Z and January-December styles. These supplies are available from a good office supply store or catalog. Incidentally, you'll often see the names **Oxford** and **Pendaflex** together when you're trying to find Pendaflex filing supplies in a catalog. Both are registered trademarks of the Esselte Pendaflex Corporation (located in Garden City, New York).

**That Reminds Me** is a tickler slip system designed to help tickle upcoming deadlines, appointments and delegations. The system is based on a rotating three-month daily breakdown. It also allows planning as far ahead as 12 years. The system uses carbonless "reminder/assignment slips" (you can make as many duplicates as you need). Each kit contains three sets of 1-31 3-by-5-inch cards; January to December cards; 12 blank, tabbed index cards; one black Rubbermaid file box; 200 Reminder/Assignment Slips; and one writing board for the slips. $49.95 for the kit; components can also be purchased separately. This product is featured in SYCOM's Professional Office catalog. SYCOM also has a forms and supplies catalog for attorneys. 800/356-8141

SYCOM, Inc.
PO Box 7947
Madison, WI 53707-7947

**TIC-LA-DEX** is a preprinted, color-coded file card tickler system that lets you systematically follow up on prospects, clients or projects. $24.95 619/281-7242, Fax: 619/281-7849

Tic-La-Dex Business Systems, Inc.
3443 Camino Del Rio South, Suite 326
San Diego, CA 92108

### *Computerized Ticklers and Time Management Programs*

**CPA Tickler** is used with Lotus 1-2-3 to monitor deadlines and commitments in a CPA office. $89 **CPA Tickler Database** is a stand-alone, comprehensive, due-date monitoring program for CPAs.
404/231-0349

Front Row Systems
PO Box 550346
3033 Maple Drive
Atlanta, GA 30355

**Homebase 2.5** is a full-featured, desktop management program that lets you track numerous calendars and schedules as well as to-do lists and time-and-expense logs. $49.95 plus $7.50 shipping. 800/523-0764 or in California, 408/559-4545

Brown Bag Software
2155 S. Bascom Ave., #105
Campbell, CA 95008

**Metro**, a desktop management program, has a complete and flexible calendar function with many features. Reminder alarms will ring even if the program isn't loaded. Notes can be attached to the calendar and appointments can be made any time of the day (or night). The

program handles several calendars and schedules on a daily, weekly or monthly basis. A mini time-and-billing program with a built-in timer will track time for 100 clients, projects or activities. $85. 800/345-1043
Lotus Development Corp.
55 Cambridge Parkway
Cambridge, MA 02142

**OnTime** is an easy-to-learn and easy-to-use computer time management program that features a lifetime calendar (through the year 2079), calendar/to-do list printouts (in a variety of formats), tickler alarm system, automatic entry of recurring events (such as weekly staff meetings), automatic rollover of uncompleted to-do list tasks and keyword searching. $69.95. 800/521-9314 or 313/559-5955
Campbell Services, Inc.
Software Division
21700 Northwestern Hwy., Suite 1070
Southfield, MI 48075

**Primetime 1.2** is a well-designed time management program that helps you set goals, organize and prioritize tasks on your to-do lists, keeps a chronological record of your accomplishments and remembers delegations and deadlines. $99.95. 800/777-8860 or 714/556-6523
Primetime, Inc.
PO Box 27967
Santa Ana, CA 92799-7967

**WHO-WHAT-WHEN** is people, project and time management software that's easy to use and has received much praise. $295. 800/777-7907 or 415/626-4244
Chronos Software Inc.
555 De Haro St., Ste. 240
San Francisco, CA 94107

## FORMS, CHECKLISTS AND CHARTS

**Abbot Office Systems** (Figure 9-22) manufactures scheduling kits, boards and systems for projects, production, plant and office layout

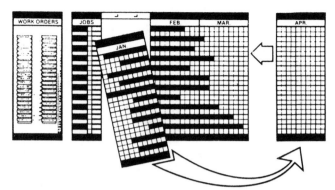

**Figure 9-22.** Abbot Office Systems Join-A-Panel lets you update your schedule by moving panels.

and applications for scheduling people and equipment. Free catalog. 800/631-2233 or 201/938-6000
Abbot Office Systems
Asbury Ave.
Farmingdale, NJ 07727

**Caddylak Systems** distributes wall planning charts and boards and has a wide array of planning and project forms. You may want to request all of their catalogs. 516/333-8221
Caddylak Systems, Inc.
131 Heartland Blvd.
Brentwood, NY 11717

**Day Runner Inc.** has time and information management forms that can be purchased together with or separately from their versatile personal organizers at department and stationery stores. 800/232-9786 or 213/837-6900
Day Runner, Inc.
3562 Eastham Drive
Culver City, CA 90232

**Day-Timers, Inc.,** offers planners and work organizers in many different sizes and formats, plus a wide range of time, information and project management forms. See these forms in their free mail order catalog. Figures 9-14, 9-23 and 9-24 in this chapter show some of their project management forms. 215/395-5884
Day-Timers, Inc.

PO Box 2368
Allentown, PA 18001

**FLEXFORM Business Templates** is a Macintosh library of electronic business forms templates designed by information management specialists. It has received a rating of "4½ mice" from *MacUser*. $89.95. 800/234-7001
Antic Software
544 Second St.
San Francisco, CA 94107

**FormFiller** lets you fill in your own preprinted forms quickly and accurately and has been selected as a *PC World* "Best Buy." $149. 800/888-4437 or 305/445-0903, ext. 2640
BLOC Publishing
800 Southwest 37th Avenue, Ste. 765
Coral Gables, FL 33134

**FormsFile** is a software program that provides access to hundreds of business forms in such categories as Memo & Office, Sales and Personnel/Payroll. An illustrated booklet catalogs and helps you select forms. You'll find Daily Planners, Weekly Reminders, Purchase Orders, Employment Applications, Packing Slips, to name a few. You can edit or create your own. 800/851-2917 or 800/223-1479
Power Up!
PO Box 7600
San Mateo, CA 94403

**FormTool Gold** helps you easily create, edit, manage and print custom forms. $99.95 (Published by BLOC–see above)

**FormWorx** is a software program that lets you create forms from scratch or modify one of the supplied forms. *PC Magazine, PC Week* and *The Wall Street Journal* had good things to say about this program. $95. FormWorx with Fill & File, which lets you fill out the same form again and again, is $149. FormWorx System 2 works with the Microsoft Windows environment and is $395. 800/992-0085; in Massachusetts, 617/890-4499
FormWorx Corp.
Reservoir Place, 1601 Trapelo Rd.
Waltham, MA 02154

**Magna Chart** is a magnetic visual control board system that comes in different styles. 800/843-3399 or 314/843-9000
Magna Visual, Inc.
9400 Watson Rd.
St. Louis, MO 63126

**Memindex Wall Planning Guides** are write-on/wipe-off planners that come in a wide selection of styles. 800/828-5885; in New York, 716/342-7890
Memindex, Inc.
149 Carter Street
Rochester, NY 14601

**Per:FORM** is a well-rounded forms software package that has received a *PC World* "Best Buy" and a *PC Magazine* "Editor's Choice." $259.95. 800/268-6082 or 716/835-0405
Delrina Technology Inc.
4454 Genesee St.
Buffalo, NY 14225

**PLANIT Board Systems Inc.** makes a good selection of dry marker white boards. 800/222-7539
PLANIT Board Systems, Inc.
515 S. 25th St.
Colorado Springs, CO 80904

**Re-Markable** boards are versatile, write-on-wipe-off wall charts. (See an example in Figure 9-25.) 201/784-0900
Remarkable Products, Inc.
157 Veterans Drive
Northvale, NJ 07647

**Reuse'it** boards are lightweight, wipe boards that come blank or preprinted and in a variety of sizes and styles. 800/826-0343 or 404/263-8893
Reuse'it Poster Board, Inc.
6687 Jimmy Carter Blvd.
Norcross, GA 30071

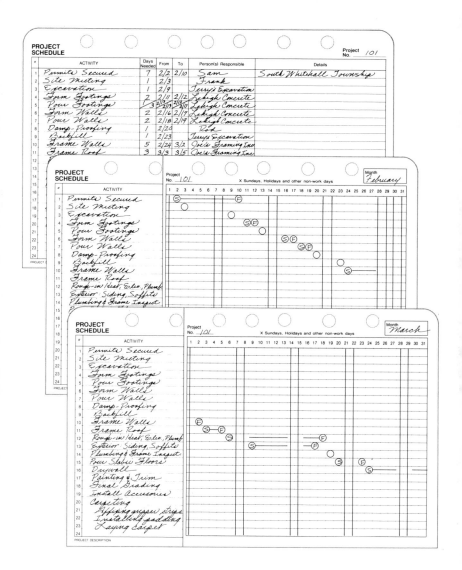

**Figure 9-23.** Day-Timer PERT/CPM Sheets include these Project Schedule forms with overlays that let you plan by the month without having to rewrite project tasks.

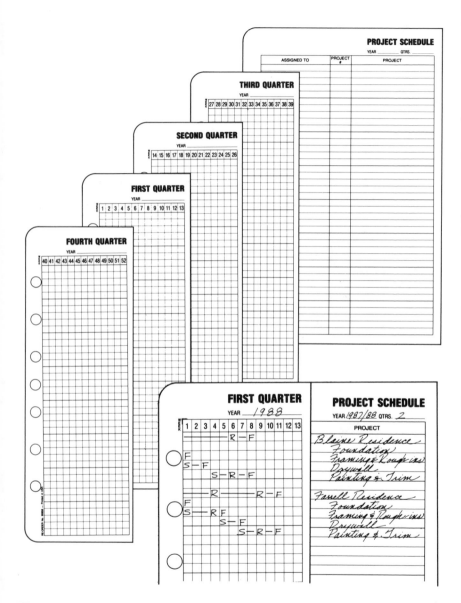

**Figure 9-24.** Day-Timer PERT/CPM Sheets are also available with quarterly overlays.

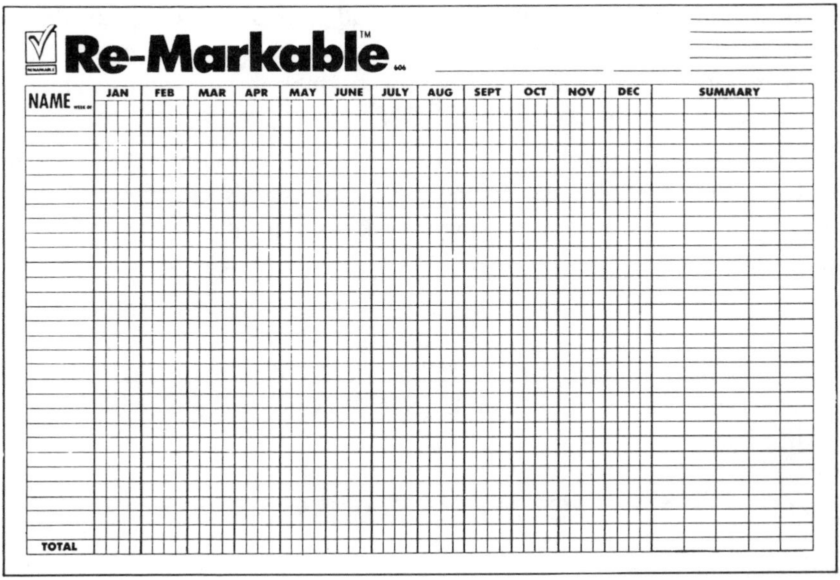

**Figure 9-25.** Project/Personnel Re-Markable board shows status of projects, assignments or personnel for the whole year on a weekly basis.

**ROL-A-CHART** visual control charts come in a dozen different models, all of which have a rotating sleeve that never runs out of space and allows for continuous scheduling. Different models are available to meet scheduling needs ranging from 13 weeks to two years. 800/824-0212 or 916/622-2437
William A. Steward Company
4708 Oak Hill Rd.
Placerville, CA 95667

**SmartForm Designer/SmartForm Assistant** are two Macintosh programs for creating and filling in forms. It has received a rating of "four mice" from *MacUser*. $399. 408/987-7000
Claris Corp. (Subsidiary of Apple Computer)
PO Box 58168
Santa Clara, CA 95052-8168

**Static Images** are white plastic easel pad sheets that cling to almost all walls. Use them as you would use a white board with dry-erase markers or with regular markers for permanent messages. They're made by Dennison. 800/DENNISON

**3M Post-it brand printed notes** (Figure 9-26) eliminate the need to write and rewrite requests for action. (You can also design and print your own custom Post-it messages–ask your printer.)

**Word Guide** templates take the guesswork and tedium out of mapping forms when you're using a program such as FormScribe on your computer. It's also a good design tool for manually produced forms, layouts and reports. $15.95 (or $9.95 when you purchase FormScribe at the same time). (See Power Up! under FormsFile above.)

## PROJECT MANAGEMENT SOFTWARE

### IBM

**AEC Information Manager** is a project-oriented database that allows you to schedule, organize and track project information. It received a "four mice" rating from *MacUser*. $695. 800/346-9413 or 703/450-1980
AEC Management Systems, Inc.
22611 Markey Ct., Bldg. 113
Sterling, VA 22170

**Manager** is a "goal-oriented management software" program useful for managing people, projects, goals and deadlines. It goes a step beyond other programs in two regards. First, there is a password protection system for privacy and security. Second, the program is "intelligent," offering suggestions and comments from time to time. For example, if you have entered only negative items related to an employee, PC Manager will suggest you enter something positive once in a while. The program also provides reminders of appointments. $59. 213/306-3020; FAX: 213/821-8122
Sterling Castle
702 Washington Street, Suite 174
Marina Del Rey, CA 90292-5598

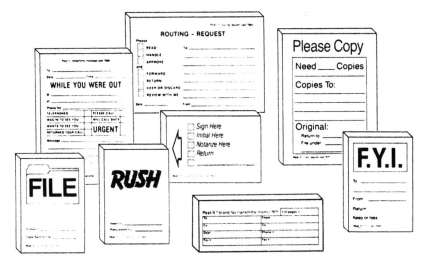

**Figure 9-26.** Post-it brand printed notes make office communications quick and easy.

**Microsoft Project for Windows** is a powerful program, particularly if you're more interested in doing Gantt rather than PERT charts. Easy to use, Microsoft Project is more for small and medium-sized projects. It has been selected a *PC Magazine* "Editor's Choice." $395. 800/426-9400 or 206/882-8080
Microsoft Corp.
One Microsoft Way
Redmond, WA 98052-6399

**Project Scheduler 4** is a good project management program that has its own graphical user interface, is easy to learn and use and gets high marks from computer magazine reviewers. $685. 415/570-7700
Scitor Corp.
393 Vintage Park Dr., Ste. 140
Foster City, CA 94404

**Time Line** is a complete project manager for planning and tracking large projects. It continues to get rave reviews (including "Editor's Choice" by *PC Magazine*). It's a powerful program with excellent documentation, a built-in tickler "alarm clock" and on-line tutorials that help reduce the learning curve. It's easy to learn and use and is flexible enough to fit the way you work. $695. 800/441-7234 or in California, 800/626-8847

Symantec Corporation
10201 Torre Ave.
Cupertino, CA 95014-2132

## MACINTOSH

**FastTrack Schedule** generates presentation quality Gantt charts and received a "4½ mice" rating from *MacUser*. $395.
AEC Management Systems, Inc. (See AEC Information Manager above.)

**KeyPlan** lets you do outlines that are converted into either Gantt or PERT charts. It received a "four mice" rating from *MacUser*. $395.
602/998-9106
Symmetry Software Corporation
8603 East Royal Palm Road, Ste. 110
Scottsdale, AZ 85258

**MacProject II** is an update of Apple's project management program. $499
Claris Corp. (See SmartForm Designer under "Forms...")

**Project Scheduler 4** (see above description under "IBM Project Management Software")

## OTHER WORK MANAGEMENT TOOLS

**BestChoice3** is a decision-support program that has received many favorable reviews. It provides analytical conclusions for a wide range of applications such as market research, personnel evaluations, capital investments, real estate purchases, or even prioritizing your to-do list. $99. (See Manager, Sterling Castle Software under Project Management Software above.)

**Crawford Slip Method** (CSM) is a manual idea generator and organizing system that is great for people who like to physically manipulate, categorize and arrange ideas on slips of paper. CSM is particularly useful for assembling employee and procedure handbooks and manuals and can be used with groups of people whose ideas you want to tap. The CSM booklet and slip box are $3 each and the classification tray is $7. 213/743-7152 (The School of Public Administration Business Office)
USC Productivity Network

School of Public Administration
University Park MC 0041
Los Angeles, CA 90089-0041

**For Comment** is a highly rated software program that allows up to 16 reviewers to revise or annotate a document. The program allows you to report or add reviewers' changes or comments in a variety of ways. $195 for one author; $995 for networks and 16 authors. 415/492-3200
Broderbund Software Inc.
17 Paul Drive
San Rafael, CA 94903

**Planmaster Information Control System** is a card/notebook organizer for managing time, projects, personnel and other priorities. You write information once and then move the PlanCards to various positions within the system without having to rewrite information. Preprinted, color-coded cards are labeled "General Purpose," "Expense," "Memo," "Things-To-Do" and "Phone Message." You can organize these cards under header cards such as the days of the week, "Next Week," etc., on three panels that fit inside a notebook. A pocket wallet for travel lets you condense the system. The system holds 306 cards but can be expanded to 510 cards. $89.95 (See Memindex under Memofile listed under Tickler Systems above.)

**PRD+** can help medical and legal transcriptionists as well as others who spend time typing double their typing speeds and production. PRD+ works with WordPerfect, WordStar, MS Word and practically every other word processing package. You type abbreviations instead of words, phrases or commands. Then, when you press the spacebar or punctuation key, the abbreviation is replaced with whatever it represents, up to 4,000 characters. PRD+ has been very favorably reviewed in *The New York Times*, *Fortune Magazine*, *PC Week* and many others. There are over 25 special editions of PRD+ for such applications as law, medicine, insurance and government. $279.95 to $429.95. 212/818-1144
Productivity Software International, Inc.
211 East 43rd Street, #2202
New York, NY 10017-4707

**ScheduleMaker** is a Macintosh program that lets you build and maintain employee schedules on hour, half-hour or 15-minute

increments. It received a "four mice" rating from *MacUser*. $395.
504/756-2322 or 504/291-6348
Craig Systems, Inc.
16717 Monitor Ave.
Baton Rouge, LA 70817

**3M dispensers** for Post-it brand notes are now available. Two handy dispensers permit easy, one-hand dispensing of special fan-folded Post-it notes. The Pop 'n Jot brand dispenser sits on the desktop. The C-300 Post-it brand pop-up note dispenser can be mounted anywhere, e.g., on your computer terminal or your filing cabinet.

**3M Laser/Copier Labels**, product number 7701, has one 8½-by-11-inch yellow label per sheet, which I use for presentations. The labels use the Post-it brand adhesive. I print out presentation comments of any length, which were inputted in my computer, onto the label sheets. Then I cut up the comments and affix to them my presentation notes. What I have is the convenience of making my own customized, removable notes that can be moved easily from one presentation to the next. Available in 25 label sheets per package from most office supply dealers.

**3M tape products** I couldn't live without: Post-it brand Correction and Cover-up Tape and Scotch brand Removable Magic Tape. Post-it Tape is a removable, opaque white tape for clean and quick copy blockout when making photocopies. Scotch brand Removable Tape is a transparent tape that attaches papers temporarily and removes easily without damaging the material it is attached to. You can write on it with ink, pencil or marker. Both tape products come in a variety of different widths.

**TopDown** is a Macintosh program that received a "4½ mice" rating from *MacUser*. It lets you break down complex projects graphically into smaller tasks. $345. 713/890-3434
Kaetron Software Corp.
12777 Jones Rd., Ste. 445
Houston, TX 77070

**WordPerfect 5.1** is the word processor we use. It's state-of-the-art and I highly recommend it for heavy-duty word processing needs. $495. 800/321-4566
WordPerfect Corp.

1555 N. Technology Way
Orem, UT 84057

**Working Hours** is a scheduling program that allows you to schedule up to 30 people, will spot schedule conflicts automatically and can show schedules in different formats. $99.95 (See Power Up! under FormsFile above.)

**Zipkey** is a shorthand program for database work. When you type in a zip code, the program automatically pops the city, state and telephone code into the correct fields. The program was recommended in a *PC World* article, "Software You Can Really Use." $30 plus $25 per update disk, at any frequency from monthly to annually. 812/339-1811
Eric Isaacson Software
416 E. University Ave.
Bloomington, IN 47401-4739

# RESOURCES AND RECORDS

## PERSONAL COMPUTER OPTIONS–IBM

### *Database Software*

Don't be fooled by the term "database software." Many of these database programs are extremely flexible and combine features such as built-in ticklers and word processors, too.

**Address Book Plus** is an easy-to-use, personal database manager that organizes and prints top-quality pocket address books that fit many organizers in sizes ranging from 2½ by 4½ inches up to 8½ by 11 inches. You can also print mailing labels, rotary file cards and envelopes. (See Power Up! under FormsFile above.)

**Alpha Four** is database software that received a "Best Buy" award by *PC Magazine.* 1/800/451-1018, ext. 117, or 617/229-2924
Alpha Software Corp.
One North Ave.
Burlington, MA 01803

**Dac-Easy Base** is touted as an easy-to-learn relational database program that provides on-screen help for an affordable price. $49.95.
214/248-0205
DacEasy, Inc.

17950 Preston Rd., Ste. 800
Dallas, TX 75252

**PC-File, Version 5.0** is the database program we use in our office. It has many useful features, including word processing capabilities that enable you to do form letters and mail merges. The program will find, list or delete duplicate records. It was selected an "Editor's Choice" by *PC Magazine*. 800/JBUTTON (orders only); 206/454-0479
ButtonWare, Inc.
PO Box 96058
Bellevue, WA 98009

**Q&A** is a top-rated, full-featured, integrated database and word processor. It features multiple file linking, instant mail merge and mailing labels and sophisticated report capabilities. $349. Symantec Corporation (See Time Line under Project Management Software above)

### *Desktop Managers/Organizers and Personal Information Managers*
The following programs go by a variety of different names. They're difficult to classify because they do such a variety of useful functions. These are among the best:

**Agenda** is a PIM that lets you organize and view your thoughts and ideas in creative ways. And it's guaranteed: if you're not productive within 30 minutes after start-up, you can return Agenda within 30 days for a full refund. $395. 800/343-5414 or 617/577-8500
Lotus Development Corp.
55 Cambridge Parkway
Cambridge, MA 02142

**GrandView** is an advanced outlining program designed for busy managers who need a powerful planning and personal organizational tool. Its outlining features help you capture and organize your ideas into action-oriented plans. Calendar and Category features allow you to delegate, assign and track tasks, schedules and priorities. You can use the word processing features along with Harvard Graphics or Lotus Freelance Plus to create business documents and presentation materials with font-enhanced text. $295. Symantec Corporation (See Time Line under Project Management Software above)

**IBM Current** is a flexible, easy-to-use PIM that allows you to organize, relate and retrieve text and graphical data such as appointments, projects, to-do lists, phone lists and expenses. It is easy to customize and is designed to operate under Windows. $395. 800/426-7699, ext. 294
IBM Desktop Software
472 Wheelers Farms Rd.
Milford, CT 06460

**INFO SELECT** (formerly Tornado) is a fast way to deal with notes, ideas, plans, contacts and all your random information. It's a personal information manager that is a free-form text database that lets you make miscellaneous notes on computer (instead of on paper slips) and search for them instantaneously. If you keep a lot of miscellaneous notes or ideas that are unrelated to each other or to particular projects or people, this could be a handy program. Features include phone dialer, hypertext, mail merge, line drawing, overviews, word processing, a tickler/reminder system and a variety of ways to search for information. INFO SELECT is based on the award-winning TORNADO, which *PC World* called "Excellent" and *PC Magazine* selected twice for its "Editor's Choice" award. 800/342-5930 or 201/342-6518
Micro Logic Corp.
100 Second St.
PO Box 70
Hackensack, NJ 07602

**Info-XL** is a PIM that offers six different windows to manage and relate six different types of information. The Manager window is for outlining information, the Records window for storing more conventional database information, the Comments window for unstructured notes, the Daily Schedule and Monthly Calendar windows for obvious functions and the Search window for searching a word or phrase. $95. 408/559-1100
Valor Software Corp.
4840 Pebble Glen Dr.
San Jose, CA 95129

**Office PC,** an upgrade of WordPerfect Library, is a desktop manager for WordPerfect users. It includes a file manager, database, calendar, calculator and an editor that manages up to nine files in memory at once. $149; **Office LAN** (the network version), $495 for the 5-pack and $1,595 for the 20-pack. WordPerfect Corp. (see WordPerfect 5.1 under "Other Work Management Tools")

**SideKick 2.0** is the latest upgrade to a popular favorite. SideKick 2.0 offers a time planner, notepad, calculator and a communications module, all RAM-resident and available at the touch of a key. Version 2.0 features network support and supports mobile office applications with connectivity to palmtop organizers, popular appointment notebooks and notebook and laptop computers. Professional-quality printouts sized to match a variety of appointment notebooks and the ability to send a message to an alphanumeric pager are also included. $99.95. 800/331-0877 or 408/438-8400
Borland International
1800 Green Hills Rd., PO Box 660001
Scotts Valley, CA 95066-0001

*Sales, Telemarketing Programs*
These programs are ideal for anyone who is managing a client database and/or is marketing products or services and wants to track these marketing efforts. Many of these programs combine features from other software such as database management, word processing, telecommunications and built-in follow-up. Consider these programs if you're in real estate, insurance, inside or outside sales, consulting, purchasing, financial services, association management, direct mail marketing, to name a few areas. You don't have to be in sales; you just need to deal with a large number of contacts on a regular basis.

**ACT!** is a powerful, easy-to-use contact management program that manages your contacts, does mail merge letters and has time management features that include a built-in reminder system and different ways to schedule your tasks, follow-ups and appointments. It was a *PC Magazine* "Editor's Choice." $395. 800/228-9228
Contact Software International
1625 West Crosby Rd., Ste. 132
Carrollton, TX 75006

**MACS** is a software package designed specially for manufacturers representatives. 800/321-1788 or 216/831-6145
Manufacturers' Agents Computer Systems

4512 Emery Industrial Parkway
Cleveland, OH 44128

**The Maximizer** is contact management software that continues to get rave reviews. It holds *INFOWORLD*'s "Best in Class" and "Excellent Value" ratings and *INBOUND/OUTBOUND*'s "Editor's Choice. The program offers a fast and flexible database. The program includes tickler and scheduling time management functions. It contains an integrated word processor that lets you do form letters, labels and envelopes. The program also includes a business calculator, as well as diary, personal accounting and calendar features. It's available in a single user version at $295 or a LAN version at $695. 800/663-2030 or 604/299-2121
Richmond Technologies & Software Inc.
Ste. 420, 6400 Roberts Street
Burnaby, B.C. V5G 4C9
Canada

**RPMS (Rep Profit Management System)** is a data management system designed for the manufacturer's rep. RPMS will track orders from quote to factory commission statement. Modules and features include invoice and commission tracking, order tracking, product tracking, direct mail, commission reconciliation and sales forecasting. $995 for Module I (Invoice and Commission Tracking), $700 for Module II (Order Tracking) and $275 to $375 each for other features. RPMS will work in a network environment. 800/776-7435 or 816/531-7257
RPMS
3822 Summit
Kansas City, MO 64111

**SaleMaker Plus** is an integrated sales and marketing software system that continues to get rave reviews by reviewer and end user alike. It's designed to build and maintain a client database and to provide quick and easy access to information for outside sales client management, inbound and outbound telemarketing, follow-up letters, targeted direct mail marketing and management reports. Pop-up windows and well-designed screens make this an easy-to-use program. $695. 800/766-7355 or 214/264-2626
SaleMaker Software
Box 531650

Grand Prairie, TX 75053

**TeleMagic** is an easy-to-use, versatile program for salespeople, executives, secretaries, customer service reps–anyone who deals with large numbers of outside business contacts. TeleMagic makes contact information instantly available–from customers, prospects and suppliers to scheduled call-backs, forecasts and to-do lists. It auto-dials, logs the date, times your call, prompts you with sales scripts and supplies answers to objections and questions. Notes are filed for instant reference later. You can generate mailing lists, labels, envelopes and mail-merged form letters. Registered users have unlimited toll-free support for one year. (See Figure 9-27 for a sample screen.) $495 for the "professional" version; $1,995 for the "network" version. Available for the PC, Macintosh, Xenix/Unix and IBM AS-400/Sys-38. 800/992-9952 or 619/431-4000
Remote Control International
5928 Pascal Court, Ste. 150
Carlsbad, CA 92008

## Text-Based Programs

**askSam** is a free-form information management environment that handles text, numbers and graphics. This program easily integrates structured and unstructured data and has a text editor. It's a full-featured text management system. 800/327-5726 or 904/584-6590
askSam Systems
PO Box 1428
Perry, FL 32347

**IZE** can search, link and generate outlines and can search extremely fast for data. $445. 608/273-6000
Persoft Inc.
465 Science Dr.
Madison, WI 53711

## On-line Databases and Information Services

**American Business Information** leases their 9.5 million U.S. business database on computer or offers hard copy directories and CD-ROM products of U.S. businesses by subject. This information is compiled from more than 5,000 yellow page telephone directories per year.
402/331-7169

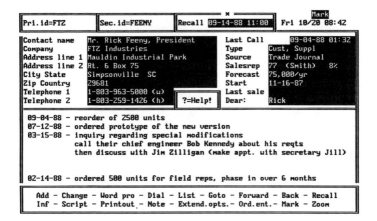

**Figure 9-27.** A typical TeleMagic screen shows you key information about a contact, including history of previous contacts and when to follow up next.

American Business Information, Inc.
5711 South 86th Circle
PO Box 27347
Omaha, NE 68127

**CompuServe,** the most popular of on-line information services, offers access to 1,400 databases. $40 one-time fee plus charges for on-line time. 800/848-8199 or 614/457-8600
CompuServe
5000 Arlington Centre Blvd.
Columbus, OH 43220

**Computer Database Plus** is an on-line database that gives you access to articles and abstracts featuring reviews of computer products from 50 publications dating back to 1987. More than 80,000 citations are available. This database "library" is available through CompuServe, an on-line information service. $40 one-time fee to subscribe to

CompuServe; usage charge is up to 61 cents per minute; $1.50 charge to display complete article and $1 to display an abstract

**Computer Library** is similar in content to Computer Database Plus but provides information to subscribers monthly in the form of compact discs, which include 45,000 citations and text from 10 publications going back 12 months. $695 for annual subscription that includes 12 discs. 212/503-4400
Ziff Communications Co.
1 Park Ave., 5th Floor
New York, NY 10016

**Congressional Toolkit** is a specialized database that provides the names and states of current members of Congress, including committees on which they serve. A built-in word processor lets you do mail-merge form letters. The program comes with the federal database or a single state database. $39.95 and $29.95 for each additional state database. 914/271-8271
BJ Toolkit
Alexander Lane
Croton-on-Hudson, New York 10520

**Datapro Directory of Microcomputer Software** is a three-volume information service that is updated monthly. I found the loose-leaf format with tabbed dividers made this comprehensive resource particularly easy to use while referring to it frequently to update software products for this book. More than 12,000 software packages are featured. Monthly updates and newsletters, along with access to the Datapro Telephone Inquiry Service, are included in the one-year subscription fee of $779. 800/328-2776 or 609/764-0100
Datapro, a unit of McGraw-Hill Information Services Co.
1805 Underwood Blvd.
Delran, NJ 08075

**FNN Newsreel** is an electronic, automatic clipping service that provides customized business news for you and access to the Dow Jones News/Retrieval (DJNR) Service and more than 55 Dow Jones databases. $179 (includes five hours of connect time to DJNR). 800/762-7538
FNN Data Broadcasting Corp.
1900 S. Norfolk St.
San Mateo, CA 94403

*Reading Up On Public Domain Software*
**Public Domain Software, Untapped Resources for the Business User,** by Rusel DeMaria and George R. Fontaine, is a good book if you're all tapped out in terms of computer expenditures. In this book you'll discover hundreds of free or low-cost programs that rival the commercial programs. You will, however, need a modem to download these programs. $19.95. 415/366-3600
M&T Publishing Inc.
501 Galveston Dr.
Redwood City, CA 94063

## PERSONAL COMPUTER OPTIONS–MAC
*Databases, Desktop Organizers and Other Information Managers*
**Double Helix** is a powerful relational database that has received excellent reviews from *MacUser*. $595. 800/323-5423 or 708/498-5615
Odesta Corp.
4084 Commercial Ave.
Northbrook, IL 60062

**Dynodex 2.0, The Instant Address Book,** is an address book manager for personal organizer users that allows you to print double-sided your name and address database directly onto standard organizer size paper (included). Works as a standalone program or a DA that lets you add, edit and dial any entry. $125. 914/876-7744
Portfolio Systems, Inc.
21 East Market Street
Rhinebeck, NY 12572

**DynoPage 1.0** prints any Mac file to personal organizer pages so you can carry spreadsheets, reports or anything from your Mac in your personal organizer. $125. (See Dyndodex above.)

**Filevision IV** is a visual information system where data can be accessed by directly attaching drawing page objects to database records. It's a complete drawing program and database management system that's ideal for desktop mapping and facilities management applications. Features include a powerful report generator, standard forms, mail merge, flexible forms design with computed fields and automatic data entry and direct graphic import. $295. 714/731-1368
TSP Software
4790 Irvine Blvd., Ste. 105-294

Irvine, CA 92720

**HyperCard** is a powerful, yet easy to use program that lets you create your own information management programs. It lets you link information by association, more like how the mind naturally works. $49; comes bundled with all new Macs. 408/996-1010
Apple Computer, Inc.
20525 Mariani Ave.
Cupertino, CA 95014

**MORE** combines outlining, word processing, desktop presentations and financial charting so that you can quickly create a broad spectrum of business documents and presentations. From bullet charts to tree charts, choose from over 100 templates and layouts. $395. 415/964-6200 or 408/253-9600
Symantec Corporation
10201 Torre Avenue
Cupertino, CA 95014-2132

**Personal Training for HyperCard** is a six-hour training program designed to make HyperCard even easier. The program offers four modules including *Using HyperCard, Creating Cards and Stacks, Basic Scripting* and *Advanced Scripting*. Each module contains a disk, audio cassette, command summary card and exercise card at $79.95 each. (Personal Training Systems also provides tutorial products for Microsoft Excel, Word & Works−Aldus PageMaker, Persuasion & Freehand−Claris FileMaker and QuarkXPress.) 408/559-8635
Personal Training Systems
828 S. Bascom, Ste. 100
San Jose, CA 95128

**QuickDEX Classic** is a text database that uses a friendly file card/rotary file card approach for keeping track of personal information such as names and addresses. It's a desk accessory that retrieves text strings very quickly. It comes with an auto-dialer. The program will load up to eight "card decks" or databases at a time. $60. 408/624-8716; FAX 408/624-7865
Casady & Greene, Inc.
PO Box 223779
Carmel, CA 93922

**RecordHolderPlus** is an easy-to-use, inexpensive, multi-featured database program good for simple database management such as maintaining mailing lists and creating customized forms. It offers excellent report and search capabilities. It received a "93" rating in *MacGuide*. $99.95. 203/872-1024
Software Discoveries, Inc.
137 Krawski Dr.
South Windsor, CT 06074

### Sales, Telemarketing and Contact Management

**C.A.T.**, which stands for "Contacts/Activities/Time," is a relational database management program that's easy to learn and use. It will help you manage all of your contacts, whether they be clients, prospects, colleagues or personal friends, as well as the tasks and activities you're doing. C.A.T. is a flexible program that works in ways you like to work, linking related information together. $495. 408/727-8096
Chang Laboratories, Inc.
3350 Scott Blvd., Bldg. 25
Santa Clara, CA 95054-3104

**Market Master** is a sales and marketing program that tracks people and helps you design sales programs complete with designated follow-up, form letters and sales scripts. This program received a "99" rating in *MacGuide* and was described as the "best sales follow-up software you can buy." **Market Master for the Macintosh**, version 3.0, includes a Results Analysis module to track results of sales activities, $395; **Market Master Manager** (for use by a group of salespeople at a location), from $595 to $1995, depending on the number of sales people. 916/265-0911
Breakthrough Productions
210 Park Avenue
Nevada City, CA 95959

**TeleMagic** is an easy-to-use contact management program that is now available for the Mac. (See Telemagic under the IBM "Sales, Telemarketing and Contact Management" section above.)

*On-line Databases and Information Services*

**CompuServe Navigator** is a software program designed to help guide you through CompuServe, the on-line information service that has the greatest numbers of subscribers. $99.95. (See CompuServe under IBM "On-line Databases" above)

**MacInfo** is a monthly service (and software program) that makes available current magazine articles and abstracts on the Macintosh and related products. $120 yearly subscription rate; $99 for educational institutions. 415/649-8176
Niles & Associates, Inc.
2000 Hearst Ave., Ste. 200
Berkeley, CA 94709

## RECORD KEEPING SYSTEMS

*Manual Record Keeping Systems*

**Expense booklets** for tracking auto and travel expenses are handy and let you keep records as you go, while you're on the go. Look for them at office supply dealers. **Keith Clark** is a good brand name.

**LPI Expense Record** and **LPI Time Record** allow for easy, as-you-go manual record keeping related to time and billing. Even though these systems are designed for attorneys, they are easily adaptable to a variety of professions. 800/222-0510
All-state Law Office Catalog
All-state Legal Supply Co.
One Commerce Drive
Cranford, NJ 07016

**Safeguard One-Write Bookkeeping System** (available in 200 formats) is great for a private practice or a small office. With Safeguard, you keep a check journal and your tax records as you go. We've used this system for years. 800/523-2422
Safeguard Business Systems, Inc.
400 Maryland Drive
PO Box 6000
Ft. Washington, PA 19034

## *Record Keeping Software*—IBM

**Acroprint Time Recorder Co.** offers Badger 6000 and ATR 6000—an automated time keeping system that can tie into your computer for tracking and printing reports on time-and-attendance, labor distribution, job costing, payroll, overtime, tardiness, shift summaries and more. 919/872-5800
5640 Departure Dr.
Raleigh, NC 27604

**Kronos Time Accounting Systems** offers a family of time keeping systems that can link with your computer system to reduce time for payroll processing, increase payroll accuracy, improve employee scheduling and control labor costs. 800/225-1561 or 617/890-8768
62 Fourth Ave.
Waltham, MA 02154

**NYNEX CallView Information System** works with your computer and phone system to track billable calls, eliminating the need to keep time sheets manually. It's designed for firms with three or more professionals who make billable calls. 800/346-9999 or 617/273-0057
NYNEX Business Information Systems
1000 Abernathy Rd.
Atlanta, GA 30328

**Project Billing** is a time billing program for ad agencies, graphic designers and print shops. It tracks billable time and expenses, prints reports and prepares invoices. 206/443-0765
Satori Software
2815 Second Avenue, Suite 560
Seattle, WA 98121

**Timeslips III** is a top-rated time and billing system featuring a memory-resident software stopwatch to time activities. Version 4.0 has many new features including improved reporting capabilities, security, bill formatting and ease of use. Timeslips III also links with many of the top selling general ledger accounting systems (requires TAL, Timeslips III Accounting Link, $79.95). Single and network editions are available for both DOS and Macintosh platforms. $299.95, single user; $699.95, network edition. 800/338-5314 in USA; 800/359-3343 in Canada; 508/768-6100 in Massachusetts.
TIMESLIPS Corporation
239 Western Ave.

Essex, MA 01929

*Record Keeping Software—Mac*

**MacInUse, Version 3.0** keeps track of your Macintosh usage for your tax records (particularly if you use your Mac at home for business). The program runs in the background but can also be automatically called up to add extra information. The program received a "95" rating in *MacGuide*. $99. 800/662-6829 or 805/385-5000
Softview
1721 Pacific Avenue
Oxnard, CA 93010

**Shopkeeper-3** is a simple point-of-sale, invoicing, inventory, accounts receivable and billing program for shop owners and other small business owners, including some consultants. $195. 904/222-8808
ShopKeeper Software Inc.
PO Box 38160
Tallahassee, FL 32315-8160

**Timeslips III** (see description under "Record Keeping Software—IBM")

Note: Always check with vendors for the latest version of software products and the compatibility with your existing hardware and software.

# 10

## FOR COLLECTORS ONLY: HOW, WHEN AND WHAT TO SAVE

*Quick Scan: If you're an inveterate collector or you're in a profession that simply requires you to save many records, documents or resources, this chapter is for you. Here are some guidelines that will help you save only the essentials.*

I'm convinced the world is divided into two groups of people–those who save and those who don't. And there has to be a Murphy's Law somewhere that says, "If you're a collector, you're probably living or working with someone who isn't."

I admit it. I'm a collector. Not only do I have many interests and avocations (I suffer from the "Da Vinci Syndrome"), but I have chosen occupations that attract collectors. I have been a school teacher, an editor and a manager. Today I am a professional speaker, writer and consultant and I continue to maintain well-organized resource material.

I am not against collecting. Certain professions demand it. But collecting requires strict guidelines and routines if you ever hope to stay in control.

Consider the degree your collecting habit is taking control over *you*. Recognize that it can be tamed and turned into a constructive resource that will give you a professional edge.

## TYPES OF COLLECTORS

Sometimes it's helpful to see the different kinds of collecting traps we fall into. People with a "possession obsession" like to buy new things and add to their growing collection. And once something enters their environment, it remains for the duration.

"Chipmunk collectors" don't go out of their way to purchase new possessions. Instead, they squirrel away everything for the winter—*every* winter. "Waste not, want not" is their motto. Chipmunks were taught to hold onto everything for dear life. Beware of thoughts like these: "I might need this someday" or "Somebody else might need this" or "This could really come in handy."

People who love the printed word are "information junkies." These are people who love to learn, read, write, improve themselves and find out what the experts have to say. And even if you're not an information junkie per se, you still live in an "information age," where there are 1,000 specialized publications every year and 1,000 new book titles each day throughout the world. The sum of printed information is doubling every eight years; it's likely that the 40 million PCs in the U.S. help contribute to this problem of information overload.

If you can relate to any of these collecting habits (and most of us can), you'll want to keep reading. Any of these habits can become nightmares in short order if you don't put a lid on them. The way you do that is by learning to *make decisions* about paper and possessions. But as we discussed in chapters 1 and 2, decisions aren't made in a vacuum.

## MAKING DECISIONS ABOUT "COLLECTIBLES"

The secret to making decisions and controlling paper and possessions is simple: know your goals and values. Know what's important to you and what's really worth your time and energy. According to Roy Disney, Walt Disney's brother, "Decisions are easy when values are clear."

Once you're clear about your values and goals, you're ready to establish some stick-to-'em criteria. The problem people have when they're going through papers and possessions is that they aren't using the right criteria. As a result, every item requires a major decision from scratch.

Start by recognizing that there are only three basic decisions you need to make: 1) what to **save**, 2) how to **sort** it and 3) where to **store** it.

## TO SAVE OR NOT TO SAVE... THAT IS THE QUESTION!

If you're suffering from "Discard Dilemmas," the following two general guidelines can help you with troublesome papers:

1. When in doubt, *save* tax, legal or business items.
2. When in doubt, *toss* resource information,
   especially information you seldom, if ever, use.

When you're in a discard mode (or should we say discard *mood*), use these simple guidelines along with the following criteria:

### Nine Questions to Toss Out When Deciding What to Save

1. Do you need the item now?
2. Was it used last year? More than once?
3. Will you use it more than once next year? (How likely is it that you will *ever* need it?)
4. Would it be difficult or expensive to replace? Could you get it from someone else?
5. Is it current (and for how long?)
6. Should it be kept for legal or financial reasons?
7. Could someone else use it *now*? (Or could someone else wrestle with this decision instead of you?!)
8. Does it significantly enhance your work or life?
9. Is it worth the time and energy to save?

Go back and star any that you could use. Keep them right in front of you as you make your discard decisions. Here's some space to add any others that specifically fit your situation:

Or follow the "cardinal office rule" of well-known Los Angeles attorney and philanthropist Richard Riordan, who advises, "Don't keep it in *your* file if someone else can keep it in *theirs*."

## THE SORTING PROCESS

Now that you've established your criteria for saving (or tossing), you're ready to begin the actual process of sorting your collectibles. Your best bet is to make it a game with definite time limits. You can spread out your game over a period of time, doing a little this week and a little next week. Or maybe you prefer to dig right in and work for a few days straight, such as a weekend. Or instead, try this one on for size: pretend you have to move your office in less than 24 hours to a space that is half the size. (Got your adrenalin flowing yet?)

Whichever is your style, choose blocks of time without interruptions, as this is real mental work that requires concentration. Block out at least a few hours. Have on hand the necessary supplies—a trash basket (or barrel), a pencil, a timer, empty cardboard boxes (Fellowes Bankers Boxes or other cardboard file boxes with lids are great) and space to work.

Tackle a small area at a time—one pile on your desk, a file drawer, a section of a file drawer, etc. Begin where the need is greatest. If your file cabinets are packed to the gills, start there. If you haven't seen your desk in years, there's no better place to begin. It's best to choose something small and be able to work through it. Set your timer to establish a reasonable time limit (an hour or less).

Begin by sorting through the designated area, deciding what to save, what to toss and what should be stored elsewhere. As you decide which items to save, sort them in categories based on *types* of items (e.g., books, files, supplies, personal items to take home), as well as *how often* you intend to use them (e.g., daily, several times a week, once a month). **Only things you use or refer to regularly during your working hours should be in your office.**

The process is not simply willpower, of sitting down and forcing yourself to go through your stuff (although a little willpower won't hurt). What you need is a **plan of action**, particularly if you have "long-term buildup." (Chapter 14 will help you design a simple plan of action—you may wish to read that chapter before attempting to tackle long-term buildup.)

**Write as you sort.** It's helpful to list your criteria and your sorting categories as you do the process. This list, along with a written plan of action, will help you tremendously. Carefully number and label boxes and drawers *as you go.* Keep a written record of any items going into storage.

I use my computer to keep a record of boxes that are stored off site. It's easy to update my word processing document, which is named "Files." I also keep a printout of "Files" in my manual filing system. My boxes are labeled alphabetically (I'll double up on letters should I ever get to "Z," heaven forbid!) I share an off-site storage room with my husband, who uses a numbered box system.

An attorney who is a solo practitioner keeps track of open and closed client files with index card boxes—ones for "Open" files and others for "Closed" files. Each card has the name of a client, the number and location of files for the client and when those files were opened or closed. The cards are filed alphabetically in the appropriate boxes (open or closed).

*What if you inherited somebody else's clutter?* I received a letter from Sharon Lawrence, a student of mine who ran into this problem several months after taking two of my seminars. She had just accepted a position as a financial management analyst in a California county administrative office. She writes:

> I have a new job and a new challenge to being organized. I left my organized office for a complete disaster area. I couldn't believe my new office; when I walked in, my mouth fell open. There were three inches thick of papers strewn over the entire surface of the desk, a bookcase filled with a year's worth of obsolete computer printouts and two file cabinets filled with five-year-old data, which belonged to other analysts.

I informed my boss that I couldn't function until I had gotten organized. It was hard to know where to begin. By the end of the second day, I had thrown away four trash cans full of obsolete reports and duplicate copies of letters and reports. I had also managed to clear the desktop. I was still faced with four piles of paper which had been sorted into broad categories.

Working a little each day for two weeks, I have now managed to organize the piles of information into file folders. I have also given away two file cabinets and distributed their contents to the appropriate analysts.

People now walk by my office and say things like, "Wow, what a difference!" I tell them about your classes and how this is the new me.

This is great, you say, if you know what you're going to need on the new job. But what if the job isn't second nature to you? When Nancy Schlegel became a systems engineer for IBM she waited a year before she tossed out information. "After a year, I knew what I needed and what I didn't and I was in a better position to set up a filing system."

## WHERE TO STORE IT

Deciding where to store your records and resources depends on four factors:

1. Up-to-date sorting and purging
2. Frequency of use
3. Size, shape and quantity of materials
4. Proximity to related items.

First, have you completed the sorting and purging process *before* you buy that extra filing cabinet or bookcase? Where to house something should only be considered after you decide *if* you should keep it.

Second, the more frequently you use an item, the more accessible it should be. Identify *prime* work areas in your office–those areas that are most accessible. If your desk top and a deskside file drawer are the most accessible areas, do they contain items that you use most often in your office?

Third, the size, shape and quantity of your resources will suggest the types of containers, accessories or pieces of furniture you select to hold those resources. If you have 12 inches of file folders you probably won't be choosing a five-drawer lateral file cabinet. If you're a graphic designer or a printer you may need special cabinets to hold large, oversized art boards.

Fourth, things that go together should generally stay together. Group similar types of books, files and supplies together. Sound like common sense? You'd be amazed to see how many items that are unrelated to each other end up together—sometimes for years.

## HOW TO PREVENT LONG-TERM BUILDUP

Having a philosophy about paper helps Revlon's Kathy Meyer-Poppe, Corporate Fleet director. She says, "File a paper or toss it out—it's either important enough to be filed right then and there or it's not that important. So throw it away."

Bill Butler, president of Butler Consulting Group in Indianapolis, makes it a point to clean one file a day. Butler says, "One file you can manage. As a result, you have fewer files, which means fewer places to lose things."

There are no rules to maintenance. You may like to adopt Butler's "one file a day" or Poppe's "file or toss" routine. On the other hand, once a week or once every six months may work better for you. Or perhaps you want to wait until the need arises—bulging file cabinets or an impending move. Some people tell me the only way they can get organized is by moving—so they actually plan a move every few years!

It can be thrilling to "clear a path" as one client described making headway on her collection. It's also thrilling for me to get letters like the following from Coleen Melton, a California art teacher:

> I'm writing to report to you that my goal is accomplished:
> 20 years of art placed into retrievable order thanks to
> your "Positively Organized!" class and your notes of
> support. I even have my husband wanting to organize his
> filing cabinet, and that is a miracle in itself.

Even lifelong collectors can learn and use the art of organization.

# RESOURCE GUIDE

(Addresses and phone numbers are included for mail order items and generally *not* for products that are widely available through office supply catalogs and stores.)

## ART WORK, BLUEPRINTS
## AND PHOTOGRAPHIC MATERIALS

### ARTIST AND DOCUMENT STORAGE FILES

**Artists portfolios, art folios, art cases, presentation cases** are all different names of portable containers for storing, transporting or displaying art work. Check out good office supply or art stores and catalogs.

For storage rather than display, consider the following items available in most office supply catalogs:

*For Flat Storage*

**The Art Rack** by Safco (Figure 10-1) is a modular, vertical filing system with eight large compartments. It's 29 by 24 by 36 inches and costs $139.95. This and other Safco products in this book are available nationwide through office products dealers, industrial supply dealers and art and engineering dealers. For a catalog or more information, contact a local dealer or write:
Safco Products Company
9300 West Research Center Road
New Hope, MN 55428

**Safco Portable Art and Drawing Portfolio** or **Smead Artist Portfolio** are low-cost, durable files with handles useful for transporting art work, film, drawings and large documents. See Figure 10-2. From $3.85 to $20

**Fellowes Portable Storage Case** is used for carrying, shipping or storing large documents flat. It includes a handle. See Figure 10-3. $23 to $27 each.

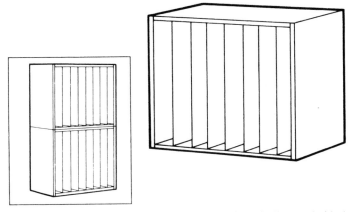

**Figure 10-1.** The Art Rack by Safco can be stacked vertically, used side-by-side or alone.

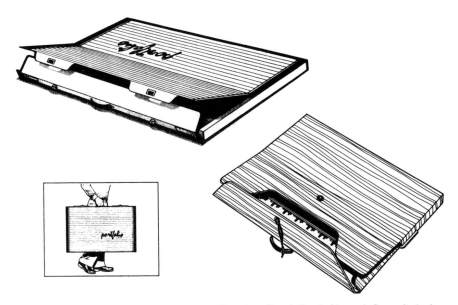

**Figure 10-2.** Safco Portable Art and Drawing Portfolio (left) and Smead Artist Portfolio

**Figure 10-3.** Fellowes Portable Storage Case

**Plan Hold** is a manufacturer of flat storage equipment that provides many different solutions. Call them for their catalog at 800/854-6868 or in California, 800/432-7486.

**Safco 5-Drawer Corrugated Fiberboard Flat Files** and **Safco 12-Drawer Budget Flat File** are economical alternatives to expensive metal files for art boards, blueprints, film, drawings, drafting paper and other oversized documents you want to store flat. See Figure 10-4.

**Figure 10-4.** Safco 5-Drawer Corrugated Fiberboard Flat Files (left) and Safco 12-Drawer Budget Flat File

**Safco 5-, 7-, and 10-Drawer Steel Flat Files** come with or without open or closed bases. See Figure 10-5. From $479 to $1,150.

**Safco Vertical Filing Systems** offer efficient systems for keeping

Figure 10-5. Safco 5-, 7-, and 10-Drawer Steel Flat Files

large sheet materials well protected, yet organized and easily accessible. Hanging Clamps form the basic unit and hold up to 100 sheets each. Choose from three systems shown in Figure 10-6: the Drop/Lift Wall Rack, $28; the Pivot Wall Rack, $125; or the Mobile Stand, $274.

### For Rolled Storage

**Safco Corrugated Fiberboard Roll Files** (Figure 10-7) are an economical way to organize and store large materials. The roll file comes in three different tube lengths.

**Fellowes Roll/Stor Stands, Perma Products Vertical Roll Organizers** and **Safco Upright Roll Files** in Figure 10-8 are good choices for deskside filing of rolled documents. They come with four rubber feet to raise the units off the ground. Choose 12 or 20 compartments. From $33 to $37.95

**Fellowes Roll/Stor Files** (Figure 10-9) feature a space-saving tambour sliding door for easy access and a neater appearance. Units can be stacked and interlocked to form a storage center for rolled blueprints, drawings, charts, etc. From $70 to $89.

**Plan Hold** offers rolled storage solutions. See listing under "Flat Storage" above.

**Safco Tube-Stor KD Roll Files** (Figure 10-10) provide an ideal low-cost system for active or inactive storage. There are two convenient

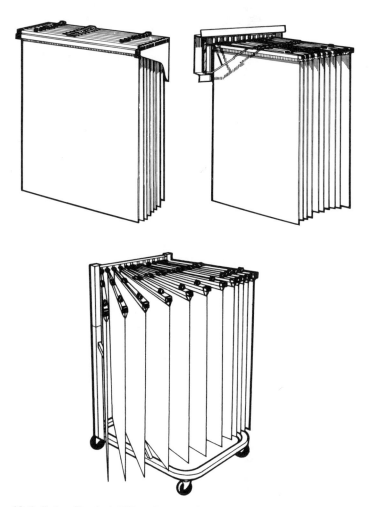

**Figure 10-6.** Safco Vertical Filing Systems Drop/Lift Wall Rack (left), Pivot Wall Rack (right) and Mobile Stand (bottom)

label areas on the inside and the outside to list rolls and locations. Units come with 18 or 32 tube spaces. Built-in tube length adjusters let you customize tube length. $39 to $52.

**Safco Mobile Roll Files** (Figure 10-11) are good for active rolled materials. The units themselves can be "rolled" to areas where they're being used. From 12 to 50 compartments.

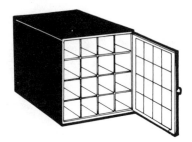

**Figure 10-7.** Safco Corrugated Fiberboard Roll File

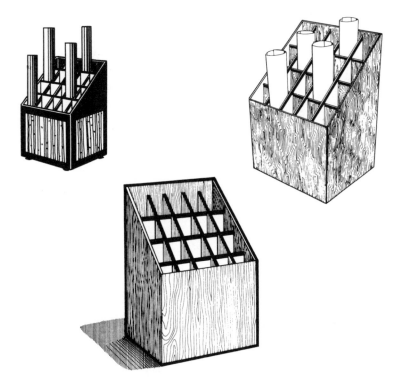

**Figure 10-8.** Fellowes Roll/Stor Stand (left), Perma Products Vertical Roll Organizer (right) and Safco Upright Roll File (bottom)

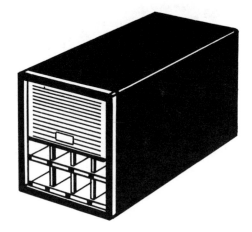

**Figure 10-9.** Fellowes Roll/Stor File

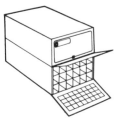

**Figure 10-10.** Safco Tube-Stor KD Roll File

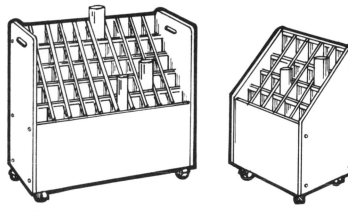

**Figure 10-11.** Safco Mobile Roll Files

## PHOTOGRAPHIC STORAGE–SLIDES AND PRINTS

**Abodia Slide Storage Cabinets** organize and store slides for easy access, scanning and assembling and have a built-in viewing screen. Cabinets hold from 1,000 to 12,000 slides. Call 800/950-7775 for information.

**Light Impressions** is a photographic and fine art storage and presentation catalog featuring archival supplies and equipment. A sampling of their products is included in this chapter. To get their catalogs contact them 800/828-6216 (or in New York, 800/828-9629).

431 Monroe Avenue
Rochester, NY 14607-3717

The following two Light Impressions items are of special interest to photographers:

**Nega\*Guard System** preserves and indexes hundreds of negatives (see Figure 10-12).

**PrintFile** (Figure 10-13) is a complete negative filing and storage system that provides rapid access to negatives and consists of transparent, polyethylene protectors in a wide range of styles and formats. Many can be filed in binders.

Simple **slide boxes** to metal **slide cabinets** will hold hundreds or thousands of slides. Light Impressions carries many of the Neumade metal cabinets. For the full line of cabinets call 203/866-7600:

**Neumade Products Corp.**
PO Box 5001
Norwalk, CT 06856

**System 4000** slide cabinets offer a complete system for storing, viewing and retrieving slides and have a viewbox for viewing 120 slides at a time. 800/325-3350

Multiplex Display Fixture Company
1555 Larkin Williams Road
Fenton, MO 63026

**20th Century Plastics** is an excellent source for photo, slide and negative pages and albums. To get their catalog call 800/767-0777:

PO Box 30022
Los Angeles, CA 90030

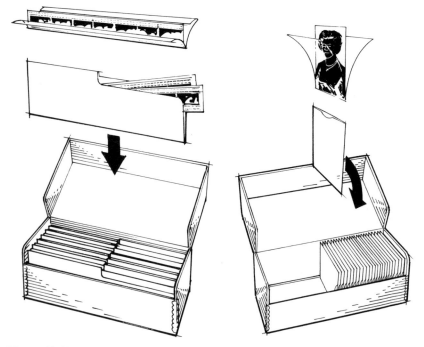

**Figure 10-12.** Nega*Guard System

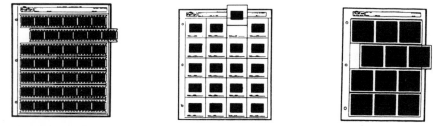

**Figure 10-13.** PrintFile Archival Preservers come in a wide range of formats for storing negatives and slides. Shown here are sleeves for 35mm negatives, 35mm mounted slides and 120 film negatives.

**Visual Horizons** offers a good range and selection of slide storage solutions, as well as other presentation materials. 716/424-5300, FAX: 716/424-5313
180 Metro Park
Rochester, NY 14623

**Figure 10-14.** Top, Perma Products Perma Pak and Fellowes Bankers Box (both lines feature boxes with separate or attached lids) and bottom, Oxford pull-drawer file, which is stackable and more accessible. Perma Products also makes a line of 100 percent recycled, recyclable boxes called EcoSafe.

## FILES AND RECORDS

When you have inactive records, look in your office supply catalog or store under the category "storage files." There you'll find boxes made of corrugated fiberboard that come in a variety of sizes and styles (see Figure 10-14). If you'll need access to files, consider getting drawer style storage boxes. Some of these are available with metal reinforcement, which provides greater durability for stacking.

If you have many, many boxes of records you want to store off site, look in the Yellow Pages under headings such as "Business

Records Storage" and "Off-site Records Storage." See also Chapter 5 for more information on filing.

If you need permanent storage boxes that are moisture resistent, consider those made by Rubbermaid shown in Figure 10-15. If you need a box that's durable and folds down when not in use, take a look at the Rubbermaid Quickcrate, also shown in Figure 10-15.

## LITERATURE ORGANIZERS

**Magazine files** or **holders** sit right on a shelf or table and are great for storing magazines, catalogs, manuals or reports. The Oxford DecoFile is made of high-impact plastic and comes in eight colors (which you could use for color coding different types of literature). Made of corrugated fiberboard, the Fellowes Magazine File costs less but will still do the job. (See Figure 10-16.)

**Literature sorters** and **organizers** come in many different styles and sizes and are great for catalog sheets, brochures and forms that you use frequently or that need to be assembled into kits. See Figure 10-17.

**Figure 10-15.** Rubbermaid Long-Term Storage File (top), Utility File (middle) and Quickcrate (bottom)

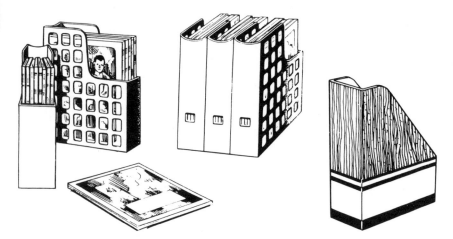

**Figure 10-16.** The Oxford DecoFile (left and middle) and Fellowes Magazine File

**Figure 10-17.** Perma Literature Trays (top left), Fellowes Premier Line Mail/Literature Center (top right), Fellowes Literature Sorter (bottom left) and Safco All Steel E-Z Stor Literature Organizer

# 11

# WORK SPACE BASICS: ENHANCING YOUR PHYSICAL WORKING ENVIRONMENT

*Quick Scan: Whether you're planning a move or you just have a sneaking suspicion your office design is missing the mark, this chapter will reveal the physical features your office should have to be a more productive, comfortable environment. Many of these features are inexpensive and easy to implement. You'll be amazed to see how the little things can make a big difference in your office, especially if you're one of the 26.6 million people in the U.S. who works at home some or all of the time.*

Do you feel like everything in your office has been put in place with Krazy Glue?

Once you get used to an office, it usually feels pretty permanent. Everything seems as if it's always been there (and always will be.) But when you become too used to your environment, you don't see the possibilities. Or if you do, you figure you can't do anything about them anyway.

I love the story that stockbroker Alan Harding shared at one of my seminars many years ago. Harding had wanted a window office. As he saw it, though, he didn't need to change offices—he just needed to install a window in a wall that faced the outside. So Harding asked his boss to have a window installed but his boss refused. For most people that would have been the end of it.

Not for Harding. You see, he spent a good part of every day in that enclosed office. He had been with the company awhile and was planning on staying a good while longer. Since he really wanted that window, he decided to spend his *own* money to have one installed—to which his boss agreed.

But that's not the end of the story. After seeing how serious Harding was about the window, his boss then decided to chip in and split the cost. What's more, when Harding came in on a Saturday to physically do the installation, his boss ended up helping. Harding says, "The whole thing wound up as a cooperative effort." It's amazing what can happen when you keep open the "windows of your mind."

There are three types of physical factors related to your office over which you have some control: your physical space, your furnishings and your total environment.

## HOW TO ORGANIZE AND MAXIMIZE YOUR WORK SPACE

Look at where and how your work space is organized. Two space factors come into play: location and layout.

## LOCATION, LOCATION, LOCATION

Where is your office located? It sounds like a simple enough question. But you probably could provide many answers.

For example, any of the following could be truthful responses: near the freeway, 40 miles from home, next to the water cooler, on the fifth floor, far away from clients or close to the marketing department.

The last time you probably thought about your location was when you changed jobs or moved to a different office. But so often we just forget about location factors. We may even experience some irritation and not realize that that irritation is directly related to our location.

So just take a moment to think about the location of your work space, to see if there are some aspects that really bother you. Take this little survey. Next to each item, write "O" for Outstanding, "S" for Satisfactory, "N" for Needs Improvement or "NA" for Not Applicable (or not important):

1. Commuting distance
2. Proximity to colleagues
3. Proximity to vendors or suppliers
4. Proximity to your market–clients, customers or patients
5. Traffic flow in or near your office
6. Privacy
7. Noise
8. Lighting
9. Proximity to equipment and supplies
10. Proximity to personal or professional services–e.g., restaurants, shops, attorney, accountant

Take a look at any "N's" you've marked. Are there any ways you could change or modify undesirable locations? Don't just accept things the way they are, especially if your performance and productivity are really suffering. Be creative–like Alan Harding.

## LATITUDE IN YOUR LAYOUT

Now take a look at your **layout**–the location and arrangement of the furniture and equipment within your own office space. There are two essentials of every good office layout: adequate **work space** and **storage space**. Sometimes it's hard to tell, however, if work and storage spaces are adequate, especially if a desktop hasn't been seen in years, filing is less than routine and a move hasn't occurred in more than a decade.

Differentiate between work and storage space. Unfortunately, in far too many offices, the distinction is nonexistent. Work and storage spaces are all lumped (and I do mean lumped) together. You'll be making great headway if you can separate these two basic spaces.

The biggest problem comes when your desktop becomes more a storage space than a work space. Too often the desk becomes a place where things are *waiting to happen*; instead, make it a place for *action*. Think of your desk as an airport runway. If you were a pilot, you wouldn't find spare parts in the middle of the runway. They would be in the hangar. So, remove the obstacles from your work surface and **clear your desk for action!** Get out of the habit of keeping *everything* at your fingertips.

How do you break the keep-the-clutter-close habit? First, **set up appropriate systems for paperwork and projects** (see Chapter 4 on desktop management, Chapter 5 on paper files and Chapter 9 on managing details).

Second, **put only those items you *use most frequently*–**be they accessories, supplies, furniture or equipment–**closest to you.**

Third, make sure you have enough work space! I generally recommend at least **two surfaces plus adequate, accessible storage space** for most people. The surface right in front of you should be your primary work surface and ideally should contain only things you use every day. This is the area where you are doing your most common work activities. A secondary surface off to the side or behind you could be used as a work area for a particular activity, such as telephoning or using your computer. This secondary area could also provide storage for items you use frequently such as your daily paperwork system, telephone/address directory and stapler.

An **L-shape** layout uses two surfaces–a primary one such as a desk and another one off to the left or right side, which when attached is called a **return.** A return is a small, narrow extension of a desk that is designed to hold a typewriter (or can be adapted to hold a computer terminal). See a desk with a return in Figure 11-1. You can order a desk with either a right or left return.

You can see in Figure 11-2 how to easily create an L-shape layout by putting a table alongside your desk. Or if you don't like using a desk at all, try two tables at right angles shown in Figure 11-3.

A **U-shape** layout, as in Figure 11-4, gives you more work surface and usually more accessible storage. I use a modified U-shape in my office–I call it a **J-shape.** I have combined modular computer furniture with two two-drawer filing cabinets and a three-shelf bookcase to provide additional work surfaces and storage space. Figure 11-5 shows my office layout.

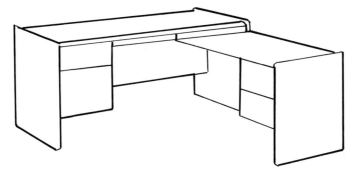

**Figure 11-1.** Desk with right return

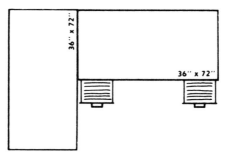

**Figure 11-2.** L-shape layout with table alongside desk

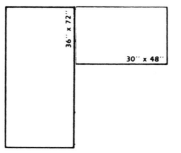

**Figure 11-3.** L-shape layout with two tables at right angles.

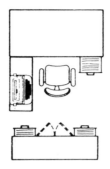

**Figure 11-4.** U-shape layout

The **triangular** layout in Figure 11-6 takes advantage of a corner, makes good use of angles and plays up the importance of the desk as a focal point.

A **parallel** layout, shown in Figure 11-7, places the main work surface, such as a desk, parallel to and in front of a storage unit (a credenza or lateral file cabinet, for example) or another work surface, such as a table.

### DESIGN YOUR OWN LAYOUT

Get objective about an existing or proposed office layout. Make a quick, little sketch of your layout. Or better yet, particularly if you're planning a move, buy some graph or engineering paper (quadrille pads work great), draw an outline of your office to scale and make paper cutouts of your furniture to scale. Cutouts work great if you have a small office space and your furniture is going to be a tight fit. Also, it's a lot easier moving cutouts around on paper than moving the real things. I've yet to see anyone throw out their back moving cutouts around.

Another option is to buy a Stanley Tools Project Planner Office Designer kit to help you with your space planning. The kit, as shown in Figure 11-8, comes with a grid sheet called a GRIDBOARD and hundreds of reusable, peel-and-stick office furniture and equipment symbols pre-drafted by an architect. Just press the symbols on the GRIDBOARD to design your layout. (The kit is listed in the chapter resource guide.)

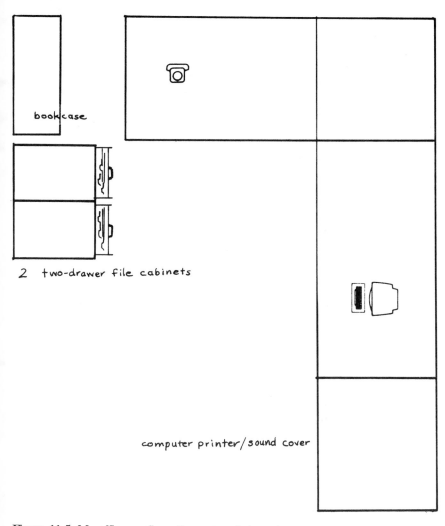

bookcase

2  two-drawer file cabinets

computer printer/sound cover

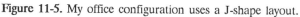

**Figure 11-5.** My office configuration uses a J-shape layout.

Even if you're not moving, remember you're allowed to move things around. I consulted with a public relations executive who had one of the most beautifully designed and equipped offices I had ever seen. But she had been designed into a corner.

She had a huge pedestal desk, with a large, cumbersome chair. Behind her was a custom-built, corner credenza with all kinds of

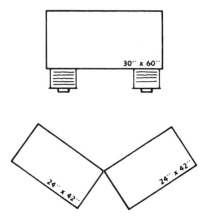

**Figure 11-6.** Triangular layout

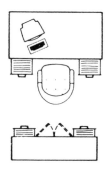

**Figure 11-7.** Parallel layout with a desk and credenza

shelves and drawers, which she never used. Instead the surfaces of her desk and credenza were piled high with papers.

Why didn't she use the credenza? Simple—she didn't have enough space to easily move the chair and access the credenza. My solution: move the desk farther out from the credenza! Why hadn't she thought of moving the desk? Probably because the designer had indicated where the furniture was to go and there it remained. Also, the desk top was a heavy piece of glass. These factors suggested real *permanence.*

Alexis Kyprianou, a colleague of mine, related how she once had a boss who spent a lot of money on a design that wasn't functional.

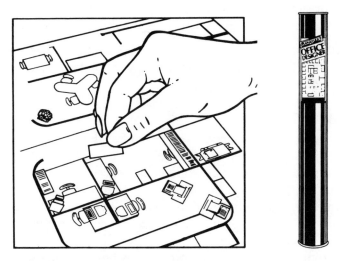

**Figure 11-8.** Stanley Tools Project Planner Office Designer kit (many of the figures for this chapter were done using this handy kit)

The boss insisted, "We'll make it work!" What he didn't realize was that it becomes *real* work when the design doesn't work.

Once people are in their offices or have been designed into a corner, the thought of changing a layout simply doesn't occur. Here's a chance to check out your layout. Quickly sketch out the main elements of your office space–furniture, equipment, walls, windows, light sources, plants. Don't worry about scale at this point.

Ask yourself these questions:

- Is your layout convenient?
- Are the things you use most often close at hand?
- Do you have enough storage and work space?
- Do you have enough space for your equipment, especially your computer equipment?
- Do you like the way your office is configured to meet with others–co-workers, clients or customers?
- Does your layout invite irritating distractions? (For example, do you always catch someone's eye as he or she walks by?)

• Do you have different areas in your office for different types of work or activity, e.g., telephoning, computer work, meeting with clients? How and where do you like to do various kinds of work?

All of these factors may enter into the kind of office layout you can live with. Some of these factors are very subtle but their subtlety shouldn't diminish their importance.

## PROXEMICS

One subtle factor concerns **proxemics**–the study of spatial configurations and interpersonal relations. Did you know that the seating arrangements in your office influence the relationships you have with your colleagues as well as your clients? Your seating arrangements make subtle statements. If, for example, in Figure 11-9, you are "A," sitting behind your desk, and you're meeting with "B," you are in a distinctly authoritarian, powerful position. This configuration may be totally appropriate when meeting with a client but if you're meeting with a colleague, perhaps the side by side configuration in Figure 11-10 would be more effective.

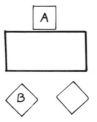

Figure 11-9. Authoritarian configuration with "A" having the advantage

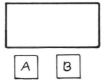

Figure 11-10. Side by side configuration

## THE DOORWAY

Decide, too, where to place your desk in relation to the doorway. If you're facing the doorway (or the opening of your cubicle) and you're in a high people traffic zone, you may find interruption is your constant companion. Turning your back to the doorway may appear too severe or even anti-social. You may prefer instead to angle your desk so as not to catch everyone's eye but to remain responsive.

When Kim Villeneuve was a divisional vice president for The Broadway department store in Southern California, she changed her position toward the doorway, depending on the type of work she was doing. Since she needed to remain open to staff most of the day, she generally sat facing the door. But when she used the telephone and didn't want interruptions, she would swing her chair around to the credenza behind her. Her telephone sat on the credenza and there she did her phone work without inviting interruption. The credenza became an area designated for important telephone work, without interruptions of people as well as any distracting paperwork on her desk.

If you have meetings in your office and you tend to run meetings in which you assert your authority, you would select a rectangular table, as shown in Figure 11-11, and sit at the head. If, however, you tend to meet informally and you're trying to foster that "good ol' team spirit," select a round table.

Of course space considerations as well as purpose will affect your final layout decisions.

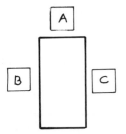

**Figure 11-11.** Meeting at a rectangular table with "A" in charge at the head of the table

## YOUR EVOLVING WORK STYLE

Finally, consider how you like to work when you design your layout and remain flexible. As your work style needs change, so should your design.

Dr. David Snyder, a physician in Fresno, California, had a desk in his private office with a credenza behind him. Then he eliminated the credenza. He used his desk to process patient files and other paperwork quickly and efficiently. He said, "I will never have a credenza again–that's where I put stuff I didn't have time to do."

Today he has added a two-drawer lateral filing cabinet behind him. The close proximity of the cabinet gives him access to reference files. He uses the top of the cabinet for his daily paperwork system, which includes a vertical rack that holds active project files.

## FURNISHINGS THAT FIT

Walk into your office as if you were walking into it for the first time. Pretend you've just arrived from Mars (some days don't we all feel that way!). Look at your office with fresh eyes and notice all your furnishings–your furniture, equipment, accessories and supplies.

Are they all well-organized, in good repair and well placed? Are they as functional as they should be? Do you have enough storage space?

## FURNITURE AND EQUIPMENT

With today's changing technology and workforce, *flexibility* is a key word to apply to your choice of furniture and equipment. **Modular** furniture (often called "systems furniture") with interchangeable components works great, particularly in automated offices, because it's flexible, can save floor space and yet can increase the amount of work surface.

The flexibility and functionality of modular furniture is particularly important if you'll ever be moving your office. Since buying modular furniture for my office, I have moved once. Each of my offices required a different configuration. Figure 11-12 shows how I was able to take my original configuration from my old office and simply reverse the components to fit my current office requirements.

Figure 11-13 shows you components from The WorkManager

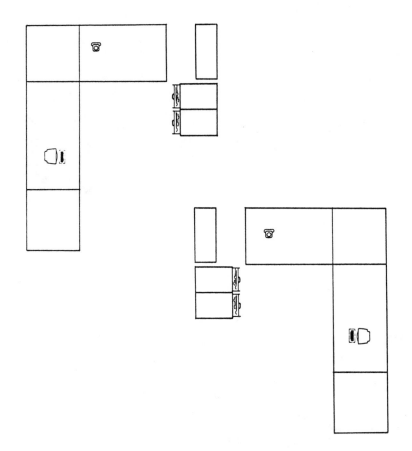

**Figure 11-12.** I was able to take my old layout (top) and easily reverse it (bottom) to fit my new office because I have modular furniture.

System, well-designed modular computer furniture made by MicroComputer Accessories, Inc. Notice that the combination of a single compact pencil drawer and the notched side panels provide completely unobstructed leg-room, making sure you don't wrack up your knees as you swivel to different areas. If you need more drawers, consider getting a portable drawer unit or file cabinet on casters. MicroComputer Accessories makes a desk height file cabinet with two file drawers and an underdesk file cabinet with a utility drawer and a file drawer. Sometimes such portable units are called **pedestals.** Some modular work stations, such as those by Biotec, are

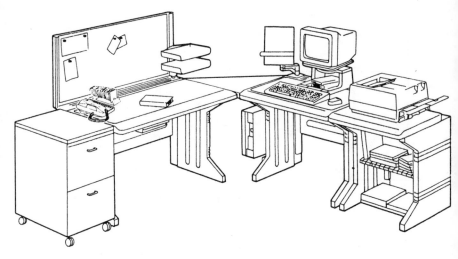

**Figure 11-13.** The WorkManager System features a variety of modular, computer work station components and accessories, many of which are shown here.

also available with recessed shelves under each work table for storage.

## ERGONOMICS

The WorkManager System is a fine example of applying **ergonomics** to office furniture design. Ergonomics is the science of making the work environment compatible with people so they can work more comfortably and productively. Ergonomics looks at the dimensions of work tables, desks and chairs and matches them to the wide range of body sizes and shapes according to certain recommended standards that are illustrated in Figure 11-14.

When you pay close attention to these standards you can avoid such symptoms as fatigue, eyestrain, blurred vision, headaches, stiff muscles, irritability and loss of feeling in fingers and wrists. The longer you work at a desk or computer, the more you need to consider the importance of correct angles of eyes, arms, hands, legs and feet.

Use a good **ergonomic chair** whose back and seat are adjustable. A good chair is more than a piece of furniture; it's a necessity for long hours of computer work. A bad one is literally a pain in the back. Adjust the height of your chair so that your thighs are parallel

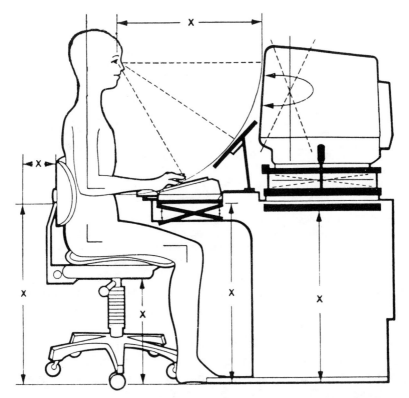

**Figure 11-14.** Ergonomics—The Human Factors (adapted from Biotec chart)

to the floor when your feet are resting flat on the floor. You should have lower back support from the backrest, which should adjust to fit your spine's contours. The seat of the chair should be curved.

Apply ergonomics from head to toe (see Figure 11-15). Putting an **anti-glare filter** on your computer screen reduces glare and eyestrain. A **foot rest** not only supports the feet, but the angle is beneficial for the back and circulation.

Don't underestimate the importance of ergonomics in relation to your **computer keyboard.** Do you like the touch and feel of the keys, the sound they make and the design of the keyboard? I like the clickety-clack touch and feel of the keys on my Dell keyboard (which is manufactured by Alps) as well as the raised dots on the "F" and "J" keys, which keep my fingers in correct alignment. But I'd prefer that the function keys were on the left as on my previous

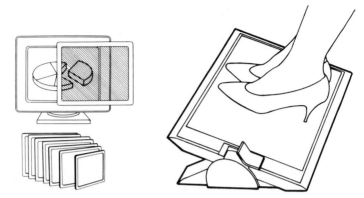

**Figure 11-15.** From head to toe: Curtis Glass Filter Plus reduces glare 95 percent, absorbs up to 98 percent VLF radiation and comes in seven sizes; FootEase is an adjustable foot rest made by MicroComputer Accessories, Inc. that lets you change the angle and height of your feet, thereby benefitting ankles, knees, hips and back.

IBM keyboard. While life's a tradeoff, you can easily buy a replacement keyboard for your computer if you're not happy with the standard issue.

In fact, your keyboard is one of the most important factors that determines just how happy you are with your computer as a whole. It's not expensive to replace your keyboard—it will cost you anywhere from $60 to $150.

Remember, too, that good ergonomic *work habits* will make a big difference in addition to selecting the right furniture and equipment. Be sure to stay at least 28 inches (about an arm's length) from your computer monitor, especially if it's a color monitor. You should also maintain a distance of 4 feet from the sides or back of any other monitor in your workplace, even if a wall separates you from the other monitor. Many studies show that electromagnetic fields emitted from monitors at unsafe distances are linked to cancer, miscarriages, birth defects in unborn babies and other health problems.

It's also a good idea to pause every 20 minutes or so to look away from the screen and to change your close-up focus by looking at distant objects in order to prevent eyestrain.

How you use your keyboard, especially if you use it many hours every day, can have an adverse physiological effect on your hands. There are several ergonomic measures you can take to prevent hand disorders such as tenosynovitis and carpal tunnel syndrome. Take a five-minute break every hour to relax your hands. Wrists should be straight while typing and at the same height as your elbows. Rest your wrists on the computer work surface, if there's room, or buy a wrist rest that attaches to your keyboard. I'm using a comfortable, padded wrist rest from the Daisy Wheel Ribbon Company. (They're at 3325 E. Shelby St., Ontario, CA 91764 at 800/266-5585 or 714/989-5585.)

**Positioning** and **placement** of equipment is an ergonomic factor that relates to left- or right-handedness. At my Positively Organized! Office seminars I ask participants whether their telephone should go on the right or left side of the desk if they are right-handed. Answers are usually evenly divided between "left" and "right." The correct answer is "left." If you're right-handed you'll be writing with your right hand. So place the phone on the left so that the phone doesn't get in the way. You'll want to hold the phone with your left hand to your left ear, leaving your right hand free to write.

Consider, too, how you like to turn your body in relation to equipment. Do you prefer a typewriter or computer on a left or right hand return? Where do you want to place the copy stand and materials—on the left or right side of your typewriter or computer? Most people just don't stop and think about the things that they use every day.

Check to see that your work surfaces are the right height from the floor. Your keyboard should sit on a surface that's generally 26 inches from the floor but your writing work surface should be 29 inches high.

The **accessibility principle** should influence your decisions about equipment placement, too. Even a work surface has areas that are more convenient than others. Angle your computer, for example, off to the side for occasional use; place it right in front of you for frequent or constant use.

One last tip on equipment: avoid the "$12,000 paper clip." It's the little things that count as one man found out after losing two $12,000 copiers because of paper clips that somehow became lodged inside. This man now uses a $3 magnet attached to a piece of velcro on his copier to hold paper clips.

## ACCESSORIES AND SUPPLIES

In my consulting work I notice that clients either have too few or too many accessories for their paperwork, telephone and computer. Those who have too few generally lump their work all together on the desk, on tables, on shelves, in drawers and on the floor. Those with too many (if one pencil holder is good, six are better) collect accessories along with good intentions. They buy a new accessory every time they're inspired to "get organized." Soon the accessory becomes just another catchall rather than a clearly defined tool. The original purpose is too soon forgotten.

Any time you add a new accessory to your environment, define its purpose and *get in the habit of using it.* And from time to time, check to see if it's doing its job. If it has outlived its usefulness, *get rid of it!* Let's look at some of the most useful work space accessories (see also chapters 3, 4, 5 and 10).

### PAPERWORK ACCESSORIES

One of the most versatile paperwork accessories is the **expanding collator.** It comes in plastic or aluminum with 12, 18 or 24 slots. If you're a CPA or an attorney, use it for large, bulky active client files that you're referring to daily or several times a week. (While it's always safer to put client files away each night in filing cabinets, using the collator is a good intermediate step for anyone who is still piling files on couches and floors.)

Use the collator near your copier or computer printer to store large quantities (up to 500 sheets) of different types of paper. I use a 12-slot collator that sits atop my computer printer sound cover.

You can always use the collator for its original purpose, too—collating! It's great for assembling or sorting literature and handouts. (See Chapter 4 for an illustration of a collator.)

The **stationery holder** is a wonderful accessory to hold letterhead, envelopes, forms and note paper. Some stationery holders are designed to fit inside a desk drawer; others sit on top of furniture or on a shelf. Place a stationery holder where you'll be using it.

**Magazine files** or **holders** are indispensable boxes for storing catalogs and directories as well as magazines. They're usually made out of plastic, acrylic or corrugated fiberboard. (see Chapters 4 and 10 for some illustrated examples.)

If you use a typewriter or computer, use a **copyholder** with a movable marker. There are many different types for the computer (Figure 11-16) but the main idea is to get one that can be placed at the same focal distance as the screen. It's hard on the eyes to keep refocusing to accommodate different focal lengths. The Curtis Clip attaches to the monitor and swings out of the way when not in use. The Wesystem Copy Hinge also attaches to your monitor (including a laptop) and can hold documents as big as printouts. Wilson Jones WideForm Copyholder holds two printouts at once. MicroComputer Accessories, Inc., Tilt 'n Turn+ is a combination monitor stand and copyholder in which the copyholder sits right between the monitor and keyboard. MicroComputer Accessories also makes a handy copyholder for your laptop called the Portable PC Easel.

If you have wall partitions, consider installing one of the **wall unit paper management systems** now available. As office space decreases into more flexible, partitioned "cubicles," using vertical wall space for accessories makes sense. Wall systems help you get paper off your desk and yet make it accessible and organized.

If you do a lot of hole punching, stapling, folding or trimming, consider getting accessories to help you automate these processes. **Electric hole punches** and **staplers** can save you a lot of time. (Panasonic and Swingline make several good models; Swingline even makes a 5,000-staple cartridge that's easy to load and eliminates frequent refilling.) **Letter folding machines** are available from Legal Tabs Co. in Colorado, 800/322-3022 or Premier in Indiana, 219/563-0641.

At a recent office supply trade show, I saw two **paper cutters** that caught my eye. The Ingento Office Paper Station is a paper trimmer than includes a built-in tape dispenser, stapler, staple remover and storage tray for small office supplies such as paper clips. The Ingento Personal Trimmer (Figure 11-17) is a miniature paper cutter that measures five by eight by 1½ inches. It includes a two-section storage tray inside for small supplies. (Ingento can be reached at 11000 S. Lavergne, Oak Lawn, IL 60453, 800/327-1336.)

## TELEPHONE ACCESSORIES AND FEATURES

Selecting a basic telephone today has become a major decision given all the different features and accessories that are available. Look for these features:

**Figure 11-16.** Oxford CopyKeeper (includes a side storage compartment for "to-be-typed" materials); Oxford Flexible Arm Copyholder; Oxford CopyCaddy; Oxford Desk Top Copyholder has a rolling ruler guide; Wesystem Copy Hinge; MicroComputer Accessories, Inc. Tilt 'n Turn+; Curtis Clip

**Figure 11-17.** Ingento Personal Trimmer

- speaker phone with on-hook dialing
- automatic on-hook re-dialing
- automatic memory dial
- compatibility with your headset, telephone answering machine or other telecommunications equipment.

If you're on the phone a lot (at least one to two hours a day) or you have any neck or shoulder trouble, a **telephone headset** is the answer. Besides being more comfortable, a headset frees up your hands to take notes, handle paperwork or operate a keyboard. I always use a headset whenever I do interviews for articles or seminars or when I know I'll need to write or type during the call. If you don't like the look or feel of a headset, at the very least use a **shoulder rest,** a device that attaches to your telephone handset and allows you hands-free movement.

**Make sure your headset is compatible with your phone equipment.** Some headsets will not work with *electronic* phones. If your phone has any of the typical bells and whistles—redial, speaker phone, memory dial—it's probably electronic. I discovered my first headset would only operate with a *mechanical, modular* phone, the traditional kind of phone with a removable handset (the part you

320 ORGANIZED TO BE THE BEST!

hold in your hand). So in addition to purchasing the headset, I also purchased a standard, mechanical phone that I only use with the headset. Standard phones, however, have become harder and harder to find because very few are still being made.

Where do you buy a headset? Radio Shack has headsets, as do many stores that sell telephones and other electronic equipment. Look for headsets in mail order catalogs, too, such as The Sharper Image from San Francisco. Office machine dealers may have them, also. Again, I can't emphasize enough the importance of compatibility. Very often sales people will not be aware of compatibility problems, so either bring your phone to the store to check it out or if you order a headset, make sure it is completely refundable.

Several years ago I discovered a company that sells headsets that are compatible with *any* phone. The company is called Plantronics (800/662-3902) and their headsets start at $89.95. I've been using a Plantronics headset for years (see Chapter 3 for a picture of mine).

A **telephone answering machine** is a must in our office. There are many on the market today with a variety of features from which to choose. Here are some features that are nice to have:

- ability to pick up messages off site, preferably without having to carry a special remote control unit
- ability to change outgoing messages off site
- if you have two phone lines, a two-line answering machine that can answer either line.

And to maximize your telephone time, use a **clock** placed strategically in front of you. And if you frequently place calls to another time zone, use a second clock specifically for that time zone. A **countdown timer** (available at Radio Shack) will help you consciously choose how much time you want to spend on each call.

## COMPUTER ACCESSORIES

Protect your eyes. Make sure your screen has an **anti-glare filter** (as mentioned earlier) or a protective coating. Purchase an anti-glare filter at your local computer store or through one of the catalogs listed at the end of the chapter. Or if you're buying a monitor, consider one such as the Amdek brand that comes with a protective mesh coating on the glass screen. (If you buy such a monitor, however, realize you can't touch the screen with your fingers or clean the screen with a cloth; the only way to clean it is with a mini-vacuum for computers or with a can of compressed air from a camera store.)

The best filter is a glass circular polarizer made by Polaroid (Norwood, Massachusetts). It costs about $100. (For names of dealers call 800/225-2770 or write to Polaroid Corp., listed in the resource guide.) The next-best filter is a neutral-density (gray) glass that costs about $60. Although widely available, plastic filters cost almost the same as glass but are much less durable.

Set your monitor on a **tilt stand** if you need to adjust the proper angle of the screen to your eyes.

Protect your ears. Enclose your noisy letter quality or dot matrix printer in a **sound cover.** Use a sound cover if the sound from your printer is disturbing to you or co-workers or can be heard during telephone calls. Check that your sound cover and stand have slots in the right places for feeding paper to and from your printer. Your sound cover should also come equipped with an automatic cooling fan. Make sure the switch for the fan is conveniently located.

Protect your floppy diskettes. Buy **plastic diskette boxes** with divider tabs to store programs, files and backups on disks.

To guard against the possibility of electrical power disturbances wiping out data, use a **surge protector,** also called a **surge suppressor** (see Figure 11-18).

**Figure 11-18.** WorkManager System SurgeManager is a surge protector for computers and peripherals and is made by MicroComputer Accessories, Inc.

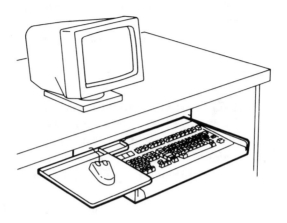

**Figure 11-19.** MicroComputer Accessories, Inc. makes a keyboard extender called the Underdesk Keyboard Drawer, which is shown here with their MouseDeck—this is a comfortable, efficient way to use and store a keyboard and mouse together.

Adapt a desk return that's too shallow with a **keyboard extender** as shown in Figure 11-19 that conveniently pulls out your keyboard and hides it under the cpu (central processing unit) and monitor when not in use. A keyboard extender is not only a space saver, but it's also a good accessory to lower a keyboard that's too high for comfortable typing.

Speaking of the keyboard, protect yours from dust, dirt and spills with a "keyskin," a special, thin, molded, plastic membrane that allows keys to be clearly visible, protected and usable. Also, be sure to cover your computer when it's not in use.

Straighten up your computer cables and wires—for aesthetics as well as safety—with cable management accessories. Velcro makes a "Wire Management" line of clips, ties and covers that will keep cables in their place.

Protect your computer system from theft with LOK-KIT from Qualtec Data Products Inc. in California at 800/628-4413 or 415/490-8911. This general purpose security kit installs in seconds without tools.

```
                    OFFICE SUPPLY REQUEST FORM
_____
_____

                                    Date:    _____

Requested by:   _____   Due by:   _____

Department:     _____   Estimated Cost:  _____

*Department Manager's Approval:   _____
(When cost estimated exceeds $25)

Description of Goods:   _____

_____

_____


Note:   Office supplies are ordered twice a week - Tuesday and
        Thursday only.  Visits to Price Club are limited to once
        every two weeks, please keep this in mind when ordering
        supplies.  Your lack of forethought does not constitute
        an emergency on our part.
```

**Figure 11-20.** This office supply form was developed by clients after participating in one of my office training programs.

## KEEPING SUPPLIES IN ORDER

Deciding what supplies to buy isn't as much a challenge as keeping your supplies organized and stocked. The following will help:

- Organize your supplies for easy access, keeping the most frequently used most accessible.
- Group supplies by type as well as by frequency of use.
- Label supply shelves, drawers or cabinets and/or use color coding.
- Replenish supplies regularly and systematically and have one person in charge of the ordering process. Develop a form like the one in Figure 11-20 to simplify the process.
- Place a re-order chart near supplies for people to indicate whenever a supply is getting low or for special requests.
- Place re-order slips strategically close to the bottom of supply boxes: whoever gets a slip turns it in to the person who orders supplies.
- Prepare a "frequently ordered items" form for each vendor you use, listing items and stock or catalog numbers; refer to these forms to speed up the ordering process.

## YOUR TOTAL ENVIRONMENT

How do you feel about your office space? Do you feel comfortable there? Is it *you*? Is there something about it that rubs you the wrong way (or the right way)?

There are five important environmental factors that affect how you feel about your office space: aesthetics, air, comfort and safety, lighting and privacy. See to what degree any of these environmental factors influence your feelings.

## AESTHETICS

If you spend at least one third of every week day in your office—that's at least eight hours a day—you deserve to have a working environment that's aesthetically pleasing.

## COLOR

Many studies have revealed the "psychology of color," showing the effect of color on our emotions and state of mind. They have found, for example, that red excites us; in fact, when red is used in restaurants it is supposed to make us salivate! But used in moderation, red can be a great accent color, particularly for a sales or marketing office where you want an upbeat atmosphere.

Blue is perhaps the most universally pleasing color and is generally a calm color, depending on the shade, of course. Grays, browns and other neutrals are even more subdued. All three can work well in professional offices.

Burgundy and deep forest green are rich colors that can work well together or separately in professional offices, too. They can be used as main or accent colors.

Use of "trendy colors" can give a more contemporary feeling, which may be important for your type of office. You do run the risk, however, of having those colors go out of style more quickly. Use of more traditional colors and color schemes avoids this problem and may convey a more permanent, solid business environment. Base color decisions on the nature of your business, who comes into your office and your own particular preferences.

Choose light and dark colors to enhance your space. Lighter colors tend to open up space and work well in smaller offices.

Darker colors make rooms feel smaller, cozier and more intimate. They work well in large office spaces that could otherwise appear too intimidating or sterile.

Don't ignore the impact of color. The question to ask is, What are the right colors for you?

## PERSONALIZATION

Color alone is not enough. Your office is not just a place to work. It should be a reflection of you. It needs to be personalized with objects you love.

In fact, why not have objects you love around you, such as art, photos or plants? Just remember, they should complement not clutter your work space.

If you've become bored with your office, consider moving personalized objects to different places. We all need variety; just moving things around or changing objects from time to time can make a big difference.

## AIR

What can you do about the air you breathe? First of all, be aware of it. Second, see if you can change any unpleasant atmospheric conditions or adapt to them.

## AIRBORNE TOXINS

The most obvious toxin in the air is cigarette smoke. Some studies have shown that cigarette smoke is more harmful to someone nearby inhaling "secondary" smoke than the smoke inhaled by the actual smoker. If smoke is a problem for you, stay away from it!

Many cities and companies now specify that smokers go outside or to other specially designated areas to smoke. If your city or company doesn't have such requirements, consider working toward establishing them. Sure it'll take some of your precious time, but isn't your health precious enough? At the very least, make sure that office workers who smoke have an air cleaner or purifier unit on their desk to remove at least some of the smoke.

As far as other toxic substances, such as asbestos, read your newspaper to stay current on new discoveries and legislation. Notice, too, whether you experience certain symptoms such as nausea and dizziness only in your office environment. Invisible toxic substances pose a real problem in detection and in identification but we're bound to see more research on this in the future.

## TEMPERATURE

Here's one of those factors that is far easier to adapt to than to change. I can't tell you how often I have complained to facilities managers about the temperature, which for me is almost always too cold in modern buildings, where you are at the mercy of a thermostat that either isn't working or is adjusted to somebody else's body!

I used to work for an aerospace company. Our department was on the same thermostat as the computer room. It was always "freeeezing" in the office. I kept a little portable heater on under my desk. (Fire regulations where you work may prohibit this solution.)

My office today doesn't usually get cold enough for a heater, but I keep an extra sweater in the office at all times, particularly during the summer when the air conditioning tends toward the cool side. I also close off most of the vents in my office in the summertime when the air conditioning is running fast and furiously. If your office is too hot, your only option may be to keep complaining or work at home if possible. But recognize that temperature is a factor in your productivity and your attitude toward your workplace.

## COMFORT AND SAFETY

Fifty percent of disabling office accidents are the result of slips or falls—most of which could have been prevented.

Keep floors clear of cords, cables and other objects. Even a rubber band on the floor can be a hazard. One office worker slipped on a rubber band, breaking his arm in two places and crushing his elbow. He lost six weeks of work.

Our discussion of ergonomics in this chapter certainly relates to comfort and safety. Check out your chair and your equipment according to the ergonomics chart and criteria discussed earlier.

# LIGHTING

Lighting is related to comfort and safety, as well as aesthetics. Select the right **amount**, the right **kinds** and the right **direction** to make lighting work best for you.

Make sure you have enough light. Some offices are too dark and depressing. Interior offices usually need additional lighting. That one panel in the ceiling just won't do it.

Make sure you don't have too much of the wrong kind of lighting in the wrong places. If you're using a computer terminal, all those overhead fluorescent lights could be causing irritating glare. Better to use a lower level of overhead lighting combined with **task lighting**, localized sources of lighting for specific tasks or areas. An example of task lighting is a desk lamp that sheds light on desktop paperwork only and stays off the computer screen.

Balance fluorescent lighting with either a natural light source (a window) or incandescent lighting. Fluorescent lighting by itself is very hard on the eyes.

In addition, some research studies indicate fluorescent lighting may be emitting harmful ultraviolet rays that cause such symptoms as fatigue and dizziness. Some retail stores are putting **ultraviolet shields** on their fluorescent lights. You may also consider replacing your fluorescent lighting with **full spectrum lights**, also called **health lights** or **Durolights**.

# PRIVACY

The last environmental factor concerns the need for privacy in your office. Privacy usually comes from some sense of *enclosure*, which can include visual as well as sound barriers. Having some barriers, be they walls, movable panels, plants, bookcases or file cabinets, is important for most people.

For one thing, effective communication needs privacy. Studies have shown that employees who sit in an open, "bull pen" environment tend to communicate less freely. On the other hand, employees who have some measure of enclosure and privacy tend to communicate more freely and openly.

Privacy also can improve productivity. Most people need to have their own space to focus, concentrate and shut out some of the distractions. A smaller, more controlled environment is also less stressful for most people.

## RESOURCE GUIDE

## FURNITURE AND EQUIPMENT

Whenever possible, see furniture and equipment "in person." At the very least, get color chips of finish or fabric or actual samples. *Never* buy a chair without sitting in it first. Suppliers are listed from different parts of the country; you can often save significantly on shipping when you order in a geographical area that's nearby.

**BIOTEC SYSTEMS** is the line of modular, computer furniture that I have in my office. One reason I selected this line was because I needed a sound cover for my letter-quality printer and its cut-sheet feeder. Biotec makes a large, roll-top sound cover and stand (Figure 11-21). To get the name of your local representative or to receive a free copy of the BIOTEC Design Guide call 800/543-1605 or in Ohio, 513/870-4400.

Hamilton Sorter Co., Inc.
PO Box 8
Fairfield, OH 45014

**Figure 11-21.** Biotec makes a roll-top, printer sound cover and stand, which I use in my office. I also use their work tables with utility shelves underneath (not shown).

**Business & Institutional Furniture Co., Inc.** mail order catalog includes the lowest prices on furniture (they'll meet or beat any price) and guarantees all products for 15 years. 800/558-8662
611 N. Broadway

Milwaukee, WI 53202-0902

**Global Business Furniture** is a mail-order catalog featuring a wide selection of furniture and equipment. 800/645-1232
63 Hemlock Dr.
Hempstead, NY 11550

**MicroComputer Accessories, Inc.** manufactures more than 100 microcomputer work station components and accessories that are as attractive as they are functional. 800/521-8270 (in California, 213/301-9400)
PO Box 66911
Los Angeles, CA 90066-0911

**National Business Furniture** is a mail order catalog that offers a substantial selection of furniture at discount prices with a guarantee for six years (except for normal upholstery wear). They provide fast shipping on 10,000 different products. 800/558-1010 (in Wisconsin, 800/242-0030)
National Business Furniture, Inc.
222 E. Michigan St.
Milwaukee, WI 53202-9956

**Omnicron Electronics** makes professional voice and time logging systems to help you automatically record and track important conversations. 203/928-0377
PO Box 623
Putnam, CT 06260

**The WorkManager System** is a complete line of modular, well-designed computer furniture and accessories. (See MicroComputer Accessories, Inc. above.)

## ACCESSORIES AND SUPPLIES

**Allsop Inc.** manufactures a line of computer and office equipment accessories and supplies that include diskette cases, computer cleaning kits and an "Office Care System" for complete office machine maintenance. These items are available through computer and office dealers or call the company in Bellingham, Washington, for more information at 206/734-9090.

**American Computer Supply** is a mail order company that offers discounts on many items, usually same day shipping (with approved

credit) and a 90-day guarantee. Call 800/527-0832 to get a sample catalog.
2828 Forest Lane
Dallas, TX 75234

**Comcor** has a complete line of telephone products with a 30-day guarantee. 800/221-3085
7 Odell Plaza
Yonkers, NY 10701

**Curtis Manufacturing Company, Inc.** manufactures more than 100 computer and electronic accessory products, which are available through dealers. 800/548-4900 or 603/532-4123
30 Fitzgerald Dr.
Jaffrey, NH 03452

**Devoke Data Products** is a mail-order catalog specializing in furniture, accessories and supplies for information processing, with a 30-day guarantee and 24-hour shipment on supply items. 408/980-1347.
PO Box 58051
Santa Clara, CA 95052-8051

**Global Computer Supplies** catalog offers computer supplies, accessories and furniture at a discount with a 30-day satisfaction guarantee, fast shipping and service. 800/8GLOBAL–800/845-6225, in New York, 800/645-1232 or 516/794-1234.
11 Harbor Park Dr.
Port Washington, NY 11050

**Inmac's** award-winning mail order catalog offers one of the best selections of quality computer supplies, accessories, furniture and data communications products. Priding itself on service, Inmac offers a 45-day trial period, a one-year unconditional refund policy and a minimum two-year performance guarantee on every product they sell. Inmac ships nearly every order the same day from one of its eight U.S. locations. The company's free technical hotline can answer virtually any product-related question you may have. 800/547-5444
2465 Augustine Dr.
Santa Clara, CA 95054

**Misco Computer Supplies and Accessories** carries a broad selection of quality products at very competitive prices. This easy-to-read mail-

order catalog also includes furniture items. 800/876-4626 (in New Jersey, 908/264-1000)
One Misco Plaza
Holmdel, NJ 07733

**Moore Computer Supplies & Forms Catalog** includes an excellent selection of computer furniture and accessories as well as computer supplies. The catalog with its alphabetical index at the front is easy to use. Moore is a very service-oriented company. 800/323-6230
Moore Business Products Division
701 Woodlands Parkway
Vernon Hills, IL 60061

**Project Planner Office Designer** kit by Stanley Tools is a kit that makes designing your office layout easy and fun. The kit comes with reusable peel-and-stick office and architectural symbols (e.g., desks, file cabinets, windows) that you press into place on a "GRIDBOARD." You can plan up to 5,300 square feet of space. In addition to the GRIDBOARD, the kit includes six symbol sheets, a scaled ruler and an illustrated design manual. Call 800/648-7654 for the dealer nearest you.

**Polaroid Corp.** makes the computer filters discussed in this chapter. 800/225-2770 or in Europe (the Netherlands), 31-053-821911.
Polarizer Division
1 Upland Road N-2
Norwood, MA 02062

**Reliable Home Office** is a beautiful catalog that features many attractive desk and office accessories for your office at home as well as at work. 800/621-4344 or 312/666-1800
1001 W. Van Buren
Chicago, IL 60607

**D.L. West Manufacturing Co., Inc.** makes Wesystem display products that let you easily insert and remove papers in a one-hand operation. 800/888-0350 or 602/290-8330
1684 S. Research Loop Dr., Ste. 510
Tucson, AZ 85710

Note: Check with dealers and catalogs for current warranty information.

# BOOKS AND OTHER READING

**9 to 5 Fact Sheets** contain valuable information about good office design, particularly for computer workers. Of special interest are: "The 9 to 5 Office Design Kit: How to Design the Work Area to Fit You," "9 to 5's Consumer Guide to Office Computers" and "Office Design for Video Display Terminals." Each fact sheet is $3 apiece or $15 for a complete set of eight fact sheets. **Do It At Your Desk** ($2.95) is a humorous book that helps computer users work out daily aches and pains through simple exercises at the desk. It also includes advice on choosing chairs and working at computer terminals. To get the fact sheets and the book and to get a complete listing of other work-related books and reports call 216/566-9308 or write:

9 to 5 National Association of Working Women
614 Superior Ave. NW
Cleveland, OH 44113

**Office At Home: Everything You Need to Know to Work Efficiently and Happily From Home** by Robert Scott (New York: Charles Scribner's Sons, 1986) provides useful tips on planning office space and selecting equipment, whether or not your office is in your home. Paperback, $9.95

**Office Furniture** by Susan Szenasy (New York: Facts on File, 1985) is a useful guide to the many factors involved in choosing furniture: aesthetics, comfort, function, strength, size and versatility. Hardback, $19.95 and paperback, $12.95

**Sunset Home Offices & Workspaces** (Menlo Park, California: Sunset Publishing Co., 1986) is loaded with ideas, illustrations and full color photos to help you design and equip an efficient work area. The book includes a variety of innovative storage options and design solutions. There are also ideas on computerized work spaces. Paperback, $7.95

**Working From Home, Third Edition: Everything You Need to Know About Living and Working Under the Same Roof** by Paul and Sarah Edwards (Los Angeles: Jeremy P. Tarcher, Inc., 1990) has several excellent chapters on setting up and equipping a home office space. (Much of this information is useful even if your office isn't in your home.) Paperback, $14.95

# 12

## THE TRAVELING OFFICE: HOW TO TRAVEL SMOOTHLY AND GET THINGS DONE

*Quick Scan: If you're away from your office a good portion of the time, you need special time management techniques and office tools to handle work responsibilities. Discover how to master paperwork and the telephone from afar. Discover the latest, high-tech telecommunications options that are now available. Read about specific tips and tricks that on-the-go professionals use when they travel. Learn dozens of ways you and your organization can keep travel costs down.*

**W**hether you travel 8 or 80 percent of the time for business, keeping up with all your responsibilities can be quite a challenge. As one executive admitted, keeping up is difficult even when you're *not* traveling. The tools, tips and techniques in this chapter could make the difference for you between travel exhaustion and exhilaration.

For many business people, traveling represents the opportunity to finally get some real work done without all the constant interruptions. Travel or commuting time can be a precious respite from the more demanding everyday routine. For Public Relations

Society of America Executive Vice President Betsy Kovacs, "The airplane is the best place to read, think and write because you're away from the telephone."

## WORKING ON THE ROAD

Make special use of your travel time.

While on a plane, Bill Butler, president of BCG Consulting, likes to make use of "creative thinking time." He'll take a sheet of paper and jot down ideas in the form of mind maps (visual idea outlines) and decision trees (pros and cons) for two or three of his current projects.

Whenever publisher Mike Welch travels, he brings along his portable Dictaphone recorder (the size of a pack of cigarettes) and some pre-stamped "Jiffy" envelopes. He mails back the tapes in the padded envelopes and he adds, "The *letters* are not waiting for my signature; what's waiting for me when I return is the *reply*."

For urgent dictation, Welch dials into his desk dictation machine, which is on 24 hours a day. And since his secretary is "super sharp," if a change has occurred since he last dictated (e.g, a certain report has already come in), she will automatically update and correct the final letter.

Welch also dictates in the car. After a recent planning meeting, he had already dictated all the thank you notes and a staff report by the time he had returned to the office.

Welch also makes good use of his commuting time by listening to tapes every morning on his daily commute by car. He particularly enjoys listening to tapes put out by ManagersEdge in Englewood, Colorado (800/334-5771). The "Newstrack Executive Tape Service" is a biweekly tape cassette series that summarizes newspapers and magazine articles. (Try listening to tapes such as Newstrack on a plane, too.)

Accomplish as much as you can in the allotted time by **consolidating activities** when you travel. Plan ahead all the meetings you want to have and the people you want to see in a particular location. Consolidate similar activities—for example, group together all your writing work. Because space is at a premium, you're almost forced to work in this linear way. It's harder to jump from one thing to another when you can't spread out all your "stuff." (And if you're one of those people who accomplishes more when you travel, perhaps you should incorporate this one-thing-at-a-time work style into your back-at-the-ranch office, too.)

## HANDLING PAPERWORK ON THE ROAD

**Planning** is the secret to handling paperwork when you travel. When you book your hotel reservation, for example, make sure the room has the basic paperwork necessities: a flat writing surface with a light and a telephone. (Isn't it inconvenient when the telephone is on the night table when you have a lot of phoning to do?) Here are some other ways to plan ahead for paperwork.

### SET UP A PORTABLE OFFICE SYSTEM

You'll need to plan a system to organize your paperwork and office supplies. As with everything else, there's no one right way to organize this system. But having a regular system in place, with the right tools and routines for you, can guarantee a more productive trip.

Select practical accessories to hold and transport paperwork and supplies. Butler carries an expandable, leather document case that contains different colored folders. He also takes along a standard manila folder to store materials collected during the trip. Butler carries a lightweight tote bag filled with reading material; when empty, the bag can be folded inside the document case. He also has a plastic folder that holds thank you notes, sympathy cards, get well cards, stamps, number 10 envelopes and letterhead.

**Categorize different types of papers.** Welch organizes his reading material for a trip into three categories. One category he calls "First Priority," which includes all of the material related to a meeting, such as the agenda and the registration list. Another category is "Fun Stuff" such as the daily paper, *USA Today* and the *Wall Street Journal*, which he says are good sources of conversation starters. A third category is "Business Reading," such as lengthy reports, industry newsletters and selected articles.

Derrick Crandall, president of the American Recreation Coalition, travels with a very heavy briefcase containing project files, his long-term projects list and a trip file that has a trip sheet on top and other related material underneath. To keep up with correspondence, he also carries three or four number ten envelopes with stamps for one and two ounces of postage as well as one large envelope with three dollars of postage.

Take pertinent resource material with you in a concise, easy-to-carry format. Duane Berger, regional sales manager for Wheels, Inc., has created an alphabetical notebook system that he takes with him when he travels. He says, "I'm not at my desk that often so I can't carry the whole file cabinet with me." So instead he carries a three-ring notebook with alphabetical tabs and reinforced paper sheets that contain summaries of clients and prospects, the latest meetings and the types of programs his company is offering.

Berger uses single word phrases, "buzz words" he calls them, so he can see information at a glance. Typical information Berger writes down would include people profile facts such as key contacts, spouse's name and special interests, and buzz word summaries of problems and solutions that would instantly remind him of next actions to be taken. If a client calls when Berger is on the road, he is prepared to talk intelligently, armed with up-to-date information. When he's in the office, he uses the book there, too, because it saves him the motion of filing.

A **loose-leaf personal notebook organizer** is an invaluable tool for carrying information you collect on a particular trip. Many organizers come with special expense envelopes that are great for keeping all your records and receipts together in one place. These envelopes make it easy to compile expense reports when you return from your trip.

Day Runner makes such expense envelopes to be used in their personal organizers. They also make a couple of wonderful items (shown in Figure 12-1) to help you keep up with correspondence on the go. Day Runner Message pages are pressure-sensitive, two-part pages for instant memos and replies. Express-it is a handy, self-mailer with a gummed edge that lets you drop someone a quick note.

**Portable file boxes** may work for you if your office is in your car trunk or you have many files to take with you on a business trip. File boxes come in all shapes and sizes and can accommodate legal and letter files and hanging file folders. Check your office supply

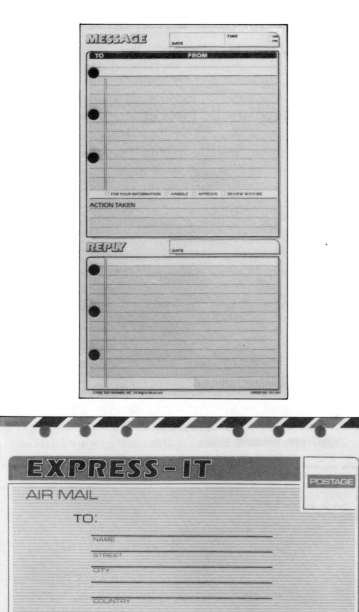

**Figure 12-1.** Day Runner Message and Express-it for easy, on-the-go communications

catalog under "file boxes" or "storage files."

Kathryn Johnson, president of *The HealthCare Forum* magazine in San Francisco, carries what she calls her "portable office," containing clear plastic folders, supplies, dictation tapes and an Express Mail envelope.

## PROCESS PAPERWORK IN TWO PLACES AT ONCE

If Johnson is away for more than three days, she takes work with her, completes it on the plane and mails it back to her office in the Express Mail envelope. She also mails back dictation tapes.

One executive has mail sent to *him* when on an extended trip. The Los Angeles Convention and Visitors Bureau sends mail and reading material to President George Kirkland via Federal Express. Backup copies of written correspondence remain in the office. Kirkland says, "Nothing is more depressing than returning from a trip to a stack of papers. When I come back, rarely do I have anything on my desk."

Neither does Mike Welch, but that's because his secretary files papers into his fifteen active projects folders in his credenza. When he returns, he checks these folders in order of their priority. At the very least, have your secretary—should you be lucky enough to have one—sort your papers into two colored folders, say, red for "urgent" and blue for "not urgent."

As for the piles of papers that accumulate on any trip, organizing consultant Barbara Hemphill, author of *Taming the Paper Tiger*, offers several suggestions. She says the time to handle those papers is during the trip *before* you get home. Throw out what you can; sort the rest into file folders. (See Chapter 4 for file folders in your daily paperwork system, which can be adapted for your traveling office.)

One of Hemphill's folders has her secretary's name. She puts papers that her secretary will handle in this folder. Then she takes out her Dictaphone recorder and dictates instructions for each paper. This saves Hemphill time when she returns from her trip and gives her secretary some control over when she processes this paperwork.

If you're uncomfortable with dictating machines, you could use Post-it brand notes. Use different colored Post-it notes to distinguish paperwork with different priorities or to categorize different types of work.

And here's a tip if you ever plan to use the hotel fax machine: check the cost first. Hotels sometimes assess high service charges—a flat rate $25 service charge per message or per-page fees of up to $10 for the first page and $1 for each additional page. An overnight mail service could be cheaper and the hotel may even have a daily pickup and delivery by such a service, which in many cases is Federal Express. (For other options see the section "More Traveling Technology" later in this chapter.)

## THE TRAVELING TELEPHONE

Today's high-tech telecommunications make traveling and staying in touch easier than ever. The biggest problem is trying to decide which tools (or toys) to use.

I did some seminar work for one Fortune 500 firm that had a problem with too many telecommunications toys. Many employees had to check five or six systems several times a day just to make sure they received all their messages. Pity those employees who were less than positively organized and forgot to check their computer's electronic mail box or the computerized message center. The more tools and systems you have, the more likely it is that something will slip through the cracks.

In addition, the company, through its strong emphasis on individualism, encouraged people to use communication channels that best fit them. This is a nice idea in theory, but when you have to remember how all of your colleagues like best to communicate and those colleagues are scattered across the country, your communications difficulties can easily multiply.

**Rule Number One is use the right telecommunications tools for you and keep them simple but effective for your applications.** Cost of the tools you select is a consideration, but be sure you measure cost in terms of time and energy savings as well as actual dollars. Let's look at some of the most cost-effective tools.

**Telephone answering machines** work great when you're out of your office. (Why is it you always seem to get more calls when you're away?) Of course, you will want to use a machine that has remote access, preferably one where you can dial a code to retrieve messages versus one that requires carrying along a special beeper.

There are also miniature answering machines small enough to take with you and install in your hotel room, such as the Code-a-Phone 3530. You'll probably need to bring a special double jack adapter and an alligator cord, which will accommodate your answering machine and the phone.

Sign up for the **call forwarding** service through your phone company if you want to be able to forward *all* your calls. If you want the option of selecting which ones will be forwarded, look into the Logos ES1 "Electronic Secretary." Easy to operate, this system will transform your answering machine into a call forwarding device. It costs $395 (plus the cost of three-way calling through your phone company) and is manufactured by Logotronix (800/442-4887). Telecommunications expert Stuart Crump calls devices such as the ES1 a **call director**. A call director is a device that plugs into your machine. Some can dial your **pager**, which beeps as soon as you get a message.

Speaking of pagers, look for the numeric type, which provides a digital readout of the phone number of the person calling you. And if you need a cross between a pager and an answering machine, consider getting the Motorola Spirit tone and voice pager. According to Barbara and Jim Suitor, who manage the Holiday Hills Resort in Eddyville, Kentucky, this pager lets someone call you on the phone and leave a 15-second live, audible message. The Motorola Bravo pager gives you a digital readout of the phone number and a message up to 60 characters in length. Look, too, for **wrist watch pagers** (Motorola makes one that is compatible with existing paging services). Motorola can be reached at 800/331-6456.

It's now possible to have a pager that is not range limited and thus confined to a local area. With SkyTel's SkyPager, for example, you can be in 200 major metropolitan regions and get a message in less than 30 seconds. If you have your callers dial a special 800 number, enter your I.D. number and record a voice message, you're instantly alerted on your SkyPager. (For more information, contact SkyTel at 800/456-3333.)

CUE Paging Corporation has regional and nationwide paging. CUE has more than 250 metropolitan areas and intends to continually expand that number. Paging costs about $34.95 to $55.95 per month depending on the region and level of service selected. (Call 800/824-9755 for more information on CUE.)

If you receive many calls and don't want to risk the chance of losing a call whenever your answering machine is handling another call simultaneously, look into **voice mail**, also called **voice messaging**. Voice mail lets several callers leave messages at the same time.

If you use your car frequently in your work or have a long commute, a **cellular telephone** is a must. Stuart Crump says to look for these three features: hands-free speaker phone, memory dialing and voice-activated dialing.

Selecting a cellular phone can be a challenge. There are about a dozen major manufacturers, each of which makes about three or four models—giving you about 40 models from which to choose. Type of use should also be a prime factor to help you select an appropriate model.

For example, if you only plan to use your phone in your car, then select a permanently installed **car phone**. However, if you need more flexibility, consider a **transportable** phone. A transportable is a briefcase-size, luggable model weighing in at about 10 pounds that's useful if you want to use the phone away from your car at another location. And if you want even greater flexibility, try a **handheld** phone. A handheld is light (under two pounds) and therefore very portable, but it isn't as powerful as the other models. You may lose some reception at times, and since it's battery-operated, you'll have to recharge occasionally.  But the fact that it can easily be carried in a briefcase or purse has led to its current popularity—that plus a continual decline in price.

Choosing the hardware is only half the story; you'll also need to select a service provider. Find out what a provider can offer in terms of coverage area, quality of customer service, clarity of sound, a convenient location and rates (the average monthly rate is $95). Make sure there are no hidden costs in your purchase or even your monthly service—some providers charge you for busy or unanswered calls.

Many business travelers will combine several different telecommunications tools such as a cellular phone with a pager and voice mail. They also take advantage of other telephone time and money savers such as selecting a long distance telephone company and using its credit card. And if a call just can't wait until they're on the ground, they use Airfone, which is on most major jets today.

## KEEPING UP WITH CALLS WHILE AWAY

Betsy Kovacs says, "I stay flexible about which telephone I use–I don't have to be in a hotel room. If I'm waiting an hour in an airport, I'll make calls using my MCI card."

On a more philosophical note, Kovacs says that the telephone helps her "maintain the rhythm of life," no matter where she is. Besides telephoning for business, Kovacs will place "stay-in-touch" phone calls. "The telephone works from out of town. The other person doesn't really care where you are when you're calling to wish a happy birthday." She adds that personal telephoning also helps make travel less jolting.

Most business travelers will call in at least once a day for messages and try to return calls the same day. Derrick Crandall, president of the American Recreation Coalition, says, "I'm a big believer in telephone services on the road." Crandall, with a staff of five, feels a greater need to stay in touch with his office so he calls in two or three times a day. He also calls the office's remote-controlled answering machine after business hours to leave or receive messages pertaining to staff.

Mike Welch, on the other hand, relies more heavily on his staff. He says, "If they need me, they'll call me–they know where I am." He was recently at a four-day conference and never needed to call in once.

To avoid surprise charges when calling from a pay phone or a hotel or hospital room phone, you can follow several tips. When using a pay phone, see if you can spot the name of the long distance carrier; if not, dial 0 or 00 and find out the name of the carrier and if it's new to you, also the rate quote. When using a hotel or hospital room phone, dial 0, the area code and the number and listen for the carrier name; if it's new to you, ask for a rate quote. If you want another carrier, hang up and ask the main switchboard operator how to reach it.

When you need to leave an important phone message quickly and for some reason you can't get through (e.g., a busy signal, no answer or you're just very short on time), use Message Mail, a personal voice telegram service. Each message can be up to two minutes in length, is in your own voice and costs $3.75. Message Mail automatically calls every fifteen minutes for three hours, starting whenever you say, until your message is delivered. You also get confirmation that your message was delivered, as well as a free reply message in your party's own voice. To use Message Mail, dial 800/283-2445.

## MORE TRAVELING TECHNOLOGY

When you prefer written to voice communications, you have several options. If you do heavy faxing when traveling, consider getting a **portable fax machine.** Some of the latest models are very compact and light and can even work with cellular or mobile phones.

A **fax mail network** lets you store faxes in a fax mailbox, which remain there until you're ready to pick them up. With fax mail, you can also take advantage of such features as automatic redialing, delay and send, "polling" (asking another machine if it has any messages) and sending one document to many different recipients.

AT&T, MCI and U.S. FAX offer fax mail networks; MCI FAX also interfaces with their other services for telex, electronic mail and personal computers. You might not even need a fax machine to send a fax; you could, for example, send a message via modem from your laptop computer directly to someone's fax machine. MCI also offers a special fax calling card for use with your portable fax.

If you don't have a fax machine available, you might use a **public fax station,** located at a quick printer or commercial mail station, such as Sir Speedy or Mail Boxes.

Hotelecopy, Inc., is the world's largest public access fax network with locations in more than 2,000 hotels, U.S. Post Offices, airports and other high-traffic sites nationwide. Many Hotelecopy units are sophisticated, self-service, credit card-operating fax terminals capable of performing numerous functions for traveling business people. For information, call 1/800/faxmail.

If you have a lot of detailed information to transmit that would be cumbersome in fax form, such as lengthy documents, databases or computer programs, **E-mail** (electronic mail) may be the way to go. E-mail lets you communicate via computers. You can send and receive messages as well as have access to E-mail networks and systems such as Dialcom (Rockville, Maryland), Western Union's EasyLink (Upper Saddle River, New Jersey) and MCI Mail (Washington, DC). Such systems integrate with other telecommunications channels, including fax, telex, Mailgram or cablegram. E-mail subscribers also have access to a variety of on-line databases and information services. E-mail is also useful for international business travelers who must communicate between vastly different time zones.

Whether you have major telecommunications requirements or you just need to get some work done while on the road, a **laptop computer** may be just the answer. Some models are as thin as a notebook and weigh under five pounds. In fact, such laptops are often called simply "notebooks." Make sure you like the keyboard design and feel as well as the clarity of the screen. Compaq LTE, NEC UltraLite, Dell System 316LT and Toshiba T1000XE are some of the more popular laptops receiving good, solid reviews. MicroComputer Accessories makes a handy copy holder for your laptop called the Portable PC Easel (800/521-8270 or in California, 213/301-9400).

A laptop computer can be an invaluable tool if you're in outside sales, giving you a real customer service edge. That's the case for the salespeople who work for City Provisioners, Inc., a food distributor based in Daytona Beach. Armed with laptops and order-taking software, the 35 sales reps call on restaurants, hospitals and other institutions. Sales reps save customers time and money by providing on-site analyses and up-to-the-minute dollar and supply figures, transmitting and verifying orders on the spot and printing out the final order for the customer (sales reps also carry portable printers). Joseph Bendix, president of City Provisioners, sums up the benefit of using laptops like this, "It's transforming the way we look at our relationship with customers. We're more like a partner in their business now."

A number of products and accessories will help to make your laptop more productive. If you use a battery-powered laptop, Battery Watch is a small (about 15K) and inexpensive ($49) software program that tracks how long your battery will last and works with most battery-powered laptops. A **connector** is especially handy in a hotel room when you want to connect your modem-equipped laptop computer (or compact fax machine) into the hotel room's telephone system. If your laptop isn't equipped with an internal modem, consider getting an external **pocket modem**. If you plan to do much faxing, an external **fax modem** with 9,600-bps capability may be the way to go or better yet, make use of an E-mail system such as MCI which receives ASCII text from a standard modem and can send it as a fax. If you're on the road with your laptop and you want to use files from your office PC, a **remote control program** will let you do so. (Check the chapter resource guide under "High-Tech Travel Tools, Accessories and Services" for more specific product information.)

Beware that some hotels are changing their telephone systems to make it impossible to operate your computer and modem from your hotel room and are establishing "business rooms and floors" that cost you extra dollars. If you're planning to do extensive work from your hotel room, check the status of their telephone system and business rooms before you get there.

If you don't need the price nor capabilities of a laptop, but would like automatic access to a phone and address database, calendar, scheduler, calculator and other handy features, get yourself a **palmtop.** In general, stay away from palmtops that don't have a "QWERTY" (standard keyboard) design, because it takes too much time to enter information on a keyboard that's too small or awkward. Look for products like The Pocket Electrodex and The Electrodex Plus by Rolodex that can exchange information with a PC. These products and others are listed in the "Portable Office Products" section of the resource guide.

## ONE DOZEN TRAVEL TIPS
## YOU NEED TO KNOW

Let's face it: traveling is time consuming and energy draining, particularly when you're out several days at a time and you're crossing different time zones. All the more so if you tend toward disorganization. So part of maintaining an effective traveling office is learning to handle the logistics of travel. Here are twelve travel tips that will make your trips less hectic and maybe even pleasurable.

### ONE: TAKE TIME TO PREPARE

You are only as organized as you are prepared. "I pack my suitcase, my briefcase and my mind for each trip," says Mike Welch. "I really think it through. Like great athletes who picture themselves leaping

over the bar, I picture myself at the business meeting." In addition
to packing all the pertinent meeting materials, Welch commits to
memory all the important details concerning the agenda.

Bill Butler advises, "Read any briefing papers or material
pertaining to your trip *before* you leave. State Department research
indicates information is not absorbed and retained as well when
you're in a travel mode."

*Los Angeles Times* writer David Shaw leaves nothing to chance.
He recently wrote a story describing how he does long-range trip
planning even for his vacations—six to eight months out. But he also
is able to combine spontaneity with organization.

"I have hotel and dinner reservations each night, for example,
but my wife and I play each day's sightseeing by ear...I don't see
any charm in spending an hour or two at the end of a long day of
sightseeing, wandering around the countryside in the hope of finding
a hotel..."

Take time to prepare to prepare your clients or customers for
your trip. Trish Lester, president of a business communications
company, writes her clients three weeks before she leaves for an
extended period of time. She encourages them to call her before
she departs, but also assures them they have the option of leaving
messages on her answering machine while she's away.

If you're planning to meet someone at an airport, hotel or
restaurant, be sure you each have a backup plan. Having
prearranged contacts, such as secretaries, at each respective office,
can help with any last minute change in plans.

## TWO: SELECT AIRLINE AND TRAVEL CLUBS, PROGRAMS AND SERVICES

Savvy business travelers who fly frequently look for ways to get the
most value from their travel. They limit, for example, the number of
airlines they fly in order to accumulate more benefits more quickly
through airline "frequent flyer" travel clubs.

Derrick Crandall, who is based in D.C., flies United almost
exclusively and is part of their Mileage Plus Premier Executive
program. Since he flies 150,000 miles a year, he is upgraded to first
class about 50 percent of the time. Crandall says he has never paid
more for a ticket to fly United but he is willing to be more flexible

with his schedule in order to get the first class upgrade bonus. That bonus also enables him to board before the other passengers so he gets first crack at overhead storage.

By the way, here's another technique to secure overhead storage, especially if you're a woman. When the airline announces "first class passengers and all those needing assistance may board now," I rush to the front of the line. No, I don't fly first class (yet) but I generally require an extra hand to help lift my garment bag up into the overhead storage. This isn't a 100 percent sure bet but it works most of the time when I'm flying alone.

When on the ground, attorney Joseph M. Malkin takes advantage of Hertz' "Number One Club Gold Service." This service saves Malkin, who is managing partner of the O'Melveny & Myers San Francisco office, at least 10 to 20 minutes every time he rents a car because he can go immediately to his car, bypassing the paperwork and wait at the rental car desk.

Be sure to check all travel benefits, including rental car discounts, that are available to you through your company or any professional association memberships. As a member of the National Speakers Association, I have access to Hertz discounts, for example. Always ask about special deals, such as a "corporate rate," but don't assume that's the best deal. A discount through an association may be better.

## THREE: TAKE RESPONSIBILITY FOR YOUR TRAVEL ARRANGEMENTS

Many business travelers believe that trip logistics such as flight and hotel are too important and costly to take lightly and so frequent business travelers are becoming more knowledgeable about this and involved in their travel decisions.

Savvy travelers have found a way to keep airline costs down by booking a seat on the off-hour, last leg of a transcontinental flight. If you don't have to fly on the hour, but have some flexibility, you can get great reductions in ticket prices from such airlines as Delta, TWA and Northwest.

Another way to keep costs down is to purchase airline tickets through a **consolidator** or a **last-minute travel club**. A consolidator buys unsold tickets from airlines and offers discount fares to those who can travel with only 3- to 30-days notice. Last-minute clubs can offer up to 50 percent or more on rooms, tours and cruises. (See the "High-Tech Travel Tools, Accessories and Services" section of the chapter resource guide for names and numbers.)

Avoid, if possible, booking the last flight out, especially if you have a speaking engagement or a critical meeting. It's far better to spend extra time at your destination than arriving a day late because of a cancelled flight.

Before you leave for the airport, always call the airline to make sure your flight is on time. For return flights, it's also a good idea to call the day before to reconfirm your flight, even if you are ticketed.

Be aware that there are hundreds of policies and procedures hidden away in airline rule books that detail such items as passenger check-in, boarding, overbooking, delayed flights, missed connections, reservations, lost tickets and damaged bags. A *Wall Street Journal* story reported that each airline has its own rules and that it's often difficult to get copies of the rule books–and in fact, many airline employees have never even heard of the books.

To give you some idea of how airlines differ, consider how much variance exists among airlines regarding reporting periods for lost or damaged bags. I read where one airline had a 45-day deadline in which to report baggage and another a mere four hours! To get a free copy of an airline's rules, contact their main headquarters office. To be safe, notify a baggage clerk immediately regarding lost or damaged baggage and write down the clerk's name.

You may also do well to file a police report, not just a complaint with the airline. Baggage theft is a common occurrence at all airports. According to a Los Angeles Police Department detective, unopened bags may sell for $75 apiece. In a letter to the *Los Angeles Times* editor, Anita Sohus related how her bags had been recovered after the arrest of a receiver of stolen goods who had 150 stolen bags in his possession! (The thief was *not* an airline employee.)

If your bags are lost, go to the baggage counter to ask for money to handle emergency expenses. Most airlines have a nominal amount they will pay per day.

Leave nothing to chance. Bill Butler advises, "Never leave home unless you have a confirmed, guaranteed reservation in hand." That goes for airlines as well as accommodations, too.

Speaking of accommodations, you may not be aware just how much influence you can have in that area, too. For starters, you should **negotiate your room rate.** Did you know that many hotels have more than 30 different rates for each guest room? Ask about any specials–such as corporate, weekend or midweek rates or if there are any special ads or coupons running in the local paper. Some hotels offer their own clubs and extend special discounts to members. Never use a hotel chain's toll-free 800 number if you plan to negotiate. Call the hotel directly.

**Avoid checking in with your MasterCard or Visa,** which the hotel will use to pre-approve and set aside a dollar amount to cover your expected expenses. This pre-approval actually reduces your current credit limit. Instead, check in with a card without any credit limit such as an American Express, a Diners Club or a Carte Blanche card, even if you later decide to pay with a MasterCard or Visa.

Be sure to **spell out important room preferences** you may have–non-smoking, quiet and proximity to an elevator. If you're traveling in Europe, you may also want to request a room on a lower floor for safety reasons, as fire alarm systems are nonexistent in many foreign countries.

## FOUR: DON'T UNDERESTIMATE A GOOD TRAVEL AGENT

That goes not only for yourself but also for your company. For some firms, travel is the third biggest expense, after salaries and rent. Yet many companies don't have clear travel policies nor the information to establish those policies.

It's helpful to have a full-service agency that can provide computer analyses of travel expenses and savings and can secure substantial discounts on airfares, hotels and car rentals. Your company could cut its expenses by 20 percent using the right travel policies in combination with an effective travel agency.

Customer service and an exacting attention to detail are two criteria to keep in mind when selecting a good agent. "I have an excellent travel agent," says Betsy Kovacs. "My agent finds flights that fit in my schedule with the least number of connections. I am price conscious but I won't settle for inconvenience."

Make sure your agent asks questions every time you fly, such as what airline you want to fly and whether you need a rental car. Does your agent always remember to credit your mileage to your frequent flyer club? Embassy Travel in Tulsa, Oklahoma, uses a quality checklist, which includes the frequent flyer number, to make sure all the details are handled all the time. This checklist is printed on the front cover of the special jacket that holds airline tickets.

The ideal agent will ask for and keep up-to-date travel information regarding your frequent flyer numbers, your billing procedures (perhaps you use two different credit cards, one for business and the other for personal travel, which is a good idea) and your travel preferences (such as airline seating, rental cars and hotel rooms). If you have to start from scratch for each trip, your agent just isn't organized enough.

Your agent should routinely provide you with seat assignments and boarding passes so that you don't have to wait in line at the airport.

Find out the day of the week your travel agency actually pays for the tickets they write. Often it's Tuesday. If you purchase a non-refundable ticket and you need to cancel, your agent may be able to void the transaction, provided the agency hasn't paid for the ticket.

If punctuality is a concern, have your agent compare the different airlines. Your agent's reservation computer can call up punctuality data for each airline on a particular flight. Also ask if they have the latest on-time survey and ratings of all the airlines; you'll see such surveys in the travel section of the paper from time to time. (Know, however, that many airlines add 29 minutes to their schedules in order to improve these on-time statistics.)

## FIVE: CHOOSE THE RIGHT FLIGHT AND SEAT

For flight times to avoid, Bill Butler comments, "I look with a jaundiced eye at the first flight out which is often a very popular flight for business. I will usually avoid it because it's too crowded and hectic."

While you may not want the first flight out, do travel early in the day, if you can. You have more options if a flight is cancelled. Avoid connecting flights but if you must schedule them, leave enough time between them—at least double what the airline tells you. If you must book a connecting flight, try to do so through a smaller airport. Also avoid traveling during holidays.

Many business travelers prefer aisle seats because they offer a little more leg room and are less confining. But not just any aisle seat will do. Derrick Crandall likes an aisle seat close to the boarding ramp since he carries on luggage rather than checking it in.

Mike Welch's seat preference is a no-smoking, aisle seat. His preference is so strong that he jokes, "I'll sit on the wing rather than sit anywhere else."

Some people prefer the "bulkhead," which has seats with the most leg room—more leg room than aisle seats. The disadvantages are that you have no underseat storage and you'll have to move if you want to see the movie screen.

If you're safety conscious, you may prefer to take the advice of one air safety engineer who recommended an aisle seat next to the rearmost overwing exit. He also recommended reading the emergency card in the seat pocket to find out how to open the various door and window exits and locating the four exits that are closest to your seat. He also suggested counting the rows of seats to each exit; you might not be able to see the exit signs in an emergency but you could still feel and count the seats.

## SIX: USE TRAVEL RESOURCE INFORMATION TO HELP YOU PLAN YOUR TRIP

Bill Butler stays current on flight information by subscribing to the pocket-size *OAG Pocket Flight Guide* (North American edition), which is available by subscription (12 issues a year) for $65 plus postage from Official Airline Guides, 2000 Clearwater Drive, Dept. M563, Oak Brook, IL 60521-9953, 708/574-6487.

Butler stays current, also, by following industry reports included in the *New York Times* travel section. He has learned, for example, that Atlanta often shows extra delays because of a big problem with early morning ground fog. On the other hand, Memphis, which has Federal Express' major terminal, is considered the "all weather airport." Butler points out Chicago is noted for lots of traffic so you need to allow extra time between connecting flights.

Butler used to travel 50 to 60 percent of the time; he now travels 30 to 40 percent. With such a heavy travel schedule, it makes good sense to have fingertip travel information. Butler maintains files on major cities he visits frequently, such as New York and Washington, D.C., and he subscribes to *New York* and *Washingtonian* magazines.

Butler also keeps his own travel notebook, which is arranged by client and location. The notebook contains directions, places to stay, ground transportation, how long it takes to get to the airport at various times of day, the "leading food adventures to the locals," restaurants to avoid and hotel history, in particular his room preferences. (Nonsmokers may also want to request and note for future reference which hotel rooms and floors are smoke-free.)

## SEVEN: CONSOLIDATE YOUR TRIP LOGISTICS

Organized travelers have a trip form they carry with them that lists their itinerary, transportation, lodging, key contacts and phone numbers. They also leave at least one copy of their trip sheet with a staff member, as well as with their family. Butler has an expense report printed on the back of his form, which makes for a convenient system.

Mike Welch uses a typewritten sheet that lists such things as the airlines and types of planes he'll be flying, seat assignments, who confirmed his reservations, rental car arrangements and who will pick him up. Along with this sheet, Welch also brings photocopies of airline guide pages he may need. He carries these items in his pockets, which have been specially organized for travel so that he doesn't have to look in a million places. Having a simple and dependable system, even when it comes to organizing your pockets, can make a big difference when traveling.

## EIGHT: HOW TO SELECT TRAVEL CLOTHING

"Keep it simple" is the best advice when it comes to selecting clothes for a trip.

Betsy Kovacs buys clothing that doesn't wrinkle. She says, "If they are wrinkled on the rack, you know they will wrinkle on the road." (Anything with wool travels great, as well as knits and polyester blends.) She also wears (never packs) one all-purpose coat appropriate for a particular trip.

Bill Butler simplifies his travel wardrobe. Butler packs black shoes and socks, makes sure shirts go with all suits and relies on neckties to provide color. Designer Bill Blass, I understand, limits his travel wardrobe to two basic "colors"–black and white.

Image consultant Jill Sprengel, of Redondo Beach, California, suggests women stick with solid colors and separates. Use accessories such as belts, print scarves or necklaces to add variety and choose ones that bring up the bottom color from your skirt or pair of slacks. Some handy items to include are a dressy blouse and belt to go out in the evening and a tweed jacket that has many colors. Sprengel advises you to take no more than three pairs of shoes–one for walking or sports (such as tennis shoes), a pair of flats and low heels that match your hair or skin color. Have at least one belt to match the main pair of shoes you'll be wearing.

Wear the right clothing when you're flying. Several layers of light-colored, well-fitting (but not tight) clothing are best. From a safety perspective, select clothes made of wool, a naturally flame retardant fabric. It's better than most materials, especially synthetics and leather, which should be avoided. (A good way to test flammability is to snip off a small piece of fabric and set it afire. If it melts rather than chars, don't wear it.) Also avoid high-heeled shoes.

## NINE: HOW TO CHOOSE AND USE LUGGAGE ON THE GO

When it comes to luggage, Sprengel recommends a small suitcase that you can take on the plane. (Try to get one with wheels that you can tow behind you as you go through the airport.) Butler, on the other hand, checks two pieces of Ventura luggage–a large case (which will hold three suits) and an overnight case. He suggests buying luggage where the airlines send theirs to be repaired. "These places know what holds up and what doesn't."

Other than a briefcase, the only thing Butler likes to carry on board is a good attitude, "There are two things you can do if your suitcase goes south and you go north: get angry or plan for this eventuality. I'm always dressed in a suit when I travel."

You might also try taping a copy of your itinerary to the inside top of your suitcase or suit bag. Perhaps an airline will contact you and ship your baggage.

Many business travelers, myself included, prefer taking their luggage on board so as to avoid the hassles of lost, stolen or misdirected luggage. But the latest FAA (Federal Aviation Administration) guidelines may put a crimp in this practice.

The guidelines advise that passengers carry on no more than two pieces of baggage. Here are three options from which to choose:

- an underseat piece that is 9 by 14 by 22 inches maximum
- an overhead bin item that is 10 by 14 by 36 inches maximum
- a cabin closet hanging piece that is 4 by 23 by 45 inches.

Fortunately, personal items such as purses, coats, hats, umbrellas and cameras don't count as carry-on luggage; unfortunately, briefcases do.

Apparently, there may be some variation in how the guidelines are administered by different airlines, depending on factors such as aircraft size and the number of passengers on a flight.

I always recommend carrying luggage on board. I never check luggage on my way to any destination if I can help it; occasionally, coming back I will, however, depending on my own energy level or if I have a particularly heavy load. Even if you check most of your luggage, be sure to pack toiletries, prescriptions, underwear, a change of clothing, important documents and any other critical items in a carry-on bag.

I bring a heavy duty garment bag by Ventura which has loads of zippered pockets. Pockets are labeled with round colored key tags (you can get them in stationery stores). I have written the names of articles contained in each pocket on each tag. (Having all those pockets can be a blessing or a curse, depending on whether you stay consistent and always keep certain items in them.)

I usually take my Janssport tote bag, which has four roomy pockets plus the main compartment. I keep the bag under the seat in front. The bag holds my cosmetic case, reading and work material and other items that I want to have accessible (or that fit better in this case than the garment bag). I also take my organizer (it has a shoulder strap). And I never go anywhere without my trusty luggage carrier. My model is sturdy enough, with its large, heavy-duty wheels to take stairs and curbs without missing a beat—or dropping my luggage. I put the luggage carrier in overhead storage, along with my garment bag. (If I'm lucky, I'll hang my garment bag in the airplane's closet.)

## TEN: PACK SYSTEMATICALLY

Betsy Kovacs starts by making a list that is divided into two parts: day and evening. She decides exactly what she is going to wear and which accessories will go with each outfit. She lays her accessories and clothes out on the bed before she packs them in her garment bag. (Her tote bag holds shoes and cosmetics.) She also has a permanent list of basics that she keeps in a pocket of her garment bag. Kovacs tries not to take too much but she also puts great emphasis on looking her best. When it comes to cosmetics and toiletries, Kovacs packs each item after she uses it the last time before the trip.

I keep many items in my garment bag all the time, in between trips. I have a cosmetic case that duplicates the cosmetics and toiletries I have at home. Packing time can be cut in half when you have an extra toiletry kit that is ready when you are. The ideal time to replenish any supplies that are low is when you unpack at the end of each trip. Dental, medical, body care and makeup supplies in travel-sized containers are convenient. For extra protection, fill containers three-quarters full and secure them in self-sealing plastic bags. I keep four small, zip-lock bags in my cosmetic case for four different types of toiletries—dental, facial, hair and eye care.

I also keep an extra hair dryer and several brushes in the bag, too, as well a couple of large plastic bags and a bathing suit (I'm a native Californian).

Pack your wallet systematically, too, or should I say, *unpack* it. Leave behind unnecessary credit cards, papers or accessories. Make a list of the credit cards you decide to take and their numbers and keep that list separate from your cards. Include any phone numbers you may need to call if your credit cards should become lost or stolen. (By the way, you should already have a complete, up-to-date list of all your credit cards.) Don't keep all your money or traveler's checks in your wallet, or any one place for that matter; stash some of it in other places for reserve.

## ELEVEN: CHECK OUT TRAVEL CHECKLISTS

It's always a good idea to maintain at least one travel checklist of items you always take on a trip. See Figure 12-2 for an example. In addition, you may want to keep sample packing lists for different

**Figure 12-2.** THE POSITIVELY ORGANIZED!
               TRAVELING OFFICE CHECKLIST

Here are some items to include in your traveling office. Check off the ones that you already have, circle the ones you want to get and add any others that would come in handy:

[] Briefcase
[] Attache case
[] Tote bag
[] Document case
[] Notebook—size:
[] Organizer
[] Calendar/appointment book
[] Telephone/address book
[] Paper—pads, loose sheets, personal or company stationery, business cards–underline any of these items or add what you'll need:

_____

[] Writing tools—pens, pencils, markers:

_____

[] Accessories: tape, scissors, stapler, clips, portable office kit

_____

[] Equipment: pocket calculator, dictaphone, small tape player, portable computer

_____

[] Labeled file folders, file pockets, expansion pockets, plastic folders

_____

[] Stamps, return envelopes, Jiffy envelopes, Express/Federal Express envelopes

_____

[] Work: schedule, agenda, files/info related to business trip, reading material, paperwork, project work

_____

[] Travel materials: itinerary, tickets, legal documents—driver's license, passport, visa, certificate of registration (from U.S. Customs for items such as cameras and watches made in a foreign country); travelers checks, cash, credit cards

_____

[] Any extra conveniences you can think of: _____

_____

types of trips that you will take again. If you have a computer, keep your lists there. Whether you prepare packing lists manually or on computer, group items by category. Some useful categories are: clothing, underwear, personal care, business materials and recreation.

## THOSE EXTRA CONVENIENCES

You may want to include, for example, some of "Bill Butler's batch of things to carry": the *OAG Pocket Flight Guide*, a small atlas, a name and address book, a list of restaurants in the major cities you'll be visiting, a digital alarm clock that keeps both current time and home-based time, a pocket calculator, extra shoelaces, a sewing kit and safety pins, aspirin, antacid tablets, foil-wrapped granola bars, a nasal decongestant in case you have to fly with a cold, cough drops, pleasure reading such as a John McDonald or Agatha Christie book and gifts wrapped with yarn instead of ribbon, which tends to become mashed in a suitcase.

Writer David Shaw takes Scotch tape, packing tape, extra glasses and contact lenses, a Swiss army knife, a spot remover, a laptop computer, rope, his own gourmet food (he refuses to eat airline fare), pre-addressed post card labels and a small pocket tool kit with pliers, chisel, hole punch, file, stapler, screwdrivers, measuring tape and scissors.

I bring along lots of dollar bills and change for tipping and phone calls. I also stash pre-moistened towelettes in my carry-on bag to freshen up.

Mail-order travel catalogs listed in the resource guide feature such handy items as nylon "hidden pocket" money pouches, inflatable neck pillows for long plane or train rides and emergency dental kits.

Take important phone numbers with you, such as those for credit card companies, which could come in handy should a card become lost or stolen. For a Visa card, call 800/VISA-911 in the U.S. and outside the U.S., call 214/669-8888 collect. For MasterCard, call 800/999-0454 and if overseas, call 314/275-6690 collect.

Have your doctor write up extra copies of prescriptions you may need while away or in case you lose any medication.

Here's some space to write in your own extra conveniences:

## TWELVE: COMBINE HEALTH AND PRODUCTIVITY WHEN YOU TRAVEL

To maintain your rhythm and your effectiveness throughout your trip, recognize that as you travel you are subjecting yourself to different demanding environments. Part of staying organized on the road is preparing in advance for the adjustments you and your body may need to make and then following through while on the trip.

## TAKE CARE OF YOUR BODY

Bill Butler says avoid unnecessary travel. "Make sure you need to make the trip in the first place, that there is no other way you can possibly accomplish your goal. See if they can come to you. Traveling is mean to your body."

Butler suggests you avoid overeating and overdrinking. He also suggests drinking bottled water wherever you go. "Just the different chemicals in the water can have an adverse effect."

Don't forget to exercise. Betsy Kovacs suggests running or even jump roping. A jump rope is an easy item to pack, too.

Derrick Crandall keeps his body on Washington, D.C., time. He never resets his watch (unless he's on an extended trip for a few weeks, several time zones away). "I like to maintain East Coast mentality and body time," he says.

## TAKE SPECIAL CARE OF YOUR BODY WHEN YOU FLY

Most airlines are cramped and uncomfortable, but fortunately, there are steps you can take to help your body adjust.

**Protect yourself against dehydration.** When you're on board a jetliner you will experience dehydration of body and skin because of the cabin's low humidity. Dehydration leads to weariness.

Be sure to drink enough liquid—one expert recommends one glass of water every hour. Apple juice, cranberry juice or fruit punch are also good. Avoid tea, coffee, alcohol and soft drinks, all of which can have a diuretic effect.

Bring along lip balm and hand cream to combat cracked lips and dry skin, likely symptoms from exposure to cabin air. Don't forget a lubricant for your eyes, especially if you wear contact lenses.

**Order your airline meals ahead of time, if possible.** Most airlines will allow you to order special meals such as fruit and cheese; vegetarian plates; low-salt, low-fat, low-cholesterol fare; and special selections for frequent travelers. Ask each airline what kinds of meals are available one or two days before you fly. Or better yet, place your order at the time you book your reservation. Remember to avoid high-fat, salty foods, which cause body swelling and retention of fluid.

**Keep your body limber and comfortable.** There are four steps you can take.

First, wear comfortable shoes you can slip on and off. Remove them shortly after takeoff.

Second, to reduce swelling in feet and ankles, elevate your feet. (Body swelling and bloating occur because of an airplane's lower barometric pressure.) Elevating your feet even a few inches really helps; try placing your feet on the carry-on case you've stashed under the seat in front.

Third, take short exercise breaks. Frequency of breaks is more important than time duration. Once every one to two hours is ideal. Take walks around the cabin and do simple stretches at your seat. Hold each stretch for 30 to 60 seconds. (You might want to tell your neighbors beforehand what you're doing.)

Fourth, help improve your posture by placing a pillow in the small of your back. The pillow provides extra support and helps you sit up straighter.

## COMBINE BUSINESS WITH PLEASURE

Crandall has a real advantage because the members of the association he directs are actively involved in recreation. The good news is that Disney is one of his members. The bad news has been when he has had to tell his six-year-old, "You can't come."

Crandall, however, tries to fly three to five trips a year with his family—his wife and his two, young daughters. He looks for ways to combine business trips with family vacations.

## PACE YOURSELF

"You have to really pace yourself when you travel," says Kovacs. "If you have to wait," she advises, "find a comfortable place, know you're there for the duration and roll with it." If there's a delay at the airport, Kovacs like to go to the airport restaurant to read, work or relax.

In fact, much of pacing yourself is just learning to relax. "Don't get too excited, don't rant and rave," says Welch. "A lot of people create a crisis to be a hero. Don't let anything get to the crisis stage. The whole secret boils down to communication—up, down, sideways. Don't take anything for granted."

What do you do if, after all your planning, your airline cancels your flight? The best course of action, especially if you have a non-refundable fare, is to have the airline place you on the next available flight. If you try to make a new reservation or rebook yourself, you may lose out on your low fare.

If you miss a flight, be sure to call the airline immediately so that all of your other reservations aren't wiped out as well. By the way, if you don't board the plane at least 10 or 15 minutes before takeoff, you stand a chance of having your seat sold to a standby passenger.

There are always options, according to Bill Butler, even if you find yourself next to the little old lady from Des Moines who wants to talk your ear off. "I have a friend who speaks Spanish when she doesn't want to be disturbed. I'm tempted to learn a few words of something myself."

One final suggestion:   Believe Murphy's Law next time you're on the road. Or as Butler says, "You have to anticipate that things won't be perfect, but most of the time you can organize and prepare."

# RESOURCE GUIDE

## PORTABLE OFFICE PRODUCTS

Company addresses and phone numbers are provided unless products are widely available through office supply dealers. Product prices are approximate and may vary.

**Auto Office Seat Desk System** by Rubbermaid (Figure 12-3) provides a multi-purpose work organizer that combines the best elements of an office desk, filing cabinet and briefcase. The system stores hanging folders and files for instant reference, and optional clip-on bins hold up to 25 extra hanging files. The system also has small storage compartments for office supplies, while oversized items such as cellular phones, tape recorders, sales catalogs and samples are concealed under a secure latch.

**Design-a-Space** portable office accessories by Rubbermaid, shown in Figures 12-4 and 12-5, let you take your office with you. If you need to write while on the road, consider the **Storage Clipboard** with a durable clip and pencil holder and a divided inside compartment that

**Figure 12-3.** Auto Office Seat Desk System by Rubbermaid is an in-car office organizer that fastens securely with seat belts and can easily be transported by means of a carrying strap.

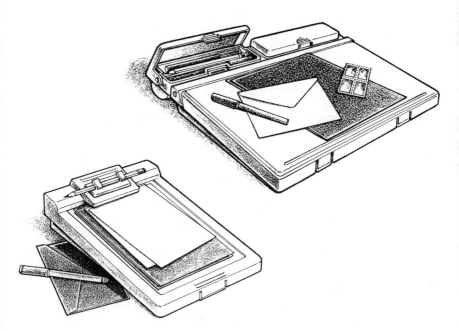

**Figure 12-4.** Rubbermaid Storage Clipboard and Portable Desk

stores notebooks, paper, pens and pencils. The **Portable Desk** is lightweight and easy to carry, with a large comfortable work surface. There are five divided compartments (two outside and three inside)

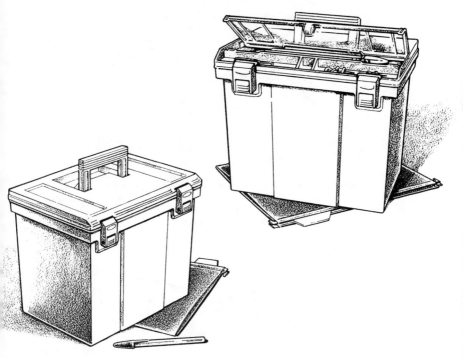

**Figure 12-5.** Rubbermaid Large File and Box Office File; the Junior File (not shown) is also available and holds a smaller number of files

that can hold a variety of paperwork and supplies. The **Large File** and the **Box Office File** are file/storage boxes that have ridges to accommodate hanging file folders. The Box Office File has a clear compartment in the lid to hold pens, pencils, calculator and other small office supplies. These Rubbermaid items are reasonably priced and are available in such stores as K-Mart and Target. For a store in your area, call Rubbermaid at 216/264-6464.

**The Executive Toolbox** ($19.95) and **The Portable Desk** ($39.95 to $89.95) from Memindex fit easily into a briefcase and help you keep traveling office supplies and paperwork organized and accessible. 800/828-5885, in New York, 716/342-7890
Memindex, Inc.
149 Carter Street
Rochester, NY 14601

**Fellowes Bankers Box R-Kive Organizer** is a complete portable filing

**Figure 12-6.** Fellowes Neat Ideas Portable File (left) and Personal File

system made of corrugated fiberboard in woodgrain styling. It includes a cover and two handhold grips for easy carrying and it comes with 12 letter size hanging folders. $14.95

**Fellowes Neat Ideas Portable File** and **Personal File**, as shown in Figure 12-6, provide great ways to transport paperwork and files. The Portable File comes with 10 letter-size hanging files.

**File-N-Shuttle** is a waterproof, dustproof and virtually damage-proof way to store and carry your files and supplies. It's great for car trunk "offices." A special stand with casters lets you roll your file to different areas of your office. The file has a clear, plastic lid that is hinged in the middle. Letter-size file, $39.95; legal-size file, $44.95; stand for letter- or legal-size files, $32.95. (See Memindex above under The Executive Toolbox.)

**Oxford File-It Portable File Box** (Figure 12-7) is a locking file box that includes a colored Pendaflex filing system–10 folders, 10 indexing tabs and one set of A-Z, household and blank headings. An expandable front makes files accessible even when the box is full. It's made of durable yet lightweight plastic with a flip-up handle and comes in six colors.

**Oxford ToteFile** is a compact, portable corrugated file that comes with a Pendaflex filing system–10 hanging folders in red, yellow or blue. The file box is white with a lid that matches the folder color.

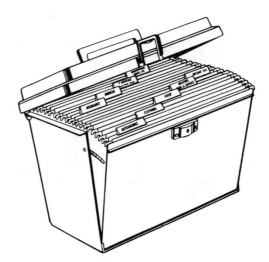

**Figure 12-7.** Oxford File-It Portable File Box

**Figure 12-8.** Oxford ToteFile

$14.89. See Figure 12-8.

**Plastic files** are great for your car trunk office or for transporting between office and home. See Figure 12-9 for some examples from W.T. Rogers.

**Portable Desk Accessory Kit** (Figure 12-10) is a zippered carry-all that packs 15 tools, including stapler, staple remover, hole punch,

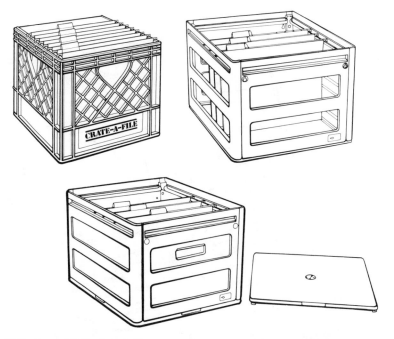

**Figure 12-9.** Crate-A-File (top left) comes with four hanging file folders; File Pal I (top right) stacks for compact storage or mounts to the wall; File Pal II is a fully enclosed file that holds 90 letter-size or 70 legal-size hanging file folders (illustrations from W.T. Rogers).

tape dispenser/pencil sharpener, tape, scissors, knife and notepad. $19.95. 215/395-5884
Day-Timers, Inc.
One Day-Timer Plaza
Allentown, PA 18195-1551

**Portfolio cases/notebooks** are convenient tools to transport a note-taking pad and key documents. Some come equipped with a flap pocket or special pocket folders, a business card holder, a calculator and a pen/pencil strap. Look for portfolios by Ampad, Hazel and InteliDesign. (These portfolios are not to be confused with the art portfolios discussed in Chapter 10.)

**W.T. Rogers Auto Clipboard** (Figure 12-11) is a handy note pad and pen for your car that attaches to any smooth, shiny surface (such as your windshield) by means of a suction cup. $5.95

**Rolodex "Companion"** is a portable file with 500 Rolodex brand

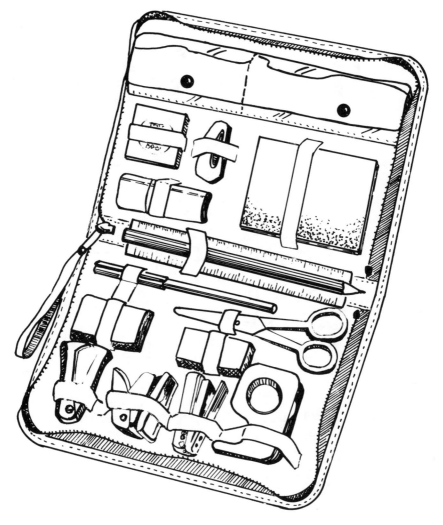

**Figure 12-10.** Portable Desk Accessory Kit by Day-Timers, Inc.

cards and is equipped with a retractable handle and sturdy latch.
**Rolodex electronic organizers, the Pocket Electrodex** and **the
Electrodex Plus,** (Figure 12-12) can exchange data between each
other as well as with a PC. The Pocket Electrodex ($179), the more
compact of the two, is the thinnest, smallest, lightest 64K pocket
computer on the market. It includes a daily organizer, calculator,

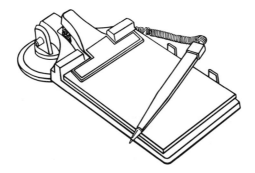

**Figure 12-11.** W.T. Rogers Auto Clipboard

**Figure 12-12.** The Pocket Electrodex and Electrodex Plus by Rolodex

currency converter and memory backup system. The Electrodex Plus ($199) has all the features of the Pocket Electrodex but is the desktop model. They each come with a free 20-minute training video, as well as a coupon for a free interface for your PC. 201/348-3939 Rolodex Corp.
245 Secaucus Rd.

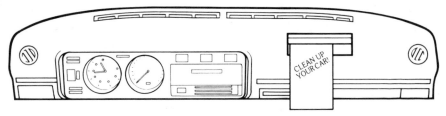

**Figure 12-13.** Wesystem Car Clip

Secaucus, NJ 07094-2196

**Wesystem Car Clip** (Figure 12-13) unobtrusively attaches to car doors, visors or dashboards to hold maps, directions, receipts or phone numbers. Papers can be inserted or removed with one hand. 800/888-0350 or 602/290-8330
D.L. West Manufacturing Co., Inc.
1684 S. Research Loop Dr., Ste. 510
Tucson, AZ 85710

## TRAVEL RESOURCE INFORMATION AND SERVICES

**AirKit** is a consolidator that gives discount airline fares for last-minute (3- to 30-days notice) travelers. 800/456-5660

**Airline Passenger's Guerilla Handbook** by George Albert Brown (Washington, DC: Blakes Publishing, 1989). This is a handy and entertaining survival guide for frequent flyers. $14.95. 800/SLAWSON

**Amtrak** is the organization to call if you want to travel by train in the U.S. 800/USA-RAIL

**The Center for Disease Control** (the Division of Quarantine in Traveler's Health Section) can provide information on immunization or vaccination when traveling overseas. 404/639-2572 (Atlanta)

**Consumer Information Catalog** is free and lists free and low-cost travel booklets such as "Fly Rights" and "Your Trip Abroad."
The Consumer Information Center
Pueblo, CO 81009

**Encore Marketing's Short Notice Club** is a "last-minute travel club" that requires a charge card number to get information. $36 per year. 800/638-8976

**"GETTING DOWN TO BUSINESS TRAVEL: A Guide to Making Your Business Travel More Productive, Profitable and Pleasant** is a 56-page pocket guidebook that features more than 200 travel secrets from seasoned business travelers. $2.25. 800/MBTI-876
Marriott Business Travel Institute
PO Box 40114-5114
Philadelphia, PA 19106-5114

**"Guide to Car Rental Agreements"** is available from the Federal Trade Commission, Bureau of Consumer Protection, in Washington, DC 20580

**International Association for Medical Assistance to Travelers (IAMAT)** is a nonprofit foundation that provides a list of American and English-speaking doctors abroad as well as up-to-date health information (immunization requirements, local diseases, safety of food and water, etc.) Membership is free but a donation is requested. 716/754-4883
417 Center St.
Lewiston, NY 14092

**The Medic Alert Foundation** provides special identification tags for those travelers who have special medical conditions such as diabetes or heart problems. Each tag lists the name of the condition and a world-wide toll-free number to call to get the wearer's medical history. The cost starts at $28. 800/344-3226 or 209/668-3333.

**Moment's Notice** is a "short-notice" discount travel club that acts as a clearing house for the travel industry's unsold space. Substantial discounts apply to cruises, tours and flights. Membership is $45 per year. 212/486-0500
425 Madison Ave.
New York, NY 10017

**Per Annum City Diaries** are attractive, pocket planners for business travelers that include a weekly calendar section, color maps and 60 pages of useful information on a particular city or group of cities. You'll find vital, current information on restaurants, stores, transportation services, 24-hour services and numbers and entertainment. The Metropolitan Diary includes information on 14 U.S. cities. 800/548-1108 or 212/213-8230
Per Annum, Inc.

114 East 32nd St., Ste. 1200
New York, NY 10016

**Plugged in for Profit: Take Your Office Anywhere** by Jefferson Bates and Stuart Crump, Jr. (Reston, VA: Acropolis Books Ltd., 1991). This book is loaded with information and resources on technological tips and tools that are particularly useful for business travelers. Here's a useful guide to laptop computers, cellular telephones, electronic mail, on-line services, dictation machines, not to mention some great organization and travel tips. Paperback, $12.95 plus $2 shipping and handling for first book, 75 cents for each additional book through the publisher located at 11250-22 Roger Bacon Dr., Reston, VA, 22090, 800/451-7771 or 703/709-0006.

**Rand McNally Commercial Atlas and Marketing Guide** features detailed and accurate maps of the 50 states, economic data, transportation and communication information, population summaries and marketing statistics. Updated annually, each edition costs $295, or $225 if you sign up as a "subscriber." 800/627-2897, Operator 450 Rand McNally, Publishing Direct Mail
8255 N. Central Park Ave.
Skokie, IL 60076-9809

**State Department Overseas Citizens Emergency Center** provides information on health conditions and current epidemics abroad. 202/647-5225

**State tourist offices** for each of the 50 U.S. states are great sources of information when you're planning a trip. Many of these offices have 800 numbers. These offices are usually located in the capital city of each state and go by many a name. Key words to look for: "Department of Commerce," "Convention and Visitors Bureau" and "Office of Travel and Tourism."

**Streets on a Disk** is a software program that provides travel routes and detailed maps with up to a half million street segments. $150 for the base package; spot map packages range from $20 to $640. 805/583-1029
Klynas Engineering
PO Box 1666
Simi Valley, CA

**Telecommunications Research & Action Center** (TRAC) will provide away-from-the-office advice on phone service. They also have a brief consumer guide for $3. 800/332-1124
PO Box 12038
Washington, DC 20005

**TeleMap Travel Routing Service** can give you time-saving "Directions-on-Demand" for travelers across town, across the country or around the world. Subscribers can call live operators 24 hours a day via a toll-free hotline for address-to-address driving directions prepared by professionals and delivered by phone, fax, modem or electronic mail. Annual personal subscriptions: $48. Corporate plans are available. 800/843-1000 (from the U.S. and Canada); 415/256-4560; FAX: 415/947-1867
TeleMap Corporation
1327 N. Main St., Ste. 105
Walnut Creek, CA 94596

**Tip Computers International** makes several credit-card-size tools to help you with tipping: Tip Computer, which calculates 15 and 20 percent tips on dollar amounts up to $100; Travel Tips USA, a two-card set that provides customary tipping amounts or percentages by service category for all travel-related situations; and Everyday Tips, a two-card set for everyday services. I've carried and used Tip Computer for years. 800/527-9493 or 619/488-7332
1236 Wilbur Ave.
San Diego, CA 92109

**Travel Smart** is a monthly newsletter that tracks the best travel deals. $44 per year. 800/327-3633
40 Beechdale Rd.
Dobbs Ferry, NY 10522

**Traveler's Advantage** provides regional telephone numbers for taped information about travel discounts on fares, rooms, etc. $49 per year. 800/548-1116

## HIGH-TECH TRAVEL TOOLS, ACCESSORIES AND SERVICES

**The Atari Portfolio** is a hand-held computer that is more powerful than palmtop electronic organizers. Weighing in at one pound, it

has a 40-column-by-8-line screen, built-in spreadsheet and word processing, 128K of RAM, a calendar with alarms, a phone directory and a calculator. $299.95. 800/443-8020
Atari Computer
1196 Borregas Ave.
Sunnyvale, CA 94088

**Battery Watch** is a software program that tracks how long your laptop battery will last and works with most battery-powered laptops. $49.95. 800/662-2652
Traveling Software, Inc.
18702 N. Creek Pkwy.
Bothell, WA 98011

**Canon BJ-10e Bubblejet** is a portable, 4.6-pound, quality printer with a sheet-feeder option. $499 for the printer; $90, sheetfeeder; $50, battery pack; $25, replacement print head/ink cartridges. 800/848-4123
Canon USA
1 Canon Plaza
Lake Success, NY 11042

**The Casio BOSS** (*B*usiness *O*rganizer *S*cheduling *S*ystem) is a 64K pocket-size organizer that can exchange data with a PC, has a "Business Card" function, a scheduler, an alarm feature, a calendar, a calculator, a memo pad and a world time function that can determine the time in 127 cities in 24 time zones. There are several different models (one even has a built-in spelling checker dictionary and thesaurus). About $260 (plus $119.95 for the computer interface). 800/272-0272 or 201/891-9466
Casio, Inc.
PO Box 7000
Dover, NJ 07801

**A connector** is useful to connect laptops and compact fax machines into a hotel room phone system. You can get it as part of the Road Warrior Toolkit, listed below, or separately for $99 from Unlimited Systems, which calls it **Konnex**, at 619/277-3300 in San Diego, CA.

**Connector, the corporate mobility company**, makes custom, fiberglass, travel cases for your telecommunications tools, such as laptop, handheld phone, fax and accessories. The cases meet airline regula-

**Figure 12-14.** ALLSOP Disk File/5 (left) holds five 5¼-inch disks and the Flip 'N' File Travel Pak from Innovative Concepts, Inc., (San Jose), holds up to four 3½-inch diskettes.

tions for underseat storage. Under $200. 800/937-1900 ext. 1300 or 818/843-0998
724 S. Victory Blvd., Ste. 202
Burbank, CA 91502

**Dictaphone recorders** offer many state-of-the-art choices in portable dictation equipment. To get your local Dictaphone representative, either call the 800 information number at 800/555-1212 and ask for an 800 Dictaphone number for your state or look in the yellow pages of your telephone directory under "Dictating Machines & Supplies," where you'll probably see a Dictaphone listing.

**Diskette files** come in small, durable cases that are ideal for popping in a briefcase. Two are shown in Figure 12-14.

**E-mail systems** offer business travelers convenient, high-tech telecommunications options. Here are three to consider: **AT&T Mail** (AT&T Corp., New Brunswick, NJ, 800/367-7225); **EasyLink** (Western Union Corp, Dallas, TX, 800/527-5184); and **MCI Mail** (MCI International Corp., Washington, DC, 800/444-6245)

**Filt-Air** is wonderful, new filter that is great for business travelers who are in their car and are exposed to smog and other pollutants. I'm a user of this $10 activated carbon auto filter that removes up to 90 percent of hydrocarbons before they reach the driver/passenger section. It also reduces dust and pollen—a nice plus for allergy sufferers. It does not, however, fit every model of car, e.g., Volvo. 800/283-7287 or 714/583-7287
ISE (Inspections System Engineering, Inc.)
7 Whatney, Ste. 200
Irvine, CA 92718

**Interstate Travelmate** is a pocket-size computer guide that shows travel services, such as gas stations, motels/hotels and restaurants, that are available at 14,000 exits along major interstate highways. $99.95. 800/421-0911, outside California, or 213/657-4800, in California
Beverly Hills Motoring Accessories
200 S. Robertson Blvd.
Beverly Hills, CA 90211

**MISCO Computer Supplies and Accessories** computer mail-order catalog features a section on handy laptop accessories, including travel cases. 800/876-4626 or 908/264-1000
One MISCO Plaza
Holmdel, NJ 07733

**North American Official Cellular Users Guide** includes cellular local service rates, roaming usage costs and dialing patterns while traveling in over 300 systems in the U.S. and Canada. Annual updates. $20, includes shipping and handling. 313/561-3339
Cellmark Publishing Company
PO Box 2619
Dearborn, MI 48123

**The Poqet PC** is a palmtop MS-DOS computer, with a full 80-column-by-25-line screen, that won the *PC Magazine* award for technical excellence. It's fully DOS-compatible and supports graphics. $1,995. 408/737-8100
Poqet Computer Corp.
650 N. Mary Ave.
Sunnyvale, CA 94086

**Remote Control Programs** let you link computers that are in different physical locations, such as your on-the-road laptop with your office PC. The following programs have received good reviews, are easy to use and show prices that include setup on both host and remote computers:

**Carbon Copy Plus,** $398 (Microcom Software Division, 500 River Ridge Dr., Norwood, MA 02062, 617/551-1999)

**Close-Up Customer/Terminal,** $195, and **Support/ACS,** $245 (Norton-Lambert Corp., PO Box 4085, Santa Barbara, CA 93140, 805/964-6767)

**Co/Session,** $195 (Triton Technologies Inc., 200 Middlesex Turnpike, Iselin, NJ 08830, 800/322-9440 or 201/855-9440)

**pcAnywhere III,** $145 (Dynamic Microprocessor Associates, 1776 E. Jericho Turnpike, Huntington, NY 11743, 516/462-0440)

**Takeover,** $295 (SoftKlone Distributing Corp., 327 Office Plaza Dr., #100, Tallahassee, FL 32301, 800/634-8670 or 904/878-8564)

**Road Warrior Toolkits** include all of the peripherals, tools and accessories that enable people who travel with computers to use their modems to send and receive data and faxes through telephone systems in hotels, offices, homes and field sites. The Toolkit, $49.95; Deluxe Toolkit with CP+Connection II, $139.95; and Tele-Toolkit with Telecoupler, $279.95. Each includes complete instructions and comes in a compact nylon case. 800/274-4277
Computer Products Plus (CP+)
16351 Gothard Street
Huntington Beach, CA 92647

**Stowaway 2400 Pocket Modem** is the first full-featured 2400/1200/300-baud, line-powered pocket modem that gets its power from the computer and phone line and requires no adapter, battery or UPS backup system. $295. 203/356-1837
Vocal Technologies, Inc.
143 Hoyt, Ste. 4K
Stamford, CT 06905

**Targus cases** are versatile, quality cases in nylon or leather for transporting laptop computers. $55 to $199. 800/243-8088 or 603/446-7721
PC Connection (a highly-rated computer mail-order company)
6 Mill Street

Marlow, NH 03456

**Telocator** is a trade association serving the interests of the paging, cellular and PCS (personal communications services) industries. Telocator has a magazine and newsletter and holds professional education seminars and industry trade shows. 800/326-TNET
2000 M Street NW, Ste. 230
Washington, DC 20036

## TRAVEL ACCESSORIES AND SERVICES

**Day-Timer Quick Trip Carry-All** (Figure 12-15) doubles as an overnighter and as a briefcase. $149. 215/395-5884
Day-Timers, Inc.
One Day-Timer Plaza
Allentown, PA 18195-1551

**Hazel Business Portables** is a good-looking, practical line of soft-sided travel pieces that includes portfolios, briefcases, carry-on bags, garment bags and overnight bags.

**Magellan's** is a 36-page mail-order catalog featuring hundreds of travel accessories, including the "hidden pocket" money pouch. 800/962-4943.
Box 5485
Santa Barbara, CA 93150-5485

**Selectronics** makes electronic, credit-card-size translators based on Berlitz Phrase Books and Dictionaries that sell for $99.95 and $149.95. 800/828-6293 or 716/248-9150

**Traveler's Checklist** offers about 40 travel items through mail order including voltage converters, adapter plugs, an inflatable back support pillow and AcuBand, a special, non-medicated wrist strap that prevents motion sickness about 85 percent of the time. The catalog is 50 cents. 203/364-0144
335 Cornwall Bridge Road
Sharon, CT 06069

**Travel Mini Pack** is a 14-page mail-order catalog that features miniature-sized, brand-name, grooming and first-aid products along with a complete line of travel accessories. 914/429-8281
PO Box 571
Stony Point, NY 10980

**Figure 12-15.** Day-Timer Quick Trip Carry-All has a large pocket that holds a change of clothes, reading material or planner and 13 leather-trimmed pockets that hold portable office supplies.

**Travel Science** offers shirt-pocket-size foreign language tools consisting of basic phrase card "Pacs" using "Natural Phonetics" by language and regions of the world. Pacs are $4 each. 505/265-9619
812 Charleston NE, Ste. 6
Albuquerque, NM 87110

# 13

# WORKING
# WITH OTHERS

*Quick Scan: If you have customers, co-workers or both, you need to read this chapter. Mastering the other chapters without mastering this one will leave you organized, but working in a vacuum. The real purpose of organization in today's competitive marketplace is to find better ways of working with others. In the other chapters you focused primarily on yourself. Now in this chapter you'll discover how to bring others into the fold by first building a philosophy of quality, service and teamwork and then developing organized solutions to improve operations.*

---

The first 12 chapters focused largely on what you as an individual can do in the work place. As a consultant and a trainer, I have found this is the best place to start. But for dramatic results, you need to spread the word so that everyone with whom you work has a chance to be their best and make exciting contributions toward helping your organization–whether it be your office, department or company–reach its goals.

## WHY EVERYONE YOU WORK WITH
## IS YOUR CUSTOMER

You have probably heard about the importance of customer service and customer satisfaction. You may not, however, realize the extent to which it applies to you and your job. The point is, no matter what kind of job you do or organization you work for, customer focus needs to be the bottom line.

To compete and be profitable in today's world economy, your organization can no longer be doing "business as usual." The old maxim, "if it ain't broke, don't fix it," isn't true any more. Change is the name of the game and to stay competitive in business, you need to **improve continuously** in order to **provide quality** goods or services **for your customers.**

Notice I've highlighted several key words. "Customers" need to be your primary focus. There are two kinds of customers for every organization: **external** and **internal.** Some consider external customers to be the most important. They're the ones who are paying for your goods or services. They're the ones you need to satisfy first to stay in business.

Internal customers are the team members with whom you work to provide the goods or services for your external customers. They could be office co-workers, contacts in another department or division or part of your supplier base.

For many, internal customers, are a close second. That's not so, however, for Hal Rosenbluth, CEO of the highly successful Philadelphia travel agency, Rosenbluth Travel Inc., which was featured in *INC. Magazine* and was a Tom Peters Service Company of the Year award winner. Rosenbluth, who calls his internal customers "associates," says, "We don't believe our customers can come first unless our associates come first. If we have happy people here, then they're free to concentrate only on our clients." Stated another way, if your internal customers aren't happy, chances are good your external customers won't be either.

Ralph Stayer, CEO for Johnsonville Foods Inc. in Sheboygan, Wisconsin, talks about employee happiness as a starting point.

> At Johnsonville, we want people to be happy, but never
> satisfied. We want people to see themselves becoming

> something. People should be continuously learning and striving to make something bigger and better of themselves. We try to make sure that happens. We aren't making just sausage here. I use the business to make great people. I don't use people to make a great business. If everyone is moving forward and working together, then the sausage will take care of itself.

So in a very real sense *everyone* with whom you work or interact is your customer. Even if you're a sole proprietor, you simply don't work in a vacuum. Once you recognize this fact, you've begun to get on board the quality revolution that is sweeping the globe.

Quality, or more precisely **Total Quality Management**, is more than a buzz word or a fad; it's a way of doing business that permeates every aspect of a business. My colleague, Dr. Susan Resnick-West, has summarized Total Quality Management as a comprehensive business strategy that 1) focuses on the customer, 2) focuses on the work process and 3) develops the organization so that the first two are possible.

To focus on the customer means to provide service and quality *as the customer sees them*. You stay close to your customers (both external and internal) by listening to them, asking them questions and working diligently to solve their problems. Customer focus means following through, doing what you say—which all involves good organizational skills and systems.

Focus on the work process is the means by which you provide customer service. It's examining the effectiveness of your organizational skills, tools and systems to check whether they're the best means for providing goods and services on time, within budget and to the customer's satisfaction. Work process has been the main focus of this book.

Developing the organization involves upper and middle management's genuine commitment to quality and customer service as well as their support of all internal customers. An openness to change and continuous quality improvement is evident at *all* levels of such an organization. In a quality-conscious organization you'll see a driving emphasis on training, communication, innovation, flexibility, employee involvement and teamwork.

Look at where you work. See if there's at least a spark of *caring* about quality, service and external/internal customers. If so, you should be able to use at least a few of the ideas in this next section to help develop your organization and create the right climate and context for customer-focused continuous improvement to occur.

## SUREFIRE WAYS
## TO INCREASE QUALITY AND TEAMWORK
## WHETHER OR NOT YOU'RE THE BOSS

There's no great mystery to producing a winning team that offers quality goods or services. It takes a consistent, organized approach that addresses three key areas: communication, employee involvement and training.

Underlying these areas, however, should be a genuine foundation of *caring about people*. Without this foundation, many of the ideas in this section could be perceived as insincere and manipulative. It doesn't matter how many great, innovative ideas you introduce into your organization if an uncaring attitude exists. As the saying goes, "People don't care how much you know until they know how much you care."

## COMMUNICATE WITH INTERNAL
## AND EXTERNAL CUSTOMERS

People in the workplace often take communication for granted and assume that enough of it goes on. There's plenty of talking and memo writing every day. And just look at all the communication toys that they're using–from voice mail to electronic mail (E-mail). But the sheer quantity of communication that takes place doesn't insure quality in the communication.

Quality communication is a two-way street. First, **keep people informed.** As Thomas Jefferson observed, "When you don't keep people informed, you get one of three things: rumor, apathy or revolution." (And he ought to know.)

**Use multiple channels of communication**, if possible. Different channels can include any of the following: memos, meetings, company publications, the boss, co-workers, bulletin boards, voice mail and electronic mail. Multiple channels make communication more interesting and less likely to fall prey to distortion or bias from information that's conveyed through only one channel or source.

Be on the lookout for communication channels that are innovative, creative or humorous. I discovered one such channel several years ago and always show it in my seminars on office organization. It's called *SEC'S TALK: Every Secretary's Instant Communication Kit* and can be used by anyone in a busy office. Originally devised for secretaries to communicate with busy bosses on the phone, it can be used anytime and for a variety of different office scenarios. It is a comb-bound book of typical office communication messages, some with fill-in portions, in large print and tabbed for easy reference. Included are such messages as "URGENT CALL HOLDING," "YOUR _____ APPOINTMENT IS HERE" AND "_____ IS ON THE PHONE." More assertive messages include "I COULD USE A COMPLIMENT ABOUT NOW!," "HOW ABOUT A RAISE?" or if things get really bad, "I QUIT!" (The book is $9.95 and available from publisher Price, Stern, Sloan in Los Angeles; the phone number is 800/421-0892 or 213/657-6100.)

On the other hand, **beware of using too many channels or communication tools.** I worked with one Fortune 500 high-tech company in which each person had several means by which they could communicate with others inside the company. Everyone had to not only check *all* of the communication channels (voice mail, electronic mail, central message center, inter-office mail) but had to remember how a colleague preferred to receive messages.

Keeping people informed is only half of the communication story. To complete the story, **ask people what they think.** This needs to happen regularly for both internal and external customers. Be prepared, however, that once you ask people what they think, you really *listen*, take the information seriously and *act on it.*

Conducting a survey is an excellent way to see what's on people's minds. Keep surveys as simple as possible. Design a major benefit into the survey—why should anyone want to take the time to complete it? Tell survey participants *what's in it for them.*

Harvey Mackay discusses three surveys he uses in his envelope business in his two best-selling business books, *Swim With the Sharks Without Being Eaten Alive* and *Beware the Naked Man Who Offers You His Shirt.* His surveys aren't intended for others to take; they're used individually as information-gathering tools to provide insight and help with decision making. According to Mackay, these forms will "help you systematize your information in a way that will make it more useful and accessible."

"The 66-Question Customer Profile" in *Swim With the Sharks* is designed especially for a sales person or manager to complete about his or her external customers in order to understand them better. "The Mackay 33 for Employees" in *Beware the Naked Man* is designed for workers to evaluate the companies for whom they work (or would like to work). Many of these questions are the kinds of questions that should be asked in company-wide surveys of employees across the board (e.g., "What is the company's attitude toward education? Pays tuition? Maintains employee library? Basis for promotion?").

Also in *Beware the Naked Man,* "The Mackay 33 for Managers" is a profile form managers complete in private for each employee, as well as for themselves. Many thought-provoking questions are included and could be adapted to the performance appraisal process.

Mrs. Fields Inc. stays in touch with more than 600 retail managers by using personal computers that link the managers to the corporate headquarters in Park City, Utah. Besides putting information at the managers' fingertips, the computers have electronic mail systems that allow managers and all employees to send ideas directly to Debbi Fields, chief executive officer. A reply follows within 48 hours.

"The President's Luncheon" is one way the IBM Endicott/Owego Employees Federal Credit Union in Endicott, New York, asks employees what they think. Every month, six or seven employees are chosen at random to have lunch with the president and discuss any topics they feel are important to them, to the credit union or to management.

The suggestion box can be a good way to get feedback but one department discovered a new twist. This was a busy mail and phone department, where phones rang off the hook and ten disgruntled employees didn't work well together. The department replaced the suggestion box with a "Gripe Box," and employees completed "Gripes and Complaints" cards anonymously. Though the Gripe Box sounds negative, it worked because it reflected how people were feeling and gave them a chance to vent those feelings. Gripes and complaints were handled openly at department meetings, solutions were generated and today everyone gets along very well.

Pat Bruner, president of T.L.C. Child Care Centers in Green Bay, Wisconsin, offers an open dialogue for her 22 employees every other month over pizza. She takes them out for pizza and then they meet for two hours. The first hour is an open gripes session about anything and anybody, including management. The second hour is spent on positive comments and solutions to gripes.

Just staying close to your customers and having your eyes and ears open can be a very effective way to find out what people think; convey that information back to your customers and you have real two-way communication. That's just what a new, local caterer-restaurant did. Zabie's in Santa Monica, California, published a beautiful, two-color brochure for their customers, in which they affirmed their "commitment to quality" and acknowledged customers' contributions. Owner Zabie Vourvoulis writes:

> We struggle constantly with the issue of service and how best to fill your needs. Many times, small suggestions or comments from you have led to big changes (paper biodegradable disposables for instance). We've also purchased new, more comfortable and sturdier stools, and we've developed an interesting, reasonably priced dinner menu...Your support has been wonderful. It's encouraging to know that effort and caring have a place in this fast-paced world of ours. We certainly appreciate yours and we hope that ours shows every day.

When I talked with Vourvoulis by phone she emphasized the importance of being able to listen to criticism. "When I hear the same critical comment several times in a short period of time, an alarm goes off and I know we have to do something."

It's the ability to listen, act and develop close relationships with both employees as well as customers that sets Zabie's apart. In business since September, 1988, Zabie's has 22 employees on several different shifts working in 1,475 square feet. She acknowledges both employees and customers in the brochure. In the restaurant, she's provided special recognition for those repeat customers who have been with her from day one: there is a name tag for each long-standing customer on every stool.

**Personalize your communication,** whenever possible. There are certain words people can't hear enough: their own names and "thank you." Take time to thank people for their thoughtfulness, hard work or good ideas. Sitting down to write a thank-you note is such a simple, but very powerful method of communication. It shows that the recipient is worth your time and you're organized enough to make time for it. Writing quick, two- or three-sentence notes on personalized note cards can be accomplished easily during spare moments, such as waiting in a doctor's office or sitting on a plane. (By the way, it's more effective to send a note right away but better to send a note late than not at all.)

Learning and using people's names can have a big impact on opening up communication. I recently had a dramatic example of seeing that it's "all in a name." Around 4:30 every afternoon, a postal carrier makes the last pick-up at several boxes near our office. Occasionally, I will go out to the boxes right at 4:30, when the postal truck arrives and hand my mail to the carrier.

Over the years, there have been several carriers, each of whom was very friendly. This year a new carrier assumed the route but he seemed very different. He was very serious and wouldn't look up when you handed him mail. He appeared almost upset that you were breaking his routine. He seemed, in a word, anti-social. Normally, I would have introduced myself and made small talk but I figured that was a real waste of time with this guy.

Weeks went by and I avoided making any contact with the carrier. Being normally a very outgoing individual, I decided one day to simply introduce myself. Much to my surprise, when I told him my name and learned his was Richard, he really lit up and began to talk. Every time I see him now, he calls me by name and has something pleasant to say.

Richard is an internal customer who is part of my supplier base. The service he provides makes it possible for me to be of service to my external customers. Because he's a part of my team, it's important to be able to communicate with him.

## ACTIVELY INVOLVE EMPLOYEES

Once you've begun implementing effective communication strategies, you've opened the door to employee involvement, the secret to quality and teamwork. Let's look at some ways for you and all employees to get involved.

Start by zeroing in on the **mission of your company or organization.** Everybody should have a copy of the company mission statement, as well as the company's guiding values. Mission and values statements are often buried in long-range planning documents that the upper management team may have generated. Progressive companies distribute copies of these statements to all employees, reprint them in company publications and may even make special posters that appear around the company. See Figure 13-1 for an example of the mission statement and guiding values for PDQ, a personnel agency in Los Angeles.

**Figure 13-1.** PDQ PERSONNEL SERVICES, INC. MISSION AND VALUES

*Mission:*
We serve the business community in a sincere and thorough manner by providing timely, cost effective results in meeting their regular, temporary and long-term staffing needs. We continually invest our talents to establish and maintain long-term relationships with both our clients and employees. Through innovation and education we strive to maintain the competitive edge.

*Values:*
**Heritage of Excellence**—We maintain the highest levels of professionalism to be the best we can.

**Customer Service**—We provide all of our customers with quality personnel services by treating each of their staffing needs as if it were our own.

**Employee Responsiveness**—We treat people in all positions with fairness and dignity. We provide opportunities for earned growth to reach their potential both inside and outside the organization. Our people are proud of their high standards and are equitably rewarded.

**Civic Spirit**—The community benefits from both our individual and company commitments to continually participate in the community's growth. Our people are educated and enriched through community involvement.

**Adaptability**—We test and try new concepts and services. We understand that one key strength in maintaining the competitive edge is our ability to identify and benefit from change.

**Teamwork**—We communicate openly and with trust in mutually pursuing opportunities and meeting challenges. Each person plays an integral role in the success of the PDQ team.

If your company has no written mission statement or guiding values, suggest that a committee or action team be formed to develop them. This group could have representatives from all different levels or departments in the company. This is a great way to build participation in the company and co-ownership of the mission statement and values. And ideally, the mission statement and guiding values will include the importance of employee involvement.

## THE SPECIAL ROLE OF MANAGERS

If you're a manager or you work for one, recognize that the role of the manager today must be that of **team leader, teacher and coach** who facilitates employee participation. Old, autocratic, traditional management styles of "do it my way" no longer work. Interesting enough, a recent study showed that women more naturally exhibit the kind of nontraditional traits needed in today's managers—the ability to share information and power, encourage employee participation and demonstrate how both individual, personal goals may be reached while attaining organizational goals.

According to management consultant and author Lee Cheaney, today's managers should also "manage on the behavior of 95 percent of employees and not on the five percent who cause problems." He suggests dealing with that five percent promptly and fairly, spending the bulk of your time developing your team.

To develop the 95 percent, today's manager needs to help form work teams that have real authority to make decisions and to act. One General Mills cereal plant has given such authority to its work teams and has realized a 40 percent higher productivity rate compared with traditionally managed groups.

We're seeing this kind of shift taking place in manufacturing circles but we also need to see it in service areas and in the office. Speaking of the office, every few years Steelcase Inc. has Louis Harris and Associates do a survey on what office workers want. Each survey has workers rank 17 key job factors in order of importance. The following continue to come out on top, above pay and promotion opportunities: honesty and ethical behavior of management, the opportunity to develop skills, the desire to have management recognize workers' contributions, having a challenging job and being able to contribute.

Managers today have the opportunity to address these factors through a more participatory management style that gives more responsibility to workers and work teams.

Participatory managers encourage their people to make decisions and come up with solutions of their own. Sun Microsystems CEO

Scott G. McNealy jokes, "When our people have difficulty making a decision, then I threaten to make the decision. That notion gets people scared enough to make the right decision themselves."

When I presented a seminar to a credit union group in Portland, one manager shared his policy, "Don't come to me with a problem unless you have at least two solutions."

## TEAM MEETINGS

Traditional meetings, as someone once put it, are all too often a place where minutes are taken and hours are lost. They've also been a place where, according to one recent survey, many participants feel uncomfortable freely sharing their opinions and believe that most meetings are dominated by hidden agendas.

Participatory team meetings are an important way for workers to develop their skills and make contributions. They're also important for dealing with problems, making decisions by consensus, promoting communication, developing leadership, building commitment, sharing information, setting goals and improving operations.

To improve your meetings, why not have a meeting on meetings? Have your work team come prepared to share at least one idea on how to make more productive, participatory meetings.

Consider having a training session on meetings. I recently conducted such a session for one company and used an entertaining, informative video called "Meetings, Bloody Meetings" starring English actor/comedian John Clease (available from Video Arts, 800/553-0091).

In a nutshell, here are the ten tips I teach about effective meetings:

1. **Every meeting should have a stated purpose or goal** that is determined in advance of the meeting and that is defined in a **prepared agenda** to which participants have had a chance to contribute. The agenda should be distributed far enough in advance so participants can prepare. Each agenda item should be as specific as possible, should include the individual who's introducing it and should cite the purpose of the item at the meeting, e.g, "For Discussion," "For Information" or "For Decision."

2. **Limit the size of the group.** Include only those who need to be there. Four to seven people is an ideal number of people for a planning or problem-solving meeting. A training session or informational meeting could handle many more.

3. Ideally **arrange participants in a circle to encourage more participation** and provide refreshments to set a more informal atmosphere.

4. **List start and end times for the meeting on the agenda and stick to them.** It may be helpful to use a countdown timer to stay on schedule.

5. Each meeting should **have a facilitator who keeps the meeting moving,** clarifies and summarizes key points, acknowledges contributions of participants by name and ends the meeting on time. The facilitator can provide a quick verbal summary at the end, reviewing the goals of the meeting and how participants contributed to reaching those goals. To build leadership, use a "rotating facilitator," a different person from the work team to lead each meeting.

6. **Have a recorder take minutes** that reflect key points, decisions, action items and the responsible participants. Minutes should be prepared and distributed to attendees within a few days of the meeting. Underline action items, deadlines and names of responsible individuals so that they stand out. Have a different recorder at each meeting.

7. Have either the facilitator or someone else **use a flip chart, overhead projector or a computer with a large screen to record key ideas** and make them visible to everyone at the meeting. Such an ongoing record serves as a "group memory," is useful reference for the recorder when preparing minutes and can be used at future meetings. Visual tools also can help improve retention of the information by 50 percent.

8. **Action items, decisions and delegations listed in the minutes** should be brought forward to appear **on the next meeting's agenda** for a status report follow-up.

9. **Be flexible and creative** with your meetings and **use different formats** that are appropriate. For manager/assistant teams I recommend **short, but frequent daily meetings** that take no more than five to ten minutes. Certainly a formal agenda for such meetings would be inappropriate but a "standing agenda,"

that covers routine items, such as the day's schedule, correspondence, telephone calls and certain ongoing clients, would be a good way to standardize and streamline this business meeting.

10. To solve problems and build teamwork, use "Quality Circle" meetings, also called "brainstorming sessions" and "Nominal Group Technique." Such meetings have a time limit and typically include four parts: 1) identification and definition of the problem (because as Charles Kettering once said, "A problem well-stated is a problem half-solved"); 2) brainstorming suggestions, alternatives and solutions without discussion; 3) discussion and evaluation of the brainstormed ideas; and 4) selection of one to three ideas for implementation.

## OTHER EMPLOYEE INVOLVEMENT PROGRAMS

Many companies today have a whole variety of **employee recognition programs** that encourage and reward employee-generated, innovative, cost-saving ideas; a superior work effort; surpassed performance goals; and employee longevity. Forms of recognition vary widely from certificates of appreciation (University of California, San Diego Medical Center has a Pride-O-Gram) to cash and prize incentive awards.

Some companies, a recent newspaper story reported, are rewarding employee risk-taking even to the extent of doing things wrong because such companies are encouraging employees to *think* for themselves and try to solve company problems. Esso Resources Canada has an "Order of the Duck" award consisting of a wooden duck's head mounted on a plunger; the duck's head symbolizes vision and the plunger represents sticking your neck out. The award goes to an employee who challenges management or does something without the boss's approval.

Some employee recognition programs are more successful than others. The sincerity and caring on behalf of management may have much to do with how these programs are perceived and hence, their success. In addition, the programs should reflect the mission and values of the company.

These programs need to be spiced up from time to time as they can become old hat in a hurry. And what works well in one company may not work well in yours.

Survey employees to see what they think of such programs and the program awards and what changes they'd like to make. (You may find, for example, that employees rate a trip to Hawaii for two as a much greater incentive than an equivalent cash award.)

**Performance management** in which employees set and evaluate their own performance objectives is an important way to involve employees. Be sure to build in recognition and reward for good and/or improved performance.

As a part of their performance management process, the Tennessee Teachers Credit Union in Nashville has each employee complete a thought-provoking, two-page, self-evaluation form for past and future performance. The form asks employees to list their performance objectives for the coming 12 months, any necessary behavior changes they'll need to make and significant achievements during the past 12 months. In addition, employees are asked to "stretch" themselves—to make a special effort to accomplish something in the next 12 months and identify what that effort will be. There is also a chart for listing strengths, weaknesses, problems and opportunities.

## THE BENEFITS OF CAMARADERIE

Building camaraderie is a fun way to encourage employee participation, teamwork and creativity. Many companies are finding that the group that plays together, stays together. Odetics, Inc., an electronics company in Anaheim, California, that was featured in the book *The 100 Best Companies to Work for in America*, even has a "Fun Committee." Joel Slutzky, Odetics chairman and CEO, notes that since people spend more time at work than anywhere else, it makes sense to encourage them to look forward to coming to work. Besides low absenteeism, his company has a very low turnover rate and low medical costs for his industry. He also believes his employees are more innovative.

Slutzky emphasizes that fun events don't have to cost a lot but should be creative and different and go beyond the typical company picnic. Past events have included a '50s party; a "couch potato" contest that included miniature golf and paper airplane activities for employees "who wanted to get into fitness without working up a sweat"; plays put on by the company repertoire theater; a surprise bash to celebrate the company's 20th birthday; and a Secretaries

Day celebration that had managers dress up as waiters and serve lunch to company secretaries in the cafeteria.

Every year, Payday, a payroll company in San Francisco, invites employees' children in for a visit. The children play games, have lunch with their parents and watch their parents work. A side benefit is that employees get to discover something personal about their co-workers.

You may spend at least eight hours a day at work, yet know very little about your co-workers. The Tennessee Teachers Credit Union has a voluntary Employee Profile form that asks about such areas as hobbies, outside interests, children and background. These forms are compiled and published periodically in an employee directory that helps employees become better acquainted.

## TRAIN TO SEE A REAL GAIN

To maintain a quality-oriented team that focuses on continuous improvement, you'll need an ongoing, quality training program. Such a program results from meeting needs identified through excellent communication with customers (both internal and external) and a high level of employee involvement.

It also requires the support of top management and should reflect a continuous improvement, growth philosophy of your company. Unfortunately, in all too many businesses, training is perceived as an unnecessary frill. But top companies, who seek to attain and maintain the competitive edge, recognize that training is an integral, essential part.

**Get involved in your own training.** Assess areas where you could use some additional training. Progressive companies frequently conduct needs assessment surveys for employees and their managers to identify training areas. Some training departments have identified and organized skill areas by category and by level or position and invite all employees to evaluate their own skill strengths and weaknesses. Training programs and materials are developed or brought in-house, based on these identified needs.

Notice whenever you feel uncomfortable in doing a new job or taking on a new responsibility. Don't pretend you know something when you don't. Don't worry about feeling inadequate. Let it be a signal that it's time for you to learn something new, and whenever you do, there's usually some feeling of discomfort that's natural.

This feeling often occurs when someone delegates something new to you. You may remember the four steps to delegation discussed in Chapter 3. The second one had to do with training. It's your responsibility to make sure you get the necessary training to do the delegated task. In a larger sense, it's your responsibility to make sure you get the necessary training to do your entire job. Of course, it's easier in a corporate culture that actively supports training. But it's still your responsibility.

## CAPITALIZE ON CROSS TRAINING

One way to get training, aside from a formal training department, is to take advantage of **cross training**. This kind of training lets you see, and in some cases lets you do, other people's jobs. There are many advantages to this kind of training. First, you have a chance to learn new skills or new aspects of your company. Learning additional skills could add to your marketing and career potential. Second, it can be helpful from an operations standpoint to have someone else fill in for you if you're out sick or on vacation.

Third, when you can see what procedures are followed by other people or departments, you have a chance to see why these procedures are necessary. You may be more cooperative when you're asked to fill out a form, for example, because you've seen firsthand, just how important it is to another department.

Building a real sense of cooperation is a major reason to cross train. Teledyne Systems Company in Northridge, California, has a chart that reads:

YOUR PROBLEM
Cooperation is spelled with two letters: "WE."

## DESCRIBE WHAT YOU DO AND HOW YOU DO IT

Your department or office should develop its own **training manual** that describes all of the different jobs and responsibilities in detail. You (and everyone) should write a description of your responsibilities, functions and processes. All of the information should be checked, tested and updated from time to time. Writing the manual on a word processor makes updates easy.

Normally, training for a new position is handled by one other person, often a predecessor. When the training isn't in some written format, vital items can become omitted.

It's important to document all that you do on your job in a manual. Such documentation might even justify why you need an assistant (or a raise!). Plus it's a real help when you train someone else to do your job—temporarily, when you go on vacation, or permanently, when you get that promotion.

## MAX YOUR FAX AND OTHER WAYS TO IMPROVE OFFICE OPERATIONS

When you've incorporated some of the important interpersonal aspects we've just discussed into the workplace, you're in a much better position to suggest and implement organizational, operational changes that affect many people. You've laid the groundwork for change.

I'd like to offer my suggestions regarding several operational areas and recommend you share these areas and suggestions *as a starting point* with those in your office or workplace.

### MAX YOUR FAX

It's amazing how in a very short period of time the facsimile (fax) machine has become almost as indispensable as the copy machine. In some offices, however, the fax machine (like the copy machine) is used too much.

Every office needs to develop suggested guidelines or a policy regarding fax use. Here is a baker's dozen I've developed that may apply to your office:

1. As a rule, don't have your fax number printed on your business card, unless the fax is specifically designated for a purpose, such as taking orders. Making your fax number too easy to get encourages junk fax and also encourages people to rely too heavily on the fax as a communication tool.

2. If you do need to include your fax number on your business card or letterhead, make the phone number larger or in bold face to differentiate it from your fax number.

3. To fax or not to fax—make fax decisions (especially for lengthy documents) based on urgency, not simply because it's easier and more convenient to fax than mail.

4. Faxing may seem like it saves time and money, but consider the cost of fax paper (which isn't biodegradable) plus the cost of photocopies you may have to make if you don't have a plain paper fax machine. Then, too, if the fax machine is being overtaxed on your end or your recipient's, you may find it takes many attempts to get through.

5. Limit the number of pages to be faxed—*before* they're faxed. Before someone faxes to you, find out how many pages will be coming. You may decide on another method. As a courtesy to someone *you* fax, let them know how many pages you'll be faxing and see if that is acceptable.

6. Number pages to be faxed.

7. Don't send unsolicited faxes.

8. Make sure your fax machine has enough memory to store a message in case your machine runs out of paper. In fact, make sure your fax is automatic enough for your business—that besides memory, it has such features as an automatic document feeder, an automatic document cutter, delayed transmission (to take advantage of lower phone rates), on-hook dialing, automatic dialing and activity report (printout of the date, time and phone number of each fax that's sent and received).

9. Get a fax board for your personal computer if you prefer getting confidential fax messages, want the option to print them out or not and you want to automate the process of sending multiple faxes.

10. When designing your own fax transmission forms, include a section called "Method/Urgency of Delivery," that has four boxes: one for "Urgent...Notify Recipient as Soon as Possible"; one for "Confidential"; one for "Regular Interoffice Mail Delivery"; and another marked "Other...(Specify). Also include the following: the sender's name and telephone and fax numbers; the company name and address; date and time sent; recipient's name, company and fax number; number of pages, including the cover sheet; subject or "RE:" section; a "Special Instructions" section that lists options to check, e.g., "Please reply," "For Your Information" and "As You Requested"; and

space for a "Message" section for a hand-written or typed message.

11. To save time and money, use Post-it brand Fax Transmittal Memos, which measure 1½ by 4 inches and attach to a corner of the original document to be transmitted. Eliminating a separate transmittal cover sheet saves paper costs as well as telephone transmission charges. See Figure 13-2.

| Post-It™ brand fax transmittal memo 7671 | # of pages ▸ |
|---|---|
| **To** | **From** |
| **Co.** | **Co.** |
| **Dept.** | **Phone #** |
| **Fax #** | **Fax #** |

**Figure 13-2.** Post-it brand Fax Transmittal Memo

12. If you want a record of your fax activity, besides the built-in activity report feature your fax may have, use the Avery FAX Cover Sheets Duplicate Copy Book. Available in two sizes, 8½ by 11 inches or 8½ by 5½ inches, the duplicate copy remains as a permanent record in the comb-bound book. You'll save telephone transmission charges with this form, which includes lines in non-transmittable ink; if you can get by with the smaller form, you'll save even more.

13. If a document doesn't need a cover sheet, type or print "Sent via fax" on the document along with the page number on each page, e.g., Page 1 of 2 and Page 2 of 2.

## VALUE YOUR VOICE MAIL

Voice mail has become a valuable, timesaving telecommunications tool. Yet, if you value voice mail over the needs of your customers, you can quickly lose the advantages this multi-user, computer-driven answering machine has to offer.

The trick is learning how to make it serve your external as well as your internal customers. Once again, I encourage you to evaluate your system and set up some guidelines. Here are nine I offer you:

1. Focus first on serving your external customer. Determine if all the options and directions of your voice mail maze encourage or discourage contact. Regularly check out the system yourself for any bugs and survey your customers' reactions.

2. Always give your caller the option to speak to a real live person. (But make sure that the referral's voice mail isn't on, though!)

3. Limit, if possible, the number of options to no more than three. Too many choices can be confusing.

4. Ideally, have a well-trained receptionist handle your company's main phone number. So few companies do anymore that you'll really stand out. (I almost always tell such receptionists how nice it is to speak with a real person and I'm often told they've heard that from other people as well.)

5. Your outgoing message should tell the caller how long they have to speak, especially if it's less than a minute.

6. On your outgoing message always ask callers to leave the best time(s) to call them back to prevent telephone tag. Assure callers that their call is important and will be handled in a timely fashion.

7. Make sure your system has an electronic telephone directory so that callers can easily get a person's extension number, even after business hours.

8. Your system should let callers speed up or bypass messages and enter the extension number or correct code to move quickly through the system.

9. When calling someone else's voice mail system, be sure to leave your name and number and a brief message that indicates the purpose of your call and any action you may need from the person you're calling. You may even want to leave your phone number twice—once at the beginning and once at the end of your message. Let them know the best times to reach you. Also speak slowly and distinctly, especially when giving your name and number.

## RENEW RESOURCES THROUGH RECYCLING

Implementing a recycling program where you work is an ideal way to improve operations because it involves *everyone*, is an "easy sell" because of all the national media publicity on recycling, offers financial rewards for companies, makes people feel good about participating and builds teamwork that extends beyond your organization to your community, country and indeed, the world. It's a real "win-win" kind of operation, where the benefits are plainly visible.

The following are sample actions to take and products to use in your recycling program (see how many you're already doing or using):

- Whenever possible, try to buy and use **recycled** and **recyclable** products. Recycled products contain a certain percentage of used materials (for example, recycled office paper has to have at least 50 percent recovered material). Recyclable means the product has the *potential* to be recycled. Look for 3M Post-it brand recycled paper notes (3M also has a list of recyclers nationwide that will accept the notes as recyclable office waste—you can write 3M at 3M Commercial Office Supply Division, 3M Center Bldg. 225-3S-05, St. Paul, MN 55144-1000); recycled file folders such as Esselte Pendaflex's EarthWise brand and those in the Quill catalog described in Chapter 5; Perma Products EcoSafe record storage boxes made from 100 percent recycled corrugated fiberboard that are 100 percent recyclable; 100 percent recycled bond paper and envelopes for letterhead and ruled writing pads through the All-state Law Office Catalog (800/222-0510); and Avery's EarthSmart line that offers multi-purpose white labels, file folder labels, phone message books, insertable indexes, computer labels and fax labels.
- Form a recycling committee and designate a coordinator in your office, department or better yet, company.
- Design a recycling program that identifies which materials will be recycled and which recycled materials will be purchased; provides a collection and storage system; offers ways to deal with confidential material; and develops an employee education and suggestion program.

- Consider recycling these materials: aluminum cans, glass containers, paper (computer paper is the most valuable), envelopes and cardboard.
- Try to reuse items such as file folders and boxes. Subway Sandwiches founder, Fred DeLuca, did just that in designing a cardboard box to transport packaged meat supplies. Once refolded, the box is used by customers as a carryout carton.
- Use paper clips instead of staples. Paper clips can be reused and staples interfere with paper recycling.
- Use paper shredders not only for controlling access to sensitive material but also to help you in your recycling program. Shredded paper makes great packing material or you can sell shredded paper directly to recycling houses.
- Get a short but helpful free pamphlet called "How to Set Up a Recycling Program" from the Texas Young Lawyers Association, PO Box 12487, Austin, TX 78711, 512/463-1446.

## HOW TO ORGANIZE OTHERS

A question I'm often asked by well-organized individuals is how they can organize a boss or a co-worker. Impossible as it may seem, there are a number of steps you can take.

Broaden your definition of "organize." Make sure it goes well beyond clean desks to include the importance of goal setting, prioritizing and working more effectively. Make sure it also complements your "corporate culture" or the philosophy and mission of your organization as a whole.

In addition, recognize that organizing others is a communication issue and a training issue. The communication issue focuses on how to *motivate* someone to *want* to be better organized. The main way to motivate anyone is to ask yourself, "What's in it for them?" There have to be real benefits for them in terms of power, prestige, profits or whatever is a real motivator. They have to clearly see a connection between getting organized and any benefits that are motivators.

Once you can show a positive connection, you have a good shot at helping them begin the organizing training process. As with most training, this is a process that takes place over time. There are skills to learn and habits to practice. If you yourself are organized and are a patient teacher, who acknowledges and reinforces small successes, you have a chance to see some exciting results. If you're a team player, not a dictator, you could even transform your entire organization. Let's see how Linda was able to apply these techniques to solve a paper organization problem that she faced with co-workers.

## PREVENTING THE DUMP-IT-ON-THE-DESK SYNDROME

Linda, an administrative assistant for a small but successful public relations firm, had a problem. Everyone would feed work to her by dumping it in the middle of her desk. They also had the habit of interrupting her from other work to explain what they wanted done.

Together Linda and I devised a special daily paperwork system that helps Linda better control interruptions and incoming paperwork. She now uses colored, two-pocket presentation folders, a different color for each person. She puts mail in the right-hand pocket and staff members feed back work to her in the left-hand pocket once a day. If a special project or deadline comes up during the day, she has a red folder on her desk to handle these top priorities.

Designing the system was only half the story, since her system involved the other staff members who needed to "buy into it." So I suggested she make a presentation at a staff meeting to introduce the system and ask for everyone's support in *trying it out* for a week. Then everyone was to get together at the following week's meeting to evaluate this new *office* system (not Linda's system). The system is still working well several years later.

It's very important to get everyone's agreement and support whenever one person introduces a new system. Otherwise, the office staff may be resistant to a system that appears to be imposed upon them.

When introducing a system such as Linda's presentation folders, remember that good communication and training skills come into play here. First, communicate the benefits to everyone. Second, clearly train people in how you see the system functioning. Be open to reasonable modifications at this point. Encourage people to be involved in this initial discussion (which is really a training session). Give up ownership of the system—it's no longer "my" system, it's "ours."

## LEADING BY ORGANIZING

As an organized member of your work group, you have a special ability to lead. Another way to say it is, "As you organize, so shall you lead."

As an organized person, you're a doer but you can also be a leader if you master the art of delegation. (Review Chapter 3 for a discussion of delegation.) When you're organized, *Positively Organized!*, you have a good view of both the macro and the micro—the big picture as well as the details. You can see more clearly what needs to be done, when and how.

Review this chapter, as well as the rest of the book. Look for ways to improve how you and your co-workers can get things done. Sometimes it's the little things that can make a big difference. I suggest, for example, that a manager/secretary team take five to 10 minutes daily to meet and discuss the day's schedule, projects and priorities. Or use a well-designed form such as the one in Figure 13-3 to help organize work flow.

If you're not in management, don't be afraid you won't have enough impact. An organized person with vision, creativity and drive can accomplish miracles. But don't do it alone. Look for other like-minded individuals who are open to change, quality improvement and innovation.

If you *are* in management, you have a special responsibility to influence and inspire others. That does not mean, however, having others do it *your* way. It means facilitating change, teamwork and an exchange of ideas and information.

## RESOURCE GUIDE

## READING AND REFERENCE

**Beware the Naked Man Who Offers You His Shirt** by Harvey Mackay (New York: William Morrow and Company, Inc., 1990). This best-selling book includes insightful anecdotes and prescriptions for effective management, career advancement and interpersonal

```
                                        DEADLINE DATE        TIME

                    SECRETARIAL WORK REQUEST
                                                       Agenda Date

                                          COUNCIL      _____
                                          ORA WORKSHOP _____
     TYPE

     _____  DEPARTMENT LETTERHEAD      SPECIAL INSTRUCTIONS

     _____  INTEROFFICE                _____

     _____  FORM                       _____

     _____  XEROX PAPER                _____

     _____  ROUGH DRAFT/DOUBLE SPACE   _____

     _____                             _____

     FILE                              _____

     _____  EXISTING FILE (SEE SPECIAL _____
            INSTRUCTIONS FOR TITLE)    _____

     _____  MAKE NEW FILE (SEE SPECIAL _____
            INSTRUCTIONS FOR TITLE)    _____
     MAIL                              _____

     _____  SEE SPECIAL INSTRUCTIONS   _____

     MISCELLANEOUS                     _____

     _____  SIGNATURE ONLY             _____

     _____  NOTARIZATION               _____

     _____  COPIES/_____ OF EACH PAGE  _____

     _____  ATTACHMENTS PENDING W/INITIATOR _____

     _____  INFORMATION COPY TO INITIATOR  _____


     INITIATED BY _____ DATE_____   cc: _____

                                              _____

     COMPLETED BY _____ DATE_____

     CORRECTIONS NEEDED_____       bcc: _____

     CORRECTIONS MADE  _____            _____

     APPROVAL FOR FINAL SIGNATURE_____

     COMPUTER FILE NAME_____
```

**Figure 13-3.** This Secretarial Work Request form serves as a useful checklist and organizing tool for a busy city government office.

skills. You'll find the "Mackay 33 for Employees" and "Mackay 33 for Managers" surveys in this valuable book. $19.95

**Business Book Center** is a wonderful source of business books. You can request books by subject in such categories as "Quality and Productivity," "Leadership," "Training and Development," "Customer Service," "Interpersonal and Communication" and "Management." The center will help you select the right one(s) for your needs and can send you an annotated catalog of books they handle by business subject area. Human resources training videos are also available. 800/554-1389 or 404/233-5435
Thompson Mitchell & Associates, Inc.
Seven Piedmont Center
Atlanta, GA 30305

**The Deming Management Method** by Mary Walton (New York: Putnam Publishing Group, 1986). This book summarizes the 14 quality management principles of quality guru W. Edwards Deming and shows how they have been applied in American industry. $10.95

**How to Avoid the 5 Most Common Mistakes in Buying a Paper Shredder** is a free, informative booklet to get before you buy a shredder. 800/245-2497 or 412/468-4300
Allegheny Paper Shredders Corp.
Old William Penn Highway East
Delmont, PA 15626

**How to Manage Your Law Office** by Mary Ann Altman and Robert I. Weil (Albany: Matthew Bender & Co., Inc., 1989). This comprehensive reference work with annually updated pages features efficient ways to manage law office operations. $95 plus the cost of annual updates (about $65). 800/833-9844 or 518/487-3384.
1275 Broadway
Albany, NY 12204

**International Productivity Journal** is a tri-annual periodical that gives you an international perspective on quality and productivity programs around the globe. $50 per year. 202/523-7464
International Productivity Service
200 Constitution Ave., NW, Room N-5409
Washington, DC 20210

**Midland City** is a delightful book written as a novel combined with how-to text and instructional appendices that show how to bring growth and prosperity to any community with a declining economy. Incorporating quality principles into real-life business situations, the book is as inspiring as it is informative. $36.95. 800/952-6587 or 414/272-8575
Quality Press
American Society for Quality Control
310 West Wisconsin Avenue
Milwaukee, WI 53203

**Modern Office Technology** is an excellent monthly magazine that gives you the latest in business and information systems for your office.
1100 Superior Avenue
Cleveland, OH 44197-8032

**Out of the Crisis** by W. Edwards Deming (Cambridge, MA: MIT Center for Advanced Engineering Study). This is Deming's famous textbook on quality. $60. It's available by contacting 617/253-7444, MIT Center for Advanced Engineering Study, 77 Mass. Ave., Rm. 9-234, Cambridge, MA 02139.

**Productivity, Inc.** publishes English translations of Japanese quality experts. It sells 40 titles of its own as well as other books on quality, productivity, customer service, continuous improvement and employee involvement. 800/274-9911 or 617/497-5146.
PO Box 3007
Cambridge, MA 02140

**Quality & Productivity Management Association** (QPMA) is a professional association that was founded in 1979 to "encourage, facilitate and serve as a catalyst for improving organizational effectiveness in productivity, quality and customer satisfaction." I'm a member of this association, which has excellent publications, chapters ("councils") in the U.S. and Canada, conferences and workshops. 708/619-2909
300 N. Martingale Rd., Ste. 230
Schaumburg, IL 60173

**Quality First** by Myron Tribus, is a collection of essays describing how to apply W. Edwards Deming's philosophy of management to

various kinds of enterprises. The collection also includes **A Template for Creating a Community Quality Council,** which provides a step-by-step guide to creating a quality revolution not only in the place you work, but also in your community. $18, ppd. 703/684-2863; FAX: 703/836-4875
National Society of Professional Engineers
1420 King Street
Alexandria, VA 22314

**Quality is Free** and **Quality Without Tears** by Philip Crosby (New York: McGraw-Hill, 1979 and 1984, respectively). These books by quality guru Crosby are important resources for your quality library.

**Quality Press** is the publishing arm of the American Society for Quality Control and has a complete catalog of their publications as well as those by other publishers, all dealing with quality principles and processes. (See address above under *Midland City*.)

**Swim With the Sharks Without Being Eaten Alive** by Harvey Mackay (New York: William Morrow and Company, Inc., 1988). This book was Mackay's first best-seller and is jam-packed with savvy tips on management, negotiation, sales and life. His famous 66-Question Customer Profile is included. $15.95

**The Team Handbook** covers almost every aspect of creating successful improvement teams. $35. 415/329-1978. Available from:
Fuller Associates
200 California Ave., Ste. 214
Palo Alto, CA 94306

**Thriving on Chaos: Handbook for a Management Revolution** by Tom Peters (New York: Harper & Row, 1987). This is a must-read book if you're serious about implementing a quality revolution where you work. Filled with stories, anecdotes and prescriptions, this book will inspire and inform you at the same time. $10.95

**The Training Store** is a catalog for trainers and other human resource professionals. It features resources such as full training programs, books, videos, slides and accessories–all under $500 and most under $100. 800/222-9909 or 717/652-6300.
Five South Miller Road
Harrisburg, PA 17109

# 14

## POSITIVELY ORGANIZED! IN ACTION

*Quick Scan: This is the companion chapter to any other chapters you've read. It's the most important chapter because this is where you commit to action. Discover how to dramatically increase your own level of organization easily and quickly. Learn how to focus on your key areas and goals for improvement in order to increase performance and achievement and become the best you can be.*

If you want to be the best, it helps to be Positively Organized! But remember that's *Positively* Organized, not *perfectly* or *compulsively* organized.

I tell my clients, "**Be only as organized as you need to be.**" Don't become compulsive or guilty about organization. This is a tool to help you *prevent* stress, not add to it. Organization is not another thing to feel guilty about.

## AN ACTION ORIENTATION

Now's the time to act. While organization is a process that evolves over time, you can facilitate this process by taking action and using this book as a springboard for action.

## DESIGNING EVOLVING ORGANIZATION SYSTEMS THAT WORK FOR YOU

As you organize, focus on this phrase: "evolving organization systems."

Just as you're working in a time of change, so, too, must your organization systems evolve and change. Be sure to involve anyone who will be affected by a new organization system. If you don't, you will probably encounter great resistance. As support operations manager Stan Morel once said, "People don't like change unless they had something to do with it."

Every organization system you and/or co-workers develop should be a flexible set of tools and work habits for managing one to three of the following resources:

1. Time–planning, scheduling, recording, completing and tracking current and future meetings, appointments, commitments, activities, projects and goals
2. Information–developing productive paperwork and work flow procedures; keeping manual and computerized information accessible and up to date
3. Space–creating a functional and pleasing physical working environment both in the office and on the road.

For many, organizational systems have evolved quite by chance over the years. Your own style and degree of organization will depend on a number of factors–your level of activity, whether you have any support staff, if you deal face to face with the public, how you like to work and the "corporate culture" where you work. It's up to you just how much and what kind of organization you need.

## WHERE TO BEGIN

Start small but think big. If you've read more than one chapter, go back to the table of contents and look at the titles of chapters that you've read. Which chapter will make the biggest difference to you and/or others in your career or life?

Now go back to that chapter and skim the headings and subheads as well as any underlines or notes you made. What jumps out? Find a small change you can make that will make a big difference. It might be changing a work habit or using a new system. Many clients find, for example, that setting aside five minutes a day to plan the next day is helpful. Some clients decide to set up and use a daily paperwork system. Others work together jointly to create or streamline an office system or procedure.

## YOUR PLAN OF ACTION

**Dare to put your intentions in writing.** When you write something down, you're giving a message to your subconscious. Besides reinforcing your subconscious, writing also helps you clarify your thinking so that you're better prepared to take action. Many, if not most people, though, are afraid that if they write something down, they'll forget about it. These people need to combine the act of writing with *reading* and *doing* what has been written. If you make a daily to-do list, for example, *read* it over several times during the day and *do* the listed activities.

**Don't be afraid of change.** Tropophobia, the fear of change, is the biggest stumbling block to action for most people. Once you accept and *initiate* change in your life, you'll have more control over it.

I have my clients write a **plan of action** at the conclusion of a seminar or consultation. The plan can take a number of different formats—it can be a simple letter to yourself or a prepared form such as the one in Figure 14-1.

**Commit to yourself, commit to a deadline.** The plan of action is basically a *written commitment to yourself.* Ideally, your first plan should focus on an organizational habit, tool, project or system that can be put into action in a *one- to four-week maximum block of time.* Create an experience of success. Don't overwhelm yourself with a six-month project where you may become discouraged or disinterested.

**Be specific.** Instead of the general "improving my time management skills," for your project, select something more specific, such as "I will take five minutes to plan and write tomorrow's to-

**Figure 14-1.**          **PLAN OF ACTION**

Today's Date: _____

Organization Project or Activity:
_____

Benefits or

Results:_____

Ideas/Sketch/Brainstorm:




Action Steps                How long/often?   Calendared?
_____
_____
_____
_____
_____
_____

Rewards_____

_____

Completion Date _____

do list at the end of each day." Instead of cleaning out all your file
cabinets from the last 12 years, complete one file drawer in one
week.

**What's in it for you?** Besides some hard work, you better be able
to rattle off a whole list of benefits or results you hope to gain.
Better yet, pick the *most important benefit*. Underline and star that
benefit.

**Plan step by step.** If your project has more than two or three steps try "mind mapping" your steps before you put them in linear order. Mind mapping is a way to pour out your thoughts and ideas in a visual, picture outline. Once you can "see" your ideas, then you can determine their sequential relationship to one another. (See also Chapter 9 for a discussion of mind mapping.)

**Make appointments with yourself.** Once you've charted out your steps, schedule blocks of time to complete these steps. Schedule appointments with yourself and don't break them! Have calls screened (or turn on your answering machine), go off by yourself where no one can find you or pick a time when you won't be disturbed. Your plan of action should indicate how long steps will take—total time or time per day/week. Then write appointments in your calendar or planner based upon your plan of action projections.

**Reward yourself!** Make your plan of action more enjoyable by providing any or all of the three main types of rewards—tangible, psychological and experiential. Tangible rewards include physical things you give yourself—new clothes, a deluxe appointment book, a car phone. Psychological rewards are positive messages you tell yourself—stating positive affirmations and giving yourself little "pats on the back." Experiential rewards are a cross between tangible and psychological—getting a massage, taking a trip, dining out in a special restaurant are examples.

Getting others involved in your organization project can be a rewarding process in and of itself. Whether you engage a "buddy" who will offer positive reinforcement or you actually share the work with another, you will more likely increase your accountability and success rate as well as lighten your load. Encourage others to support you in your goals and do the same for them.

## HOW TO CHANGE HABITS

Getting more organized almost always involves habit-changing behavior. But don't worry, it doesn't take a lifetime to change a habit. Actually it takes 21 to 30 days, provided you do the following:

1. Decide what new habit or behavior you intend to practice.
2. Write it down on paper. List *how, when* and *why* you're going to do it.
3. Share your new habit with someone else.

4. Reward yourself. Psychological affirmations before, during and after you practice a behavior can be particularly helpful.
5. Practice, practice, practice. You need to repeat the behavior, preferably every day, to create the habit.

## COMMITMENT TO BE THE BEST

You will succeed with your plan of action and habit changes only if you are truly committed to being the best.

But what does being the best mean? For some, it's beating out the competition. For others, it's "doing your best"–being in competition with yourself.

It's fine tuning what you're already good at. Award-winning athletes, such as world champion whitewater canoeist Jon Lugbill, are always fine tuning, looking for a better way. See if you can relate Lugbill's whitewater canoeing description to your work or life:

> I love the sport and I love being good at it. The challenge is that you constantly have to search out all the little advantages: techniques in the boat, types of boats, what you eat, how much sleep you get, everything down the line–you've got to learn to get the most out of everything you can. The combination of physical and mental goals, that's what's exciting about the sport for me.

How about being the best human being you can be? When all is said and done, isn't that what *really* counts?

Define it for yourself. After all, the way you live your life makes a statement about you–why not make the best statement?

According to Dr. David Viscott, author and radio psychiatrist, we each have at least one special gift to give the world. I agree that your gifts should extend beyond yourself in some way to make a better world. What are your gifts and how are you making the *best* of them?

Being Positively Organized! will help you *use* those gifts so you can indeed be the best.

# A PERSONAL NOTE

# FROM THE AUTHOR

**I want to hear from you.** Please write me in care of Adams-Hall Publishing with your results from this book as well as any comments or suggestions for future editions. You, too, could be in print! (There's a simple, quick 'n easy communication box on the next page.)

Upcoming editions of *Organized to be the Best!* will feature your contributions and keep you up to date on the latest organizational tools and techniques. You'll see how others are dealing with the challenges we all face. What's more, you'll be part of an ongoing process that's on the cutting edge of quality, performance and achievement.

You can also be a part of that process even more directly. Work with me through a personal consultation or a customized "mini-training" program designed to produce positive results in a minimum amount of time. I work with individuals, offices, companies and professional organizations. My bio is on the next page.

## AUTHOR BIO

Author **Susan Silver** is a nationally recognized author and organizing expert who directs the Santa Monica, California, firm **Positively Organized!** Ms. Silver helps clients enhance personal productivity, improve office management and streamline day-to-day business operations.

Susan designs and conducts training programs for corporations and other professional organizations. Her private practice includes individuals in a variety of fields and professions.

Susan blends more than a decade of experience as a management consultant, manager, educator, writer and entrepreneur. A recognized expert on organization, she frequently appears in the media. She is past president of the Los Angeles Chapter of NAPO–the National Association of Professional Organizers and is an active member of the Quality & Productivity Management Association.

Susan shows professionals easy, effective ways to manage time, track projects and activities, use personal computers, organize work space, simplify paperwork, maximize filing and information systems, improve communications and teamwork and achieve goals.

Here's a simple, Positively Organized! way to communicate with Susan or to get your ideas in print for the third edition of her award-winning book. Make a photocopy of this page, complete the box and mail it to her c/o Adams-Hall Publishing, PO Box 491002, Los Angeles, CA 90049. (Their toll-free number is 1/800/888-4452.)

---

HERE'S WHAT I THINK, SUSAN.....

1. This is what I liked about the book:


2. Next time include:


3. I'm interested in (check all that apply):
   - [ ] an individual consultation
   - [ ] Positively Organized! consulting/training programs
   - [ ] purchasing multiple copies of the book at a discount

PLEASE ATTACH YOUR BUSINESS CARD.

---

# |NDEX

*Quick Notes: To the best of my knowledge, all products listed in the index and the book are trademarks and/or registered trademarks of the companies manufacturing the products. Numbers in **boldface** indicate an illustration or chart. The abbreviation (RG) indicates the listing is in a chapter resource guide and/or includes a phone number and often an address as well.*